Forging the Peninsulas
Michigan is Made

by David B. McConnell

selected art by
Theresa L. Deeter
David B. McConnell
George L. Rasmussen

cover art by George L. Rasmussen

Hillsdale Educational Publishers

Made In Michigan

PRINTED WITH
SOY INK™

PRINTED ON
RECYCLED PAPER

Advisors

James K. Cameron, M.A.
Saline Public Schools

Linda K. Ecklund, M.A.
DeWitt Public Schools

Eric T. Keiber, M.A.
Hillsdale Public Schools

research assistant: Elizabeth B. Dewey, M.A.
editorial assistant: Stella M. McConnell
editorial assistant: Elizabeth A. Pechta
layout and development: Lori E. Wells

© 1989, 1995 David B. McConnell

Hillsdale Educational Publishers, Inc.
39 North Street
P.O. Box 245
Hillsdale, Michigan
517-437-3179

99 98 97 96   — 7 6 5

Library of Congress Cataloging in Publication Data

McConnell, David B. (David Barry), 1949-
    Forging the Peninsulas: Michigan Is Made / by David B. McConnell : selected art by Theresa L. Deeter, David B. McConnell and George Rasmussen, cover art by George Rasmussen.
       p. 416 cm. 22x28
    Bibliography: p. 398
    Includes index.
    Summary: A history of the state of Michigan designed for use as a junior high-high school textbook. Includes photographs, maps, artwork, and study questions.
    ISBN 0-910726-75-2
    1. Michigan—History--Juvenile literature. [1. Michigan--History.] I. Title.
F566.3.M34 1989
977.4--dc20
                                                89-15206
                                                  CIP
                                                   AC

1995 edition ISBN 0-910726-83-3

Acknowledgments

No textbook is the work of a single person. It is the product of many hands, both directly and indirectly.

First, without those individuals who took the time to record history as it happened we would not know it. I am indebted to missionary, priest, explorer, pioneer, soldier, farmer, and industrialist— both the humble and the mighty— who put down in diaries, notes and letters what was happening around them.

Next, I thank those who are the professional caretakers of historical information, those who work in the archives, libraries, and museums. I appreciate those individuals who took extra time to assist me during my visits:

Nancy Bartlett, Bentley Historical Library, University of Michigan
John Curry, Michigan State Archives
Dorothy Frye, University Archives and Historical Collections, Michigan State University
Dr. James Griffin, National Museum of Natural History— Smithsonian Institution
Melissa Keiser, National Air and Space Museum— Smithsonian Institution
The staff of the J.M. Longyear Research Library, Marquette
Cynthia Read-Miller, Henry Ford Museum and Greenfield Village
Dr. William Mulligan Jr., Clarke Historical Library, Central Michigan University
Gordon Olson, Grand Rapids City Historian
Theresa Sanderson Spence, Michigan Technological University Archives

Thanks also to Phyllis Sponseller for allowing me to photograph items from her Native American artifact collection and to Janet Johnston and the helpful staff of the Mitchell Public Library in Hillsdale.

For their many hours spent producing the color maps I tip my hat to: Bonnie Jones, Mary Lois Moss, Ellen R. White, and the staff at the Center for Cartographic Research.

I appreciate the assistance of Governor John Swainson for arranging the use of the Manchester forge and the cooperation of blacksmith Tim Armentrout who posed for the cover art. The artists Theresa Deeter and George Rasmussen have done much to enhance this publication.

I am especially thankful for the many helpful comments and ideas so willingly given by teachers throughout the state. No textbook can have any measure of success without the input of classroom teachers.

Thanks to Diane Beem and my father Robert McConnell whose extra hours in the office gave me more time to devote to this project. I thank my wife Janice for reading the manuscript and taking vacation time to visit archives.

Finally, I take full responsibility for any errors. I would appreciate these being brought to my attention and I will endeavor to correct them in future editions.

Contents

1 **MEET MICHIGAN**
1 Learn the Basics
8 What's Underfoot
12 The Time at the Edge of the Ice

2 **MICHIGAN'S NATIVE AMERICANS - PEOPLE OF NATURE**
17 First Michiganians: Two Amazing Groups
22 Unwritten History
29 Life Among the Tribes

3 **FRANCE COMES TO NORTH AMERICA**
37 The Pathway to Michigan
44 Search for Souls: Missionaries & Priests
52 The Explorers: Through Woods and Over Waters
62 Fur Is King!

4 **THE BRITISH - A NEW FLAG ON THE FRONTIER**
66 A War in the Woods: French, British & Indians
71 Chief Pontiac on the Offensive
78 Michigan - While Our Nation is Born: 1774-1783

5 **MICHIGAN JOINS THE U. S. - FROM WILDERNESS TO TERRITORY**
85 The British Hang On!
90 United States Takes Possession: 1796-1812
99 The War of 1812: The Last Tussle for Michigan
105 The War of 1812: Victories at Last!

6 **THE PATHWAY WIDENS - PIONEERS ON THE WAY**
111 Yankees Move West
121 Forging the Landscape: Farmers Arrive!
127 Those Frontier Days

7 **TOWARD STATEHOOD - GROWING LIKE A WEED!**
137 Becoming a State: No Simple Matter
146 Boom and Bust
153 Canals & Copper

8 A STAND AGAINST SLAVERY

165 A Way to Freedom: The Underground Railroad
174 New Politics From the Woverine State
181 Michigan's Army Goes Off to War: 1861-1865

9 WE TAKE FROM NATURE'S STOREHOUSE

191 Lumbering: Rugged People and the Smell of Sawdust
204 Copper and Iron by the Ton
214 A Farming Revolution: More Food For All
223 Fishing on the Great Lakes

10 THE FOCUS CHANGES - FROM FARM TO FACTORY

233 We Made It Here - Cereal, Stoves & Cigars
243 In the Factories - The Worker's Viewpoint
248 Time for Reform: Who Was Potato Pingree?
253 Great Lakes Ships and Cargoes

11 WE PUT THE WORLD ON WHEELS - FORGING AMERICA

264 From Quadricycles to Corporations
274 Ford, Durant, Olds, and Others Help the Auto Industry Grow
282 Life Just Isn't the Same: Changes in Society

12 AN AWESOME WAR & AFTERWARDS - WORLD WAR I

290 From the Plow to the Gun
298 Rum Runners, Gangsters and the 1920s
306 Modernizing Michigan

13 BLEAK TIMES LEAD TO ANOTHER WAR - 1930s & 1940s

315 Michigan Bends Under the Depression
326 Unions: A New Friend at the Factory
334 Tension and Triumph in Democracy's Arsenal: World War II

14 MICHIGAN AS WE SEE IT TODAY

346 Settling Down: Colleges, Homes, and Highways - 1950s
357 Going In New Directions Under New Stresses - 1960s
368 Twists and Turns: A New Era Is Coming - 1970s & 1980s
378 Environmental Concerns
384 Beautiful Places & Interesting People

399 **Bibliography**
407 **Glossary**
419 **Index**

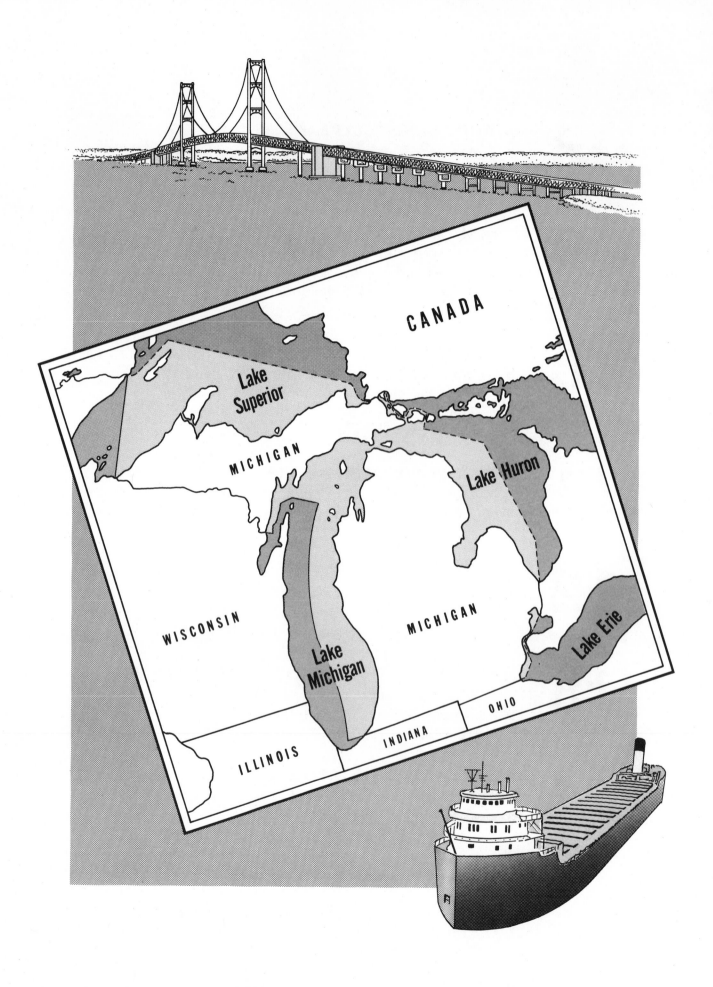

1 MEET MICHIGAN!

Chapter 1 Section 1

Learn the Basics

Here are the key concepts you will find in this section:

How the Great Lakes affect Michigan.

Information about the size and location of Michigan.

Facts about the many different groups of people living in Michigan.

What a county is.

Names of the largest cities in Michigan.

You Live in a Unique State

A quick glance at any map shows Michigan is unique. Why? Because it is the only state made of two *peninsulas. A peninsula is a portion of land nearly surrounded by water.* This is the only state on the mainland of the United States which is divided by water.

In the past, each peninsula was more on its own. The water of the Straits of Mackinac (MACK in aw) kept the people apart. Today this problem is not as great. The Mackinac Bridge connects the Upper and Lower Peninsulas. Air travel and modern communications make it much easier to keep in touch. Before, the only way to reach the other peninsula was by boat.

What else is unusual about Michigan? Take another look at the map. This state is in the center of several large bodies of freshwater known as the Great Lakes.

These lakes play an important part in our past and present. Michigan has the longest coastline of any state except Alaska! Michigan's 3,000 miles of coastline borders on four of the five Great Lakes. They are Lakes Huron, Michigan, Erie, and Superior. Which Great Lake does not touch Michigan? It is Lake Ontario. An easy way to remember the names of all five Great Lakes is to take the first letter of each and spell HOMES. The Great Lakes are quite important because they hold one-fifth of the world's supply of fresh water.

The St. Lawrence River (St. stands for Saint) carries water from the Great Lakes to the Atlantic Ocean. It also allows ships from the ocean to reach Michigan. Michigan has ports which receive ships from many foreign countries.

The Great Lakes Affect Us In Many Ways

Even the name Michigan relates to the Great Lakes. It comes from the Native American words for great or big lake. Michi, mishi, or kitchi mean great quantity. Gami is one word for lake. Over the years these different words were combined and the spelling changed until, finally, the word Michigan was officially used in 1805.

The Lakes are very important to Michigan. They even affect the climate. Winds from the west are warmed as they pass over the Lakes in the winter and are cooled by them in the summer. Moisture is picked up by the winds as they pass over the water and this gives extra rain and snow to some areas.

Michigan's actual boundaries go through four of the Great Lakes. Large parts of Lakes Michigan, Superior, and

Huron are in the state of Michigan. There are over 38,000 square miles of Great Lakes water within our borders. Altogether, Michigan is about 60 percent land and 40 percent water, including parts of the Great Lakes.

Michigan's Land

Of course, most people think about the land in Michigan instead of the water. Michigan's land covers over 58,000 square miles. Which peninsula is larger? The Lower Peninsula is. It has about three-fourths of the land area. Much of the land is gently rolling hills.

The Upper Peninsula has higher places. Usually, Mt. Curwood is thought to be the highest point. But recent studies show nearby Mt. Arvon to be a bit higher at 1,979 feet. The Porcupine Mountains are another high point. But Michigan has nothing as high as the Rocky Mountains. Most of the state is between 500 and 1,000 feet above sea level. Study the color maps on pages M-4, M-5, and M-6. Learn how these maps show the elevation of the land.

Michigan spans quite a distance corner to corner. Traveling from the southeast corner to the northwest corner the distance is 475 miles. Using state highways it is even further—620 miles from Ironwood to Monroe. Going 475 miles south from Detroit, would take a person to the Smoky Mountains in Tennessee, after crossing all of Ohio and Kentucky! Heading east from Detroit and traveling 475 miles almost reaches New York City. The western tip of the Upper Peninsula is as far west as St. Louis, Missouri. The eastern edge of the Lower Peninsula is directly north of Tampa, Florida. Some towns in the western end of the Upper Peninsula are actually closer to the capitals of Wisconsin, Minnesota, and Iowa than they are to Lansing, the capital of Michigan.

Florida and Georgia are the only two states east of the Mississippi River which are larger than Michigan. Michigan is even larger than several foreign countries including Greece and Nicaragua. On the other hand, it is smaller than England or France.

Finding Michigan

Where exactly is Michigan? It can be spotted easily on a map by looking for the Great Lakes. But, let's be more precise. There is a sign north of Traverse City which shows where 45 degrees north *latitude* crosses Michigan. This spot is exactly halfway between the equator and

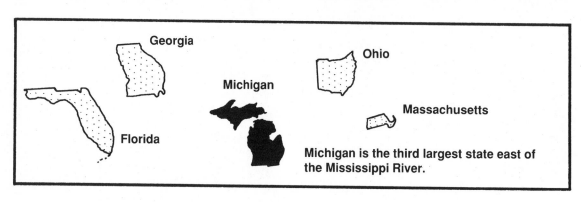

Michigan is the third largest state east of the Mississippi River.

the North Pole. *Latitude is a measurement going north and south from the equator. If you look on a globe or map of the world you will see lines of latitude. In a sense, they are like the rungs of a ladder, going across the globe or map.*

Another line, 83 degrees west *longitude,* passes near Detroit. *Longitude is a measurement going east or west from a city in England. This city has been given the location zero (0) degrees longitude and everything else is measured from there. You can see these lines which connect the North and South Poles on the globe.*

Follow the latitude and longitude lines which cross Michigan as they pass other places in the world. Remember, Traverse City is about 45 degrees north latitude. An imaginary trip to the east along the line 45 degrees north latitude goes through France and eventually crosses just north of Japan. Look at the globe above. If you follow the 85 degrees west longitude line to the south, you pass through Central America, finally ending in the Pacific Ocean off the coast of South America.

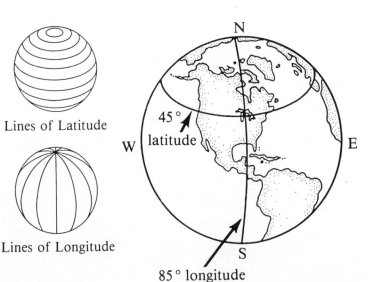

Lines of Latitude

Lines of Longitude

45° latitude

N

W

E

S

85° longitude

Michigan's Foreign Neighbor

People often forget Michigan is next to a foreign country, Canada. A large part of our border is international because of this. Several bridges and a tunnel connect Michigan to Canada as all of the boundary between us is water. Three rivers form this border at the nearest crossings. The Detroit River is between Detroit, Michigan and Windsor, Ontario; the St. Clair River is between Port Huron, Michigan, and Sarnia, Ontario; and the St. Mary's River is between Sault Ste. Marie, (Soo Saint ma REE) Michigan, and Sault Ste. Marie, Ontario. Ontario is the Canadian *province* next to Michigan. *A province is much like a state in the United States.*

It is easy to cross the border to Canada, but everyone does have to stop and answer questions at check points. Each government is concerned with who crosses the border and what people might be carrying with them. People are often asked where they were born. They may also be asked if they have anything besides their personal belongings with them. Special permits are needed to carry merchandise which can be sold. Of course, it is against the law to carry handguns or illegal drugs into Canada.

The people of Canada and Michigan have been friends for many years. Many Michiganians take vacations in Canada. There are no soldiers to guard the border as there are in many countries. We have other things in common with the people of Canada. One of these is sports. The Detroit Tigers play baseball with the team from Toronto, Canada!

There is considerable trade between Michigan and Canada. Products made on either side of the border are often sold on the other side. Canada and the United States have more trade between them than any other two countries in the world.

Michigan's People

One of the most exciting things concerning a state is learning about its

4

people. Each of us and the things we do are a little part of Michigan's history. In the beginning this was the land of the Native Americans, the first Michiganians.

Today, Michigan is a mixture of over 20 ethnic groups. As a matter of fact, Michigan has more *ethnic groups* than almost any other state! *An ethnic group is one based on race or place of origin. People in the same ethnic group have similar customs.* These people have come from the far corners of the world.

Even as you read this, new people are arriving from Mexico, Vietnam, Cuba, Jordan, Lebanon, Syria, and other places. Perhaps they have come to escape war or poverty. They may have come to find a new sense of freedom or a chance to worship as they choose. Many of them are discovering Michigan for the first time. People who have lived here for generations are still proud of their roots and can tell you from where they originally came. Their ancestors may be from Africa, Asia, Europe, or Canada.

How has this affected the makeup of our people? If a survey were made of everyone living in the state, it would show the largest ethnic group is German. The second largest group has ancestors from England. Those from Africa come in third with about 13 percent of the population. The Polish are the next largest group and there are many more groups as well. Each has brought its own special culture with it.

Each group has added its own unique heritage and produced its own outstanding individuals. They have all had an impact on Michigan. The Dutch, those originally from the country of Holland, are a major portion of the people living

Michigan's Ethnic Groups

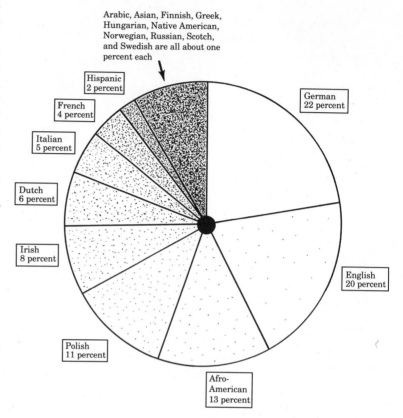

Arabic, Asian, Finnish, Greek, Hungarian, Native American, Norwegian, Russian, Scotch, and Swedish are all about one percent each

Hispanic 2 percent

French 4 percent

Italian 5 percent

Dutch 6 percent

Irish 8 percent

Polish 11 percent

Afro-American 13 percent

German 22 percent

English 20 percent

around Grand Rapids and Holland, Michigan. Today, there are more Arabic people living near Detroit and Dearborn than anywhere else in the United States. Actor Danny Thomas is one Arab-American from Michigan. The people from all of these nations and places add *ethnic diversity* to Michigan. *Diversity means many kinds. Ethnic diversity provides a variety of customs, ideas, and artistic styles. It makes for a more interesting place to live.*

Michigan is the eighth largest state in population with about 9,200,000. However, the people are not evenly distributed. Most live in the southern third of the Lower Peninsula. In fact, just three counties have 43 percent of the whole population! They are Wayne, Oakland, and Macomb. Comparing the combined population of these three counties to the number of people living in some states is

© 1989 Hillsdale Educational Publishers

Michigan's counties.

interesting. Thirty-six states have smaller populations than this three county area! Obviously, these counties influence much of what happens in Michigan.

The Purpose of Counties

Just what is a *county? It is a unit of state government.* Having counties is one of the ideas brought to this country by the early pioneers. The county system was developed in England. Each state in the United States, except Louisiana, has counties. A state is usually a large area and it is hard to be in touch with all the people. Counties make it easier to govern.

Each county has its own county seat, almost like a state capital. A courthouse is at the county seat. The courthouse has a court and several offices to keep county records.

Each of you will have information about yourself kept at the courthouse! Birth and death records are kept there. When real estate (a home, a farm, an office building, etc.) is sold, records known as deeds are filed in the courthouse. These records are used to see who will pay

6

property taxes and how much they owe. When you decide to marry, you must go to the courthouse to get a marriage license.

Michigan has 83 counties. Each is an area of land, usually shaped like a square. Keweenaw County is farthest north. Marquette County has the most land. Benzie County is the smallest in size and is about one-sixth the size of Marquette County. It is a good idea to know in which county you live and the counties next to it.

Why do the counties of Wayne, Oakland, and Macomb have so many people? At one time most Michiganians worked on farms or in small villages. The expansion of the automobile industry in the 1910-1925 period caused many people to move off the farms into the cities. Soon, Detroit, Dearborn, Livonia, Pontiac, Sterling Heights, and Warren grew to be among the largest cities in the state. These cities are all located in the *tri-county* area of Wayne, Oakland, and Macomb counties. As time passed, more cities started in between the larger ones. *Suburbs* developed as the cities became too crowded. *Suburbs are smaller towns on the edge of a large city.* Now, most of these three counties are "wall to wall" cities and towns.

The Largest Cities

Detroit is by far the largest city in the state. In 1990 it had 1,027,974 people. Grand Rapids is the second largest, but

© 1989 Hillsdale Educational Publishers

Selected larger cities in Michigan. The bigger the circle, the greater the population. The state capital is marked with a star.

it is not nearly as big. It has some 190,000 people. Warren and Flint are next in size. Warren has a population of 145,000 and Flint 140,000. Lansing is fifth with roughly 123,000 people. Of course, populations change all the time. These figures are based on the U.S. census which is taken every 10 years. Recently, most Michigan cities have lost people who have moved to smaller towns and to other states which have more jobs. The number of jobs in Michigan industry seems to be shrinking.

Michigan is a state with an exciting past and there is more to learn. Here are just some of the basics about Michigan so far:

Michigan is unique because it has two peninsulas.
Michigan touches 4 of the 5 Great Lakes.
Michigan is halfway between the North Pole and the equator.
Canada is a foreign country which borders Michigan.
Michigan is the third largest state east of the Mississippi River.
People from many ethnic groups live in Michigan.
Michigan's population is concentrated in three counties.
Michigan has 83 counties.
The largest cities are Detroit, Grand Rapids, Warren, Flint, and Lansing.

Questions

1. Name the four Great Lakes surrounding Michigan. Explain how the Lakes affect Michigan's climate.

2. Explain what the line 45 degrees north latitude has to do with Michigan.

3. How many miles does Michigan span from southeast corner to northwest corner? How does Michigan compare in land size with other states east of the Mississippi River?

4. Using the circle graph in the book, tell which are the four largest ethnic groups in Michigan.

5. Which three counties have the largest populations? What percentage of Michigan' people live there?

6. Name Michigan's five largest cities in order of their size.

Chapter 1 Section 2

What's Underfoot

> *Here are some key concepts you will find in this section:*

Several great changes affected the land long ago.

These changes caused valuable minerals to be formed here.

Interesting facts about ancient life can be learned from fossils.

Our Dirt Has History!

Michigan has not always been as it is today. Since the time the earth formed, this land has gone through some really radical changes! *Geologists* tell us a very long time ago a saltwater sea covered Michigan and much of the area around it. *A geologist is a scientist who studies rocks and the formation of the land.* Many geologists think the land may be three billion years old. During this time seas may have covered Michigan for 500 million or so years. These numbers are the best guesses available today.

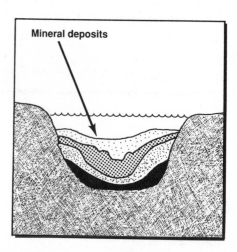

Giant Mountains Here?

Michigan may have seemed a dull place as it sat under water for all this time, but nature was planning some excitement. The land started to push together from the north and from the south. What was in between was squeezed up to make mountains. Geologists believe these mountains in Michigan may have reached 25,000 feet in height! They stretched through Canada and covered the Upper Peninsula. The ancient mountains are known as the Killarney Range.

Have you ever seen any 25,000 foot mountains in the Upper Peninsula? Whatever happened to such huge mountains? They were destroyed by one of nature's most powerful forces, *erosion. Erosion is the wearing away of soil or*

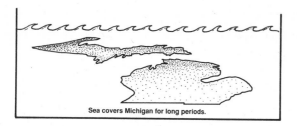

Sea covers Michigan for long periods.

Interesting Deposits

When one of the great seas covered northern Michigan, an unusual thing happened. Material containing iron began to settle to the bottom. It continued to collect until it was 300 to 750 feet thick in some places. This would become the iron ore which is mined today.

rock by wind and water. Erosion works very slowly but it continues for millions of years without stopping. Each drop of rain or breeze carries away a tiny particle. The great mountains were actually blown and washed away!

Ancient mountains

Michigan Volcanoes!

About 1.2 billion years ago the earth began to tear apart in the western Upper Peninsula. A weak spot had developed there. Molten rock or lava pushed through to the surface and volcanoes formed. During this process pure copper and silver metal flowed with the lava! It would have been an exciting event to see take place, but there were no people in Michigan to watch. As far as scientists know, the only living things at this time were algae and bacteria.

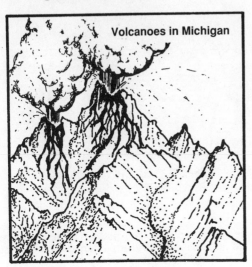

Volcanoes in Michigan

Clues from the Great Seas

Can you think of any ways to prove that great seas once covered Michigan? In the Upper Peninsula, there is sandstone which was once under one of these seas. During millions of years the pressure and weight from the earth above turned the sand to sandstone. Nature's process of erosion has removed the earth and rock which was once above the sandstone and now it is on the surface!

About 500 million years ago the sea shrank until it only covered the Lower Peninsula. Because the sea no longer covered the Upper Peninsula, the under-

The horn-shaped fossil on the right is a Rugose Coral which was in Michigan about 220-500 million years ago, while the Atrypa Costata, the shelled creature on the left, lived in the Michigan area 355 million years ago.

ground rocks of the two peninsulas are quite different now. Eventually the smaller sea could not hold all of the minerals dissolved in its water and they began to collect at the bottom. Valuable deposits of lime, salt, and gypsum were left behind, mostly under the Lower Peninsula. The existence of these kinds of mineral deposits is another way to prove there were once great seas which covered Michigan.

During the time of the great seas, fish and other sea creatures lived in the water. Some of the earliest had shells and we can find these shells as fossils. But there may have been other life forms which did not turn into good fossils. We may never know for certain what exactly lived or swam in the seas over Michigan!

One fossil is common. It is of a sea coral. Similar corals still live in the oceans of the world. This coral turned into a rock

Petoskey stones are actually fossils of sea coral polished by the waves of Lake Michigan. The stone was named after the city of Petoskey where many fossils have been found.

which is the Michigan state stone, the Petoskey stone. It has this name because it is often found on the shores of Lake Michigan near Petoskey. If you find a Petoskey stone, you are holding something in your hands which is about 350 million years old!

Michigan Sharks and Whales!

Other strange things lived in those seas. Geologists know some of the fish looked like sharks and many of them were larger than a human! Even a few fossil remains of whales have been uncovered in Genesee and Iosco counties.

Besides the coral and fish, there were sea plants. These plants have become another resource for Michigan. Large amounts of them rotted and decayed. After millions of years they turned into oil and gas.

Other plants grew along the shore of the sea. We would think these plants looked strange indeed! They also died and fell to the ground. Great quantities piled up and decayed. Over a very long time these shore plants became coal. Some Michigan coal has been mined but it doesn't have the quality of coal from other states and the deposits are smaller.

279 Million Years Missing!

There is a big mystery in Michigan's past. While there are many fossils of plants, fish and other sea creatures; no one has ever uncovered dinosaur fossils. As a matter of fact almost no fossil or rock exists for a long period of time. This period is called the "Lost Interval." The "Lost Interval" spans from about 280 million years ago to about 1 million years ago. There are very few clues which tell what happened in Michigan during these millions of years!

It is a real mystery as to what could have happened to all the material from this time span. Geologists do have some theories. This does not mean that dinosaurs never lived in Michigan, just that there are no fossils to prove it. One explanation is Michigan was thought to have been higher than the land around it at that time. Because of this, the rocks and bones or fossils were worn away by erosion. It is also possible glaciers of ice later scraped away the fossil remains.

How Old Is This Rock? Where Is It From?

The rocks on the surface of the Upper Peninsula are generally older than those in the Lower Peninsula. This is because the lower peninsula rocks were

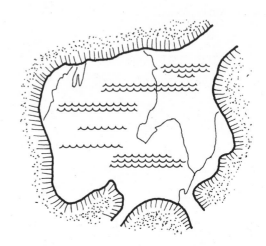

A sea once covered the state. The sea slowly dried up and left behind important deposits. (Art by David B. McConnell)

formed from the sea bed which covered that area.

Within the Lower Peninsula the older rocks are on the outside edges. Can you think of a reason why this would be so? The sea covering the land slowly dried up, and as this happened, older deposits were left on the outer edge. Finally the newest rocks were created as the last of the sea disappeared near the center of the Lower Peninsula.

The rocks of Michigan tell the story of the past. They hold clues about what took place millions of years ago. If you were to drill an oil well in the center of the Lower Peninsula and look at the drilling core, you could actually see many layers of rock with the oldest usually being at the bottom.

Why is any of this important today? Michigan is unique among states because the two peninsulas are geologically separate and distinct. Understanding rock formations is necessary to find the valuable mineral resources. Knowing what is underground helps geologists discover oil, gas, limestone, gypsum, salt, copper, silver, gold, and iron. All in Michigan! It has been said that Michigan has a wider variety of minerals than most places of its size on earth.

All of these minerals have been an important part of Michigan's economy and history. The minerals in our state have affected the lives of many people over the years and will continue to be important to us in the future.

Questions

1. List three minerals which are in Michigan because the land was once covered by great seas.

2. List two valuable metals left here because of ancient volcanoes in Michigan.

3. What actually is a Petoskey stone? Why does the Michigan state stone have this name?

4. Why have no fossils of dinosaurs been found in Michigan?

5. Write a paragraph to explain how geological events of the far past are affecting human activities in Michigan today.

Chapter 1 Section 3

The Time at the Edge of the Ice

Here are the key concepts you will find in this section:

Thick sheets of ice once moved over Michigan from the north and made many changes to the land.

Our first people arrived about the time the last ice sheet was melting.

Just after the ice sheet melted, several strange animals lived here. Now these animals are extinct.

Every City & Town Covered By Ice

This land was once covered with ice. Not ice from a cold winter but hundreds to thousands of feet of ice. Billions of tons of ice. It all started 1.6 million years ago. Every place where any city or town is today was under all of this ice. You may not believe it! But there are still clues left behind for the doubtful. The whole surface of the land shows signs of what the ice did. If you know how to look, clues are everywhere. This kind of ice is called a *glacier. A glacier is a very thick ice sheet which slowly covers a wide area of land because more snow falls in the winter than can melt in summer.* The ice began to form around the North Pole and it moved inch by inch to the south. Michigan was covered by four glaciers over a long period of time.

The glaciers pushed down over Michigan just like a bulldozer. Tremendous amounts of gravel, rock, and dirt were pushed south by the ice.

When the ice finally melted, much of this material was left behind. This rock and gravel often formed hills. Studying the shapes of the hills helps you to see

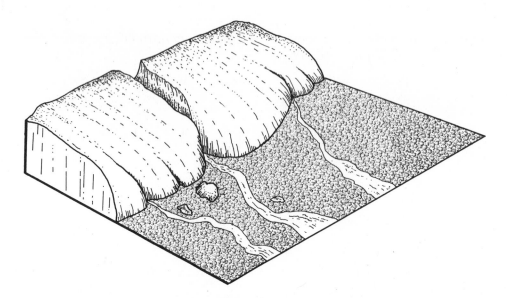

Glaciers advanced over the state moving gravel, rock, and dirt as they went. The hills that were left behind help us understand the path of the ice. This picture shows the glacier beginning to melt and the water running off. (Art by David B. McConnell)

the "footprints" the glaciers left behind. The hills are one of the clues that show glaciers were really here once. If you visit a gravel pit in Michigan, you will probably see many kinds of rock. Each type was made in a different place and perhaps at a different time. It was all brought here by the bulldozer action of the glaciers. When geologists see so many kinds of rock in one place, they realize it is further proof that a glacier once passed over the area.

What did the glaciers do here?

The mass of ice which came over Michigan was truly great. The ice weighed so much it actually pushed the land down! Careful studies by scientists show that Michigan is still slowly rising because weight of the ice has been lifted.

Glaciers did much to form the Great Lakes. The ice acted as a bulldozer and scraped away softer rock making depressions which became Lakes Michigan and Huron. As the last glacier melted, a tremendous amount of water filled up the low places and created the Great Lakes. The Great Lakes may be one of the most valuable gifts left by the glaciers.

Melting ice was also responsible for making many smaller lakes in Michigan. Often huge chunks of ice fell away from the glacier as it slowly returned north. The ice chunks made depressions in the ground and as the ice melted, the depressions were filled with water. In some places, this kind of lake still exists. Just

imagine, the first water in these lakes arrived over 10,000 years ago!

Besides bringing gravel and rock to Michigan, glaciers pushed dirt to the south. Much of the dirt found in the Lower Peninsula originally came from the

The topsoil in the southern Lower Peninsula was left behind by the last glacier as it melted. This area is better for farming because of the soil which was brought south along with the ice.

Upper Peninsula or even Canada. This is why the southern Lower Peninsula has better soil for farming than most of the Upper Peninsula and the northern Lower Peninsula. The better soil of this part of Michigan is another gift from the glaciers. So you see, our dirt does have history!

Were There Any Witnesses?

Did anyone ever see this great glacier? Perhaps, but it is doubtful we

14

will ever know for sure. The last of the four great glaciers melted 12,000 to 13,000 years ago. *Archaeologists* believe the first people moved to Michigan at about the same time. *An archaeologist is a scientist who studies about past human life and activities. They often study remains found buried in the ground. Fossils, bones, lost tools and ruins are some of the clues they use to help them form their ideas.* There may have been a time when the first human in Michigan looked north and saw a wall of melting ice. They probably stood in awe; the ice could have been 5,000 feet high! There would have been many rivers and rushing streams carrying away the water from the melting glacier.

The First People

We don't know too much about the first people who lived here. We don't know

The first people who lived in Michigan were the Paleo Indians. Paleo means ancient. These Indians are believed to have been here from 9,000 to 11,000 years ago. (Art by David B. McConnell)

what they called themselves or even if they had a language at all. Today they are known by the name of Paleo-Indians. Paleo means ancient and is a name made up by archaeologists. We really can't say where they came from, except to say they must have moved here from the south. The last glacier probably still covered the land to the north. The archaeologists have found bits of animal bone and stone spear points which lead them to think

Animals like these wooly mammoths once lived in Michigan, perhaps 9,000 to 12,000 years ago. Evidence tells us they were hunted by the Paleo Indians.

these people moved from place to place to follow game which they hunted. And what animals they were, large hairy beasts which looked like elephants!

Animals You Won't See In a Zoo!

At this time, Michigan was home to many animals which no longer exist. Now they are extinct. The ones which looked like hairy elephants are called mastodons and mammoths. Fossils and bones of many more mastodons than mammoths have been found here. Many farmers have been plowing their fields and found huge mastodon bones!

Saber-toothed tigers were also in the region! Would a stone spear be any defense against such a big cat?

What other animals might the Paleo-Indians have seen? Fossils of giant beavers which were as large as a bear have been uncovered! There are traces of musk ox and a long legged pig-like animal; not to mention the more familiar deer, moose, wolves, and bears.

How Old Did They Say?

Can we believe scientists when they say that all of this happened 10,000 to 13,000 years ago? Why do they tell us this age? Archaeologists from the University of Michigan and other colleges have tested fossil bones to come up with this answer.

The test they used is called *radiocarbon dating,* also known as carbon 14 dating. Delicate equipment measures very tiny amounts of radioactivity in the fossils to estimate their age. *First, small samples are burned to form carbon. Then the amount of radioactivity is measured. It is from this measurement of radioactivity that an estimate of the age is made. Each living creature takes in a bit of radioactive carbon dioxide while it is alive, but as soon as it dies the radioactivity slowly disappears. After 50,000 years the amount of radioactivity is too low to detect, so this method only can work for samples less than 50,000 years old.*

Prehistoric Time Line

All items are noted by years ago.

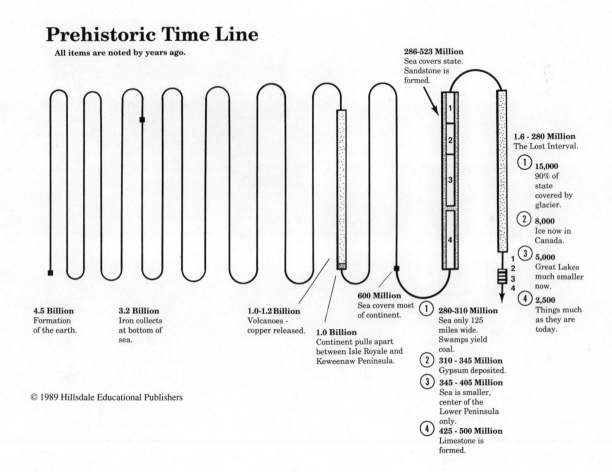

286-523 Million
Sea covers state. Sandstone is formed.

1.6 - 280 Million
The Lost Interval.

① **15,000**
90% of state covered by glacier.

② **8,000**
Ice now in Canada.

③ **5,000**
Great Lakes much smaller now.

④ **2,500**
Things much as they are today.

4.5 Billion
Formation of the earth.

3.2 Billion
Iron collects at bottom of sea.

1.0-1.2 Billion
Volcanoes - copper released.

1.0 Billion
Continent pulls apart between Isle Royale and Keweenaw Peninsula.

600 Million
Sea covers most of continent.

① **280-310 Million**
Sea only 125 miles wide. Swamps yield coal.

② **310 - 345 Million**
Gypsum deposited.

③ **345 - 405 Million**
Sea is smaller, center of the Lower Peninsula only.

④ **425 - 500 Million**
Limestone is formed.

Questions

1. Give examples of two clues which help to prove Michigan was once covered by a glacier.

2. What animals might the Paleo-Indians have hunted?

3. What clues do we have that there were indeed Paleo-Indians, mastodons or giant beaver once living in Michigan?

4. How many years ago do archaeologists believe the first Paleo-Indians and mastodons lived in Michigan? What is the name of the test which leads them to say this?

5. Imagine you are a Paleo-Indian in Michigan. Write a paragraph about the surroundings where you live and your activities.

2

MICHIGAN'S NATIVE AMERICANS
—PEOPLE OF NATURE—

Chapter 2 Section 1

First Michiganians: Two Amazing Groups

Here are some key concepts you will find in this section:

The first people to work metal in North or South America lived in Michigan long ago. We call them the Copper Culture people.

Later a more advanced group of people with unusual burial practices lived here. They are called the Hopewell people.

Prehistoric Copper!

You may have heard Michigan had copper mines. Do you know when the first miners started work? It was over 6,000 years ago! They were the first to work with metal in either North or South America. Archaeologists have found ancient copper spearpoints, tools, and bracelets which they believe were made that long ago from Michigan copper.

If you visit Isle Royale or the Keweenaw Peninsula, you can still see the remains of 5,000 or so small pits where the first miners worked. Thirty feet is about as far down as they go. Those miners did not have heavy equipment and high explosives. They had to be content with wooden and stone tools. But fire and cold water were most helpful. The copper metal was in layers between solid rock. To make the rock release the copper, it was heated with fire. Then cold water was thrown on the hot rock causing it to crack. Large stones were also used as hammers to break the rock apart.

Who Worked These Mines?

The people who worked those mines are known as Copper *Culture* people. *Culture refers to the ideas and ways of doing things that a group of people share in common.* Cultures differ in many ways.

Copper Culture people took copper from pits they dug. (From the Michigan State University Museum)

18

Each may have its own language, beliefs, and ways of living that help people meet their needs in their own unique situation.

The Indians of that culture used the copper they mined to make knives, spear points, axes, fishhooks, and needles. Besides the practical items, bracelets and other jewelry were made. Small pieces of copper were rolled up and used to decorate their hair.

The Copper Culture people also traded their copper to tribes from other regions. Copper items from the early pit mines have been found as far west as North Dakota and as far east as Quebec,

A Copper Culture man may have looked like this. The ornaments in his hair are small copper tubes. He also has a necklace of copper pieces. (Art by George Rasmussen)

Canada. When the people of the Copper Culture were not mining, they hunted and fished. They probably traveled in dugout canoes.

How Do We Really Know?

How can archaeologists be sure copper items found in these other places came from Michigan? First, they look at the way the items are made and ask if they seem to be made in the same way as those from Michigan. Second, they do chemical tests on the copper to see if it has the same tiny amounts of impurities as the Michigan copper. It is not likely that copper from two places would have exactly the same impurities.

We might know more about the Copper Culture people if it were not for the fact that the water level of the Great Lakes is higher now than it was then. Scientists think some of the places where they lived are now under water.

Gone Long Ago!

No white person ever met any of the Copper Culture Indians because they disappeared about 3,500 years ago. We do not know exactly why they disappeared. Perhaps the climate changed; perhaps the animals the people hunted moved away. But they did not leave because they ran out of copper. There was still plenty of it left.

When Europeans finally did arrive, the Indians in Michigan continued to have things made of copper, but they did not mine it.

Roughly 2,500 years ago, a second amazing group lived in part of Michigan. While the Copper Culture

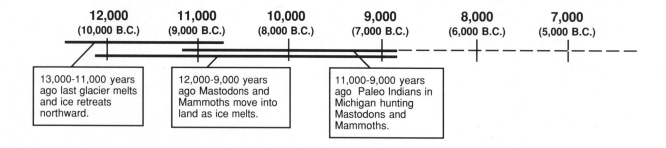

| 12,000 (10,000 B.C.) | 11,000 (9,000 B.C.) | 10,000 (8,000 B.C.) | 9,000 (7,000 B.C.) | 8,000 (6,000 B.C.) | 7,000 (5,000 B.C.) |

13,000-11,000 years ago last glacier melts and ice retreats northward.

12,000-9,000 years ago Mastodons and Mammoths move into land as ice melts.

11,000-9,000 years ago Paleo Indians in Michigan hunting Mastodons and Mammoths.

people were found in the Upper Peninsula and Isle Royale, this second group lived in the southern Lower Peninsula. They are called the Hopewell people. They would be surprised at that name because it is really that of a farmer named Hopewell. One day he was clearing some of his land in Ohio and he dug into a large mound of dirt. He was amazed to find it contained skeletons, arrow points, pottery, and more. After that, similar mounds were labeled with his name.

Since the first discovery of a mound by farmer Hopewell, many more mounds have been uncovered. Some of the best-known mounds in Michigan are the Norton mounds just outside Grand Rapids. Michigan was only a small part of the Hopewell area but it is quite exciting that such mounds have been found here!

These items pointed far into the past and began the study of an early people who buried their dead under mounds of dirt. The Hopewell people lived in the Ohio River Valley and southern Michigan for 1,000 years or so and they seemed to have been quite an advanced group. They made beautiful art objects and traded with other groups far away.

Since the Hopewell people lived long before written history, we can only learn about them from the objects found in their burial mounds. Along with the bodies, they put many other things. It is believed things were placed with the dead person so their spirits could use them. Some of the dead were buried with great riches.

One mound in Ohio contained thousands of pearls, shell beads, and ornaments of precious metals. One mound is as much as 100 feet high! The Michigan mounds though are smaller.

The Hopewells did many other remarkable things. They had outstanding artists who made decorations for the living and the dead. Mysterious figures have been found that were cut from glasslike mica. Tobacco pipes were carved from stone in the shape of falcons, frogs, and other animals. They had musical instruments too. A set of small copper panpipes was in one mound. Some things were even made of gold and silver. Those

The Hopewell people buried members of their culture in mounds. (Art by David B. McConnell)

ancient Indians were very good potters too. Pots made from fired clay were common.

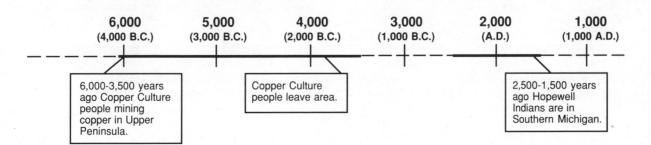

6,000 (4,000 B.C.)	5,000 (3,000 B.C.)	4,000 (2,000 B.C.)	3,000 (1,000 B.C.)	2,000 (A.D.)	1,000 (1,000 A.D.)

6,000-3,500 years ago Copper Culture people mining copper in Upper Peninsula.

Copper Culture people leave area.

2,500-1,500 years ago Hopewell Indians are in Southern Michigan.

20

The Hopewells traded widely. Much of the materials used to make their artistic objects came from other places. They used mica from the Appalachian Mountains near the East coast. Volcanic glass came from Wyoming where Yellowstone National Park is today. Shells were brought from the Gulf of Mexico and the Atlantic Ocean.

Those ancient Michigani- ans wore well-made clothes crafted from furs, tanned animal skins, and woven cloth. From the remains in their mounds, it is believed both men and women wore earrings made of copper. They also had necklaces of bear claws and pearls.

Why did the Hopewell people bury their dead in mounds? Did they have some strong religious beliefs which caused them to do it? Were the only people buried in the mounds just certain special persons in their society? Had some of them earned great wealth through trading? There may never be positive answers to these questions.

After nearly 1,000 years, the Hopewells faded from the scene. Some other groups carried on a few of their practices. There were still some burial mounds, but they did not contain the same skilled artwork.

One fact about the Hopewells is certain—they left us with more questions than answers.

This Hopewell man is wearing copper earrings. Hopewells were noted for their skilled artwork. They were named Hopewell after the man who discovered one of their mounds. (Art by George Rasmussen)

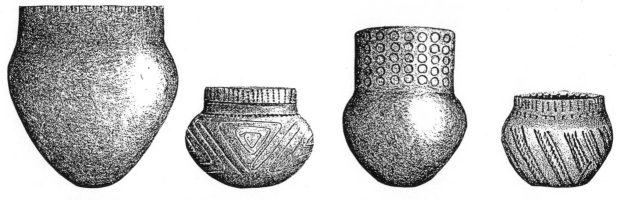

These artifacts were discovered in the Hopewell mounds near Grand Rapids. (Courtesy Dr. James B. Griffin and the University of Michigan Museum of Anthropology)

Questions

1. How did the miners from the old Copper Culture get the copper from the rock?

2. Give examples of the things these first miners made with the copper?

3. How do we know the Hopewell people must have traded with groups far away?

4. Name three things which you feel were outstanding or unusual about the Hopewell people.

5. Write a paragraph giving your opinion whether it is right or wrong to dig up the resting place of the dead to learn about them. If it is right to dig up a Hopewell grave, what about one in an old cemetery?

Chapter 2 Section 2

Unwritten History

Here are some key concepts you will find in this section:

Several major tribes of Native Americans lived in Michigan about the time the Europeans arrived.

The three main tribes living in Michigan are related and speak similar languages.

Each tribe had its own area but they moved about from time to time.

The names by which we know the tribes are often not the names they actually used for themselves.

The tribes did not have a written language; therefore, much of the information about them was written by Europeans and is sometimes inaccurate.

From the Beginning

The Native Americans or Indians were the first citizens of Michigan. Michigan has been their home for 10,000 to 13,000 years. These first people did not leave a written history of themselves. They used picture writing and we can see a few examples of their history painted on cliffs, carved in stone, or on birch bark.

Besides picture writing, the tribes had a strong tradition of telling their history through stories. In that way, information of great events was passed from one person to another and from one generation to the next. Sometimes the stories were fictional and made into legends. The tribes had legends about how the Sleeping Bear Dunes were created and why rabbits have short tails, etc. Much of the oral (spoken) history of the tribes is factual however.

Be Careful of Viewpoints

The written history we do have has been mostly done by European newcomers. No history was written before the Europeans arrived, which was just over three hundred years ago. The Europeans wrote from their own viewpoint and included many biased remarks. Some of the things they believed about the native people may have come from a single observation and may not have represented everyone.

Most of us have our own *biased ideas* which are not really true. *A biased idea is one which we have formed without actually studying the facts. They may be*

This carving on sandstone made by prehistoric people is called a petroglyph (PEH tra glif).

ideas which are just based on our own or someone else's opinions. A biased idea would be to think that all people from a certain country are evil.

We may also have *stereotypes. That is to say, we think that everyone in an ethnic group is alike and can fit into the same mold.* In this case, a stereotype would be that all Indians are alike. Within all groups of people, there are those who are good and those who are bad, those who are smart and some who are not as smart.

Grouped by Tribes

The Europeans gave the name Indian to all of the native people living in America. Of course, the Europeans used that name because they were lost. They first thought they had discovered India! The name Americans would have made more sense as that is what the land was finally called. At first, the Europeans lumped all the native people together as one group with the name Indians.

But, the native people did not see themselves that way. They lived in groups which were similar to small nations. We call their groups tribes. Each had different customs and beliefs. Tribes were divided into *clans. A clan is a group where everyone has a common ancestor.* Members of a clan had a responsibility to help each other. If you went to a large family reunion, you could think of that as a meeting of your clan. Indians are not the only ethnic groups to have clans. The Scotch are well known for their clans too. A tribe was not a close-knit government unit like a city or state. They were scattered over large areas and did not necessarily get together each year for formal meetings or to elect one chief over all the people.

Tribes moved, or *migrated*, from time to time. *A migration happens when an entire group of people leave one area and move to another. Usually such moves are caused by a lack of food, disease, a war, a change in climate, or other serious problems.* Since the tribes migrated or moved their locations, they should be considered as tribes of the Great Lakes region, not just the tribes of Michigan.

In most Indian marriages, a young man offered gifts to the mother and father of the young woman he wished to marry. If the gifts were returned, the proposal was rejected, and the gifts would be offered to a different family. (Art by George Rasmussen)

Where Did the Tribes Come From?

How are the tribes in Michigan related to the ancient people who lived here during the time of the Copper Culture and the Hopewells? This is a very difficult question to answer. Archaeologists have found bits and pieces of pottery, arrow heads, and other items from groups living in Michigan during the time in between but it is hard to know much about the people. It is a time of mostly unknown history.

Most historians believe the more recent tribes migrated into Michigan after the time of the Hopewells. Ojibwa oral history says their tribe once lived by

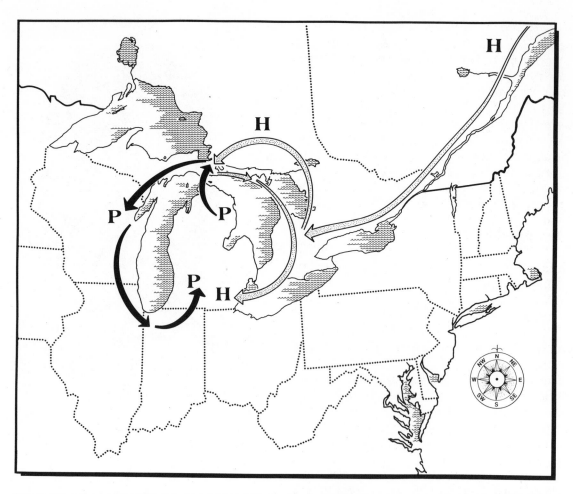

The Indian tribes of the Great Lakes region did not stay in a permanent location. This map shows the migration over a span of some 200 years of two tribes, the Huron (H) and the Potawatomi (P).

the Atlantic Ocean. When they reached the north shore of Lake Huron, they followed it until a new home was found around the rapids at Sault Ste. Marie.

There are other clues about large groups of Indians migrating. When the French first arrived in Canada, they observed a large Indian village on the St. Lawrence River at Montreal where many Indians lived along the river. Upon the return of the French 60 years later, there were only a few Indians living along the river and the village was empty. Certain historians have suggested that the Indians caught European diseases when they first met white people. Since the Indians had no resistance to those diseases, the results could have been terrible. The Ojibwa might have moved

because of diseases caught from the early French explorers or even from Viking explorers who visited the East Coast before the French and English.

War was another reason for migrating. Parts of the Huron tribe moved to Michigan because they were attacked by the Iroquois (EAR a quoy) tribes and forced out of their home in Ontario.

Names of the Tribes

How many tribes lived in Michigan and what were their names? There were three major tribes and three or four slightly less important tribes who lived here. The list is for the years around 1750. The Ojibwa are thought to have been the largest of the tribes who lived in the area in the last 300 years.

The first three tribes were part of a loosely organized group known as the "Three Fires." They had common traditions and thought of themselves as belonging to the same family.

Three main tribes living in Michigan:

Ojibwa (Also called Chippewa or Ojibway) [CHIP eh wah, O JIB way]
Ottawa [OT ah wa]
Potawatomi [POT a WAT o me]

Smaller tribes living in Michigan:

Menominee [meh NOM eh nee]
Huron (Also called the Wyandotte) [HYOUR on, Wy n dot]
Miami [my AM ee]

That, however, is not the end of the list! Other tribes lived in Michigan earlier. Examples of those are the Sauk (SALK), the Fox, the Kickapoo (KICK eh poo), and the Mascouten (meh SKOOT en). Those four tribes are known to have traveled long distances on foot and did not use canoes. Though by the end of the 1700s, all four tribes had left the area.

The Neutrals (NEW truls) came from the east in Ontario and lived in parts of Michigan for a while. Some Sioux (SOO) lived here too, although they were generally found west of Michigan.

You Called Me a Snake! or Who Made These Names?

A careful study of tribal names will show they are not necessarily the names used by the tribes themselves. Neutral and Fox are not Indian names, but English ones. Some of the names are not flattering at all. They might be the name an enemy tribe used. Sioux came from an Ojibwa word for snake, which was shortened by the French. Several names have been changed by the French or English. Some have just been given to a tribe and are nothing like the name the tribe used.

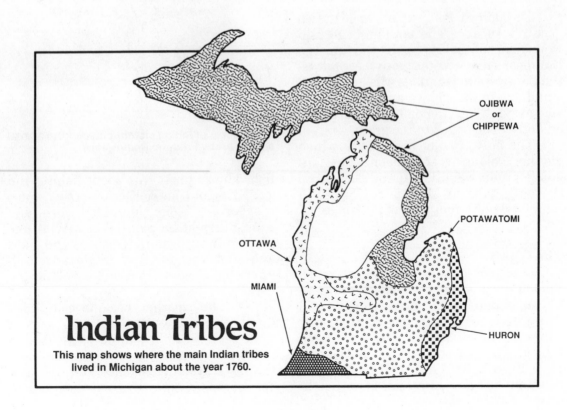

Indian Tribes
This map shows where the main Indian tribes lived in Michigan about the year 1760.

For example, the Ojibwa or Chippewa actually called themselves the Anishinabe (ah nish in A bey). This means "first man" or "original man." Ojibwa was what neighboring tribes called them because of their puckered moccasins. The word Chippewa developed as the English said Ojibwa with a silent "O." The French also used Saulters (soo TUR) as another name for the Ojibwa. They first met the tribe near the rapids on the St Mary's River and the French name for rapids is sault (soo). This name means people of the rapids.

Their Languages

Michigan's main tribes belonged to the Algonquin (al GON quin) language group. Once again, that is what the French thought as they lumped together all tribes which spoke a similar language. The French probably used the name Algonquin because it was similar to the name of a tribe who worked closely with them when they first reached Canada. It was not a word used by the Michigan tribes.

The Ojibwa, Potawatomi, and Ottawa once all spoke a similar language and were a part of that group. By the time the Europeans made contact with those tribes, the Potawatomi language was not understandable to the Ojibwa and Ottawa and vice versa. The Menominee, the Sauk, and others belonged to the group as well.

The only tribe of importance which did not belong to the Algonquian language group was the Huron. They were the only tribe in Michigan to speak a completely different type of language.

The Ojibwa

Let's look more closely at each tribe. The Ojibwa was the largest tribe in Michigan and has the most members still living here. They were one of the larger tribes north of Mexico and their area ranged from Ontario to North Dakota. They lived mostly in the Upper Peninsula and the Lake Huron side of the north-

ern Lower Peninsula. The Ojibwa mainly hunted and fished for their food. They were experts in using birchbark canoes and often fished from them.

What did the Ojibwa look like? Indian agent Henry Schoolcraft said about half of the men were over six feet tall. They tattooed their faces and foreheads with blue or black lines. The number of lines indicated the band to which each person belonged. Bands were smaller groups within a tribe. The women wore their hair very long and braided it. Men and women used bear grease on their hair and bodies. The grease served as hair tonic and lotion for their bodies. Remember, they were outdoors almost all the time with the sun and wind drying out their skin.

Members of the Ojibwa tribe had summer and winter homes. Each spring the tribe gathered on the shores of the Great Lakes for the spawning runs of

An example of Indian clothing made from animal skins. (Art by Frederic Remington)

fish. The summer was spent fishing and gathering blueberries, cranberries, and raspberries. Some pumpkins, corn, and squash would be planted too. Wild rice often grew in swampy areas around lakes and that was another important food. Many foods were dried and saved for the winter.

As the weather became cold, each family left and went out on its own. It could be hard to find animals for food in the winter and people might starve if they all stayed in one place. But the early spring was a time of great excitement.

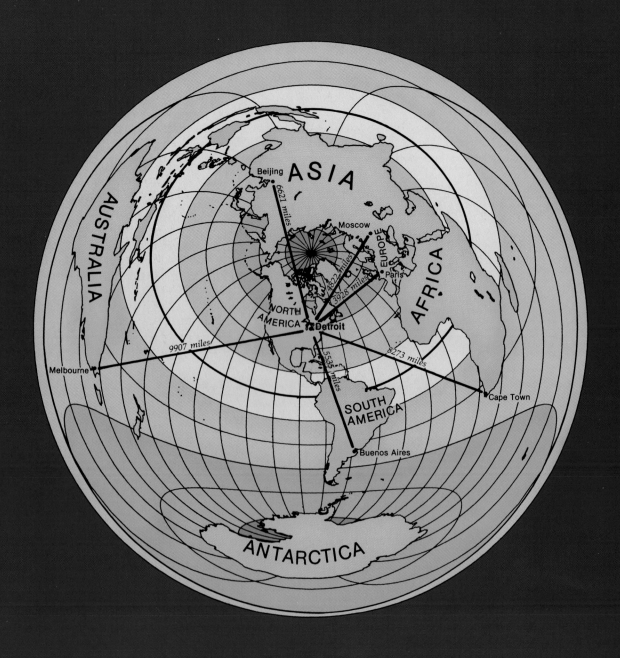

A View of the World from Michigan

This is a special map of the world. A straight line from the center to anywhere else will show the distance and direction to the place. Only straight lines starting at Detroit are accurate. Do not use this map to compare sizes. The greater the distance from Michigan, the more the shapes and sizes of continents have been stretched.

93°W
48°N

90°W

87°W

Ontario

84°W

Minnesota

Grand Portage

Lake Superior

C A

Duluth

Superior

M i c h i g a n

Sault Ste. Marie

Sault Ste. Marie

St. Croix River

Menominee River

Manitoulin Island

Wisconsin

St. Paul
45°N

Lake

Huron

Iowa

Mississippi River

Green Bay

Fox River

Manistee River

River

Wisconsin River

Madison ☆

Muskegon River

Saginaw River

Milwaukee

Grand

River

Lansing ☆

Lake

St.

Clair

Thame

Dubuque

Lake

Detroit

42°N

Michigan

Chicago

Fox River

Gary

Kankakee River

Toledo

Lake

Des Moines River

Fort Wayne

Maumee River

Cleve

Illinois

River

Ohio

☆Springfield

Illinois River

Indianapolis ☆

☆Columbus

39°N

Mississippi River

Indiana

Cincinnati

Missouri River

River

☆
Jefferson City

St. Louis

Wabash

Vincennes

River

Frankfort ☆

Missouri

M2

Ohio

Louisville • Lexington

Kentucky

V

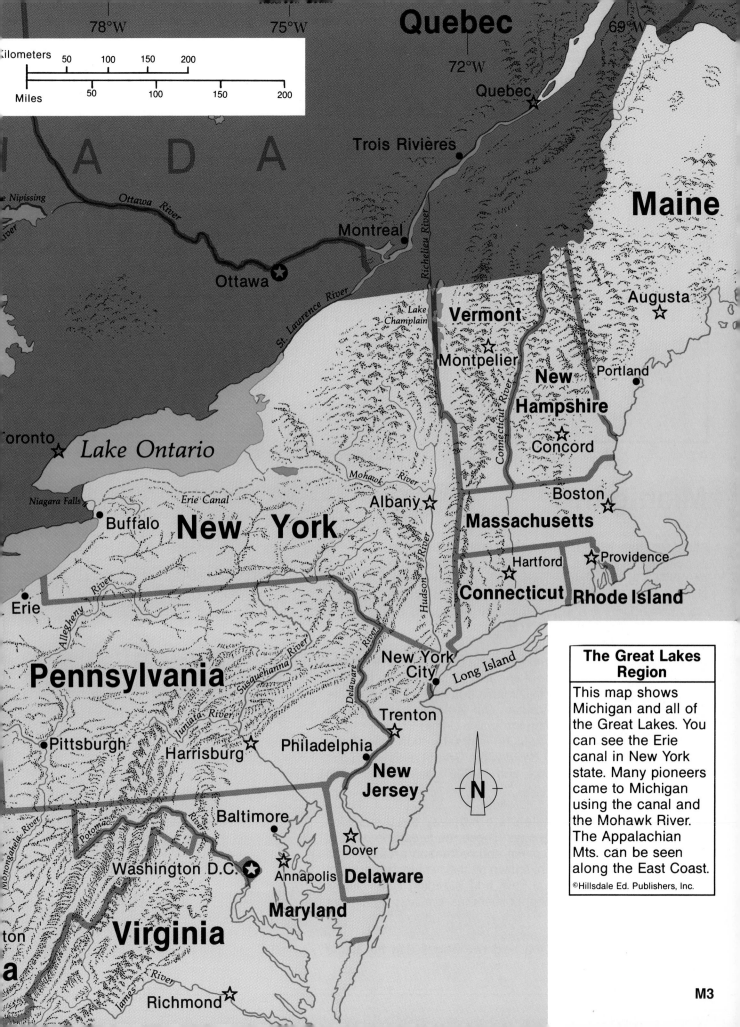

The Great Lakes Region map showing the northeastern United States and parts of Canada.

Scale:
Kilometers: 50, 100, 150, 200
Miles: 50, 100, 150, 200

Labels visible on map:
- Quebec
- 78°W, 75°W, 72°W, 69°W
- Quebec
- Trois Rivières
- Maine
- Lake Nipissing
- Ottawa River
- CANADA
- Montreal
- Ottawa
- Richelieu River
- St. Lawrence River
- Lake Champlain
- Vermont
- Montpelier
- New Hampshire
- Augusta
- Portland
- Connecticut River
- Concord
- Lake Ontario
- Toronto
- Mohawk River
- Boston
- Niagara Falls
- Erie Canal
- Albany
- Massachusetts
- Buffalo
- New York
- Hartford
- Providence
- Connecticut
- Rhode Island
- Erie
- Allegheny River
- Hudson River
- New York City
- Long Island
- Pennsylvania
- Susquehanna River
- Delaware River
- Trenton
- Juniata River
- Pittsburgh
- Harrisburg
- Philadelphia
- New Jersey
- Monongahela River
- Baltimore
- Dover
- Delaware
- Potomac River
- Washington D.C.
- Annapolis
- Maryland
- Virginia
- James River
- Richmond
- N (compass)

The Great Lakes Region

This map shows Michigan and all of the Great Lakes. You can see the Erie canal in New York state. Many pioneers came to Michigan using the canal and the Mohawk River. The Appalachian Mts. can be seen along the East Coast.

©Hillsdale Ed. Publishers, Inc.

M3

Michigan

Michigan has a population of roughly 9.2 million people, which ranks it 8th among the 50 states. The population is not evenly divided. Wayne County has more people than any other and over 43% of the state's residents live in just three of Michigan's 83 counties, Wayne, Oakland and Macomb!

Michigan is 23rd in size among the states with 58,216 square miles of total land area. There are also 38,575 square miles of Great Lakes water within Michigan's boundaries. Four of the five Great Lakes touch Michigan. Our Great Lakes' shoreline of 3,200 miles, is longer than the entire United States Atlantic Seaboard. The Michigan shoreline is greater than that of any single state except Alaska. Besides the Great Lakes, Michigan has over 11,000 inland lakes and 36,000 miles of rivers and streams.

Michigan has a 9,500 mile state highway system which includes 1,800 miles of freeways. These roads can be used to reach Michigan's 86 state parks and recreation areas. Ten of the larger of these parks are shown on the next three pages of maps. Isle Royale National Park and Sleeping Bear Dunes and Pictured Rocks National Lakeshores are also within our borders.

Note: Maps on this, and the next two pages use the same map legend and are drawn at the same scale.

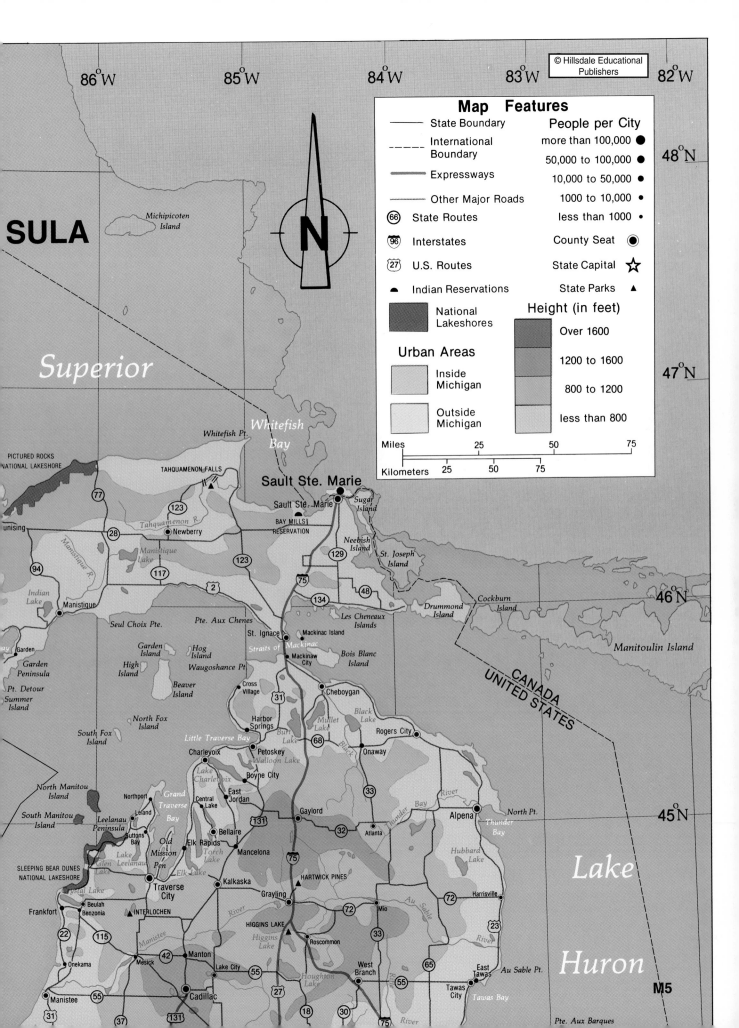

86°W   85°W   84°W   83°W   82°W

© Hillsdale Educational Publishers

48°N

47°N

46°N

45°N

SULA

Michipicoten Island

Superior

Map Features

——	State Boundary	**People per City**	
- - -	International Boundary	more than 100,000	●
━━	Expressways	50,000 to 100,000	●
——	Other Major Roads	10,000 to 50,000	●
⑥⑥	State Routes	1000 to 10,000	•
⑨⑥	Interstates	less than 1000	·
㉗	U.S. Routes	County Seat	◎
◣	Indian Reservations	State Capital	☆
		State Parks	▲

National Lakeshores

Urban Areas

Inside Michigan

Outside Michigan

Height (in feet)

Over 1600

1200 to 1600

800 to 1200

less than 800

Miles   25   50   75

Kilometers   25   50   75

PICTURED ROCKS NATIONAL LAKESHORE

Whitefish Pt.

Whitefish Bay

TAHQUAMENON FALLS ▲

Sault Ste. Marie

Sugar Island

⑦⑦

⑫③

Tahquamenon R.

Unising

②⑧ ● Newberry

BAY MILLS RESERVATION

Sault Ste. Marie

Neebish Island

St. Joseph Island

Manistique R.

Manistique Lake

⑨④

①①⑦

⑫③

② ⑫⑨

⑦⑤

④⑧

Indian Lake

● Manistique

Seul Choix Pte.

Pte. Aux Chenes

①③④

Les Cheneaux Islands

Drummond Island

Cockburn Island

46°N

Garden

Garden Peninsula

Garden Island

Hog Island

High Island

St. Ignace

Straits of Mackinac

Mackinaw City

Mackinac Island

Bois Blanc Island

Manitoulin Island

Pt. Detour

Summer Island

Beaver Island

Waugoshance Pt.

Cross Village

③①

Cheboygan

CANADA
UNITED STATES

North Fox Island

Harbor Springs

Mullet Lake

Black Lake

South Fox Island

Little Traverse Bay

Charlevoix

Petoskey

⑥⑧

Rogers City

Onaway

Walloon Lake

Boyne City

Black River

North Manitou Island

Northport

Grand Traverse Bay

Central Lake

East Jordan

Gaylord

③③

Atlanta

Alpena

North Pt.

45°N

South Manitou Island

Leelanau Peninsula

Leland

Lake Charlevoix

Bellaire

①③①

③②

Thunder Bay

Thunder Bay

Suttons Bay

Elk Rapids

Mancelona

Hubbard Lake

Lake Leelanau

Old Mission Pen

Torch Lake

⑦⑤

Lake

SLEEPING BEAR DUNES NATIONAL LAKESHORE

Glen Lake

Elk Lake

Kalkaska

HARTWICK PINES ▲

Crystal Lake

Traverse City

Grayling

Au Sable River

Huron

Frankfort

Beulah

Benzonia

▲ INTERLOCHEN

Manistee River

⑦②

Harrisville

②②

①①⑤

HIGGINS LAKE

Higgins Lake ▲

⑦②

Mio

②③

Onekama

④②

Manton

Roscommon

③③

Au Sable Pt.

Mesick

Lake City

⑤⑤

West Branch

⑥⑤

East Tawas

● Manistee

⑤⑤

Cadillac

②⑦

①⑧

③⑩

Houghton Lake

⑤⑤

Tawas City

Tawas Bay

M5

③①

③⑦

①③①

⑦⑤

River

Pte. Aux Barques

MICHIGAN'S LOWER PENINSULA

Map legend and mileage scale on preceding page.   © Hillsdale Educational Publishers, Inc.

THE DETROIT AREA

This map also shows current and historic points of interest.
Windsor, Ontario and Canada are colored gray.

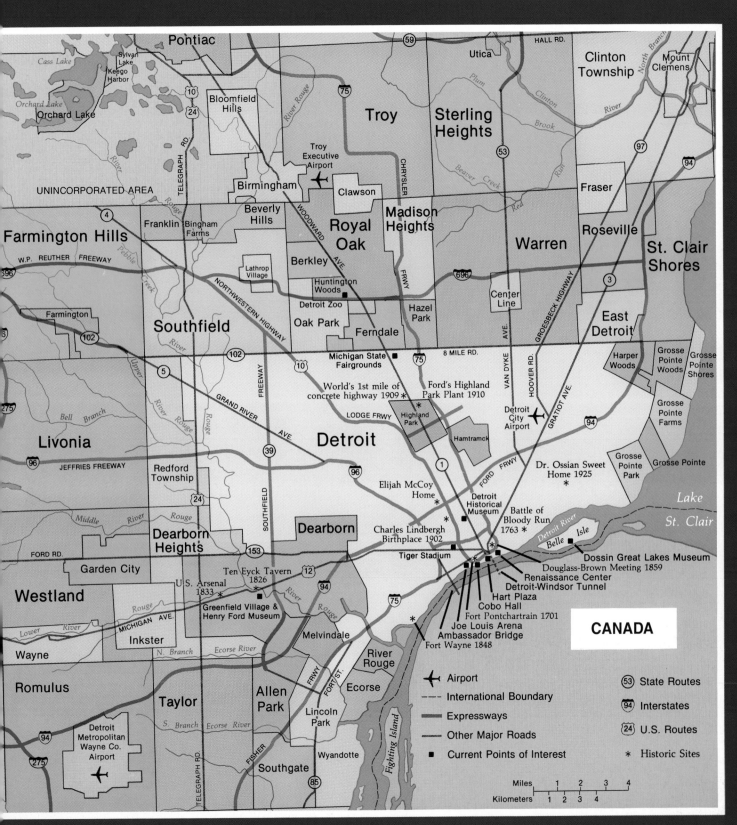

Cass Lake • Sylvan Lake • Keego Harbor • Pontiac • Utica • HALL RD. • Clinton Township • Mount Clemens

Orchard Lake • Orchard Lake • Bloomfield Hills • Troy • Sterling Heights

UNINCORPORATED AREA • Troy Executive Airport • Birmingham • Clawson • Madison Heights • Fraser

Farmington Hills • Franklin • Bingham Farms • Beverly Hills • Royal Oak • Warren • Roseville • St. Clair Shores

W.P. REUTHER FREEWAY • Berkley • Center Line • East Detroit

Farmington • Lathrop Village • Huntington Woods • Hazel Park • Grosse Pointe Woods • Grosse Pointe Shores

Southfield • Detroit Zoo • Oak Park • Ferndale • 8 MILE RD.

Michigan State Fairgrounds • Harper Woods • Grosse Pointe Farms

World's 1st mile of concrete highway 1909 * • Ford's Highland Park Plant 1910 • Grosse Pointe

Livonia • LODGE FRWY • Highland Park • Hamtramck • Detroit City Airport

JEFFRIES FREEWAY • Detroit • Dr. Ossian Sweet Home 1925 * • Grosse Pointe Park • Grosse Pointe

Redford Township • Elijah McCoy Home * • Lake St. Clair

Dearborn Heights • Detroit Historical Museum • Battle of Bloody Run 1763 *

Dearborn • Charles Lindbergh Birthplace 1902 * • Belle Isle

Garden City • Tiger Stadium • Dossin Great Lakes Museum

Ten Eyck Tavern 1826 • Douglass-Brown Meeting 1859
U.S. Arsenal 1833 * • Renaissance Center
Westland • Detroit-Windsor Tunnel
Greenfield Village & Henry Ford Museum • Hart Plaza
Cobo Hall
Inkster • Melvindale • Fort Pontchartrain 1701
Wayne • River Rouge • Joe Louis Arena
Ambassador Bridge
Romulus • Ecorse • Fort Wayne 1848

CANADA

Taylor • Allen Park • Lincoln Park

Detroit Metropolitan Wayne Co. Airport • Wyandotte

Southgate

Legend

+ Airport
- - - International Boundary
— Expressways
— Other Major Roads
■ Current Points of Interest

(53) State Routes
(94) Interstates
(24) U.S. Routes
* Historic Sites

Miles 1 2 3 4
Kilometers 1 2 3 4

THE LAND AND ITS USES

Wayne County
3,801.4 persons per square mile

Key to Colors

 Forests

 Fruit

 Industry

 Grains & Dairy

 Beans & Sugar Beets

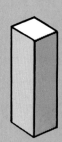 1 inch equals 500
people per square mile

WHERE PEOPLE LIVE IN MICHIGAN

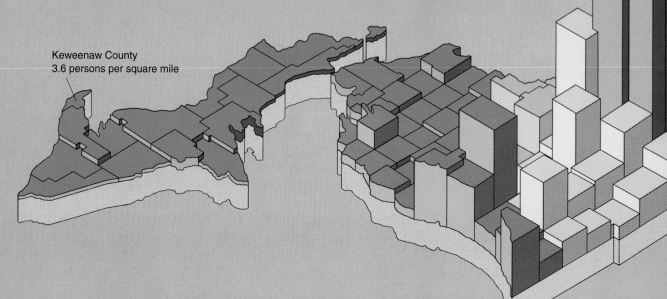

Keweenaw County
3.6 persons per square mile

Designed by the Center for Cartographic Research and Spatial Analysis,
Michigan State University. ©Copyright Hillsdale Educational Publishers.

M8

Families gathered in the maple forests, called sugar bush, to collect sap from the trees and boil it down to make maple syrup and maple sugar.

The Ottawa

The Ottawa tribe's name came from the word *adawa* or *adawe* (ah da wah) which means to trade. They traveled hundreds of miles to trade woven mats and furs for pottery and sea shells. Corn, sunflower oil, tobacco, and medicinal herbs were also traded with other tribes. Their many travels helped the Ottawa to become expert in the use of their canoes.

Their tribe lived in the western part of Michigan. They had lived to the east in Ontario, around the area of Manitoulin Island, but they were driven to Michigan by raids from the fierce Iroquois.

Since they were related to the Ojibwa, many of the Ottawa customs were similar.

The Potawatomi

This tribe finally settled in southern Michigan, northern Indiana and Illinois, parts of Ohio, and Wisconsin. Their name is from an Ojibwa phrase which has to do with fire. It has two possible origins. It may mean "keepers of the fire" because they always carried some of their fire from place to place. Another meaning for their name is "people of the place of the fire" because they used fire to clear the grassland for farming.

The Potawatomi could depend more on farming as they lived in a warmer part of the state than the other two main tribes. They did use fire to burn off grass before they planted their corn, squash, beans, tobacco, melons, and sunflowers.

Menominee—Wild Rice in the U.P.

The Menominee tribe lived in the central Upper Peninsula and along the Menominee River. Their name is an Ojibwa word for "wild rice people." They used the wild rice which they gathered from swampy areas as a major source of food. Their customs were much like those of the Ojibwa people who also lived in the

Upper Peninsula. Little is known of the history of the Menominee.

Miami—They Walked along Rivers

In 1673, French missionaries found the Miami tribe living along the St. Joseph River in southern Michigan. Their main village was in northern Indiana on the Kankakee River. There is a point where these two rivers are only a few miles apart and other tribes carried their canoes from river to river. Even though the Miami lived along these two important waterways, they usually traveled on foot!

The Miami farmed and stayed in permanent villages unless attacks from nearby tribes forced them to move.

The Huron men had unusual haircuts so the French gave them the name Huron which meant "hair of a wild pig". (Art by Frederic Remington)

Huron—The People with a Different Hair Style!

One of the first tribes contacted by the French along the St. Lawrence River was the Huron Tribe. They became good friends and traded furs. The homeland of the Huron at that time was around the southern end of Georgian Bay on Lake Huron.

The tribe called itself Wendat, but the French used the word Huron because the men of the tribe had a haircut which reminded the French of the hair on a wild pig. All of the hair was cut off except for a ridge down the middle of the head which stuck straight up.

The Huron were related to the Iroquois tribes and spoke their language. For some reason, other Iroquois tribes became enemies of the Huron. The French missionaries set up work in Huron villages which eventually became fairly successful. However, in 1649, the Iroquois began an all-out war against the French and the Huron. Many of the survivors escaped to Michigan. But the tribe never regained its strength.

The Huron were forced to migrate and they circled counterclockwise around the Lower Peninsula trying to find a new home. They lived near Mackinac, also in Wisconsin, and finally near Detroit where they were known as the Wyandotte.

The Iroquois—Warriors of the Lakes

The Iroquois did not live in Michigan, but they had a powerful effect on those who did. They were not just a single tribe but rather a group of five tribes. They were sometimes known as the Iroquois League. They lived in the land south of Lake Ontario in what is now New York state. After the Europeans arrived, a sixth tribe joined the League. The Iroquois had a more organized form of government than other tribes. Some of the colonists even took ideas for the United States Constitution from the League!

The Iroquois became very warlike and powerful. They were among the first tribes to have guns which they received in trade from the Dutch. They attacked neighboring tribes, often forcing them to move.

The Iroquois destroyed the Erie tribe in Ohio. They constantly fought the Huron in southern Ontario. The League sided with the British against the French, making it harder for the French to reach Michigan. Most of the Iroquois fought with the British in the American Revolution. After the war, many migrated to Ontario and still live in Canada today.

Questions

1. List the three main tribes living in Michigan about 1750 and tell approximately where each one lived.

2. Give two reasons why tribes migrated to Michigan. Name a tribe and their reason for moving.

3. List two examples of tribal names which are not Indian words and two which are Indian words.

4. Write down four new facts you have learned about the Native Americans in Michigan from studying this section.

5. Explain how the Michigan tribes passed their history on from generation to generation. How has most Native American history been passed on to us today? Give some reasons why the European accounts of Native American history can have errors.

Chapter 2 Section 3

Life Among the Tribes

Here are some key concepts you will find in this section:

The Michigan tribes were self-sufficient in meeting their needs by using the natural materials around them.

The Michigan Indians believed men and women did not own land, animals, or the things of nature. These things were to be shared and used by all people.

The Michigan tribes have left us a living legacy. Indians introduced many things which continue to touch us. These include foods, tobacco, games, names, and useful items like the snowshoe and canoe.

If You Had Been There!

What was life like among the tribes? Would you enjoy being a member of one of the tribes living in Michigan 200 or 300 years ago? Would life be an adventure or would you be lost without the modern conveniences we enjoy today? Let's take a look into the past. Understanding the culture of Michigan's Indians will help in understanding what happened to them and why.

Finding Food

Nature provided all of the food for Michigan's Indians. Lakes and rivers were important places to find food. Fish often supplied just as much or more meat to the tribes than animals. Many of the settlements were on rivers or lakes so they could be close to a source of fish in both summer and winter.

Long ago, Michigan fish were plentiful and large. Sturgeon reached six feet in length and weighed over 100 pounds; lake trout weighing 50 pounds were sometimes caught! The men used hooks, spears, and nets to catch fish. Another way to catch fish was from a canoe at night. Fish were attracted by the light from a torch and then speared.

Some people believe the Indians could not make fish nets before Europeans sold them rope and twine. The tribes, however, were able to make their own twine long before that. They used fiber from basswood bark, wild hemp and nettles. By twisting these together they could produce a strong and useful cord.

Traps and snares were favorite ways to catch animals. A snare could be set up which used twine and a bent branch acting as a spring. Traps for rabbits and smaller animals were made from hollowed-out logs with a door falling in place to hold the catch.

Bows and arrows were the weapons used for hunting most large animals. Sometimes the hunting was done at night using torches to catch the attention of a deer until a hunter could get close enough to use his bow.

Passenger pigeons were plentiful and could be caught in well-placed nets. Hunters also shot turkeys, ducks, and other birds. A special arrow with a blunt end was used for small birds.

Hunting was not without dangers and difficulties. A hunter might be badly injured by a charging buck, not to mention what an angry bear could do! Fishing through the ice on a freezing winter day might lead to frostbitten fingers. Quite often the hunters had to travel far and wide to locate game. Supplying meat for the village was hard work.

Sometimes there was no food or no time to prepare it. For those emergencies a high-energy food called pemmican (PEM eh kan) was made ahead and kept on hand. Pemmican is a mixture of sun-dried venison pounded into a paste with fat and berries. It was usually stored in skin bags. If the pemmican was kept dry, it could last for years. It was probably not a taste treat, but served its purpose.

Indians obtained all of their food from nature. Venison from deer was one source of meat. (Courtesy Michigan State Archives)

Crops

Corn, beans, squash, and sunflowers were grown along with tobacco. Corn was an important food for all tribes. It was dried and used in many ways. The women ground corn using two stones or pounded it into a flour. The corn flour went into bread.

Dried corn was usually stored for the winter. Each village dug several deep holes to hold their corn. The holes were covered to keep animals out. Corn provided a nutritious food which could be stored for a long time.

Indians used these rocks to pound corn into a flour to make their bread.

The Bow and Arrow

We think of the bow and arrow as the main weapon associated with Native Americans. But the weapon was actually developed over hundreds of years. The spear was used first; many mastodons and other prehistoric animals were killed

These are examples of Indian stone tools, spear points, and ornaments. They were all found in Michigan. A quarter is included in the photo to compare size.

with spears. We know that because thousands of spear points have been found along with animal bones. The bow and arrow was used more after 500 A.D.

Have you ever found an Indian arrowhead? Many people have! Large numbers of arrowheads and spearpoints have been unearthed in Michigan, often by farmers. Points were normally made of a hard stone called flint. They were made by using larger stones to strike and chip away pieces of the flint.

Their Homes

What would you have seen long ago in the home of a Michigan Ojibwa or Potawatomi? They only had the natural materials which were at hand to build

Wigwams were used by tribes in the Michigan area. The shelters covered with birchbark could easily be taken down and moved as the Indians traveled and hunted. (Art by David B. McConnell)

their homes. The houses of all the Great Lakes tribes were built of the same materials and in about the same way. They began with a frame of branches. The frame was covered with reed mats or tree bark. Size and shape were the big differences. The size depended on whether a tribe lived in a permanent village or moved from place to place.

The Ottawa, Potawatomi, and Miami tribes all lived in small villages during the summer. When winter came, the village would break into small groups who traveled through the country hunting and fishing. Those three tribes used one- family wigwams. Wigwams were dome-shaped and about 15 feet across. They could easily be taken down and moved. The Great Lakes tribes did not use tepees covered with animal hides, though sometimes a tepee-shaped frame was covered with birchbark. Tepees were the homes of tribes living in western states.

The Huron built the largest homes. They were mostly farmers and lived in the same place all year. Their homes were 20 to 80 feet long, about 20 feet wide, and 14 feet high. They were known as longhouses because of their length. Holes in the tops of the houses let out smoke from fires. It could be crowded at times since as many as 20 families lived in one longhouse!

The Huron tribe built longhouses instead of wigwams. Longhouses were more permanent homes which could hold as many as 20 families. Hurons might stay in the same location for several years.

To protect themselves from unfriendly tribes, the Huron villages had fort-like walls of logs which stood on end.

Huron villages lasted about 10 years. By that time the soil was usually worn out and the firewood supply in the area was gone. Then the community would move to a new place.

Values

Sharing was an important part of all Indian cultures. When a hunter brought back food, it was shared by anyone in need. It was an honor to be able to give! That was true with all things. Status was built on the ability to give rather than on the ability to acquire.

The tribes felt men and women did not own things of nature. They could not individually own the land, forests, or animals. The Michigan tribes had no notion of a person owning the land. Land was a resource to be used by all the people. Families would usually return to the same hunting and fishing grounds each year and their rights would be respected by other members of the tribe.

According to their religion, the creator had made each creature to be equal and everything had a soul. All things on earth were tied together in a natural harmony. An Indian hunter felt the deer was like his brother, but he knew he must kill the deer in order for his family to survive. Killing animals just for fun was rare.

Religion

All the tribes in Michigan were very spiritual. They felt each object or animal had a spirit or soul. In a sense, bears, rocks, lakes, or waterfalls all had spirits. Their religion and nature were tied closely together. This does not mean they attended worship services or went to church. When European missionaries arrived in Michigan they generally felt the tribes had no religion, or at best were just superstitious. But the tribes did have religious beliefs; they just weren't the same religious beliefs the Europeans had.

Tribal Government

The Native Americans had unique ideas about government. *They felt no man had the right to control another person's fate.* Chiefs and other leaders were chosen because of the people's respect. They picked leaders they knew were generous, wise, and humble. Ambition and political drive didn't bring the responsibility of leadership. There were chiefs for war and other chiefs in times of peace. Chiefs could only advise; they could not force anyone to do something. If a war chief made too many mistakes, the warriors wouldn't follow him and would just go home.

Their beliefs about sharing, ownership of land, and democracy made the culture of the Great Lakes tribes much different than the culture most people live in today!

Tobacco

Smoking tobacco is a very old custom in America. It was the Native Americans who first taught the Europeans about it when they arrived.

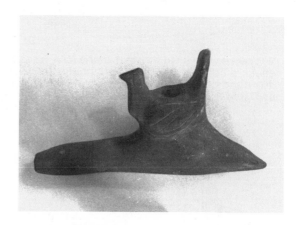

Two pipe styles are shown here. The bird stone is a decorative one. It would have a stem attached to it like the bottom example.

In many ways smoking meant much more to the tribes than it does to people today. It was often a part of special ceremonies and was viewed as having spiritual significance. The French missionary Father Marquette said there was nothing more mysterious or respected among the tribes than the pipe. Smoking a pipe together was a way to seal a bargain or end an important agreement.

Tobacco was grown in the Great Lakes area, especially Ontario. It probably grew in Michigan as well. One tribe in Ontario was even named the Tobacco Nation.

Europeans called the Indian pipes calumets, from a French word meaning tubes.

Artwork

The Great Lakes tribes used natural materials to make beautiful everyday

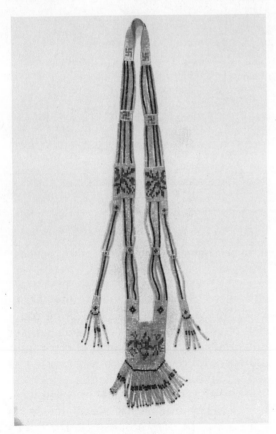

Europeans introduced beads to the Indians. This necklace is an example of the intricate work done by the Indians.

objects. Their tools, weapons, and clothing were carefully decorated.

Men were usually the carvers. They used wood, stone, and bone. From wood they made canoe paddles, war clubs, pipe stems, spoons, bowls, and cradleboards. Stone was used to make the bowls on their pipes.

The women made colorful clothing, bags, and moccasins from fur and leather. Deerskin was often dyed black with a dye from oak or butternut bark. Moose hair and porcupine quills were also dyed. A red dye was made from bloodroot, yellow from sumac stems, and blue from wild blueberries.

For the northern tribes, porcupine quills were a favorite craft material. The women pulled the quills through their teeth in order to flatten them. The quills were added to clothes, bags and moccasins. After European traders brought tiny glass beads, those were often used for decoration in place of quills.

Games and Sports

The Indian men especially enjoyed games of chance using dice. There were many variations and quite often large bets were placed.

Another of their sports was baggataway (beh GAT eh way) or lacrosse (la cross). It is considered the grandfather of modern hockey. It is the oldest organized sport in North America. Baggataway was played with large teams, sometimes whole villages. A wooden or deerskin ball was used and the goals might be very far apart. Each player had one or two webbed sticks. There were few rules and stomping, kicking, tackling, and hitting were permitted. Such a rough and tumble sport could result in serious injury and possibly death!

The Living Heritage of the First Michiganians ...

Inventions

We often make use of Indian inventions without even realizing it.

The Michigan counties selected on this map have Indian names. Names of some of the other counties sound like Indian words, but actually have other origins.

Three methods of transportation came from the tribes; the canoe, the snowshoe, and the toboggan. The basic design of some modern tents is taken from the dome-shaped wigwam. The bow and arrow was probably developed by the Indians on their own but was not unique to them.

Trails to Highways

Driving on I-96 from Detroit to Lansing doesn't remind you of an Indian trail as you look out to see miles of concrete. But you are taking the same route used by Michigan's Native Americans for thousands of years! Several of our major highways follow the same routes used as ancient Indian trails.

The shape of the state and the location of many important places cause us to travel to the very same spots the tribes wished to reach. Because of this, I-75, I-94, I-96, and other highways follow along the same routes as the old Saginaw

Trail, the St. Joseph Trail, and the Grand River Trail.

Many Indian Names

Any time you look at a map, you will discover Indian names are everywhere in Michigan! Even the name of our state comes from Indian words for big lake.

And the states around us, Wisconsin, Illinois, and Ohio, have Indian names. Illinois is a tribe and Ohio is an Iroquois name for a river.

Thirty-three of Michigan's counties use Indian names or the county name is made from several Indian words. "Place of the river's outlet" is one meaning for Saginaw. Lenawee (len AH way) is a Shawnee word for people. In the Upper Peninsula, Keweenaw means "place where a portage is made." One meaning for Kalamazoo is "churning water." Look on the map to check if your county has an Indian name.

Michigan cities use many Indian names too. Some are named for proud chiefs. Pontiac, Tecumseh, Okemos and Tawas are examples. Petoskey is the last name of an Indian family.

Others are not as exciting. Muskegon is a name meaning swamp or marsh, Escanaba means flat rock. Several of the names have been changed from the original tribal words. For example, Munising comes from the word "*minissing*" which means "at the big island."

All of these Indian names remind us of the first people who lived here and that Michigan is rich with their history.

Where Are They Now?

The United States government acquired the lands of the Indians through treaties between 1807 and 1842. Settlers moved where the Indians once lived and the Indians were often forced to leave the state. After the 1840s, many were taken to government reservations in the Southwest, while others fled to Canada. Today there is an Indian community on the Canadian side of the border at Walpole Island near Algonac.

Take as an example, the members of the Sauk tribe who once lived in the Saginaw Valley. First, they were moved to Iowa and then to Kansas. Later, they were forced on to Oklahoma where they live today.

Many of the Native Americans who stayed in Michigan had to live on reservations. There are four federal government reservations in Michigan and some other very small ones including two state reservations. (Look at the color maps M4, M5, and M6. Federal Indian reservations are marked by a half circle.) Three are in the Upper Peninsula while one is in the Lower Peninsula. Michigan's largest reservation is the Isabella Reservation near Mt. Pleasant. These reservations are similar to small towns. Tribal councils govern each one. The

Indians continue to live in Michigan today. These tribal members are at a meeting concerning fishing rights. (Courtesy Michigan State Archives)

Bureau of Indian Affairs, through the federal government, holds this land in trust.

Few Native Americans are on reservations today. Some are farmers, but many live and work in cities. The highest Native American population in Michigan is in Wayne county. The first Michiganians remain proud of their heritage and continue to hold tribal meetings. Many prefer to be called Anishinabe (ah nish in A bey) which means "original people."

Questions:

1. Make a list of eight foods or dishes eaten by the Michigan tribes. Were the tribes able to catch or grow all of these things by themselves?

2. Name one of the two main types of homes used by tribes living in Michigan. Briefly describe the home. Tell how that type of home suited the lifestyle of the tribe who used it.

3. Explain what Michigan Indians thought about the values of sharing and owning land.

4. Michigan's first people left us many things which touch our lives today. Some of them are names of cities and counties, inventions, games and foods. Give five specific examples.

5. Write a paragraph explaining in what ways you would have enjoyed, and the ways you would not have enjoyed, living among a Michigan tribe 200 or 300 years ago.

In his own way Michael Wawro is keeping Native American traditions alive. He spent six months building this Ojibwa style birchbark canoe. Following the traditions of Michigan's first people, the canoe was built in the woods with no clamps, glue or power tools. (Courtesy Sandy Fish, Alpena)

3 FRANCE COMES TO NORTH AMERICA

Chapter 3 Section 1

The Pathway To Michigan!

Here are the key concepts you will find in this section:

The St. Lawrence River was the pathway which finally brought the first Europeans to Michigan. They were the French. Michigan became a part of the French empire.

The fur trade and the search for a way to the Orient were two important reasons the French explored this area. Both of these activities involved rivers and the Great Lakes water system.

The French became involved in a war between two groups of Native American tribes. This had a great impact on what the French did later.

Life for the early French was not easy and settlement was slow.

If you stop thinking of America as highways and start thinking of it as rivers, you get closer to the country.

Charles Kuralt, *Reader's Digest*.

Pathway to Michigan

The St. Lawrence River is like a sword driving toward the heart of North America. This river became a pathway into the continent. Today it is hard for people to realize how important rivers were to travelers when the first Europeans arrived in North America. Imagine the worst dirt road you have ever seen and realize there was nothing then in North America as good as that to use! Also imagine the thickest forest or woods you have ever seen and realize such forests covered most of the continent at that time!

The St. Lawrence was a highway ready to be used by sailing ships and canoes. The Indians had been using it for centuries. It was only a matter of time before the adventurers from Europe began to use the river to go southwest into North America.

The pathway of the St. Lawrence River eventually became the pathway to Michigan. Much of our early history is tied to this great river and the people who used it. It reaches the Great Lakes—the same Great Lakes which surround our state. It brought the Europeans here and the Europeans changed forever the land now called Michigan.

Rivals in a New World

The conquest of North America by the Europeans was a contest by four countries: England, France, Holland, and Spain. The Spanish settled in the southern United States and Central and

The St. Lawrence River became a major trade route for the French. Each year they brought in trade goods and supplies; then returned to France with fish and furs. (Art by David B. McConnell)

South America. The Dutch from Holland settled in what is now New York State. Only a few Dutch traders ever went as far west as Michigan. Therefore, Spain and Holland did not have a big part in Michigan history, but England and France did.

The first great explorer to use the St. Lawrence was Jacques Cartier (car tee YAY). In 1534 he was sent by the king of France to find a route to the *Orient. The Orient refers to the modern countries of China, Japan, India, and the others in that part of the world.* The king was interested in finding a way through North America so the French could reach those lands by sailing west. No one at that time had any idea how large North America was, or how far it was to the Orient; so it seemed to be a reasonable idea.

Their Motives

Why did Europeans want to get to the Orient? Did they enjoy sailing for

months at a time on dirty little ships with a bunch of smelly sailors and eating half-spoiled food? No! Finding a shortcut to the Orient was a business venture, a way to make a great deal of money. Europeans had discovered the people in the Orient had some interesting products. Spices and silk were two which attracted their attention. Silk made very nice clothes and the spices helped European food to taste much better, especially if the food had not been kept cool or wasn't very fresh!

Up the St. Lawrence!

Cartier left France with two ships and searched for a way to continue across North America. He explored the mouth of the St. Lawrence River and finally landed on the Gaspé Peninsula. There he made friends with some Indians. In the fall, he took two of the Native Americans back to France. The next spring Cartier returned with the Indians. He anchored near an island on the day honoring the death of a Christian saint named Lawrence. To Cartier, remembering religious heroes was important, so he named the bay at the beginning of the river after Saint Lawrence. Thus, the mighty St. Lawrence River got its name.

His Indian friends guided him as he sailed up the river. They stopped at an island where the tribesmen told Cartier he was in a kingdom called Canada. Canada is the Huron-Iroquois word for village. Cartier continued to use the word for the land he visited. Eventually all the land north of the United States came to be known as Canada.

Cartier could not find a route to the Orient and that caused the French rulers to lose interest for many years in further exploration of the area.

Fish and Furs Keep Them Coming

Although French explorers did not come back right away, fishermen did. In the early 1500s it was discovered the ocean near Newfoundland was excellent for fishing. Each summer the sea was dotted with white sails. Sailors met the natives when they went on shore to collect food or to dry their fish. Some ships even went up the St. Lawrence River.

The tribes they met were interested in European metal knives, hatchets, fish hooks, and pots. Such items would make life much easier for them.

What could the Indians give the sailors so they could get these things? Furs! The sailors were happy to exchange their knives and fishhooks for the beautiful Indian furs. The French fur trade with North America developed quite nicely in that long-range manner. The historian Samuel Morrison says in 1583 the Paris fur market sold about $12,000 worth of North American furs.

Furs for the Rich and Famous

In Europe, furs had been used in expensive clothing for a long time. The kind and amount of fur people wore was related to their rank in society. Beaver hats had been worn in England since the late 1300s. Also, coats were trimmed with fur collars. But by the 1500s, many fur-bearing animals were hard to find in Europe. The last beaver was seen in England in the 1520s; after that time, it became *extinct* in that country. *Being extinct means there were no more of these animals left alive.*

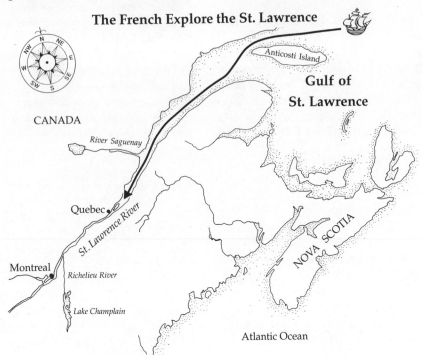

The Frenchman Cartier explored and named the St. Lawrence River.

The French King Takes Action

The Spanish had built a good business by stealing gold from the natives in Mexico. They had developed their colonies and had set up government, farming and religious missions. England had also been busy, but was not quite so far along in North America as Spain was in the south. England sent several sailors to explore the coast of North America.

About 1600, the king of France felt left out of the activity in the New World. He decided to begin a settlement in North America but didn't want to pay for it himself. So he offered to give exclusive fur trading rights to any company willing to start the settlement. Thus, the company had a fur trading monopoly. *A monopoly is the total control of a market.* Monopolies and fur trading companies would be important in the future of Michigan.

The first company had a rough time starting their settlement. So, eventually, the monopoly was taken away and given to a new company. The area to be covered in North America by their monopoly was between latitudes 40 degrees north and 46 degrees north—a large piece of land!

A Great Frenchman Challenges the Wilderness

An important member of the second company was Samuel de Champlain (duh sham PLANE). He was an experienced soldier and sailor. He knew about Canada and the St. Lawrence because the fishing ships stopped at his hometown in France.

In 1604 they tried to start a settlement on the southwest side of Nova Scotia. That did not seem to be a good location so an expedition searched for a better site. The expedition sailed down the coast of America as far as Plymouth, Massachusetts. Champlain even made charts of the harbor. That was years before the Pilgrims arrived!

Did the company with the monopoly really keep all the furs from such a huge region? No they didn't. Over 80 competing ships took home furs each year without bothering to give any to those who had the monopoly! It would have taken a whole navy to stop them! Illegal fur traders continued for a long time to be a problem in New France. So Champlain suggested they settle far up the St. Lawrence to be closer to the furs they wanted.

First Settlement on the St. Lawrence

Three ships left France in the spring of 1608 to make a fresh try. Champlain had chosen a place where the river narrows, about 375 miles up the river. The Native Americans called the place *Kebec* which means narrow place in the river. The French changed the name to Quebec (kay BECK) and a great city was about to be born.

Monopoly— So What!

Trouble was waiting for Champlain! When he arrived, angry fur traders were already there. The traders didn't like the idea of a monopoly and killed one of Champlain's men and wounded another in a fight. Champlain had to do some fast talking to control the situation.

He was not, however, one to slow down because of problems. Soon buildings were finished and winter wheat and rye planted. But it was a very cold winter. Several of the men died. By spring, only eight of the 24 were alive! Two of them were boys, Etienne (ay TYEN) and Nicolas. The boys spent the terrible winter learning the Indian language from the local tribe. Their ability to speak with the Indians was later very important.

Helping Friends with Musket Balls!

When Champlain was exploring the east coast of America, the Indians told him of the problems they had with the Iroquois tribes. (They were five tribes who worked closely together. They were also called the Five Nations.) Even though they were bullying other tribes, Champlain hoped he could lead them to be peaceful. At that time, the Iroquois lived in a large area south of the

St. Lawrence River, in present day New York state. The Huron and other tribes with whom the French traded lived north of the river and were often attacked by the Iroquois.

Finally, Champlain felt talking was useless and decided to help the friendly tribes. He reasoned that if they did not have to spend time fighting, the Indians would get more furs. He said he would go with them to battle the Iroquois. About 60 friendly warriors and 20 Frenchmen went in canoes up the St. Lawrence, and then south on the Richelieu (Rish i loo) River. They found a beautiful lake which Champlain promptly named after himself.

History was waiting to be made at the southern end of the lake. After dark on July 29, 1609, Champlain's group met an Iroquois war party of about 200 men. The Iroquois had built a crude log fort to protect themselves. That night the two tribal groups exchanged insults and boasts. The next morning the Iroquois came out and the Huron charged forward, stopped, and urged Champlain to show his power. His power was a match-lock musket loaded with four lead balls.

This picture is similar to one Champlain drew showing himself during the 1609 attack on the Iroquois. (Art by David B. McConnell)

Three chiefs wearing eagle feathers walked in the lead of the Iroquois. With a single shot, Samuel de Champlain killed two of the chiefs and left the third dying! The course of history was set. Now the French had entered the war between the Iroquois and their enemy tribes. The surprise of the thunderous French muskets caused the Iroquois to turn and run, but it would be for the first and last time!

Did Champlain do the right thing? Could he have helped the two groups of Indians find peace instead? Today we can only guess the answers. But the attack on the Iroquois helped close the pathway of the St. Lawrence to the French. It changed the way they eventually came to Michigan.

The "Friendly" Dutch

The Dutch seemed to get along fairly well with the Iroquois. They were settling New York which they called New Amsterdam. (Amsterdam is the capital of Holland.) From here the Hudson River goes north and almost reaches Lake Champlain. It flows into the heart of Iroquois country. This was certainly to the advantage of that group of tribes because they learned about guns and eventually traded furs to the Dutch for the new weapons. The government of New France was quite unhappy with the Dutch trading practices.

More French Exploring

Remember, the French wished to find a way to the Orient, to locate a passage through North America. Champlain continued to look in his "spare" time. Various Indians told him of a salt sea to the west. But how far away was it and how could he get there? He also heard of a great sea to the north. Champlain wanted to try to find it but the Native Americans were not interested in giving away all of their secrets. He could not find anyone who would guide him there.

The two boys, Etienne and Nicolas,

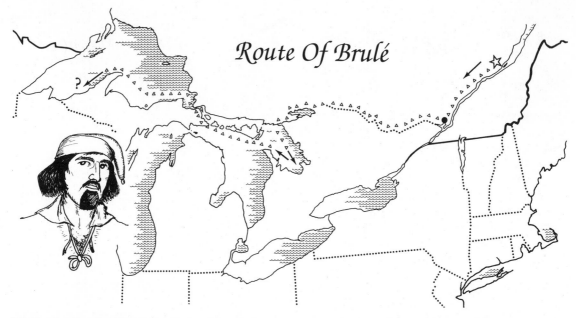

Route Of Brulé

Brulé, who lived most of his life in the woods, may have looked like this although there is no known picture of him. He is believed to be the first European to visit Michigan. (Art by David B. McConnell)

who survived the first winter at Quebec, knew the tribal languages well. They spent much time with the Indians and easily learned their customs. Etienne, to whom historians gave the last name of Brulé (broo LAY), eagerly went on several canoe trips. On one of them he traveled west using the Ottawa River and passed through Lake Nipissing, Georgian Bay and finally into Lake Huron. He was the first European to see Lake Huron and probably several of the other Great Lakes.

The trouble with Brulé was he never bothered to write anything down about his travels. Sometimes even Champlain didn't know where he was! Brulé would be gone for long periods of time, living with the Indians, practically disappearing, and then coming back to Quebec. Nonetheless, Brulé and Champlain discovered Lake Ontario in 1615. Brulé and a companion named Grenoble helped find the way to Michigan. They probably reached the Upper Peninsula about 1622. Look on a map and see the route they used. By now the French knew about most of the Great Lakes and had found the land which was to become Michigan!

They did all of this by following the rivers and lakes.

A Competitor Takes Over!

In 1630 the British decided to sail up the St. Lawrence and take over New France. Champlain was caught alone in the fort and he had no choice but to surrender. He was shocked to find Etienne Brulé and Nicolas helping the British. Knowing he was outnumbered, they had gone over to the other side!

Champlain was taken prisoner and put aboard a British ship. Luckily by the time it reached England, peace had been declared. Soon he was able to head back to New France. Champlain was more than a little upset at his two lads who had turned traitor!

The End of Brulé

Etienne Brulé, the first European to see Michigan and explore so much of the Great Lakes, met a sad end. Before Champlain could bring him to trial, a group of Huron Indians turned on him, tortured, and killed him.

The Jean Nicolet Story

By 1634 Champlain was an old man. He decided to make one more try to locate that mysterious passage to China by sending Jean Nicolet (JHAN nee ko LAY) up the Ottawa River. Nicolet had spent many years living with the various tribes and was experienced in that part of the country. He was an interpreter and agent for the fur company. A beautiful Chinese robe was provided to impress the Chinese who might be found.

He traveled through the Straits of Mackinac and followed the north shore of Lake Michigan. At Green Bay, Wisconsin, he thought he might have found a waterway further west. Unfortunately, he soon came to the end of the bay and realized it didn't connect with an ocean. Deciding he might as well impress the Native Americans, Nicolet put on the robe and announced his presence to the first Indian village he found. Then he shot his two pistols in the air. It made a great show and scared away the women and children! The news of the newcomer attracted 4,000 or 5,000 Indians who came to see Nicolet and provided him with a fine feast. But his search for a way to the Orient was not successful.

The Father of New France Dies

Champlain died in 1635. Today he is known as the "Father of New France." He suffered many hardships. He struggled to start a new country in a wild land. He used the St. Lawrence River as a pathway into North America.

Champlain really wanted to build cities and develop New France as a great country but working with the company of fur traders created difficulties. They were more interested in making money than anything else. They did not bring many families or supplies to Quebec. There was only a tiny 1.5 acre farm to provide food for everyone! He could not get much help from the merchants in the company or from the king.

We know much about Champlain and what life was like because he wrote four books about his adventures. Without those books, we would not know about life in New France.

Questions

1. What were the French doing in North America when they first started to trade furs with the Indians?

2. List three countries which were rivals of France in North America. Tell two problems caused by these rival countries.

3. What was Champlain's purpose when he joined the attack against the Iroquois?

4. What part of Michigan did Jean Nicolet see on his trip to find China? Where did his trip end?

5. Write a paragraph on the importance of the help the Indians gave the French in exploring North America. Back up your ideas with as many facts as possible.

Chapter 3 Section 2

Search for Souls: Missionaries & Priests

| Here are the key concepts you will find in this section: |

The priests accomplished these things:
- They spread French influence throughout the region.
- They gained knowledge about Indian life.
- They learned about the geography of the land.
- They kept the only written records of many historical events.

Priests On the Way to Michigan

In the 1600s the people of France had an increased interest in religion. Almost as soon as the first attempt was made to start a settlement in North America, French men and women were ready to come. They wanted to make Christians of the Indians in the new land.

The missionaries were members of several religious organizations. In North America there were three main Catholic groups. The Jesuits (JEZH wits) were the most aggressive in their work. They were not just in New France, but also in many other parts of the world. At about the same time the French missionaries were arriving in North America, the Jesuits were also starting missions in South America and Vietnam.

The missionaries, who were generally well-educated, willingly gave up the more comfortable life they had in France. Here they had to work hard, often with poor facilities.

They had an impact on what happened in New France. Their desire to reach the Indians meant they would travel far from French settlements. By doing that, the area under French control expanded. They studied the tribal languages and customs which made it easier for the French to know how to work with the tribes.

Not Easy Work!

Early missionary work was not for the faint-hearted or lazy! The historian Francis Parkman wrote a description of the winter experience of one missionary trying to live with Indians in a wigwam. The fellow shared a wigwam about 13 feet by 13 feet. The missionary listed his

French priests traveled thousands of miles on Michigan's rivers in their efforts to reach the tribes. (Courtesy Michigan State Archives)

main grievances under four categories; *cold, heat, smoke, and dogs!* This is what he said:

"Put aside the bear skin and enter the hut. Here were packed 19 men, women, and children with their dogs, crouched, squatted, coiled like hedgehogs, or lying on their backs, with knees drawn up to keep their feet out of the fire. The bark covering was full of crevices, through which icy blasts streamed in upon him from all sides; and the hole above, at once a window and a chimney, was so large that as he lay he could watch the stars as well as in the open air. While the fire in the midst, fed with fat pine knots, scorched him on one side, on the other he had much ado to keep himself from freezing. At times, however, the crowded hut seemed heated to the temperature of an oven. But these evils were light, when compared to the intolerable plague of smoke. During a snow storm and often at other times, the wigwam was filled with fumes so dense that all were forced to lie flat on their faces, breathing through mouths in contact with the cold earth. Their throats and nostrils felt as if on fire; their scorched eyes streamed with tears. When he tried to read, the letters of his prayer book seemed printed in blood. The dogs were not an unmixed evil, for by sleeping on and around him they kept him warm at night; but, as an offset to this good service, they walked, ran and jumped over him as he lay, snatched food from his birch dish or, in a mad rush at some discarded morsel, now and then knocked over both dish and missionary!"

"Father Le Jeune and the Hunters" in Parkman's *The Jesuits in North America.*

The Huron Were First

The early missionaries worked with the Huron tribe who lived south of Georgian Bay and north of Lake Ontario. One of the missions in that part of Ontario was called Sainte Marie.

In 1641 Father Jogues (ZHOG) and Father Raymbault (raim BOE) left the mission and traveled by canoe north to the Saint Mary's River between the Upper Peninsula and Canada. The St. Mary's River has a swift rapids. It was near that spot where the two priests found a large village of about 2,000 friendly Indians. They called that place Sault Ste. Marie (SOO SAYNT ma REE). Sault means rapids and Sainte Marie was their home mission in Ontario. The Indians invited them to stay; the two priests, however, felt they must return to the land of the Huron.

The priests' work among the Huron tribe was going well until a serious problem developed. The Iroquois tribes decided to attack the Huron and others living in that area. A large part of the Huron tribe was killed and many of its members driven far away. The Iroquois

The Huron tribe had to flee Ontario because of Iroquois attacks. Many Hurons were killed in the warfare. (Art by George Rasmussen)

also tortured and killed many of the priests including Jogues and Raymbault. Because of the Iroquois attacks, the late 1640s was a time of terror in New France! Even much of the fur trade came to a halt.

A New Priest in the U.P. --- Father Menard

The Jesuits were eager to work with the Huron again and they had heard rumors the Huron had fled toward the west end of Lake Superior. In 1660, Father Menard (may NAR) went back to the Lake Superior region with some Indians who had come to Montreal to trade furs. He followed the southern shore of the lake until he came to Keweenaw Bay. The trip must not have been easy for Father Menard as he was 55 years old. Menard spent the winter with people from the Ottawa tribe near L'Anse at the base of the Keweenaw Peninsula. Surviving a difficult winter, he parted company with the Ottawa to go farther west. One Frenchman and some Indians went with him. Unfortunately, somewhere on the way he became separated from his group and was completely lost, never to be seen again! Such was the way of the rugged land.

The Battles Stop --- More Missionaries Come

After much complaining by those living in New France, the King of France sent soldiers to attack the Iroquois villages and burn their crops. After a few months of such aggressive treatment, the Iroquois agreed to an uneasy peace.

Another missionary was then chosen to follow in Menard's footsteps. That person was Claude Allouez (clawd ah l WAY). A Jesuit from the age of seventeen, Father Allouez was a determined person. He made his way along the rocky shore of Lake Superior. As he visited the places where Menard had been, he asked if anyone knew what had happened to Menard.

Of course he could not find the other priest, but in 1667 he returned to Quebec and told of something he *did* find—pieces of copper from the Upper Peninsula! He also mentioned stories of a great river which lay to the west of Lake Superior. It was actually the Mississippi.

Father Allouez came back to do missionary work among the tribes in and around Michigan. Altogether he spent 22 years in the region and he is buried in Niles, Michigan.

Father Marquette was the founder of Sault Ste. Marie, the first permanent city in Michigan. (Courtesy Michigan State Archives)

The Father Marquette Story

In 1668 a young man, who became one of the best-known Jesuit missionaries, made his way to Michigan. He was Jacques Marquette (JHAHK mar KETT). Marquette once said he wanted to be a missionary from his earliest boyhood. Probably the desire to be a missionary in those days is similar to someone in today's world thinking about being an astronaut. Either career would be challenging and exciting, taking a person to the edge of the unknown.

The son of a lawyer, Marquette was born in 1637. He went to a Jesuit school and those missionaries who died at the hands of the Iroquois were heroes of the students. At 29, he was finally assigned to go to New France and begin his work among the Indians. It took six long weeks of uneasy sea travel to reach Quebec.

Women in the Missions

Men were not the only ones giving their time and lives in the French mission field. While Marquette was at Quebec he must have seen the school for girls started by Marie Guyard (GHEE ar) in 1639. There young Indian girls lived and studied along with the daughters of French families. Other French women worked along with Marie Guyard to train the Indians in European ways. Quebec also had a hospital run by 13 nuns. They took care of sick or injured Indians. Both the school and hospital are still operating today! Women were not allowed to become priests so they could not work with the tribes in the wilderness.

Going Into the Unknown Land

The first thing all new priests had to do was learn one or more of the Indian languages. It wasn't easy and some priests never could get them quite right. Only those who mastered at least one of the languages had much impact in New France. Marquette was able to learn parts of several tribal languages while he was at Quebec.

Before long, Marquette was in a canoe and on his way to Sault Ste. Marie. His group paddled up the Ottawa River and then west to Lake Nipissing. Their route was the one most often used by the French to reach the Great Lakes. It had 18 *portages*, and some of them were six miles long. *A portage is a place where the canoes must be carried.*

The Sault was a good place to preach to the Indians. Many visited there each summer to catch fish in the rapids. Now there would be *Black Robes* at the Sault too. *Black Robes was the nickname the Indians used for the Jesuit priests.* Marquette started a permanent mission and spent one winter there. It was the place where Father Jogues and Father Raymbault had visited earlier. Sault Ste. Marie, Michigan's oldest city, developed from that mission post.

The next spring Marquette was sent to a place just west of the Upper Peninsula into what is now Wisconsin. Here he replaced Father Allouez.

Learning About a Great River

During the first winter at his new post, Father Marquette helped nurse a sick Ottawa warrior back to health. The man was so grateful he gave the priest an Indian slave who had been captured from the Illinois tribe. Marquette spent much of the winter talking with the Illinois about the land where his tribe lived. At first it must have been difficult to communicate with the young man who spoke a language new to Marquette. Gradually he learned the Illinois man had crossed a great river flowing from north to south. It was probably the same river Father Allouez had heard called the "Mesippi." Could it be a passage to the Western Sea?

Marquette was ready to explore the river right away, but he had to force himself to wait for permission from the government and Jesuit headquarters in Quebec.

A Dream Which Comes True!

In 1672 Louis Jolliet (LOO ee zhol ee AY) arrived at the St. Ignace mission where Marquette was then working. Louis was well-educated and once wanted to join the Jesuits, but changed his mind.

The news he brought Marquette was very exciting. The government had approved an expedition to find the great river Mesippi and they were authorized to go together in the spring.

Granting permission to make the dangerous voyage was about all the help the government gave Jolliet. He had to pay all the expenses himself. The trip would cost a considerable amount. They needed canoes, food for the seven Frenchmen who would be on the trip, and trade goods as well as gifts for the Indians. In Quebec, a contract was made explaining how any profits from furs collected during the trip would be divided among the adventurers.

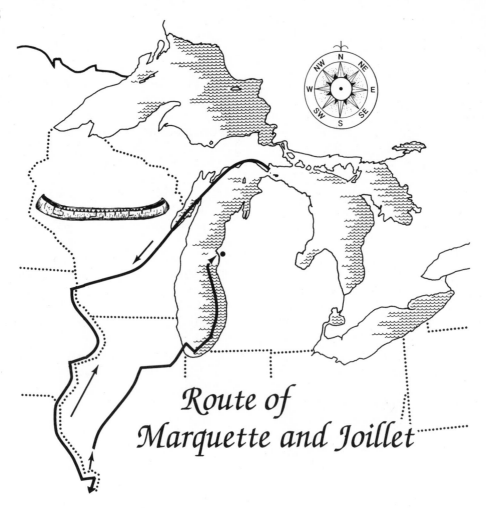

Route of
Marquette and Joillet

Marquette and Jolliet voyaged to find the Mississippi River in 1673.

Voyage To Find the Mississippi River

On May 17, 1673, Jolliet, Marquette, and five Frenchmen were on their way! Their two canoes followed the southern shore of the Upper Peninsula down the Garden Peninsula. Then they turned south to reach Summer Island and went from island to island until they reached the Door Peninsula of Wisconsin. The eastern Green Bay shore was their guide. Along the way they stopped at a Menominee village.

When they told the Menominee people their objective of going down the Mississippi River, the Indians gave them a lecture on the dangers they would face:

"There are Nations who never show any mercy to strangers, but break their heads without any cause....The great river is full of horrible monsters, which devour men and canoes together; that there is even a demon, who is heard from a great distance, and who bars the way and would swallow up all who venture to approach him."

Father Marquette in *Jesuit Relations*, volume 59, translated by Reuben G. Thwaites.

Marquette told the Indians he could not take their advice "...because the salvation of souls was at stake, for which I would be delighted to give my life...."

They took their canoes up the Fox River and stopped briefly to visit Father Allouez at his new mission. Lake Winnebago was crossed and they once again followed the Fox River. About 50 miles upstream another Indian village was sighted. They asked if two guides could take the group to a nearby river which connected with the mighty Mesippi (Mississippi).

On June 10 the French and two guides left the village as an amazed crowd watched them go. The course took them through swamps and many small lakes. Marquette wrote:

"We greatly needed our two guides, who safely conducted us to a portage of 2,700 paces, and helped us to transport our canoes to enter the river; after which they returned home, leaving us alone in this unknown country...."

Jesuit Relations, volume 59

Alone in Dangerous Country

The Indian guides helped them reach the Wisconsin River. They canoed 118 miles down the Wisconsin. On June 17 Marquette wrote "...at 42.5 degrees of latitude, we safely entered the Mississippi...with a joy I cannot express."

What did they see in the new land? They did not see any Indians at first. But they were still worried; so each night they slept in the canoes anchored away from the shore. On the eighth day someone noticed footprints on the right bank of the river! Marquette and Jolliet decided to follow the footprints while the others stayed behind to guard the canoes.

They came close to an Indian village. Both of them put their courage to the test and began to shout and yell to attract the villagers—and maybe end their lives! Marquette spoke to them in the Illinois language. Would they understand? Yes, they were from the Illinois tribe! Soon, as was the Indian custom, calumets were smoked as a token of peace. The French left the village after visiting for several days.

Onward they traveled into uncharted land filled with tribes who spoke unknown languages. After many days they were quite certain the Mississippi did not go to the Western Sea (Pacific Ocean) but went instead into the South Sea (Gulf of Mexico). When they reached what they figured was the latitude of 33 degrees, they felt they might be at risk of falling into the hands of the Spanish. If that happened, they knew all knowledge of their voyage would be lost while they rotted in prison—or worse! It was time to head the canoes north and fight the mighty Mississippi's current and paddle home.

Back Home—Almost!

Near the end of September the explorers dragged into the mission on the Fox River but no one was there. The Indians and Father Allouez had gone off to hunt for winter game. In October, Jolliet and his crew left for Sault Ste. Marie with Marquette staying behind.

In the spring when everyone returned, they found Marquette was not the healthy young man they remembered. He had chills and fever and could not eat much. He remained sick and very weak all summer.

Marquette's illness continued over the next several months. Once he tried to go back to visit the Indians he had met but was too sick to continue. Finally two French friends paddled him to visit the Illinois tribe. Marquette was an honored guest.

He was asked to stay but his health had become poor again. Marquette decided he must go back to St. Ignace, Michigan, where he hoped to get better.

The Marquette Memorial in St. Ignace, Michigan. (Courtesy Nancy Hanatyk)

50

He was highly thought of by the tribe and canoe loads of Indians followed them up the Illinois River. As they left the Indians behind near Chicago, Marquette was so sick he could not even move.

In a desperate attempt to get Marquette back to St. Ignace, the two friends decided to take a new route and follow the east shore of Lake Michigan. No Frenchman had ever seen that side of the Lower Peninsula. The priest was now only semi-conscious and he prayed often. On May 18 they came to a river and Marquette told the men it would be a good place for him to be buried. They took him ashore, probably near Ludington, and he died late in the evening as his companions prayed and wept.

Jolliet had almost reached home when tragedy struck in the rapids of the St. Lawrence. His canoes tipped over and all his notes were lost. (Drawing by Chet Kozlak from *A Great Lakes Fur Trade Coloring Book*, copyright 1981 by the Minnesota Historical Society)

Jolliet's Problems

Meanwhile, Louis Jolliet had almost made it back to Montreal when both his canoes turned over in a rapids on the St. Lawrence River. Some of the men drowned and he lost all of his notes and papers. To add humiliation on top of the disaster, his sister-in-law sued him for rent on one of the canoes which he had borrowed from her! Eventually the government did recognize his work in exploring the Mississippi and gave him the largest island in the St. Lawrence River where he set up a fishing business.

Remember to Take Notes!

Much of the history presented in this chapter would be unknown except for the journals the priests kept while in New France. The tribes did not have written languages and many of the fur traders could not read or write.

The Jesuits recorded everything they possibly could and most of their information is very accurate. The Jesuit order in France published books of what happened to the priests each year. Their books are called *Jesuit Relations*. Today there are over 70 volumes of the *Relations* and they have been translated into English. They cover a span from the time the first French priests came to New France until after the French and Indian war, about 150 years later.

At many places in this book there are quotes from letters and diaries kept by other people. Because people went to the trouble to keep accurate records we know more about the past. Someday, your notes may be studied by historians trying to find out about life during the twentieth century!

Questions

1. Besides fur trading, what brought many French men and women to America? Was this group easily accepted by the Indians?

2. Who named Michigan's oldest non-Indian settlement? Why did they give it this name?

3. Name three of the French priests who came to Michigan. Tell some of the things priests did which helped New France expand into Michigan.

4. How did the roles of men and women differ in French missionary work among the tribes?

5. Refer to the color map pages M4 & M5. Tell which modern roads and highways you could use to follow as nearly as you can to the first part of Marquette and Jolliet's route to the Mississippi.

6. What personal qualities helped Father Marquette to be successful in his work among the Indians and in his voyage to the Mississippi?

Chapter 3 Section 3

The Explorers:
Through Woods and Over Waters

Here are the key concepts you will find in this section:

The French king claimed Michigan and all of the Great Lakes in a ceremony at Sault Ste. Marie.

The first sailing ship west of Niagara Falls was built to sail on the Great Lakes.

The first Europeans saw the Lower Peninsula by walking across it.

Detroit began as a fort to keep the British out of the Great Lakes.

The first European women arrived in Michigan.

Learning About the Land

The French began exploring the Great Lakes Region as soon as they learned of its existence. You have already read about Brule´ and other French explorers including Nicolet, Marquette, and Jolliet. All used the lakes and rivers as their routes to reach new and unknown places. They were forging knowledge of the land as they drew new maps which became more and more accurate.

Not only were the French learning more about the Great Lakes but the amount of furs coming from that region was increasing each year. In 1670 the government of New France heard rumors about a British group called the Hudson's Bay Company which planned to trade furs in the land to the north. Furs were the economy of New France and such news was upsetting! It was definitely time for France to make a claim to the land in central North America.

The Hudson's Bay Company

What exactly was the Hudson's Bay Company and why was it important? The company was the basis for a British claim to the land north of New France. Now the British were on two sides of New France,

not just one. Strangely, the company was started by two Frenchmen! They were two brothers-in-law, Medard Groseilliers (grow zeh YAY) and the young Pierre Radisson (ra dee SOwn), who went to the land around Lake Superior. Radisson wrote a journal of their travels and mentioned some of the places they visited in the Upper Peninsula.

When the two returned in 1660, people noticed the fine furs they brought back with them. They even told the governor where they found them and suggested the best way to get other furs like them was to sail into Hudson's Bay and James Bay from the Atlantic Ocean.

The governor was not very open-minded and he had the two men heavily fined for going without his permission! He should have been more thoughtful. The next thing Groseilliers and Radisson did was to travel to England—the arch rival of France. In England the two were successful in finding people to back them. Eventually they formed the Hudson's Bay Company which has been one of the world's most famous fur trading businesses. It operated as such until recently, a life span of over 300 years!

Claiming Michigan and Much More!

To protect French interests, a plan was developed. It would claim the land for France and impress the tribes to continue their trade with the French and not with any British traders who might stop by.

Sault Ste. Marie was chosen as the site to make the claim because it was a regular meeting place for many tribes. The French put on a really big show, and the event was named the Pageant of the Sault.

It was a June day in 1671. A tremendous gathering of about 2,000 Indians from tribes as far away as Green Bay, Wisconsin, came to witness the ceremony. Chiefs from 14 tribes were present or represented.

A high official, named St. Lusson, had been sent by the king of France to take a leading part. He and all the French officers wore their finest uniforms to impress the Indians. Priests, including Claude Allouez, along with dozens of voyageurs were also there.

The French marched to a small hill where a large wooden cross was set in the ground. Beside it was a post showing the King's coat of arms. After a song and prayers for the king, St. Lusson held his sword in one hand and some sod in another, proclaiming in a loud voice:

"We take possession of the said place of Sault Ste. Marie, as well as of Lakes Huron, and Superior, the island of Manitoulin and of all other countries, rivers, lakes and tributaries, contiguous and adjacent there unto, as well as those discovered and to be discovered, which are bounded on one side by the Northern and Western Seas, and on the other side by the South Sea including all its length and breadth."

Jesuit Relations, volume 50

The speech was translated for the Indians by Nicolas Perrot (pe ROW) who was an important French trader. The French then shouted together and fired their muskets as a salute.

Father Allouez also spoke. He told the tribes they were now the children of the king; he would be their father. He told of the king's greatness, vast wealth, and power. Presents were given to the Indians.

It was an exciting time, and the Indians enjoyed the show; but they did not know the full meaning of what was said.

As for the French, could they live up to their claims? For a time, many would try!

A Man With Grand Plans—La Salle

One of those Frenchmen was Robert Cavelier, Sieur de La Salle, otherwise known as La Salle (la SAL). He was ambitious and adventuresome.

La Salle's family was wealthy but he did not inherit any of it. Since he had expensive plans, the problem of finding enough money to pay for them always faced him.

His older brother had joined the priesthood and was serving in Montreal. Robert learned the mission there was willing to sell land cheaply to attract settlers. He went and received over 350 acres. La Salle, however, wanted more excitement than farming provided; he preferred to explore the nearby area and learn Indian languages.

During a short time of peace, La Salle had several Iroquois stay with him. They told him about a river which began in their land and which was so long it took eight or nine months to reach the great sea. What great sea? Could it be a way to reach the Pacific Ocean?

Their name for the river was Ohio. In the Indians' view, the Allegheny, Ohio, and southern half of the Mississippi were all the same river. Because of what the Iroquois said, some members of their tribe must have actually gone to the Gulf of Mexico and back!

I Must Go!

The information set La Salle's imagination on fire and changed his life forever! There could be no rest until he explored the river. In 1669 the govern-

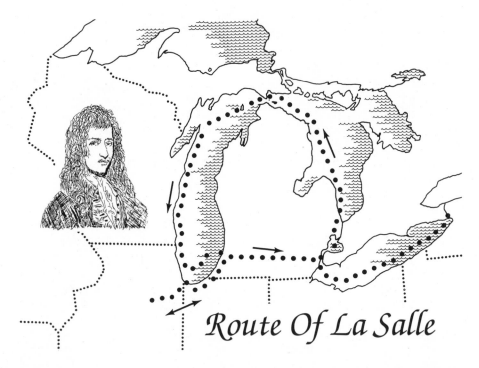

Route Of La Salle

In 1680, LaSalle and his men were the first non-Native Americans to cross the Lower Peninsula. (Art by David B. McConnell)

ment of New France gave him permission, but would not help pay for anything! La Salle somehow persuaded the mission at Montreal to buy back his land so he would have enough money!

Into Iroquois country he went to find a guide. It is believed La Salle finally located a branch of the Allegheny River which is south of Lake Erie. He traveled down the river and into the Ohio River and on to Louisville, Kentucky—perhaps even further. Unfortunately, there is not much information about what happened on his trip. Historians disagree on exactly what he did.

La Salle Upsets Traders

He returned to Quebec and became good friends with Count Frontenac (FRAHNT nak), the governor of New France. The two of them built Fort Frontenac near Kingston, Ontario. La Salle's close ties with the governor worried other fur traders at Montreal and made many of them jealous. They felt La Salle would use the new fort to take the fur trade away from them.

The fort was only a start for his ambitions. In 1677 La Salle returned to France and was given broad powers by King Louis XIV to explore and build forts along the Mississippi River. There were three requirements, however:

1. He had to do it all within five years.
2. There wasn't to be any fur trading with the tribes who came to Montreal.
3. And, he must do it with his own money.

Henri de Tonty— A Friend!

On the voyage from France, La Salle met Henri de Tonty, an Italian. He would become La Salle's trusted friend—one of the few he would ever have. Both Henri and his brother Alphonse eventually came to Michigan.

Henri had been in the army and lost one of his hands in battle. It had been replaced with an iron hand covered by a leather glove. Once or twice Tonty used his hand in fights with Indians. They didn't know the secret of his knockout blows and thought he had "powerful medicine!"

Building the *Griffon*

La Salle not only had grand plans, but he was also a hard worker. He expected to obtain furs in the west—in spite of his promise to the king. A vessel larger than a canoe would be needed to do the job. A full-sized sailing ship would be built on the Niagara River, above the falls.

La Salle was never blessed with much good luck. The boat carrying supplies to Niagara was wrecked and almost everything was lost. La Salle thought the boat's captain was either terribly unskilled or wrecked the boat on purpose. Perhaps one of the Montreal fur traders paid him to do it. During that time several men were sent ahead to gather furs west of Mackinac.

After much difficulty and concern about Iroquois attacks, the ship was finished and named the *Griffon*. This is a mythical animal with the body of a lion and the head and wings of an eagle. La Salle chose this strange beast because it was on the Frontenac family coat of arms. A carved griffon was placed at the bow of the ship. There was nothing like this ship on the Upper Great Lakes. It had room for about 45 tons of cargo and five cannons armed the deck.

Meanwhile his enemies had spread many rumors about La Salle going off on a crazy voyage. The people who loaned him money were afraid he would never come back to pay his bills so they seized all of his property!

First Stop, Detroit

The stubborn La Salle meant to continue his plans, and in August 1679 the *Griffon* set sail heading west. After three or four days they reached the narrow straits, or as the French would say *detroit*, between the Lower Peninsula and Canada. Today, Michigan's largest city is located along those straits. As they traveled up the river, they were impressed by the large number of animals they saw. Many apple and plum trees along with abundant grape vines grew on the land along the river.

The *Griffon* sailed on into Lake Huron and toward St. Ignace but had to survive a terrific storm which had the sailors praying for help.

When they arrived at St. Ignace they found a busy community with a mission

La Salle's Griffon was greeted by the Indians when it arrived at Michilimackinac. (Courtesy American Museum of Natural History, oil sketch by George Catlin)

house, homes of French traders and a village of Huron wigwams and another village of Ottawa. Crowds of Indians were awed by the *Griffon*. They gave La Salle a warm greeting.

The Furs Were Waiting

The *Griffon* continued and met the men who had gone ahead to collect furs near Green Bay! It was then La Salle felt he must make a daring choice. The furs had to go back to Montreal and be sold to pay his bills, but was the captain trustworthy? On the one hand, La Salle wanted to go back on the ship, but on the other he felt the need to supervise the next stage of his plan. Should he go down the Mississippi and build a fort and a second ship? The decision was made; the *Griffon* would have to go back without him.

Danger in the Air!

The furs were loaded on the *Griffon*, and the captain was instructed to sail quickly to Niagara, unload the furs, and return to the southern end of Lake Michigan. Near the St. Joseph River, La Salle would be waiting and counting on him to bring supplies to finish the second ship.

As they prepared the *Griffon* to sail, some of the Indians told the captain a storm was coming, but he didn't see any sign of it and left anyway. Before the ship was out of sight, the storm hit, and tossed the ship violently! La Salle and the other men were in canoes on their way. They were in trouble too. It was all they could do to keep from drowning. For five days the storm raged. No one would ever see the Griffon again and its disappearance is still a mystery!

On November 1, 1679, after a long and very difficult journey, La Salle's group arrived on the east side of Lake Michigan. It was there they built the first non-Indian outpost in the Lower Peninsula. They called it Fort Miami after the tribe living in the area.

Another Fort and Ship to be Built

In December, La Salle left two men at Fort Miami and the others went up the St. Joseph River. They used a portage and then followed the Illinois River. At a place along the Illinois, and about 200 miles south of Fort Miami, they built a new fort.

It was at that new fort, hundreds of miles in the wilderness, that Tonty was to build another sailing ship. But they still needed to get parts and rigging; so, La Salle decided to take some of his men and go for them. Their first stop was at Fort Miami, in Michigan. It was hoped the *Griffon* had returned, but it had not.

Through the Woods

La Salle's group then had no choice except to travel over 600 miles to Montreal. In March they began their journey. It was decided to walk rather than use the St. Joseph River. It would not be easy because there were no paths and the forests were thick. La Salle said, "...in two days and a half our clothes were all torn, and our faces so covered with blood that we hardly knew each other." Fortunately on the third day, the forest was no longer as thick and it was easier for them to travel.

Indians did not hunt in the southern part of Michigan at that time because it was claimed by five or six rival tribes. The only ones in the area were war parties who traveled in secrecy.

At one point, La Salle and his men had to cross a very large swamp which took three days! They didn't dare make a fire as hostile Indians might see the smoke. At night they took off their wet clothes and slept in blankets. One morning when they awakened, it was so cold their clothes were frozen "stiff as sticks." In their rather delicate condition they had to build a fire to thaw out the clothes. But there were Indians watching and when they saw the fire, they ran up to attack! Luckily by the time they came close, the Indians could see La Salle and his men were French. The Indians called out in the Illinois language to La Salle and said they had mistaken them for Iroquois. A sigh of relief went through the shivering men.

La Salle did not leave behind enough information for us to know the exact route they took across the Lower Peninsula. They probably walked across the second row of counties. They were the first Europeans to see that part of our state. Finally they arrived at the Detroit River and crossed it on a raft. The group reached Lake Erie near Point Pelee and built a canoe which they used to paddle east close by the Lake Erie shoreline until they once again saw the site where the *Griffon* was built. No one had seen the *Griffon* anywhere and La Salle went on to Montreal with a heavy heart.

After the *Griffon*

What happened to La Salle and his grand plans? In spite of it all, he managed to keep exploring and was the first Frenchman to reach the mouth of the Mississippi River. Later, he managed to get the king to back an expedition to start a French colony at the mouth of the Mississippi River. La Salle felt the French could control the whole river valley and keep out the British and Spanish. But La Salle's bad luck only got worse! From France, they sailed into the Gulf of Mexico and tried to find the river's mouth. To his dismay, his ships missed and instead, they landed in Texas, far to the west. Stranded, he was shot and killed by two of his own men. La Salle left behind his unfulfilled dreams *and* enormous debts! But there have been few men who have ever tried harder to change the course of history.

The Man Called Cadillac

Close on the heels of La Salle, was another man with great ambitions. He was known as Lamothe Cadillac (la MOT KAD el ak). Nova Scotia was Cadillac's first home in New France. He and his wife, Marie-Therese (ma REE TEH rez), had some land there.

A Spy for France

For a time, Cadillac was a pirate, attacking English ships. Through his voyages Cadillac became an expert on the British colonies. In 1692 he provided maps of the American coastline and harbors to the French government. The French Minister of Marine, like our Secretary of the Navy, was so pleased he promised Cadillac command of the first vacant military post in New France.

Reward for a Good Job

Michilimackinac (MISH ill ih mack in naw) was the post given to Cadillac, and that brought him to Michigan for the first time. It was not the fort tourists visit today. That fort wasn't built until about 1715. Michilimackinac was the name used for the whole Straits of Mackinac area. Cadillac's post was at Fort de Buade (deh BODE) near St. Ignace. While there, he traded in furs which were sent back to his wife in Quebec.

The fur trade was important to Cadillac and he did not mind doing whatever was needed to get furs, including trading brandy to the tribes. That only caused the priests to become violently upset with him.

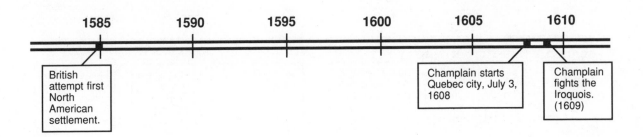

Timeline: 1585 — British attempt first North American settlement. 1590. 1595. 1600. 1605 — Champlain starts Quebec city, July 3, 1608. 1610 — Champlain fights the Iroquois. (1609)

An Idea for a New Fort

While at Fort de Buade, he began to see the possibilities for a fort which could keep the British traders out of the Great Lakes. Using his knowledge of sailing and maps, he decided the straits between the Lower Peninsula and Canada would be an ideal spot.

It could only take place, however, with the permission of the king. Off Cadillac went to Paris. He had long talks with the man who helped him get the post at Michilimackinac. The official's name was Pontchartrain and he had become Cadillac's friend. The king had recently decided to close all of the outposts in the west because there was an oversupply of furs. That did not bother Cadillac too much, and since he was such a good speaker, he was able to convince those in government that he should build his new fort at Detroit anyway.

Not Just a Fort

Cadillac's plan had several new twists. He wanted to move all the Indians from the Michilimackinac area to Detroit. There they would be trained in French schools. He also wanted to use them as soldiers! Many French families would be brought to live at Detroit where they could start farms. His ideas were radical! Very few French families lived outside the cities of Quebec and Montreal.

Just as La Salle's plans had upset many people, so did the plans of Cadillac. Can you think why? Fur traders were afraid his western location would allow Cadillac to take control by having all the Indians trade with him. The Jesuit missionaries were very upset with the idea of having Indians move away from their headquarters at St. Ignace. They also worried about brandy being traded to the tribes.

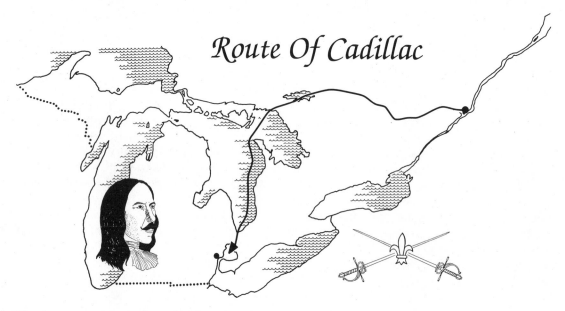

Route Of Cadillac

Cadillac began as a spy and provided maps of the American coastline to the French government. Later, he planned and settled Detroit. (Art by David B. McConnell)

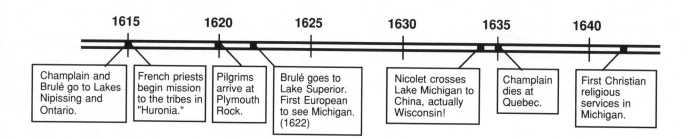

1615	1620	1625	1630	1635	1640

Champlain and Brulé go to Lakes Nipissing and Ontario.

French priests begin mission to the tribes in "Huronia."

Pilgrims arrive at Plymouth Rock.

Brulé goes to Lake Superior. First European to see Michigan. (1622)

Nicolet crosses Lake Michigan to China, actually Wisconsin!

Champlain dies at Quebec.

First Christian religious services in Michigan.

Michigan In Pictures

Upper Falls of the Tahquamenon River in Michigan's Upper Peninsula. The river has two picturesque falls located four miles apart. *(Courtesy Michigan Travel Bureau)*

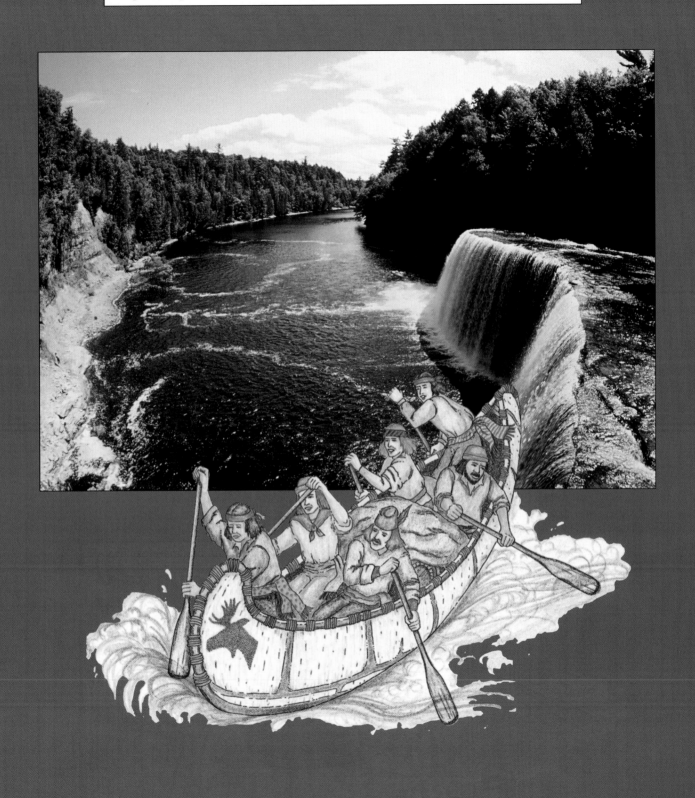

French explorers and fur traders used Michigan's rivers as highways long ago. *(Theresa Deeter)*

A Port Huron steam engine on display by the Michigan Steam Engine and Threshers Club. The club has an annual meeting in late July near Mason. This type can weigh between 15,000 - 20,000 pounds. (*Courtesy David B. McConnell*)   **1**

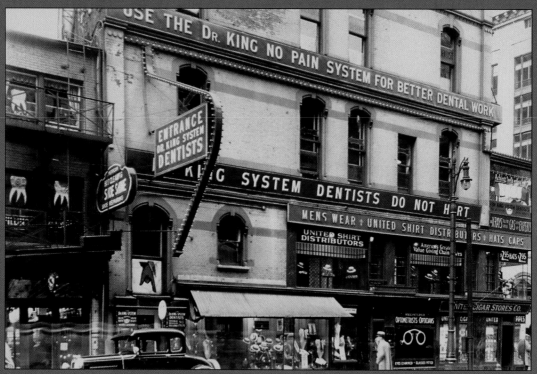

Downtown Detroit, as it appeared in 1930. (*Courtesy Michigan State Archives*)   **2**

A *Ford Model T* car. The Ford Motor Company sold 15 million Model Ts in 19 years. (*Courtesy David B. McConnell*)

C 2

The Renaissance Center, a familiar sight on the Detroit skyline, was completed in 1977. The 73-story glass hotel is one of the world's tallest and is Michigan's tallest building. (*Courtesy Michigan Travel Bureau*)

The state of Michigan has had three capitol buildings. The first was located in Detroit. In 1847, the capital was moved to Lansing, but the building quickly became inadequate. The present capitol building was then built and dedicated on January 1, 1879. (*Courtesy Michigan Travel Bureau*)   **3**

The Gerald R. Ford Museum, located in Grand Rapids, was dedicated in September, 1981. The dedication was attended by numerous celebrities, including Bob Hope, Danny Thomas, and Sammy Davis, Jr. (*Courtesy Michigan Travel Bureau*)   **4**

With its Great Lakes, 11,000 inland lakes and 36,000 miles of rivers, Michigan offers much to those looking for water recreation… whether swimming or fishing for salmon. (*Courtesy Michigan Travel Bureau*)

The 730-foot *John B. Aird* is passing in the background of this beach. The self-unloading freighter was launched in 1983. (*Courtesy Michigan Travel Bureau*)

This replica of the sloop *Welcome* was launched in 1980 and is harbored in Mackinaw City. The original was an armed ship stationed at Fort Michilimackinac during the Revolutionary War. The ship carried supplies to British outposts around the Great Lakes. (*Courtesy Mackinac Island State Park Commission*) **1**

In 1855 the first ship passed through the Soo Locks. These locks enable ships to pass between Lake Huron and Lake Superior, overcoming a difference in water levels of about 19 feet. As many as 600 vessels pass through the locks each year. (*Courtesy Michigan Travel Bureau*) **2**

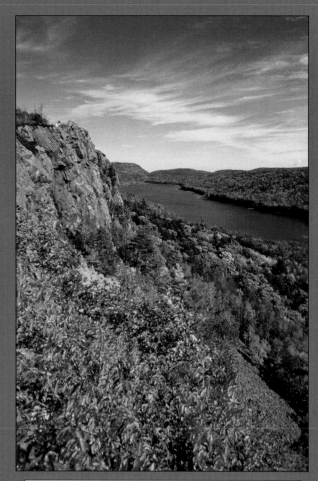

The Rock Shaft House, for the Quincy Copper Mine in Hancock stands over the No. 2 shaft. This shaft was more than 9,000 feet deep – once the deepest mine in the Western Hemisphere. (*Courtesy David B. McConnell*)　　**2**

The Porcupine Mountain Range, located west of Ontonagon, is one of the highest elevations in the State. (*Courtesy Michigan Travel Bureau*)

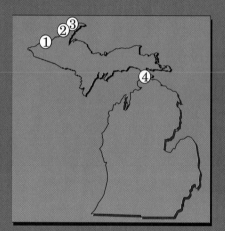

Eagle Harbor, on the Keweenaw Penninsula, was first settled in 1844 and was the site of early copper mining. (*Courtesy Michigan Travel Bureau*)　**3**

The Mighty Mac, which connects Michigan's two peninsulas, is opened each Labor Day for those who wish to walk the five-mile suspension bridge. (*Courtesy Michigan Travel Bureau*) **4**

The Eagle Harbor Lighthouse on the Keweenaw Penninsula. The first lighthouse here was built in 1851. The tower in the picture was built in 1871. (*Courtesy David B. McConnell*)

Fort Michilimackinac has been located in three places. It was established at St. Ignace in 1681, reestablished at Mackinaw City in 1715, and later moved to Mackinac Island by the British. It has now been restored at Mackinaw City. (*Courtesy Michigan Travel Bureau*)

Frankenmuth, home of the Bavarian Inn, is Michigan's top tourist attraction. Over 3 million people visit each year. The Bavarian Inn is considered the tenth largest restaurant in the United States. (*Courtesy Michigan Travel Bureau*) **2**

Holland is famous for its Dutch heritage. A street vendor makes and sells wooden shoes, a part of the Dutch costume, during the annual Tulip Time Festival. The festival takes place each May. (*Courtesy David B. McConnell*) **1**

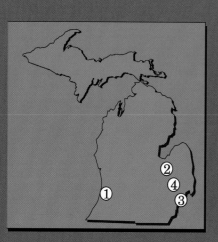

The Renaissance Festival is held during the month of September in Holly. It includes the re-creation of a sixteenth-century village, and a crafts marketplace. (*Courtesy Michigan Travel Bureau*) **4**

A Ukrainian-American woman at the downtown Detroit ethnic festival. Festivals are held every weekend from the first of May to the middle of September. Each festival emphasizes a different ethnic group. (*Courtesy Michigan Travel Bureau*) **3**

Detroit is Born!

On June 4, 1701, Cadillac left Montreal in a convoy of 25 canoes. The canoes carried 50 soldiers and 50 voyageurs along with many Indians and supplies to build the new fort. His second in command was Alphonse de Tonty. By July 23 the group had reached Grosse Ille in the Detroit River. They camped there after looking for the best location for building the fort. The next day work began. It would be called Fort Pontchartrain.

Cadillac was just barely in time because the British made a treaty with the Iroquois to build a fort on the Detroit River that very same month! When they learned about the French fort, the British gave up their plans—for the time being.

Not Just Men Anymore!

The next event in Detroit's history was a first for Michigan. Mrs. Cadillac and Mrs. Tonty arrived with their families. Cadillac's goal was to build a real settlement of French people in Michigan. He brought his wife, Madame Cadillac, as an example. It had all the Indians excited and they felt it meant the Frenchmen were there to stay. The French would be able to protect them when needed.

The ladies traveled in canoes with some of their children and several Indians and soldiers. The trip was 600 to 700 miles. They arrived to a chorus of shouts and firing of guns. Some of the local Indians fell on their knees and kissed their hands, saying, "Now we know our French brothers mean to stay and be our friends. Never before have French women been seen willingly to come to these parts."

Some Success—But Many Problems

Many Indians did come to Detroit in spite of the protests from the Jesuits. The first winter there were 6,000 Indians living around Detroit! That sounds like success, but then came the problem of finding enough food for all of them. Remember the Indian way of life was not designed to have large numbers of people live in one place, especially during the winter.

Other problems developed. It was hard to keep soldiers from deserting, and people who came to farm often decided it was easier and more profitable to trade furs instead.

The little village had some early industries. They included a blacksmith, armorer, tool maker, and brewery. There was also a large windmill, and a community bakery oven.

Cadillac and Tonty had many troubles with the fur traders at Montreal and with the Jesuits. By 1711, those in power decided to give him a promotion and get him out of Detroit in the process. So he was made governor of Louisiana.

Detroit Faces Great Danger!

Among the Indians Cadillac had asked to move to Detroit was the Fox tribe from far away Wisconsin. It was after Cadillac had gone, however, that over 1,000 of them showed up. The new commander of the fort didn't have Cadillac's courage and was afraid of so many new Indians. He asked them to leave.

The Fox Indians were naturally upset by receiving the cold shoulder from the French. The other tribes were not very friendly either. But the Fox decided to stay. However, trouble was brewing by the next summer.

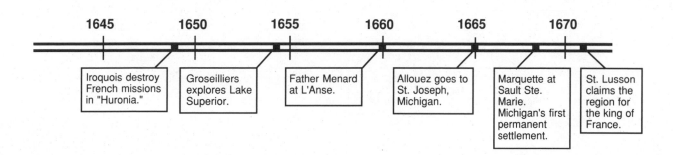

Timeline:

1645 — Iroquois destroy French missions in "Huronia."

1650 — Groseilliers explores Lake Superior.

1655 — Father Menard at L'Anse.

1660 — Allouez goes to St. Joseph, Michigan.

1665 — Marquette at Sault Ste. Marie. Michigan's first permanent settlement.

1670 — St. Lusson claims the region for the king of France.

Madame Cadillac, accompanied by her son Jacques and Madame Tonty arrived in Detroit in October 1701. The arrival of French women showed Cadillac's intention to stay on at Detroit permanently. (Courtesy Michigan Bell an Ameritech Company)

The young village of Detroit was in great danger in that year of 1712. Somehow fighting broke out. The Fox laid siege to the fort for 19 days while the French stayed inside firing back. After darkness on the nineteenth day, the Fox decided to go home and forget about the bad-mannered French. Unfortunately, the Huron and other tribes living at Detroit caught up with them. Most of the Fox were killed or captured.

When the remainder of the tribe in Wisconsin learned what had happened, they became bitter enemies of the French. Because of this, for over 20 years the French could not use the Fox and Wisconsin Rivers to reach the Mississippi!

Fortunately for Detroit, the next 40 years were quiet times on the frontier and the outpost slowly grew. Eventually it had about 900 people or roughly 90 percent of the European population in Michigan.

Marie-Therese Cadillac

Put yourself in the shoes of Madame Cadillac. Go back to New France and try to think what life was like about 300 years ago. Would you be willing to go to a wilderness outpost where there was only one other European woman? Madame

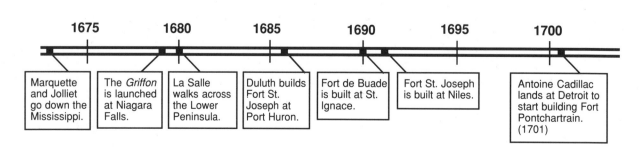

1675	1680	1685	1690	1695	1700

Marquette and Jolliet go down the Mississippi.

The *Griffon* is launched at Niagara Falls.

La Salle walks across the Lower Peninsula.

Duluth builds Fort St. Joseph at Port Huron.

Fort de Buade is built at St. Ignace.

Fort St. Joseph is built at Niles.

Antoine Cadillac lands at Detroit to start building Fort Pontchartrain. (1701)

Marie-Therese Cadillac did and lived other adventures too.

Marie's school days were spent side by side with Indian girls at the convent school in Quebec. There she must have learned about Indian ways and language. Her father was a fur trader and she saw how the business was run by watching him. Later, she became involved in fur trading when her husband shipped furs to her from Michilimackinac and Detroit.

While they were living in Nova Scotia, Cadillac sailed away to spy on the British colonies. But his ship was blown so far off course by a storm, it ended up across the ocean in France. Nothing had been provided to help Madame Cadillac take care of the family or farm. She had no idea what had happened to her husband. Was he dead?

To add to her distress, the British attacked their town and both the town and her home were burned. She and her children were left stranded on the beach. As if things could not be worse, Spanish pirates saw them and kidnapped them. They were held for ransom, which her family in Quebec paid.

Her husband eventually returned, and in time Madame Cadillac became one of the first French women to live in Michigan. They were at Detroit for 10 years.

She had six more children at Detroit and probably continued to help with the fur business. One of her many duties was to teach Indian women some of the French ways. Mrs. Cadillac may have taught them how to do needlepoint and perhaps some of the French dances.

Though Marie-Therese Cadillac went back to France and lived her last years there, she was a pioneer woman in every sense of the word!

Questions

1. Give a reason the king of France felt he needed to make an official claim to Michigan and the Great Lakes.

2. What was the Pageant at the Sault?

3. What happened to the *Griffon*?

4. What trip did La Salle take in Michigan during 1680? What was significant about his trip?

5. On his way across the Lower Peninsula, did La Salle find many Indian villages? Why or why not?

6. What was special about Detroit that would make it more than just another fort?

7. Who were the first European women known to come to Michigan?

8. Write a paragraph in your own words explaining which person from this section you think did the most to develop Michigan. Give reasons for your choice.

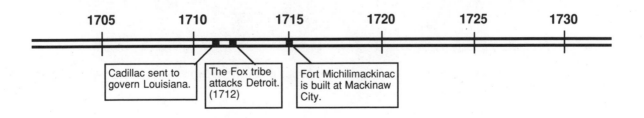

1705	1710	1715	1720	1725	1730

Cadillac sent to govern Louisiana.

The Fox tribe attacks Detroit. (1712)

Fort Michilimackinac is built at Mackinaw City.

Chapter 3 Section 4

Fur Is King !

Here are the key concepts you will find in this section:

Fur trading was the main business activity in Michigan for 200 years.

The Straits of Mackinac area was a center for fur trading in the Great Lakes region.

Beaver was the most important fur animal.

In the long run, the concentration on fur trading caused major problems.

For about 200 years fur was THE business of Michigan! The economy was based on the fur trade. Not farming. Not lumbering. Not making cars. From the 1640s to the 1820s fur was king! The search for good animal skins was what brought French traders to Michigan. Furs were what most Indians spent their time collecting.

Meeting at Mackinac

Michilimackinac was the center of the fur trade for an area much larger than just Michigan. It was in the middle of the Great Lakes region. Traders came by canoe from Montreal and Indians from far to the north and west, all to Michilimackinac. It is true that Cadillac got many traders and Indians to come to Detroit, but after about 10 years, everything shifted north once more. Some trading also took place at Sault Ste. Marie and St. Joseph. In later years much of the trading took place on Mackinac Island.

That part of the Great Lakes was a good place to meet. If traders went much further west, they risked winter weather before they could return to Montreal. In the early days the tribes did bring furs right to Montreal but as more animals were hunted, they became scarce and the Indians had to move west to find enough.

At first, the French conducted business at St. Ignace on the northern side of the Straits. Later, a fort was built on the south side of the Straits. That fort has been rebuilt at Mackinac City and today is known as Fort Michilimackinac.

For many years the canoe was the main source of transportation on the Great Lakes. (Courtesy Michigan State Archives)

Who Did the Work?

Most of the work in the fur trade system was done by Indians and *voyageurs (VOY uh zhahs). Voyageurs were men hired by fur companies to transport goods and people.* With metal traps which the Indians got from the traders, an average of six beavers could be collected in a day. Trapping could be done in summer or winter, but the animals had better furs in the winter. The colorful voyageurs paddled the canoes for the traders. As they traveled, they sang tunes to keep their paddling in rhythm. Voyageurs paddled several hundred miles each season!

Beaver is the One!

They were looking for all sorts of fur-bearing animals. Bear, raccoon, moose, deer, muskrat, mink, otter, fox, marten, wolf, and even skunk were trapped. But beaver skins were the center of the fur-trade business, even from the earliest days. Beaver skins became a kind of common denominator. Everything was measured as being worth so many beavers.

Regulations for the Trade at Michilimackinac

Large blanket-	=	*3 beaver or 4 buck-skins*
One pound of gunpowder	=	*1 beaver*
Brass kettle, each pound-	=	*1 pound of beaver*
4 Bars of lead	=	*1 beaver*
1 fathom calico cloth	=	*2 beavers*
(A fathom is about six feet)		
Earbobs (earrings)	=	*1 small beaver or 1 doeskin*

From *Michilimackinac- A Guide to the Site*

Beavers live in groups and work together. They need a pond for their community. If necessary, they will make a pond by building a dam across a small stream. Lodges are built in the pond as their homes. Once a beaver pond is found, it is not too hard to catch the animals.

Beaver pelts were used as money and traded for other items. (From Michigan State University Museum)

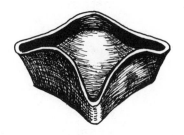

A major use of beaver pelts was to make felt for hats. The finished hat, however, did not look like fur. Three different styles are shown. (Art by David B. McConnell)

The trappers cleaned the animal skins and fastened them to a wooden hoop to dry. Dry skins or pelts were squeezed together in a fur press under great pressure. That made a compact bundle. Usually about 60 pelts went into a bundle and the bundle was covered with deer skin and sewn up. The bundles weighed between 90 and 100 pounds and were worth from $300 to $600, depending on the demand.

Many of the furs became coats and robes. But the big market for beaver was for hats. Beaver hats do not really look like fur hats because the fur is not used directly. Only the short hairs next to the skin were used. These short hairs were made into a kind of felt and it was the felt which was used to make the hat. Beaver hats came in many styles.

Let's Trade!

Trading in furs was quite profitable to those in charge. Even after the French lost control of Michigan, the British and the Americans continued the fur trade. Some historians believe profits reached up to seven times the costs, or 700 percent. Such profits lured traders and explorers farther and farther into North America.

The king of France controlled the fur trade by granting licenses to favored individuals. But the high profits attracted many to trade illegally. Those men traded without a license. The illegal traders were known as *Coureur de bois* (koo ER deh BWAH). This translates as "woods runner." They often bribed officials to look the other way.

In exchange for furs, the tribes received useful items which made their life easier; however, they were habit forming. Once a young Indian began to hunt with a gun, he needed to trap more animals to have a supply of gunpowder, lead balls, gun flints, spare parts, and tools for his weapon.

They also traded for items which weren't useful and liquor was one example. Trading liquor (brandy, rum and wine) was almost always discouraged by the government and missionaries. But it happened anyway. It was easy to trade anything you wanted when you were hundreds of miles in the wilderness. There was little law enforcement.

This list shows what was carried to Michilimackinac to trade for the year of 1775. Liquor was a large part of the merchandise.

1,150	barrels of rum and wine
38,000	pounds of gunpowder.
44,000	pounds of musket balls and shot (bullets)
1,051	muskets (guns similar to rifles)
6	bags of flour
38	cases of axes and ironware
73	bales of copper, brass and tin kettles
200	bales of tobacco
130	kegs of pork and lard
16	barrels of salt

From *At the Crossroads* by the Mackinac Island Park Commission.

Because so much depended on fur trading, it had an impact on everyone in New France and in the long run created problems. There were not many farms or other industries because most young men took to the woods. Since the men were often gone from home, the number of French people did not increase very fast. The Indians were affected too. Eventually, the many changes caused by fur trading ruined the Indian way of life. They could no longer make do with their own resources. They no longer had the skills to make many of the things needed to survive.

Questions

1. Between which years was fur trading the most important economic activity in Michigan? During that time, was the business center of Michigan in the northern or southern part of the state?

2. What was considered the most important fur-bearing animal? What was usually made from its fur?

3. How long might it take an Indian to collect enough beaver pelts to trade for a large blanket? Explain your answer.

4. Look at the list of trade goods brought to Michilimackinac in 1775. Make two columns on your paper. In the first column list all of the things the Indians got in their trading which were used up. In the second column write those things which would last for a long time.

5. What were the advantages and disadvantages of the fur trade for the Indians?

4 THE BRITISH-
A NEW FLAG ON THE FRONTIER

Chapter 4 Section 1
A War In The Woods: French, British, and Indians

> *Here are the key concepts you will find in this section:*

By the 1750s England and France began to squabble over land south and east of Michigan.

In 1754, the French and Indian War started between these two countries. Indians fought on both sides but mostly helped the French.

Both French and Indian people from Michigan played important parts in this war.

The British won this war in 1760 and took control of all of Canada including Michigan.

New France Meets New England

Over the years New France grew slowly, perhaps too slowly. By the 1750s New France had about 80,000 people while New England had nearly 1,250,000! Why was there such a difference? Government policies had much to do with it. The British allowed all those who wanted religious freedom to come to their 13 colonies. Once they got there, most started farms and communities. On the other hand, the French government would only let Catholics come to America. That meant a smaller number of French immigrants. The focus of life in New France was the fur trade. The traders often did not start farms or towns. That kept the population down.

The British and French each had their own ideas on how to manage things in America and it did not really matter which way was better until the two countries began to challenge each other. The French had been concerned about British traders for many years. They built forts to control the Great Lakes and the

waterways. But still the British kept coming; there were just too many of them to be content in the 13 colonies!

The British also were beating the French at their own game of trading furs

Westward movement by British traders worried the French. The French placed markers along the Allegheny and Ohio rivers in 1749 to affirm their control of the land to the north and west.

with the Indians. The British offered a better variety of goods and at lower prices too! Both countries competed to attract the Indians' business.

Where is the Boundary?

It was 1671 when the French made a claim to Michigan and all of the Great Lakes. By 1749 they decided to do something similar with the land south of Michigan. At that time 200 men went down the Allegheny and Ohio rivers in canoes.

They placed markers along the river proclaiming ownership of the land to the king of France. They spoke with Indians along the way and urged them to trade with the French. They were already late. One of the priests among the group said, "...Behold, the English are already far within our territory; and what is worse, they are under the protection of Indians whom they entice to themselves.... Their design is, without doubt to establish themselves there...."

So, the British were making friends with the Indians and moving into the Ohio territory! The struggle over this land would lead to war.

Spats, Arguments, and Fights

Charles Langlade from Michigan played a major role in that war. Langlade was born at Michilimackinac. His mother was the sister of an Ottawa Chief and his father was French. He knew much about the Indians' way of fighting in the woods.

Leading 250 Ottawa and Ojibwa warriors, Langlade went into Ohio to assert French control. There they attacked the village of a tribe friendly to the British traders. Many Indians were impressed and decided it was better to do business with the French after all!

Then the French and British began to act like two neighbors bickering over where to put a fence. The French built a new chain of forts in the backyard of the British colonies. Next, each side decided to build a fort where Pittsburgh is today. The British started first but were driven

off. Later, George Washington arrived with more British soldiers and fighting began. But Washington had to surrender and admit he was trespassing.

British soldiers were back the next year, 1755. The Michiganian, Langlade, fought against George Washington, the Virginian. Langlade was given credit for another French victory. The French and their Indian allies went on to attack British settlements in Pennsylvania, Maryland and Virginia. The fireworks of the French and Indian War had begun!

The war spread like a fire to all British and French territories around the world. Either side could lose its empire. At first, the French could not be beaten. They won battle after battle. The French woodsmen and Indians were a big help.

The French and British worked hard to gain the support of the Indians. The Indians fought for both sides during the French and Indian War. (Courtesy Mackinac State Historic Parks)

Everybody Wants the Indians

Both sides were tugging on the Indians to join them. It was the French, though, who led the Indians to make

68

many raids against the British with much success. The French used warriors from western tribes; many of them came from Michigan. Indians were often willing to attack the British because the British were starting farms and towns, and taking away Indian land in the process.

To get more support from the Indians, Charles Langlade met with a grand council of the Michigan tribes across the river from Detroit. It was March, 1759. A chief named Pontiac was at the meeting listening. It was reported that Langlade's speech went something like this:

"My Brothers, I will not try to tell you that the French, our friends, are still winning the war. But do not make the mistake of thinking that because there have been setbacks, the French are lost.

Now I have been asked by the Detroit commandant to call you together to ask again that you raise up your tomahawks in the French cause, which is and must be your cause as well.... you know in your hearts the French are your friends.... They love the land as you love it and know that it belongs not to individuals, but to all, to share equally. The English may ply you with great gifts to win you over, but the gifts disappear when you have won and your land disappears as well. If you do not fight him with the French, then mark what I say, the time will come when you will have to fight him alone...."

Wilderness Empire by Allan W. Eckert.

Trouble On the St. Lawrence

The St. Lawrence River was the pathway into New France and the route used to get supplies. In 1758 the British attacked a great French fortress at the mouth of the river. After 49 days, the fort surrendered. No longer could French ships bring supplies to Quebec and Montreal. The St. Lawrence became the pathway to a British victory. Soon the French no longer had materials to trade with the tribes.

Finally, it came down to a battle outside the gates of Quebec, the capital of New France in 1759. The French fort was strong and it sat on a steep hill looking over the St. Lawrence River. Charles Langlade, Chief Pontiac, and about 400 Indians from the Michigan area were there too.

Thousands of British soldiers came in 60 ships and set up camp on the other side of the river. All the time the French cannons blasted them. General Montcalm was the leader of the French army. It was his idea to stay in the French fort and let the British run out of supplies while they tried to attack. Montcalm was certain the British would have to leave when winter came. But before long, the British set up their own cannon and fired back across the river.

The siege had been on for 80 days and it was by then September. The French were having problems but it did look as

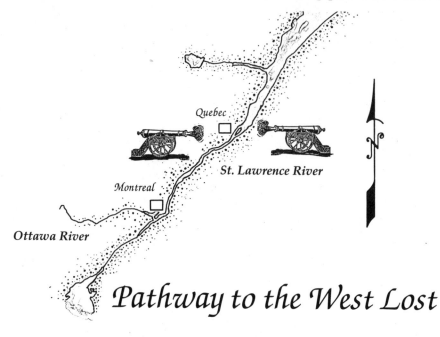

Pathway to the West Lost

French and British soldiers as they might have appeared at the Battle of Quebec.

though the British would have to leave soon. Their supplies were very low and it would not be long before the river froze. The British officers told their general to leave and come back next summer. But he wanted to try one last plan.

Will They See Us Coming?

On a rainy and moonless night, British soldiers quietly crossed the St. Lawrence River in boats and waited. If the French saw them now they would be cut down. A few men pulled themselves slowly up the great cliff. During the night more and more men scrambled to the top. The boats went back and forth across the river all night.

At six in the morning, General Montcalm got on his horse and rode around the fort to check out the situation. Once outside he saw about 4,000 British soldiers lined up on the far side of a field. He gasped, "This is serious!"

The alarm was given and thousands of French troops poured out of the fort. An intense battle began. The British general was wounded three times. He sat on the battlefield dying but smiled when he heard an officer say, "They run. Look how they run!" The French soldiers were running for the safety of the fort. General Montcalm was riding back to the fort when he too was fatally wounded. Early the next morning Montcalm was buried inside the Ursuline chapel. In a sense, the French empire in North America was buried along with the general.

An Empire Dies!

That night Charles Langlade met with Pontiac and they headed back to the Great Lakes country.

Charles Langlade returned to Michilimackinac and told the French and Indians there about the loss of Quebec. Soon he left for the Wisconsin territory where he hoped he could stay away from the British.

The French commander at Detroit didn't believe it when British soldiers came to replace him and his men. Only after he saw the papers of surrender, did he turn over the fort. Fort Michilimackinac was taken over the next summer. Michigan was indeed in British hands.

By 1760 all of New France had been surrendered to the British. Two small islands off Newfoundland were all that France could keep from their once great empire. They still belong to France today.

Questions

1. Why was New France weaker than New England at the time of the French and Indian War?

2. What was the French and Indian War about?

3. Where was the last great battle in the French and Indian War fought and when did it take place? Why was this battle significant to Michigan?

4. What argument did Charles Langlade use to convince Indians from the Michigan area to fight against the British?

5. If the British had lost the French and Indian War, give your opinions how Michigan would be different today.

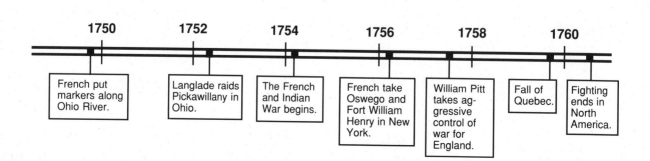

Chapter 4 Section 2

Chief Pontiac On The Offensive

Here are the key concepts you will find in this section:

After the French and Indian War, most of the French settlers and traders stayed in Michigan.

The British made several mistakes in dealing with the Indians. The Indians became quite upset.

Chief Pontiac was a great Indian leader who finally attacked Fort Detroit to drive the British out.

Soon other Indians successfully attacked several forts in Michigan and in other places.

The British Take Over Michigan

Captain Donald Campbell, a British officer, came to Detroit to take charge of Fort Pontchartrain. Its new name would be Fort Detroit. Though the French soldiers left, many of the fur traders and those with small farms stayed behind. The French continued to be the largest non-Indian group in Michigan for another 60 years! Although they lost the war, the French people appeared friendly. Captain Campbell did his best to get along with everyone. He could speak French and often had parties inviting the French traders and their families.

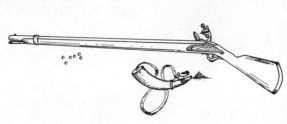

In 1761 Campbell reported some grumbling among the Indians. William Johnson, an old Indian expert, was sent to check out the situation. The Iroquois had made him an honorary chief and he had fought side by side with them in battle. In many ways he was like Charles Langlade.

The conference with the Indians went well and an ox roast ended the talks.

William Johnson gave a ball for the British officers and French merchants. Johnson's diary says, "...danced the whole night until 7 o'clock in the morning, when all parted very much pleased and happy."

Even though the French seemed friendly, some of them hoped their French soldiers would come back eventually. And they told this to the Indians too.

Bad Policies

The British government was not as wise as William Johnson and Captain Campbell in dealing with the Indians. There were new orders not to give them presents or to trade any gunpowder to them. The tribes needed gunpowder for hunting. Too many Indians had come together in one place to continue with their old life-style.

Next spring the British Northwest Company traders arrived to do business. Without the French competition, the British saw no reason to have low prices for the Indians. Everything became more

Major Gladwin, British commander at Detroit in 1763. (Courtesy Michigan State Archives)

expensive. Some traders cheated the Indians too. William Johnson warned that all of this would cause trouble.

In addition, the British wanted to control the land and that upset the Indians. The French and the Indians had always shared the land together. Now the British wanted land for farms and settlers.

The tribes were growing restless. Because the French and British were still at war in Europe, there were rumors the French army would return. At Detroit, Captain Campbell was replaced by Major Gladwin. The major was not so friendly to Indians. The Potawatomi, Ottawa, and Huron all had villages near Detroit. Chief Pontiac lived in the Ottawa village where Windsor is today.

Trouble is Brewing

Pontiac invited many tribes to come to a meeting on the Ecorse River on April 27, 1763. It was there he proposed a way to get rid of the British at Detroit. He would ask to meet with Major Gladwin in the fort. Pontiac would bring many

warriors in with him as a part of his group and each man would be wearing a large blanket.

Over the next few days Indians began to show up at the French blacksmith asking for files. Did the blacksmith ask why they wanted so many files? Did he provide the files with a curious look or just a little smile?

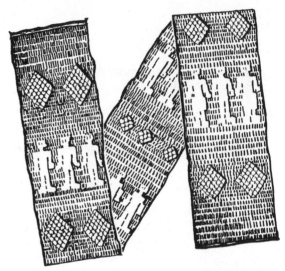

Wampum was used as a sign or symbol of a sacred pledge. A belt of wampum consists of many tiny tubes shaped from pieces of sea shells. (Art by David B. McConnell)

Pontiac's warriors were cutting the barrels of their muskets short with the files! The guns would be under their blankets when they walked into the fort! Once inside Pontiac would hand the major a *belt of wampum*. *Wampum was a belt of small white or colored tubes made from river shells. It was often used to show that a sacred pledge was being made. Wampum was very precious to the Indians.*

In Pontiac's plan, if he turned the green side up, they would throw off the blankets and shoot. More Indians would be outside ready to run in and join the fight.

Mid-morning on May 7, 1763, 11 chiefs and 60 warriors solemnly walked into the fort—their fingers close to gun triggers. But they soon realized something was wrong. The soldiers were not going about business as usual. They were armed and ready, bayonets on their muskets. Every move of the Indians was tensely watched by the Englishmen. How did they know?

There are many stories explaining how the British learned about Pontiac's plan to attack Detroit. One says a young French woman heard about the plan and wanted to warn her boyfriend who was a British trader. Here is another story:

A pretty Indian woman delivered a pair of moccasins to Major Gladwin the day before Pontiac's council meeting. The elk skin moccasins pleased the major so much, he asked her to take the remaining skin and make another pair. She said she would but she did not leave the fort. At sunset when they cleared the fort of strangers, an officer saw the woman and she did not want to go. She was then taken back to Major Gladwin. This time she said she did not want to take the elk skin because *she could not return it*. She was urged to explain her statement. Eventually, the woman told of Pontiac's plan to attack.

This is a portion of the account given by Thompson Maxwell, a British soldier at the fort in 1763. The account is preserved in the historical records at the Clarke Historical Library, Central Michigan University.

A grim Pontiac told Major Gladwin that was not the way to hold a council! He kept the green side of the wampum belt down and left the fort. The next day Pontiac asked if all of his warriors could come and smoke a pipe of peace with the British. Gladwin told him only chiefs could come.

The following day all the Ottawa came to the fort anyway. They were not allowed to go in. Pontiac was furious that his plans had not worked.

The 120 or so British inside the fort knew they were in real danger because Pontiac had about 800 warriors. A few of the British had homes outside the fort. They had no protection at all!

Pontiac Attacks

Yells and war cries came from the woods and soon the fort was under attack. Warriors rushed up to the fort and furiously tried to hack a hole in the wooden wall with their tomahawks. After many warriors were killed, the Indians became convinced they could not cut their way into the fort.

That night the Indians started fires against the wooden walls. British soldiers raced back and forth with buckets

An Indian woman may have warned Major Gladwin of Pontiac's plan to attack Detroit. (Courtesy Michigan State Archives)

74

of water to stop the flames. Officers expected the Indians would try to do the same thing the next night so they took precautions. A hole was cut through the wall from the inside and a cannon placed to fire on anyone coming close to the wall! In the darkness that night many Indians died.

For days the battle continued. The British were becoming desperate because they had only three rounds of ammunition left for each soldier and only enough food for half-rations each day.

Major Gladwin and his soldiers clung to the hope that supplies and reinforcements would come by the end of the month...just a few more days. On May 30 the soldiers could see the supply canoes in the distance on the river. As the boats came closer, however, those in the fort were horrified as they realized the canoes had Indians in them. Pontiac and his men had already captured the food and ammunition intended for the Brit-

ish. The siege went on. All of June and most of July passed with the British closed up in Fort Detroit.

Battle of Bloody Run

Finally a British captain named Dalyell reached Detroit by water with 280 men and supplies. That gave the British more confidence. They even planned a surprise attack of their own.

At 2:30 in the morning on July 31. Captain Dalyell lead his soldiers through the dark to attack Pontiac's camp. About 3,000 Indians were camped up the river. Dalyell was crossing a bridge over Parent's Creek, which is now in Elmwood Cemetery, when Indian muskets boomed from the tall grass. Pontiac's warriors had been waiting for them! The captain and many men died. Around eight in the morning the surviviors made it back to the fort. Following the tragic battle, Parent's Creek was given the nickname of Bloody Run.

Pontiac's men leave the fort after Major Gladwin discovered their plan to attack the British at Detroit. (Frederic Remington, Harper's Magazine April, 1897)

Fort Michilimackinac was attacked by the Ojibwa during a lacrosse game. Many British soldiers were killed. (Courtesy Michigan Bell an Ameritech Company)

Time Runs Out

Grimly, the British continued to hold out but the Indians were just as stubborn. Some supplies had reached the fort by boat; the Indians, however, were sure the soldiers would again run low on ammunition. But time was also against the Indians. It was fall and they needed to go hunting and gather food for the winter. Warriors began to drift away from Detroit with their families. Some of the Indian groups made peace. Near the end of October, Pontiac received a letter from the French telling him France and England had finally signed a peace treaty and the French would not be able to send soldiers to help take Detroit. Pontiac decided to call off the attack. The Indian siege of 153 days was the longest in American history and showed Pontiac's skill as an organizer and warrior.

War Spreads Far and Wide

During that long summer the British soldiers learned of other disasters. Detroit was not the only fort Indians had attacked! Many tribes all along the western frontier had risen up to throw out the British. Pontiac had sent messengers urging them to fight. Forts fell on May 16, May 25, May 27, June 1, and June 2. Only Fort Detroit, Fort Niagara on the Niagara River, and Fort Pitt at Pittsburgh held out against the Indians. Fort Miami at St. Joseph, Michigan, was gone and there was tragic news about Fort Michilimackinac at Mackinaw City.

Secret Plans for Michilimackinac

Chief Minavavana of the Ojibwa tribe had become friends with Captain Etherington at Fort Michilimackinac. The chief suggested the Ojibwa and Sauk tribes play a game of baggataway or lacrosse in honor of King George's birthday. Captain Etherington agreed it was a fine idea. The Indians could play just outside the fort.

Alexander Henry was one of the English fur traders at the Fort. He was adopted as a brother by Wawatam, an Ojibwa chief. It was Chief Wawatam who invited Henry to come on a hunt with him and his wife. Wawatam said he was "worried by the noise of evil birds." That was an Indian expression meaning there might be trouble. Since Henry was waiting for his canoes of supplies, he turned the chief down. He was touched though when Wawatam and his wife left with tears in their eyes. That same day many Indians came into the fort to trade. Henry was puzzled when the only goods they bought were tomahawks!

"The morning was sultry. A Chipeway came to tell me that his nation was going to play at bag gat i way, with the Sacs, another Indian nation for a high wager. He invited me to witness the sport, adding that the commandant was to be there, and would bet on the side of the Chipeways. In consequence of this information, I went to the commandant, and expostulated with him a little, representing that the Indians might possibly have some sinister end in view; but the commandant only smiled at my suspicions."

Travels and Adventures by Alexander Henry, 1809.

The Lacrosse Game

Many of the soldiers came out to watch the game. It was a great sight! Captain Etherington made his bet on the Ojibwa side. Even though it was a warm day, Indian women wrapped in blankets sat near the gate. Suddenly the ball went over the wall and into the fort. The players rushed inside after it. As they ran they snatched weapons from under the women's blankets. Lieutenant Jamet held off several Indians with his sword until he was killed. Few of the soldiers had time to defend themselves. It was a massacre!

Charles Langlade and his family were watching from their house. Alexander Henry ran up to the Langlades and begged them to help him. Langlade said, "What do you expect me to do?" Amazingly an Indian woman who worked in their house took Henry up the back stairs and hid him in the attic. Through a hole in the wall Henry witnessed a terrible slaughter.

He remained in hiding that night but the next day he was discovered and taken prisoner. He nearly lost his life several times during the days which followed. Wawatam eventually bought his release with presents. Henry stayed at Michilimackinac in spite of his nightmarish experience and became a successful trader in the region.

The Outcome

It was part of the greatest Indian uprising in American history and became known as Pontiac's Rebellion. Not until 1766 did Pontiac and other chiefs smoke a peace pipe with William Johnson at Oswego, New York. Pontiac kept his pledge of peace and tried to stop other plots against the British. Three years later he was in the Illinois country near St. Louis when a group of Indians became angry with him and murdered him. Pontiac was a courageous leader who was trying to keep his people's land the best way he knew.

A lacrosse stick.

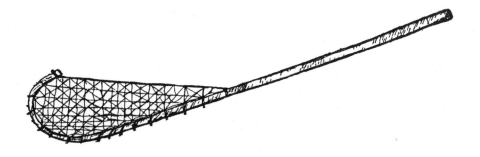

The British government was concerned there could be another Indian uprising like Pontiac's War. They wondered what they could do to prevent such a disaster. The tribes had been angry because settlers were taking their land. The government's solution was to pass a law, the Proclamation of 1763, stopping settlers from going west of the Appalachian Mountains. They hoped that would keep the Indians satisfied. Michigan would remain a land of Indians, fur traders, and some French settlers. British soldiers stayed at Fort Detroit and Fort Michilimackinac to keep control of the area.

The Black Trader

At this point in history an unusual explorer and trader made his way to the area. In the mid-1760s Jean de Sable (jhan duh SAW bul) came to Michigan. De Sable was a black man with a French background. He was born in 1745, on Haiti, an island southeast of Florida. His father was probably a French trader and his mother a black woman. He was sent to school in France, but later moved to New Orleans on the mouth of the Mississippi River. When the Spanish took over that city, de Sable traveled north and finally made his way to Michigan.

It is said de Sable became good friends with Chief Pontiac and lived near his camp, trading with the tribes. This black Frenchman moved west when Pontiac left Michigan. In 1779 he became the first non-Indian to have a permanent settlement at the portage of Chicago.

Later, during the American Revolutionary War, the British went to Chicago and took de Sable prisoner. He was kept at Mackinaw for some time and then released to trade with the Indians near Port Huron. He stayed at Port Huron until the mid-1780s. Jean de Sable died in 1818 at St. Charles, Missouri.

De Sable was well-educated and he spoke English, French and several Indian languages. He had a good reputation among both the English and the tribes. Jean de Sable was a unique person and one of the first black people in the land of Michigan.

Questions

1. What five things made the Indians angry after the British took over Michigan?

2. Who made the plan to take over the fort at Detroit in 1763? Did the French encourage or help with this plan?

3. How did the Indians plan to surprise the British soldiers at Fort Michilimackinac?

4. Chief Wawatam acted as an individual and had different feelings from the other Indians who attacked Fort Michilimackinac. What did Chief Wawatam do? Give an example to show his feelings were different.

5. What was the new British policy about settlers after Pontiac's War?

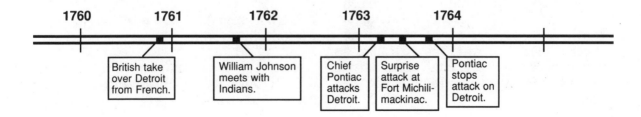

| 1760 | 1761 | 1762 | 1763 | 1764 |

British take over Detroit from French.

William Johnson meets with Indians.

Chief Pontiac attacks Detroit.

Surprise attack at Fort Michilimackinac.

Pontiac stops attack on Detroit.

Chapter 4 Section 3

Michigan While Our Nation Is Born: 1774 - 1783

| Here are the key concepts you will find in this section: |

Some British policies which relate to Michigan and Canada helped lead to the Revolutionary War

Detroit was a base for British raids during the Revolutionary War

American frontier settlers planned to capture Detroit

The success of George Rogers Clark helped Michigan become a part of the United States.

Spanish soldiers took over the fort at Niles, Michigan.

Life in Detroit

In 1773 a census was taken at Detroit. Studying the information from the census helps us learn more about life in Michigan at that time. The center of Detroit was the British fort. People had homes and farms on two sides of the fort. A few people even lived on "Hog Island," which is now called Belle Isle. The census shows the people of Detroit had many farm animals and even slaves! Slavery was permitted then under the British. In 1773 Detroit was 72 years old but still had only 1,367 people, not counting the Indians in the nearby villages.

British Policies Bring Revolution

Once the British had won the French and Indian War, England ruled all of North America east of the Mississippi River. Before the war, the 13 colonies made up most of the land under their control. For many years England let the colonies do much as they wanted. Then things began to change. The British government tried to please the Indians by keeping settlers from going west onto Indian land. That angered the Americans in the colonies. The colonists believed they had a right to live wherever they wanted.

In addition, the British taxed people in the colonies to pay for the recent French and Indian War. The Americans felt those taxes were much too high and unfair.

Next, the British government attempted to keep the many French people living in Canada and Michigan happy by passing the Quebec Act in 1774. The law provided that:

1. Catholics could practice their religion without interference from the government.
2. The people could continue using French laws for business and private property matters.

A general return of all the inhabitants of Detroit their possessions, cattle, houses, servants, and slaves taken by Phillip Dejean, Justice of the Peace for the said place the 22nd day of September, 1773.

	Men	Women	Young men Ages 10 to 20	Boys 1 to 10	Young Women Ages 10 to 20	Girls 1 to 10	Servants	Men Slaves	Women Slaves
Southside of Fort	107	81	33	112	30	76	27	6	3
Northside of Fort	124	107	45	137	24	134	36	26	22
The Fort	66	36	6	35	4	30	27	14	14
On Hog Island	1	1	"	"	"	"	3	"	"
Total	298	225	84	284	58	240	93	46	39

Reproduction of a 1773 census which was taken in Detroit.

3. Governing officials would be appointed by the king of England.

4. The boundaries of Quebec province would expand west and south to the Ohio River. Michigan was included.

It was the first time Michigan had been included in any form of official government. Before that time, the commanders at each fort carried out the law as they saw fit.

The Americans in the 13 colonies took offense at the Quebec Act. It was almost as if New France had not been defeated in the war. The colonists wondered if the British government was going to interfere with *their* freedom of religion. They wondered if *their* elected officials might be replaced too! Freedom of religion and freedom to choose government officials was very important to the people in the 13 colonies.

The Quebec Act, the taxes, and other new British laws helped push the colonies into the Revolutionary War. In that war the colonies declared their independence and freedom from England and the British government. It was the beginning of the United States.

Michigan During the Revolution

The French people living in Michigan did not see what all the fuss was about. After all, they now had a government and religious system much like the one they had lived with for the last 150 years. That attitude kept the people in Michigan from trying to fight the British during the Revolutionary War. The French did not object to being ruled by a king and they had never been allowed to elect their government officials.

80

But the French and Indians were not the only people in Michigan. There were British soldiers at Michilimackinac and Detroit. While the French people were not active in the Revolution, the British soldiers were! Detroit became a base to send out raids against the colonies and against the American settlers who had moved into Ohio and Kentucky.

Raids From Detroit

To reduce the need for soldiers, the British convinced many Indians to fight on their side in the Revolutionary War. The Indians' concern for the land and their way of life was the reason they changed sides so quickly. The Indians did not mind attacking settlers because they wanted to keep them off their land. In return, the Indians received gunpowder and supplies from the British. Detroit, in fact, served as the supply center for the entire area.

To help encourage the Indians to attack American settlers, the British offered money whenever the Indians could prove an American had been killed. How could the Indians show such proof? The British paid them when they brought back scalps!

Henry Hamilton was the commander at Fort Detroit and the British lieutenant governor. He was given the nickname of "the Hair Buyer" because it was reported he paid the Indians for American scalps.

The pioneer settlers who had gone to live in the Kentucky area were living in terror of Indian attacks. The situation got so bad that 1777 was known as "the year of the bloody sevens." Many settlers were taken prisoner and brought to Detroit to be held for ransom. The great Daniel Boone was even one of those prisoners. The Indians were so proud of catching him they adopted him into their tribe.

Let's Capture Detroit!

George Rogers Clark was a young backwoods pioneer who meant to take action. He went before Virginia's governor (Virginia claimed the Kentucky area at this time) and asked for 500 soldiers to attack Detroit. The governor and Thomas Jefferson liked the idea of taking Detroit but had no soldiers to spare. Finally Clark was given permission to get volunteers from the backwoods settlements.

After much effort, about 175 men agreed to leave their families and go after

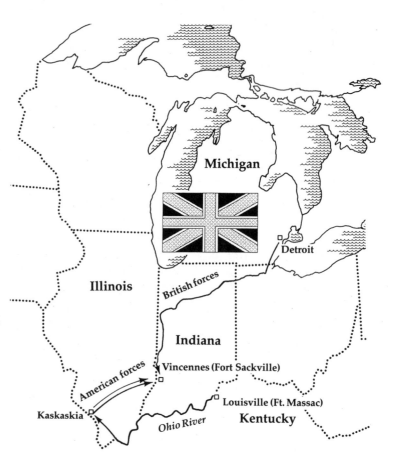

Clark's Route 1778-1779

American soldiers under George Rogers Clark left Louisville, Kentucky and captured the British forts at Kaskaskia and Vincennes. Their goal was to take Detroit from the British. This map shows how important rivers were to transportation, even in wartime.

the British. Clark decided to attack the British fort at Kaskaskia (ka SKAS kee uh) first. He probably went there because this fort was much smaller than the one at Detroit. Kaskaskia is across the river from St. Louis. It was the summer of 1778. Clark's march against Kaskaskia was such a surprise that one night he was able to walk through the gate of the fort and into the commander's bedroom. Kaskaskia, like Detroit, was really a settlement of French people. The British had told the French people terrible stories about what would happen to them if the Americans ever took over. George Rogers Clark understood the need to be friendly with the French and soon they had no fears.

But there were many Indians in the area who had supported the British. It was a bigger job to win them over! He told them how the British had become frightened,"like deer in the woods," and had hired the Indians to do their fighting for them. Clark convinced the Indians it would be better for them to stop fighting the Americans. His speeches were more bluff than anything else since he was greatly outnumbered. The Americans under Clark also marched across Illinois and captured Fort Sackville at the village of Vincennes (ven SENZ).

The British Leave Detroit To Catch Clark

When news of those events reached Detroit, "Hair Buyer" Hamilton was appalled. He left Detroit with soldiers to stop Clark. They took rafts and followed the Maumee and Wabash rivers. Hamilton easily took back Vincennes from the small American army left there.

Clark was in Kaskaskia when he learned that Hamilton was coming after him. By then it was the winter of 1779 and Hamilton would wait until spring to march toward Kaskaskia. Clark believed in making surprise moves. He knew only a fool would try to march across Indiana in the winter, especially when so much of the land between Kaskaskia and Vincennes was flooded.

George Rogers Clark and his men marched through the swamps of Illinois to make their second surprise attack on Fort Sackville at Vincennes. (Photo courtesy of Illinois Bell)

A Grueling Winter March

Off Clark and his soldiers went, through mud and ice cold water. There was no place to put their supplies to keep them dry so they had to build platforms when they stopped for the night! They ran out of food. Two canoes were used to rescue men who could not go on any longer. The flooded rivers caused his men to have great suffering. In Clark's words it was "too incredible for any person to believe."

When American soldiers arrived at Vincennes, Clark told the French people that he meant no harm to them. Then he attacked the British fort. After all the difficulties his men had experienced, it was amazing they had the strength to fire their guns! It took much more fighting to take Vincennes the second time. But Hamilton finally decided to surrender, in part, because of what Clark said he would do to the British soldiers if the Americans had to storm the fort.

Henry Hamilton's hands and feet were bound with chains and he was taken to Virginia as a prisoner of war. He was hated by many and not treated very well, even though he denied that he personally paid for scalps. Daniel Boone, however, had been impressed by Hamilton while a prisoner of the British in Detroit. To show his respect, Boone visited him. Perhaps Hamilton was not as bad as his reputation.

Detroit Stays Out of Reach

Clark waited and tried to raise enough men to attack Detroit. But he could not get men or supplies from Virginia. Everything was needed to fight the British in the East. In the end he gave up his plan of taking Detroit.

Spain Comes to Michigan!

Late in the war, Spain and France decided to try to help the colonies in the revolution against England. Spain did not do much to help, but in the winter of 1781 it sent a small group of Spanish soldiers and Indians from their post at St. Louis. They followed the Mississippi and other rivers north until they reached Fort St. Joseph at Niles, Michigan. For all practical purposes the British had left the fort empty. Some traders and supplies stayed behind.

The Spanish raised their flag over the fort, took all of the supplies they could carry, set the fort on fire and left. Because of that little expedition, the city of Niles can say it has had four flags during its history, French, British, Spanish, and American.

The Revolutionary War Comes to an End

Most of the battles during the war were far to the east of Michigan. General George Washington, with the help of the French army and navy, finally forced the British to surrender at Yorktown, Virginia. The last battle was in 1781. But it took two more years to negotiate the final peace treaty . One reason the treaty process took so long was the problem of deciding the western boundaries of the United States.

What Clark Did For Michigan

Even though George Rogers Clark did not capture Detroit, his actions had an impact on Michigan. First of all, the British were worried he would attack, so they built a new and stronger fort at Detroit, and they moved the fort at Mackinaw City to a better position on Mackinac Island. That fort is still on the island today. His actions also helped win the land north of the Ohio River for the United States. If Clark had not been successful, England would probably have

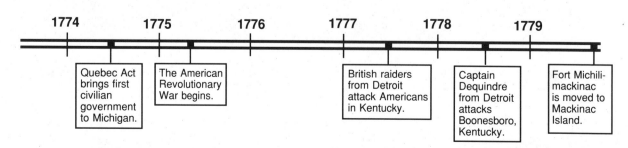

1774 — Quebec Act brings first civilian government to Michigan.

1775 — The American Revolutionary War begins.

1776

1777 — British raiders from Detroit attack Americans in Kentucky.

1778 — Captain Dequindre from Detroit attacks Boonesboro, Kentucky.

1779 — Fort Michilimackinac is moved to Mackinac Island.

kept this land after the Revolution; instead, it was included in the area given to our new country in the peace treaty of 1783. The land we call Michigan was not a state at that time. It was only a part of the much larger area known as the Northwest Territory.

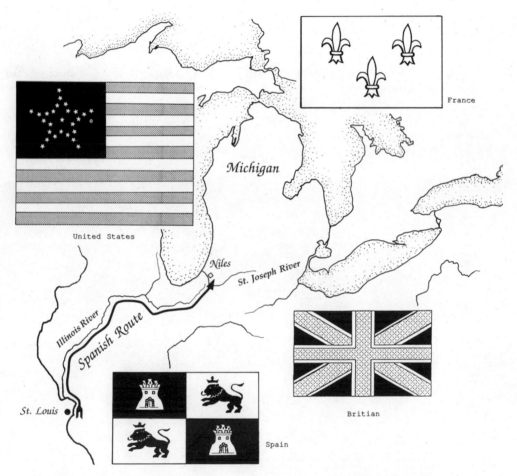

Four Flags Over Michigan

The flags of four nations flew over Niles. The American flag shown is one design used when Michigan became a state in 1837. (Map by David B. McConnell)

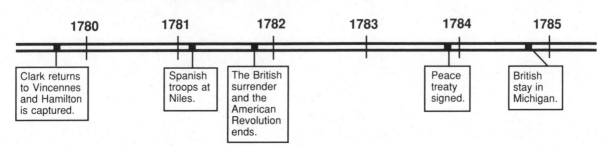

1780	1781	1782	1783	1784	1785
Clark returns to Vincennes and Hamilton is captured.	Spanish troops at Niles.	The British surrender and the American Revolution ends.		Peace treaty signed.	British stay in Michigan.

Questions

1. Why didn't the people living in Michigan join those in the 13 colonies and declare independence from the British?

2. What part did the British at Detroit play during the Revolutionary War? Mention at least three things.

3. Who made a grueling winter march to recapture Fort Sackville at Vincennes?

4. Were the British worried that George Rogers Clark might attack Michigan? Give a reason for your answer.

5. How did the victories by George Rogers Clark affect Michigan after the Revolutionary War?

6. Wilbur Cunningham has written a book about Michigan called *Land of Four Flags*. What does the title of this book have to do with Michigan? Explain your answer.

5 MICHIGAN JOINS THE UNITED STATES

FROM WILDERNESS TO TERRITORY

Chapter 5 Section 1

The British Hang On!

Here are the key concepts you will find in this section:

The British did not want to leave Michigan after the Revolution.

The British supplied guns so the Indians could attack settlers moving onto their land in Ohio.

General Anthony Wayne defeated Indians and a small force of British in Ohio during 1794.

The Indians made a peace treaty which gave up land in Ohio and Michigan.

Redcoats Still Rule

Under terms of the peace treaty with England, Michigan was to become part of the new United States. But there was one significant hitch in the plan: the British did not leave their forts at Mackinac Island and Detroit! Many British fur traders were making money in the area. They encouraged the British government to hold on. Canada continued to be under British control. Michigan was a long way from the newly formed 13 states. The mighty British were not impressed by the strength of the young United States.

Ironically, after they lost the Revolutionary War, the British forgot about the Quebec Act. After the war, many Americans who had not wanted to join the Revolution moved to Canada. The British government was no longer so concerned about the French in Canada.

Michigan stayed under British rule, and because of that, the first judge to hold court in Detroit was from Canada.

His name was Powell and he arrived in 1789. Even more unusual was the first election in Michigan. In 1792 the people of Michigan voted for members of the Parliament of Upper Canada!

In today's television programs, Michigan and Ohio are not considered the "Wild West," but in the 1790s they were just that. The British kept the Indians supplied with guns so they could attack American settlers in the Ohio River Valley. Perhaps the British thought the Indian attacks would weaken the United States and cause the young country to collapse.

British Support Indian Raids

As far as the settlers were concerned, life was about the same as it had been during the war. While the British kept control of Detroit, Mackinac Island and the Great Lakes, the settlers were not safe in the Ohio Valley and very few came into the Michigan area at all. Many

86

The Forts of General Wayne

A map of forts which were established on General Wayne's march through Ohio north toward Toledo.

General Anthony Wayne was a stern leader who carefully planned his march against the Indians in Ohio. (Courtesy Michigan State Archives)

This is the reconstructed blockhouse of Fort Recovery. This site as well as others such as Fort Wayne later became cities.

Indians, supported by the British, had their villages along the Maumee River just south of Michigan.

In 1790 President Washington sent General Josiah Harmar into Ohio to attack the tribes and humiliate the British. Indians under Chief Little Turtle massacred Harmar and the United States was humiliated instead. A second army force was sent to Ohio the next year but it could do no better. President Washington was very concerned. A national crisis was developing over the situation.

Soldiers on the March

General "Mad" Anthony Wayne was selected to lead a third army to wrestle control of the Ohio from the British and Indians. General Wayne had fought in the Revolution and was known for his bold actions in battle. That was how he got his nickname. But he had become more conservative over the years and General Wayne was determined not to be defeated. The honor of the United States was at stake!

He felt the soldiers in the first two battles had not been well trained. He spent months training his soldiers. Orders were given to shoot deserters or give them 100 lashes with a whip! He spent much time training his soldiers to use bayonets.

Beginning at Cincinnati, the army slowly marched north across Ohio toward the Indian villages along the Maumee River. To be safe from a surprise attack, General Wayne had his men cut down trees to build a blockade around the camp each night. The soldiers also built several strong forts along the way.

Little Turtle, Blue Jacket, and other Indian chiefs decided to lure the Americans into a tremendous tangle of trees which had been blown down by a tor-

This painting of Ojibwa leader Figured Stone was made during treaty talks in 1826 near Lake Superior. One day Figured Stone had a chance to show his feelings about treaties. He joined a U.S. government agent as he sat on a log. The agent moved over to make more space between them. But Figured Stone also scooted over. Again the agent moved but the Ojibwa followed right next to him. When the agent got to the end of the log, Figured Stone gave a mighty push sending the government man sprawling. Do you think the agent got the message? (Courtesy Clarke Historical Library, Central Michigan University)

nado. The place was known as Fallen Timbers. It was just south of Toledo, Ohio and only a few miles from Michigan. About 1,300 Indians and 53 British advisors had made their camp there. Not far from Fallen Timbers, the British had built a fort on the Maumee River.

General Wayne sent a messenger to tell the Indians "...experience the kindness and friendship of the United States of America and the invaluable blessings of peace and tranquility." The Indians said they would think about his words for 10 days. Wayne felt the ten days would be used to bring in more warriors. He did not wait that long.

Battle at Fallen Timbers

On the fourth day General Wayne prepared to march, even though his leg was infected from an old wound and he was in a great deal of pain. It was time to lead his men to the Indian camp and discover if the Indians would fight or surrender. When the American soldiers reached the camp, the Indians began shooting at them. Wayne had given the Americans orders to march into the trees and use their bayonets first and not fire their muskets until the enemy was on the run. Considering that their guns only held a single shot, that was wise advice. Many Indians and British were killed while trying to reload.

The Indians left the trees and ran to the British fort on the river. The British in the fort did not open fire on the Americans. They did not even open the gates to let the Indians in. They did nothing at all! It was a sad day for the Indians who had trusted and helped the British.

General Wayne's army went on to destroy many of the Indian villages and their farms. They also built one more fort and it became the city of Fort Wayne, Indiana.

An Important Treaty

The next summer, Little Turtle, Blue Jacket, and other Indians came to Fort Greenville and met with General Wayne. There they made a peace treaty with the

United States. Indians from the Michigan tribes also attended. They too pledged peace with the United States.

In the treaty Indians gave up a large part of what became the state of Ohio and some land in Michigan. In exchange for their land, the Indians were provided $20,000 in trade goods and $9,500 in goods each year forever. It may not have been a fair trade, but much more could be purchased for a dollar at that time. A sum as large as $20,000 was a considerable amount then.

The Treaty of Greenville was the first major Indian land treaty to affect Michigan. As a part of the treaty, the Indians gave up land on the Detroit River and at the Straits of Mackinac, including Mackinac Island.

The Stars and Stripes Over Michigan!

And what about the British? The Battle at Fallen Timbers made them realize they risked war with the United States if they did not leave. They were already at war with France once again. The danger of General Wayne's large number of well-trained soldiers so close to the British forts could not be shrugged off. After the way they had been treated during the Battle of Fallen Timbers, the Indians had lost their faith in England. Without help from the Indians, the British knew they would need many more soldiers to hold the area. Reluctantly, the British made a treaty and said they would leave their forts on the Great Lakes by 1796.

On July 11, 1796 Captain Moses Porter led American soldiers to take over the British fort in Detroit. It was a great day for Michigan! For the first time the American flag flew over the land won in the Revolutionary War. A war which ended 13 years before! The actions of General Wayne and the soldiers he commanded helped to bring Michigan into the United States.

General Anthony Wayne and his soldiers were great heros. Wayne was made Secretary of the Northwest Territory. Eventually, a large county in the territory was named for him. One of the officers with General Wayne was Lieutenant Colonel John Hamtramck (HAM tram ik). A Michigan city was also named for Hamtramck. General Wayne died from his infected leg on the way home.

The people in Detroit viewed the change of government with mixed feelings. William Macomb was a wealthy trader at Detroit who welcomed the Americans, though he died before they arrived. He used his influence with the Indians and urged them to go to Greenville to make a treaty. But many of the people did not want to have anything to do with the Americans. They moved across the Detroit River to live in Canada. The British soldiers left Fort Lernoult in Detroit and built a new fort on the Canadian side of the river. There continued to be much British influence in Michigan.

Wayne, Hamtramck and Macomb were three men involved in events at the time when Michigan changed hands from being British to American. Places named for them are important in Michigan today.

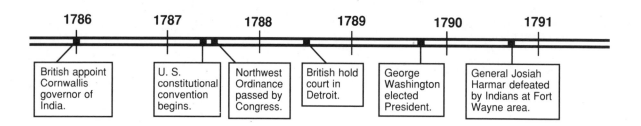

1786	1787	1788	1789	1790	1791
British appoint Cornwallis governor of India.	U.S. constitutional convention begins.	Northwest Ordinance passed by Congress.	British hold court in Detroit.	George Washington elected President.	General Josiah Harmar defeated by Indians at Fort Wayne area.

Questions

1. Give two reasons why the British wanted to stay in Michigan after the Revolution.

2. How did General Wayne's victory at Fallen Timbers help open the way for settlers to come to Michigan?

3. What part of Michigan did the Indians give up by the Treaty of Greenville? Did the tribes receive anything for their land?

4. What did many of the British people living in Michigan do when the Americans took over?

5. Write a paragraph giving your opinion on how the Indians in this area were treated by the British and Americans in the 1790s. Back up your thoughts with examples.

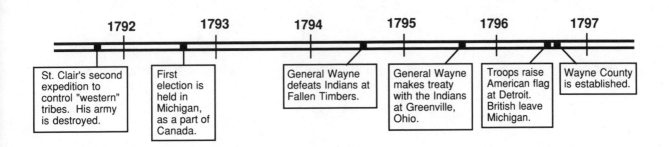

1792 — St. Clair's second expedition to control "western" tribes. His army is destroyed.

1793 — First election is held in Michigan, as a part of Canada.

1794 — General Wayne defeats Indians at Fallen Timbers.

1795 — General Wayne makes treaty with the Indians at Greenville, Ohio.

1796 — Troops raise American flag at Detroit. British leave Michigan.

1797 — Wayne County is established.

Chapter 5 Section 2

United States Takes Possession: 1796 - 1812

Here are the key concepts you will find in this section:

Several problems had to be solved before the land which became Michigan was ready to be settled. Resolving land claims by the first 13 states and surveying the land were two of these.

A set of laws called the Northwest Ordinance said how the land would be divided and governed.

Michigan was formed into its own territory in 1805. In the same year Detroit was destroyed by fire.

Five officials were appointed by President Jefferson to govern the Michigan Territory.

Bad feelings continued between Americans and British along the border.

The Settlers Must Wait!

The 13 British colonies had declared independence from England and were ready to become the 13 American states. The colonies had been in existence for about 200 years. During this time the population had grown to nearly 4 million by 1790. Land within the colonies was

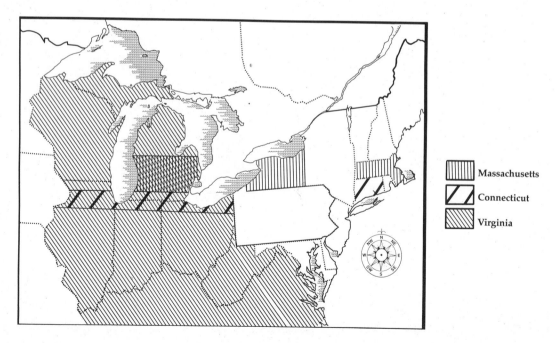

	Massachusetts
	Connecticut
	Virginia

During the early formation of the United States, parts of Michigan were claimed by Virginia, Massachusetts and Pennsylvania.

expensive and it was hard for a young family to find good land for farms. Americans were ready to move west into the new land— all the way to the Mississippi River.

The Northwest Territory, including Michigan, was a part of the new land. However, there were several problems which needed to be solved before settlers could move into the area. The first problem was with the British who would not leave. And there were the Indians who wanted to keep their land for themselves. It did help matters for the settlers when General Wayne defeated the Indians. It also helped when the British left Michigan in 1796. But not all the problems were solved yet.

Who Controls the Land?

When the colonies were first formed they often had no set western boundary. The charter for Virginia gave it all land north to 45 degrees north latitude but it mentioned nothing at all about the boundary on the west. What does 45 degrees north latitude have to do with Michigan? If you are not sure, look on a map. Would Detroit and Lansing become a part of Virginia? Connecticut and Massachusetts also claimed parts of the future Michigan land!

Thankfully, the states worked out the conflicting claims to land in the West during the process of setting up the government of the United States. By 1780 it had been decided the western land would be formed into sections which would become new states of the United States. The new states would have the same rights and powers as the first states. The concept of taking new land and forming new states which would be equal with the older states was a bold new idea! That was the way the United States grew from 13 states to 50.

Survey the Land First

Could the settlers begin to move west now? No, there were still other problems. The land was all forest and wilderness; there were no fences, no neat city lots to buy. How would people know which land

was theirs? The land had to be surveyed so it could be purchased with a proper description. *A surveyor is a person who finds boundary lines for maps using special instruments.*

Congress passed the Land Ordinance of 1785 (*ordinance means law*) which stated the land must be surveyed before it was sold and not afterwards, as had

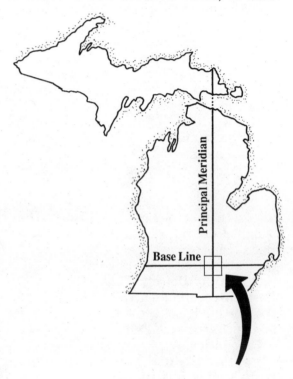

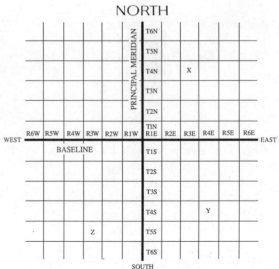

CONGRESSIONAL OR GEOGRAPHICAL TOWNSHIPS

(Each is 6 Mi. Square)

92

happened in some places. The law also said the land would be divided into square blocks six miles on a side. The blocks would be called *townships*. Each township would be divided into 36 smaller units one mile square called *sections*. A section has 640 *acres. An acre is a land measurement forming a square with a bit more than 200 feet on each side.*

The Land Ordinance also contained a new idea about how to help pay for schools. A set amount of land would be saved to be used to build and pay for schools. The sixteenth section of each township would be saved to promote education.

It would be helpful if each township could be located and identified. Surveyors had already taken that into account. Two lines were drawn on the Michigan map to give a frame of reference.

One line going east and west was marked across the Lower Peninsula. That is called the *Base Line*. Today 8 Mile or Base Line Road heads west along that exact line just north of Detroit. The Base Line continues across the north edge of the second row of Lower Peninsula counties.

Another line runs north and south up the Lower Peninsula and into the Upper Peninsula reaching Sault Ste. Marie. This line is called the *Prime Meridian*. Each township in Michigan is east or west of the Prime Meridian and north or south of the Base Line.

Data provided by the first surveyors would be used to locate land in the territory for a very long time. Even today property descriptions are based on the information gathered by surveyors tramping through underbrush over 150 years ago! Surveyors and the methods they

used forged the way Michigan was to be far into the future.

The land was almost ready to sell to settlers. Anyone would be able to go to a federal land office and buy a section of land for a minimum price of $640. But $640 was quite a lot of money at that time and 640 acres was too much land for one family to clear for a farm! At first, land speculators took advantage of this and bought whole sections and then resold the land in smaller lots for higher prices. They made large profits.

There was just one more detail. The land had to be obtained from the Indians by the United States government. A treaty with the Huron, Ojibwa, Ottawa, and Potawatomi tribes was made in 1807. That treaty obtained about a quarter of the Lower Peninsula in exchange for $10,000 in cash and goods, plus a payment of $2,400 each year. The Indians kept the right to hunt and fish on the land. That was known as the Detroit or

Indian Tribal Land Treaties

1- Greenville Treaty, 1795
2- Detroit Treaty, 1807
3- Maumee Treaty, 1817
4- Saginaw Treaty, 1819
5- Sault Ste. Marie, 1820
6- Chicago Treaty, 1821
7- Carey Mission Treaty, 1828
8- Chicago Treaty, 1833
9- Washington Treaty, 1836
10- Cedar Point Treaty, 1836
11- La Pointe Treaty, 1842

The Northwest Territory

Brownstown Treaty. It was the first really large land area given up by Michigan's Indians. However, the treaty process went on for many more years. Not until 1842 would Indians give up the last major piece of Michigan

Laws For the New Territory

Next came another ground-breaking law, the Northwest Ordinance. This law helped forge the future of Michigan in several ways. Many aspects of Michigan, which are taken for granted today, first came from that set of laws. The ordinance helped shape Michigan's boundaries; it also explained how Michigan would be governed before it became a state.

Briefly, here is what the Northwest Ordinance guaranteed to people living in the Territory:

1. Freedom of religion.
2. Protection against unjustified imprisonment
3. Trial by jury.
4. States formed in the Territory would always be a part of the United States.
5. Slavery was prohibited*.
6. All lakes and rivers leading to the Mississippi and St. Lawrence Rivers would be open to use by any U.S. citizen.
7. Indians were to be treated considerately. No land would be taken from the Indians without their consent.

8. Schools and education would always be encouraged because "religion, morality and knowledge are necessary to good government and the happiness of mankind."
* People who already owned slaves were allowed to keep them. Often the slaves were not blacks but Indians.

The ordinance was passed by Congress at New York City at the same time the Constitutional Convention was meeting at Philadelphia. In several ways, the Northwest Ordinance was ahead of the times compared to the original U.S. Constitution (before the Bill of Rights was added).

Where Will the Borders Be?

None of the land in the territory had been divided into states. The Ordinance simply said no less than three or more than five states would be carved from the area. Michigan could easily have ended up with a much different shape. In fact, for many years it looked as if it would be quite different. Borders were changed several times. Also, Michigan almost had another name. President Thomas Jefferson proposed Cherronesus, Metropotamia, and Sylvania as names for parts of our state!

Three Steps to Statehood

The Ordinance provided three stages to becoming a state. Each stage depended on the number of voters in the territory. In order to vote a person had to be a free white male who owned at least 50 acres of property. When a part of the territory had 60,000 free people, statehood was possible. Here is what the law said:

"...whenever any of the said states shall have 60,000 free inhabitants therein, such state shall be admitted by its delegates into the Congress of the United States, on an equal footing with the original states in all respects whatsoever; and shall be at liberty to form a permanent constitution and state government ...."

Until the final stage was reached, Congress had much power over the

94

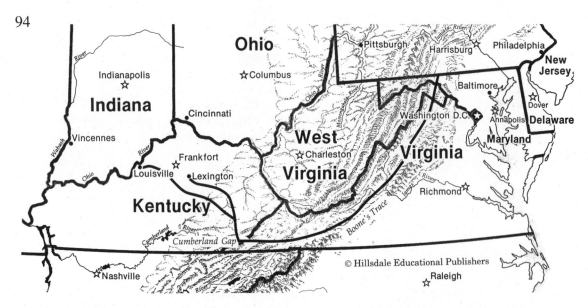

Kentucky, Ohio, and Indiana were settled before Michigan because of the ease in getting to those areas. The Appalachian Mountains blocked the direct path from the East to Michigan. Settlers used Boone's Trace and the Cumberland Gap to go over the mountains. The Ohio River was another route west.

government. The first officials were not elected at all, but appointed by Congress.

Michigan's first American election was held in the winter of 1798. It was quite different than elections by modern standards. To begin with, it was held in a tavern. Each voter had to publicly announce his choice. James May ran against Solomon Sibley for territorial representative at Cincinnati. May was supported by the former British citizens and Sibley by the pro-American voters. Mr. May protested because Sibley gave out free drinks to voters and had soldiers with clubs threaten anyone who didn't vote for him! The people in far away places like Mackinac Island didn't even get a chance to vote at all!

Other Places Grow Faster

Settlers were moving west across the Appalachian Mountains through the Cumberland Gap and down the Ohio River. Once through the mountains they spread out across the land. Since the Cumberland Gap and the Ohio River are both on the Kentucky border, it was natural that Kentucky would become one of the first "new" states. That happened in 1792. By 1803, Ohio was ready to become the first state formed from the Northwest Territory.

In Detroit—1800

Detroit was officially allowed to have village government by an act of the Territory in 1802. A five-member board of trustees was created. The first act of the Detroit trustees was to adopt a fire code. Everyone was required to help put out fires. They also had to keep buckets and bags of water, and ladders on hand to fight fires. Apparently it was not

**Talking about politics at the tavern.
(Art by David McConnell)**

Leather fire bucket. (Art by David B. McConnell)

an easy job to keep everyone prepared; reports mentioned those who didn't have fire equipment ready.

Worrying about fire was not the only problem in frontier Detroit. A police report noted: "A number of hogs are daily running in the streets, to great detriment of the public."

Birth of the Michigan Territory

After Ohio became a state, Michigan was combined with the Indiana Territory. That did not please Michiganians because the capital of the Indiana Territory was in Vincennes which was just too far away. The people of Michigan asked Congress to set up a Michigan Territory so they could be closer to their own government. In 1805 the Michigan Territory was created. Its southern boundary was to be "an east-west line drawn through the southerly bend or extreme of Lake Michigan." At that time only a small part of the Upper Peninsula was included in Michigan.

The new Michigan Territory would have a governor, a secretary, and three judges. All of these officials were appointed by the President of the United States, Thomas Jefferson. William Hull was the new governor. Hull had been a general in the Revolutionary War. He was from Massachusetts. Stanley Griswold from Connecticut was the secretary. One of the judges was Frederick Bates from Michigan. He was Detroit's postmaster. Another judge was from Ohio and he refused to serve. Augustus Brevoort Woodward was the third judge. All the laws for the territory would be made by the governor and the judges because there was no legislature at that time.

Since those people were not elected, Michiganians did not have any say in the choices and some of the men had unusual personalities. Griswold proved to be so difficult to get along with that Jefferson finally removed him from office! Bates moved to Louisiana the next year. But Judge Woodward was probably the most unusual and amazing official. He was very smart and spoke French, Spanish, Latin, and Greek. But he was quite stubborn too.

Disaster at Detroit!

In the summer of 1805 what kind of town did the officials find when they arrived at Detroit? Not much town to speak of—because it burned down on June 11! John Harvey was a Detroit baker. On that morning he was busy baking bread and he, or someone else, had been smoking a pipe. A gust of wind may have caught a piece of burning tobacco. The tobacco got into some straw or hay on the floor of Mr. Harvey's stable. No one noticed what had happened at first, but soon the stable was on fire. Fire! Fire! As flames burned through the roof, the wind picked up sparks and spread the fire to other buildings.

Everyone pitched in to help. The fire wagon was brought out. The wagon had a big barrel of water and a hand pump. People hurriedly formed a human chain to pass buckets of water to the fire. Soldiers ran across the parade ground to help. Others used axes to try to chop down a path ahead of the fire so it would burn out. Men and women raced up ladders to pour water on their own dry roofs. But there wasn't enough water to put out the fire. Even the suction hose on the fire wagon became clogged with pieces of felt from the hat maker's well and stopped working.

In about three hours, all of Detroit was a pile of smoking embers except for the military buildings! It was a very discouraging scene to everyone in Detroit. But the priest, Father Richard (ree SHARD), tried to cheer people up by saying, "We hope for better things; it will

The 1805 Detroit fire which according to legend was started by ashes falling from a pipe. (Courtesy Michigan Bell an Ameritech Company)

arise from the ashes." This saying became the city motto of Detroit.

Luckily no lives were lost. It was also fortunate that there were several farms outside the town walls. The farmers took in the homeless and gave them food. Others stayed in the fort.

A Grand Plan for the Future

Some wanted to start rebuilding right away while others thought they should wait until the new officials arrived. The new government was ready to help. Judge Woodward was fresh from Washington D.C. where that city was being designed by a French architect. He liked what he saw in Washington and presented an idea for Detroit based on the future. He thought Detroit should be a grand city with streets 200 feet wide and laid out like the spokes on a wheel. Well, the people of frontier Detroit could only sit back and scratch their heads at such a plan. Many of them had farms that were not much wider than 200 feet! In the end only small parts of the judge's plan were actually used.

The U.S. government gave each person over 17 years old a lot measuring at least 5,000 square feet. Because of the fire and the free land, Detroit developed into a city with large lots and plenty of open space—until years later when the skyscrapers came!

The Ups and Downs of Early Government

The government provided by the appointed officials had its ups and downs. Hull and Woodward often fought with each other over the way things should be done. Sometimes laws were passed by one group of officials only to be repealed when they were out of town!

Many of Judge Woodward's ideas were not practical. He wanted a $20,000 courthouse and jail for Detroit. That would be like asking people to build a $500 million courthouse today!

Governor Hull was not too popular either. Detroit had a *militia*. A militia is similar to the national guard today. *A militia consists of people who volunteer to be soldiers with the job of defending the state.* It was a common practice at that time. But Governor Hull wanted the militia to wear fancy uniforms instead of buckskins and fur hats. Officers in the militia were to wear: "dark blue coats, long and faced with red, with a red cape, white buttons and lining." Furthermore they would have cocked hats topped with red tipped black plumes, red sashes, swords, pistols, and bearskin holsters. They would be quite a sight! The soldiers were shocked into disbelief. There wasn't even any cloth in the entire territory to make such uniforms. Governor Hull, however, had it shipped in and sold it to the members.

Father Gabriel Richard was a Catholic priest from France. He is remembered for his work in education, Congress, and religion. (Courtesy Michigan State Archives)

A Hardworking Pioneer

In spite of the difficulties with early government there were bright spots in the Michigan Territory. A noteworthy person was Father Richard. Richard was a Catholic priest who had come from France to escape the French Revolution. That was a time of terror in that country when many leading citizens were beheaded. Father Richard barely escaped with his own life. He arrived in Detroit in 1798 to take charge of St. Anne's Church, the oldest church in Michigan.

Besides working in his church Father Richard did many other things to help the community. He started a school for Indian children. He brought the first printing press to Michigan and in 1809 printed the first newspaper in the territory. His press was also used to print several books. Later, Father Richard served in Congress and taught in the school which became the University of Michigan.

Tension on the Border

Bad feelings continued with some of the British Canadians across the Detroit River. An example of this took place in 1807 when Matthew Elliot came to Detroit to go to court. He sued in the Supreme Court of the Michigan Territory to recover eight of his slaves who had escaped into Michigan. Elliot lived on the Canadian side of the river and had been an official in the British Indian Department. Many Americans hated those who worked for this department. It had been responsible for giving guns to the Indians in the past and encouraging them to attack settlers. Some people said they were still doing so. As soon as people heard Elliot was coming to Detroit, a mob began to form.

While Elliot was at court, he learned about a plan to tar and feather him on his way home! Mr. Elliot was too crafty to be caught by a mob and escaped. Elliot's lawyer did not think the threats were serious but he was told: "Oh yes, they will, and if he comes over again, he will get it, and no matter at what hour of the day or night they can catch him!"

Judge Woodward decided that Elliot could not get his slaves back because the Northwest Ordinance said slavery was against the law. The only people who could own slaves were those who already had them before the law was passed. However, slaves would be returned if they escaped from the original states. The law said nothing about returning slaves from someplace else. This case is interesting because in a few years American slaves would be going to Canada to escape to freedom!

During these years Detroit and Mackinac Island were really the only two major centers of activity in Michigan. Mackinac Island continued to be the headquarters of fur trade for the Great Lakes, but the British competed from a nearby island. Detroit was the capital of the territory and the center for the government. The town was growing slowly because it was quite difficult for settlers to reach Michigan. Soon the problems with the British and Indians would boil over and stop all progress for a while. The Michigan Territory would be at war!

Questions

1. Name three problems which had to be solved before settlers could come to Michigan from the 13 states in the United States.

2. In 1800, was it clear that there would be a state called Michigan? Explain.

3. Was all of the Upper Peninsula included in the Michigan Territory?

4. Who appointed governing officials for Michigan at this time?

5. Give two examples which show that the appointed officials in the Michigan Territory were not always in touch with frontier life.

6. What serious event happened in Detroit in 1805? How did this event change the way Detroit is today?

7. What did the Northwest Ordinance say about the following: slavery, taking land from the Indians, and education? Write a paragraph giving your thoughts about how well the provisions for these three areas have been carried out over the years.

Chapter 5 Section 3

Part 1

The War of 1812: The Last Tussle for Michigan!

Here are the key concepts you will find in this section- part 1

Two Indian brothers, Tecumseh and Tenskwatawa, united several tribes against American settlers between 1806 and 1813.

Governor Harrison of Indiana defeated a large group of Indians at Tippecanoe in 1811. Then Tecumseh and his followers went to work with the British in Canada.

Problems between the British and the Americans finally led to a second war in 1812. Battles took place in and near Michigan.

Detroit and Fort Mackinac were captured by the British in humiliating defeats.

Irritations Lead to War

Even after treaties with the Indians and the exit of the British, the Michigan pioneers faced problems. Tension was increasing between the Indians and American settlers. And why not! Settlers were hungry for Indian land and were not shy about taking it. The Indians were beginning to realize what the land treaties with the Americans really meant for them.

Strong Indian Leaders to the South

Settlers had heard rumors about a Shawnee from Indiana who was becoming a powerful leader among the tribes. This man was known as The Prophet. The Prophet's Indian name was Tenskwatawa (tens QUA ta wa), which means "the one who opens the door." Indians considered The Prophet to have magical powers. A British trader had told him about a total eclipse of the sun which would take place on June 6, 1806. On that day he went before his people and told them the sun would disappear.

When it did, The Prophet called out to the Master of Life to raise the shadow from the face of the sun. Those who saw it thought a miracle had been performed!

The 'miracle' helped Tenskwatawa have a strong influence over many Indians. Other events which increased

Tecumseh is shown here wearing parts of a British military uniform.

the Indians' interest in magic were a massive earthquake which shook the entire Mississippi River valley and the appearance of a comet, both in 1811.

The Prophet had a brother known as Tecumseh (ta KUM see). His name means shooting star. Tecumseh was also an able leader. He was very concerned about the settlers taking Indian land. Indiana's governor, William Henry Harrison, made the Treaty of Fort Wayne with some of the older chiefs in 1809. When Tecumseh heard that by the terms of the treaty the Indians turned over some 3 million acres of land to the United States, he was very angry. He fumed, "Sell a country! Why not sell the air, the clouds and the great sea, as well as the earth? Did not the Great Spirit make them all for the use of his children?" Tenskwatawa and Tecumseh argued the land belonged to all Indians and not just those tribes who made the agreement.

Tenskwatawa and Tecumseh were also angry because their father and two brothers had been killed in battles with the Americans.

We Must Work Together!

Tecumseh traveled to many tribes telling them that they must unite and work together to fight the American settlers. He spoke to tribes in the north and as far south as Florida. Captain Sam Dale heard Tecumseh and was impressed with his ability. Dale commented, "His voice resounded....hurling out his words like a succession of thunderbolts.... I have heard many great orators, but I never saw one with the vocal powers of Tecumseh."

Settlers in the Indiana Territory began to feel the pain of more Indian attacks. To stop those attacks, Governor Harrison gathered a large army in 1811 to march to the main Indian camp. The camp was known as Prophet's Town. Prophet's Town was on the banks of the Wabash and Tippecanoe Rivers in Indiana. At that time Tecumseh was gone from the camp.

William Henry Harrison made the Treaty of Fort Wayne in which the Indians turned over 3 million acres to the American government. Harrison became famous for his leadership at Tippecanoe. (Courtesy Michigan State Archives)

A Fight on the Tippecanoe River

Governor Harrison's army came within sight of Prophet's Town, but Harrison was told by the Indians that they wanted peace and would hold a council with him the next day. Tecumseh had warned his brother not to attack the Americans; however, Tenskwatawa did not follow that advice. Isaac Naylor was a 21-year-old volunteer in Harrison's army. This is what he said happened on the morning of November 7, 1811:

I awoke about four o'clock the next morning, after a sound and refreshing sleep.... A drizzling rain was falling and all things were still and quiet throughout the camp. I was engaged in making a calculation when I should arrive home.

In a few moments I heard the crack of a rifle.... I had just time to think that some sentinel was alarmed and firing his rifle without real cause, when I heard the crack of another rifle, followed by an awful Indian yell all around the encampment.

In less than a minute, I saw the Indians charging our line most furiously and shooting a

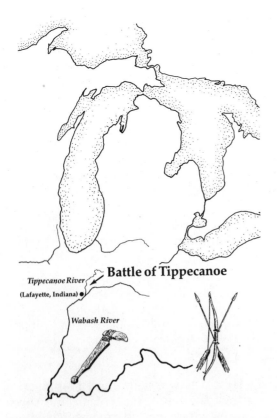

Battle of Tippecanoe

Tippecanoe River
(Lafayette, Indiana) •

Wabash River

Some of the guns were so new they were still wrapped. There were other reasons to feel the British were being bullies. British fur traders were often seen on American land. British ships had been stopping American ships on the oceans and taking sailors to use in the British navy. Americans felt the British should be driven from Canada. America should help the Canadians become a free nation.

Get Rid of the British!

America got ready for war but their defenses were not strong. In 1811 Michigan had only nine main settlements with about 4,700 non-Indian people. About four-fifths were of French background. There were only two forts; the one at Detroit had 94 soldiers and the one at Mackinac had 79 soldiers. The United States only had one warship on the Great

great many rifle balls into our campfires, throwing live coals into the air three or four feet high.

...The Indians made four or five more fierce charges on our lines, yelling and screaming as they advanced, shooting balls and arrows into our ranks. At each charge they were driven back in confusion, carrying off their dead and wounded as they retreated.

Just after daylight the Indians retreated across the prairie.... As their retreat became visible, an almost deafening and universal shout was raised by our men. Huzza! Huzza! Huzza!

Statement by Isaac Naylor,
Eyewitness Account File,
Tippecanoe Battleground Museum.

After such a disastrous battle The Prophet's leadership was questioned, and Tecumseh became the main leader of the movement. Tecumseh and his followers went to Canada and lived near Detroit.

The people in Michigan and indeed the whole country were tired of the British. Some Americans felt the British were trying to take control over land they lost during the Revolutionary War. Governor Harrison reported that each Indian at Prophet's Town had a British gun, scalping knife, war club, and a tomahawk.

General Hull served as Michigan's territorial governor and was made a general of the Northwestern Army in 1811. (Courtesy Michigan State Archives)

Lakes and it was being repaired. Actually, the U.S. was barely able to control the vast western land which included Michigan. The fact that most of the non-Indian population was French did not help.

Michigan's territorial Governor Hull went to Washington to discuss the situation. He felt Michigan was in a weak position unless the Americans could keep British warships off Lake Erie. Hull was made a general and given command of the northwestern army. His goal would be to attack the British in Canada. The first objective was Fort Malden at Amherstburg. Besides the regular soldiers, three units of the Ohio militia were called into duty. Colonel Lewis Cass led one of those units. Lewis Cass later became the governor of Michigan Territory.

The War of 1812

In April 1812, Hull headed back to Michigan by way of Ohio. There the governor of the state, Return Jonathan Meigs, put the Ohio soldiers under Hull's command. The soldiers faced a difficult march to reach Detroit. They had to cross the Black Swamp which was between Toledo and Detroit. Progress was quite slow because a road had to be built as they worked their way over the swamp.

Americans were ready for a fight and felt the British could be defeated. Canada would be freed of the British and they would be driven out of North America altogether. On June 1, 1812, President James Madison asked for a declaration of war against England. In his message he mentioned the attacks by Indians against settlers in the West and the violation of American rights at sea.

One detail was forgotten— no one told the frontier posts that war had actually been declared! The government sent Hull a letter by mail, but it did not arrive in time. Hull put his military information and supplies on a ship which was easily captured when it sailed by Fort Malden!

John Jacob Astor was a German who started a large fur trading business on Mackinac Island. Astor had sent a messenger from the east coast to Mackinac

Island to warn his traders that war had been declared. His choice of a messenger was a poor one. The man stopped to tell every British post on the way west! The War of 1812 was not off to a good start for the Americans, and it only got worse.

Canada is Invaded!

Nevertheless, General Hull invaded Canada in July. He made camp in Windsor, which was called Sandwich at that time. There was little fighting. Hull made a proclamation to the Canadian people:

"Inhabitants of Canada!.... The army under my command has invaded your country.... It brings neither danger nor difficulty. I come to find enemies not to make them, I come to protect not to injure you...."

Hull was worried about going south to attack the fort. The British had three warships which could fire on his soldiers as they attacked the fort since Fort Malden was located on the edge of the Detroit River.

The Americans decided to be very cautious. They would wait until they could bring heavy cannons across the river to keep the British warships away. The project took nearly a month. Before they were ready, news came that the British had captured Fort Mackinac! General Hull worried that the British and Indians would soon be coming south to attack Detroit. He left his plans uncompleted and returned to Detroit.

A Surprise Attack at Mackinac!

This is what happened at Mackinac Island. Captain Charles Roberts of the British forces on St. Joseph Island, not far from Mackinac, was ready to make good use of the early warning he got about war with the U.S. He took many French Canadians and Indians in canoes to the far side of Mackinac Island. Landing in the darkness the British and Canadians worked very hard to bring a cannon up the steep hill which was behind Fort Mackinac. By the next morning the cannon was aimed down inside of the fort.

Fort Mackinac was secure with its eight-foot thick stone walls high above the harbor. But British and Canadian troops moved a cannon up a hill in behind the fort forcing it to surrender. (From Michigan State University Museum)

Now the eight foot thick stone walls of the fort could not protect the American soldiers below.

Lieutenant Porter Hanks was in charge of Fort Mackinac. He was horrified when he realized that the British cannon would slowly pulverize his fort and men. He did not have many soldiers to defend the place and he still didn't know war had been declared. He surrendered without firing a single shot!

Hanks and his soldiers were sent to Detroit after they promised they would not fight against the British again.

Detroit in Danger

Hull learned that more British soldiers were on the way to Fort Malden from Fort Niagara in the east. He sent Lewis Cass, another officer, and 400 men to find some Americans bringing supplies to Detroit. The absence of Cass and his troops left Fort Detroit shorthanded.

About the same time Isaac Brock took over Fort Malden. The new British commander was a man of action. Two days after arriving at Fort Malden he told General Hull to surrender. He warned that if the Americans did not give in, he could not be responsible if the Indians attacked people living outside Detroit. Hull did not give in, so the British began to fire their cannons across the Detroit River.

Cannon balls came crashing down into the streets and homes of Detroit. As the Augustus Langdon family was beginning to eat breakfast, a cannon ball smashed through the roof of their home, through the ceiling, past their plates, through the table and into the basement! Judge Woodward had just jumped out of bed to see what was going on when a cannonball blasted through his bed! Lieutenant Hanks, who was under arrest and waiting to face a court-martial for surrendering, was killed in the bombardment.

Astonishing Surrender!

While all of that was going on, the British commander Brock crossed the Detroit River with his troops and joined a large number of Indians. When Hull learned that so many Indians were coming to attack Detroit, he became very concerned for the civilians. He was afraid of an Indian massacre. Lewis Cass and his soldiers had not returned. They could not locate the supplies and had camped only three miles from Detroit. For some reason, Cass did not come back to Detroit when he heard the noise of the British cannons. Without consulting anyone, General Hull raised a white table cloth as a sign of surrender.

The British could not believe their good luck in capturing such an important fort without a battle. The American people in Detroit could not believe the surrender either. They could not believe that Hull would give in without a fight! Lewis Cass later wrote about the surrender:

"...the general took counsel from his own feelings only. Not an officer was consulted. Not one anticipated a surrender, till he saw the white flag displayed. Even the women were indignant at so shameful a degradation of the American character."

Michigan Pioneer and Historical Collections, Volume 40

The British General Brock wrote his commander:

"I hasten to apprize Your Excellency of the capture of this very important post—2,500 troops have this day surrendered prisoner of war, and about 25 pieces of ordnance have been taken without the sacrifice of a drop of British blood. I had not more than 700 troops including militia, and about 400 Indians to accomplish this service. When I detail my good fortune Your Excellency will be astonished...."

Michigan Pioneer and Historical Collections, Volume 40

Actually both Brock and Hull thought the other side had many more soldiers than they did. General Brock went east and left Colonel Henry Procter in charge at Detroit. For the time being, Hull and the American soldiers were sent to Quebec as prisoners of war. After the war, General Hull was court-martialed and sentenced to be shot for cowardice. The army was not impressed with his concern about saving the lives of civilians. However, President Madison considered General Hull's Revolutionary War bravery and gave him a pardon.

Questions

1. What was the Indian name of the man called The Prophet?

2. After the British left Michigan in 1796, did they still have influence over what happened in the area? Explain your answer.

3. What was Tecumseh's goal?

4. Who was in command of the Indians and who was in command of the Americans at the Battle of Tippecanoe? What happened in that battle?

5. Name two places in Michigan which were captured by the British early in the War of 1812. How did poor communications play a role in the loss of both places?

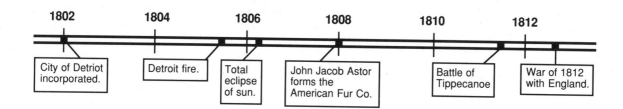

1802	1804	1806	1808	1810	1812
City of Detriot incorporated.	Detroit fire.	Total eclipse of sun.	John Jacob Astor forms the American Fur Co.	Battle of Tippecanoe	War of 1812 with England.

Chapter 5 Section 3

Part 2

The War of 1812: Victories at Last!

> *Here are the key concepts you will find in this section- part 2*

The war continued going badly for the Americans. Captured soldiers near the River Raisin were massacred by Indians who were fighting on the British side.

The American army in the West was concentrated at a fort near Toledo, Ohio. The British attacked this fort for many days but could not capture it. This left a large American army ready to go after the British when the opportunity was right.

Oliver Hazard Perry defeated the British navy on Lake Erie. This victory allowed the American army to move against Fort Malden where the main British army in the West was camped.

With the Americans in control of the Great Lakes, the British at Fort Malden felt in danger. They left and marched northeast.

The Americans under General Harrison chased the British and caught them near the Thames (TEMZ) River in Ontario. They were defeated along with their Indian warriors at the Battle of the Thames in 1814.

A peace treaty was made on Christmas Day, 1814. Lewis Cass was made the new governor of the Michigan Territory.

Remember the River Raisin!

William Henry Harrison was given command of what was left of the American army in the area near Michigan. He planned to retake Detroit. Volunteers were gathered from Ohio and Kentucky. The American troops came north and camped just south of Toledo, Ohio, not far from Michigan's southern border.

On January 17, 1813, about 1,000 Americans marched to Frenchtown (Monroe, Michigan) on the River Raisin, and chased away a small group of British.

Before dawn on January 22, the British brought about 1,200 soldiers and Indians across Lake Erie over the ice. The Americans were not prepared for this surprise. A fierce battle began, the largest to ever take place in Michigan. Some of the Americans surrendered. The British commander, Colonel Procter, promised they would be protected from the Indians if they gave up.

Procter was worried more Americans would arrive from the Toledo area and counterattack. He felt he would be much safer in Fort Malden so he marched back across the ice taking the American prisoners who could walk. Procter left the wounded Americans with two British doctors. Most of the wounded were kept in two warehouses near the River Raisin.

After the British soldiers had gone, a terrible event took place. The Indians sought revenge against the wounded Americans. The warehouses were set on fire and the soldiers killed and scalped as they tried to escape the flames. The Americans felt Colonel Procter had neglected the wounded men on purpose and violated his promise. The Americans were outraged and made "Remember the River Raisin!" a battle cry.

At Fort Meigs

In the meantime, the main group of American troops had built Fort Meigs on the Maumee River, near Toledo, Ohio. About 2,000 soldiers and their horses were inside. Even some women and wives were also living in the fort. It was a rare occasion when anyone dared to leave the fort because Tecumseh and his warriors were hiding outside ready to kill the

During April 1813, Procter marched to Fort Meigs with his British soldiers. They set up cannons across the river and fired on the fort for five days. Not content to use ordinary cannon balls, the British heated some of them until they were red hot. The balls sizzled into the earth where the Americans were taking cover. But the Americans continued to hold the fort.

Can They Hold Out?

It was getting pretty bad inside the fort. The wounded had no hospital and were lying about on the ground. There was a shortage of ammunition and food. About the time the Americans wondered how much longer they could hold out,

Fort Meigs was surrounded by Tecumseh's warriors and British soldiers in the War of 1812. (Courtesy Mackinac State Historic Parks)

unwary. Fort Meigs was built of logs to keep the troops safe from Indians, but Harrison knew these logs would be shattered by British cannons. So he had the soldiers also dig large mounds of earth to hide behind.

Tecumseh stood outside the fort and yelled to General Harrison:

"I have with me 800 braves. You have an equal number in your hiding place. Come out with them and give me battle. You talked like a brave man when we met at Vincennes, and I respected you, but now you hide behind logs in the earth, like a ground hog!"
American History Illustrated, February 1972.

Harrison was not interested in having part of his troops killed in a battle with Indians who could disappear into the woods.

Procter's army left. Perhaps there was grumbling from his own soldiers. The men in the Canadian militia needed to do their spring planting and the Indians may have become tired of the long siege. It was an important standoff between the British and Americans. Fort Meigs has been rebuilt and you can stand in the same spot where those British cannon balls came whizzing into the fort or imagine the voice of Tecumseh calling out from behind the trees.

The Lake Erie Problem

On a small island on the western end of Lake Erie, stands a tall monument to Oliver Hazard Perry. It is a monument to the services of a 28-year-old sailor who fought bravely for his country. General Hull had warned how much trouble British warships would be on Lake Erie. These ships had kept Hull from making a speedy attack on Fort Malden. They also brought critical supplies to the British and kept the Americans from getting their own supplies by ship.

The Americans did not like this situation and decided to do something about it. They began to build several small war ships on the Niagara River and at Erie, Pennsylvania. Oliver Hazard Perry was given command of the American ships.

had to take cannons from Fort Malden to use on it. Some of the American sailors were Kentucky pioneers who had never seen a ship before. The Americans under Perry had more ships than the British, but the British had cannons with longer range.

The commander of the British ships was Robert Barclay. Procter urged him to do battle with the Americans soon. Procter was feeding about 14,000 people at Fort Malden, including the Indians and their families. No supplies had come in since the American fleet had been completed.

Michigan

Canada

Detroit

Battle of Thames

Thames River

Lake Erie

Fort Malden

Frenchtown (Monroe)

Perry's Victory

Fort Meigs

The War of 1812

The Battle Begins!

On the morning of September 10, 1813, Barclay made the decision to fight. The British sailed from Fort Malden into Lake Erie. Soon Perry spotted the British ships and was under sail to meet them. The ships slowly moved toward each other; there was not much wind. The sailors on both sides were impatient. Hearts beat rapidly as they manned their cannon. Perry's command ship, the *Lawrence*, carried a flag which said *Don't Give Up the Ship*.

A puff of smoke came from one of the British ships, then the boom of its cannon carried over the water; the shell splashed harmlessly into the lake. A second British cannon fired—the *Lawrence* was

Perry needed to get closer to Fort Malden, where the British ships had their headquarters. So when the ships had been finished, they sailed to Bass Island. This is not far from Sandusky, Ohio, and the Cedar Point amusement park.

Neither side was a proper navy; the ships had whatever equipment was at hand. The British built a new ship but

hit! Perry could not even fire back; the British were out of range! But a fierce battle began once the American ships were close enough. American and British sharpshooters fired at each other from the rigging. The ships shook with the tremendous blasts from the cannons. The smell of gunpowder hung heavy over the water.

Perry's ship took a terrific pounding. Soon every officer on the *Lawrence*, except Perry and his younger brother, were dead or wounded. By 2:30 all the cannons on the *Lawrence* were out of action and only 20 of the 103 sailors were unhurt. The British thought the battle might be almost over. For some reason, one American ship, the *Niagara*, had stayed on the edge of the battle. Now the *Niagara* came closer and Perry made an unheard of decision.

He got into a rowboat and four brave sailors rowed him between splashes from British cannon balls. He took command of the *Niagara* and sailed it right between the British ships! He fired the ship's guns all at once as he passed. By this time, the British commander Barclay had been wounded twice. The added firepower of the *Niagara* caused the British to surrender. (The *Niagara* was saved and is now on display at Erie, Pennsylvania.)

What Will the British Do?

Tecumseh and the British could hear the booming cannon fire but the battle was too far away to see. Tecumseh wondered what had happened but could pretty well guess the outcome when the British ships did not come back.

All of the United States was excited by Perry's victory. Newspapers around the country told of the good news. This victory opened the door for General Harrison to go after the British at Fort Malden.

Lake Erie was the scene of a battle between British and American forces in which the British surrendered. (Courtesy Clarke Historic Library, Central Michigan University)

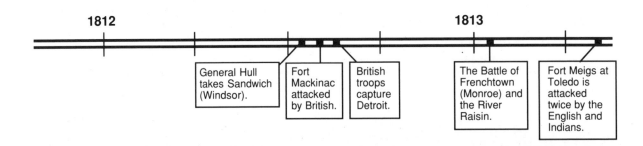

1812

1813

General Hull takes Sandwich (Windsor).

Fort Mackinac attacked by British.

British troops capture Detroit.

The Battle of Frenchtown (Monroe) and the River Raisin.

Fort Meigs at Toledo is attacked twice by the English and Indians.

U.S. First Artillery soldier from the War of 1812. (Courtesy Mackinac State Historic Parks)

The British commander Procter knew Fort Malden was in serious danger. General Harrison had several thousand soldiers ready to march from Fort Meigs. Perry could easily sail his ships by and fire on the fort. Colonel Procter decided to retreat and head northeast.

When Tecumseh heard about this plan he was shocked and angry. He made a passionate speech. He told the British he wanted to fight and keep Americans off Indian land. Throughout the war the Indians had hoped to get their land back from the Americans by helping the British. When he had finished talking, the Indians jumped to their feet with a shout and shook their tomahawks!

A Quick Retreat

Tecumseh's moving speech did not stop Procter from leaving on September 24. The British made a hasty retreat with many of the Indians going too. There were Potawatomi Indians with Tecumseh and probably Indians from Michigan. The Americans, including Lewis Cass, were right behind them. Procter's plan was to move along the Thames River and make a stand further east. But the British couldn't move fast enough so they started leaving guns and supplies along the way.

About 35 miles west of Lake St. Clair, along the north side of the River Thames, the American army caught up with the British. The British troops were not very well organized. American bugles sounded and the Kentucky volunteers charged forward on their horses. The enemy could not stop the mounted riders and they rode through the soldiers, then turned and charged back from the other side.

This was too much for the British and they were quickly overcome. Although the Indians fought bravely, Tecumseh was killed early in the battle. The British commander Procter fled and the rest of his army surrendered to the Americans. The fight became known as the Battle of the Thames.

This battle was the end of the Indian dream of keeping Americans off their land. It was also the end of a great leader, Tecumseh, who shaped that dream.

Lewis Cass was soon made governor of the Michigan Territory by President Madison. He kept this position from 1813 until 1831. In Detroit, the Americans renamed the fort after Governor Shelby of Kentucky, the state which had provided so many soldiers during the war.

Life was quite hard during this time. Some Indians continued to attack settlers. In the fall of 1814, they killed Ananias McMillan in Detroit and

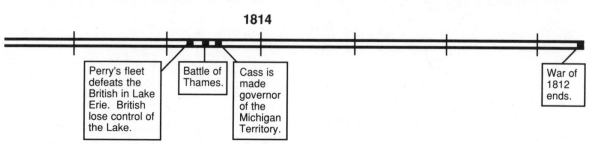

1814

Perry's fleet defeats the British in Lake Erie. British lose control of the Lake.

Battle of Thames.

Cass is made governor of the Michigan Territory.

War of 1812 ends.

kidnapped his son. Besides these attacks, the dreaded disease cholera (KOL er a) struck down both soldiers and civilians. Food and firewood were scarce which caused additional hardships.

Blunders at Mackinac

The only British stronghold left in the Michigan area was at Mackinac Island. The next summer, July 1814, American warships sailed north to capture that fort. Perry was not in charge and the whole attack was poorly planned. The Americans could not retake the island.

Peace at Last—The War is Over!

The British eventually realized it was going to be too costly to win the war and peace was made on Christmas Eve, 1814. At last the War of 1812 was over.

If Perry had not beaten the British, then Harrison might not have been able to chase them into Canada and defeat them at the Battle of the Thames. Without these two victories, it is possible Michigan would have returned to British or Canadian control.

The exact boundaries between Canada and Michigan were not decided until 1822. At that time, Drummond Island was given to Michigan, even though the British had built a fort there, and Boblo Island, in the Detroit River, was given to Canada.

In 1817 the Rush-Bagot Agreement was made between the United States and England. This agreement kept either country from having large numbers of warships on the Great Lakes.

All worries about war with England did not disappear overnight. The United States kept Fort Mackinac active for many years and later Fort Wayne was built at Detroit.

Questions

1. Where, exactly, was the largest battle ever to take place in Michigan? Which war was taking place at the time? What battle cry did the Americans use after this defeat?

2. Before September 1813, how was the war going for the Americans in the Great Lakes region? Give facts to back up your answer.

3. Why was it important for Perry to defeat the British warships on Lake Erie?

4. How did Tecumseh feel about the British retreat after Perry's victory? What did Tecumseh hope to get by helping the British?

5. What agreement says the United States, England, or Canada will not keep warships on the Great Lakes?

6. What happened to former Governor Hull? Who replaced him as governor of the Michigan Territory?

6 THE PATHWAY WIDENS-PIONEERS ON THE WAY!

Chapter 6 Section 1

Yankees Move West

Here are the key concepts you will find in this section:

The Erie Canal helped bring the first big group of settlers to Michigan.

People wanted to move to Michigan because land was cheap here. Much land in Ohio and Indiana had already been bought. Most of the early Michigan settlers were from New England and New York. They were called Yankees.

Before the land could be bought by settlers, the government had to get legal title to it from the tribes living here. The Indians gave up their land through several treaties.

Lewis Cass was governor of the Michigan Territory for 18 years and did much to promote the state and help settlers.

A New Route to Michigan— The Erie Canal

A full 200 years after the time of the French explorers, using rivers and lakes was still the easiest way to travel. But people were impatient with nature and wanted to forge new routes, to go places where no river flowed. In 1817 the governor of New York state decided to build a *canal* which would link New York City with the Great Lakes. It was named the Erie Canal.

Canals are man-made rivers. A large ditch is dug and when it is filled with water, small boats can travel as if they are on a river. By forging this canal across the land, people formed another great pathway to Michigan.

The Erie Canal, snaking 363 miles west across New York state, was a big engineering project for those times. It was 40 feet wide and 4 feet deep. It took 83 locks to raise boats from the Hudson River up to the level of Lake Erie. Over 300 bridges had to be built over the canal.

Good Roads Were Scarce

Why did people go to the trouble to build canals? Good roads were few and far between in the early 1800s. The roads which did exist were not paved and became full of deep ruts in wet weather. It was said when the ruts dried out, the roads were so bumpy they could shake out a person's false teeth!

There are many folk stories telling just how bad Michigan roads were. In one story, a traveler sees a beaver hat sitting in a mud hole. He reaches down to pick up the hat but is startled because there is a man under it! He calls for help to aid the distressed fellow, but the man objected, "Just leave me alone stranger. I have a good horse under me and have just found bottom!"

112

Early roads in Michigan Territory were very poor. Some people laid planks on the ground in an attempt to make travel easier. (Courtesy Michigan State Archives)

Many of the roads were private and each wagon had to pay a fee or toll to use the road. Some owners of toll roads tried to improve their trails by laying logs or wooden planks on the ground, but that was not much help. Trains and railroads were only a dream for the future. It was a time when many canal projects were begun. A project was even started to build a canal across the Lower Peninsula.

Why Did the Settlers Come?

Why would anyone want to leave a business or farm in the East and migrate to Michigan? The main reason was the difference in land prices. Farming was how most people in the United States made their living at that time. Farmland in the New England states was overworked and expensive. A young family seldom had enough money to buy farmland in the East. In contrast, land in Michigan and nearby states was quite cheap, especially after the Land Law of 1820 allowed small parcels to be sold. Most land sold for only a little more than the minimum price of $1.25 per acre. Besides, the whole nation seemed to have an itch to move west.

Coming to Michigan on the Canal

The grand opening of the Erie Canal was in 1825. Then it was westward-ho!

The Erie Canal opened the route to Michigan and thousands of families traveled the canal.

Horses or mules towed Erie Canal boats about four miles an hour. It took six to eight days to go the length of the canal.

Adventurous families with a pioneer spirit could take their belongings and get on board a canal boat. The boats had no oars, sails, or motors; they were pulled at about four miles an hour by mules walking along the shore.

John Nowlin and his family came to Michigan on the Erie Canal. He had bought some land that was near the present city of Dearborn. He wanted to move there with his wife and five children. Mrs. Nowlin was not so excited about his idea. Her son William wrote in his book, *The Bark Covered House*, "Many of her friends said she would not live to get to Michigan if she started...that if she did go, the family would be killed by Indians, perish in the wilderness, or starve to death!"

The Trip Begins

In spite of the misgivings of the Nowlin's friends, they headed for Michigan. They paid 1.5 cents per person, per mile, to ride on the canal boat. When the captain shouted "Low bridge!" everyone on top of the boat had to lie flat on their backs or risk being scraped off.

After spending six to eight days aboard the canal boat, the Nowlin family reached the rip-roaring city of Buffalo on the shore of Lake Erie.

The Nowlins planned to take the steamship *Michigan* to Detroit, but first they had to spend a bad night in a disreputable hotel worrying about being robbed of their life savings, $500 in silver. In the morning they quickly left the hotel and went to the dock.

Settlers crossed Lake Erie by ship. The *Michigan,* one of several steamboats in service, looked much like this.

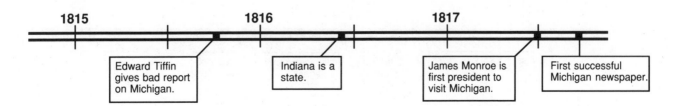

1815   1816   1817

Edward Tiffin gives bad report on Michigan.

Indiana is a state.

James Monroe is first president to visit Michigan.

First successful Michigan newspaper.

The Lake was not Pleasant

Once the *Michigan* moved out onto Lake Erie, the wind blew hard and cold dark blue waves tossed the ship violently. The young William Nowlin remembered, "I was miserably sick, as were nearly all the passengers.... The most awful terror marked nearly every face. Some wept, some prayed, some swore.... Our clothes and bedding were all drenched, and to make our condition still more perilous, the boat was discovered to be on fire!"

A bucket brigade managed to put the fire out and stopped what would have been a total tragedy from taking place. The ship did make it to Detroit in 37-40 hours and the lucky Nowlin family was glad to step ashore.

Although there were dangers, steamships offered some definite advantages to travelers. They were usually faster and they could run on a regular schedule since they did not have to wait for a good breeze. The first steamship sailed to Detroit in 1818. It was the *Walk-In-The-Water*. Traveling on it, passengers could reach Detroit from Buffalo in as little as 1 1/2 days and pay seven dollars for the cheapest fare. By 1856 the Great Lakes had 118 propeller steamers, 120 paddle wheel steamers, and 1,149 sailing ships.

The Chicago Road

The Nowlins left Detroit on the Chicago Road which connected Detroit and Chicago. William Nowlin wrote, "I could just see a streak ahead four or five miles, with trees standing thick and dark on either side." Finally they reached their land near Dearborn.

Other families also used the Chicago Road to travel into the wilderness of Michigan. The road followed the Old Sauk Trail which was the ancient path used by the Indians. Now it is known as U. S. 12.

The Chicago Road was started in 1825 and finished in 1833. It was not actually built to bring settlers west but to allow soldiers and military supplies to go from Detroit to Fort Dearborn at Chicago. The war of 1812 encouraged the federal government to build the Chicago Road and others like it.

The condition of the road was none too good. Some travelers complained they could hardly find it. Even so, much of the early settlement followed along the Chicago Road. Many of the oldest towns in the Lower Peninsula are on that route. Most of the early pioneers coming to Michigan went to live in the southern counties.

A Journey in Covered Wagons

Abraham Edwards is an example of one of these early pioneers. In 1828 Edwards brought his wife and ten children on the Chicago Road to settle in western Michigan. The diary he kept tells how few settlers were in Michigan and how difficult it was to travel from place to place:

...The first night from Detroit we slept at TenEyck's tavern, at Dearborn; the second night at Sheldon's (A small village about 6 miles east of Ypsilanti.) and the third night two miles west of Ypsilanti, where for the first time we used our tent and cooked our own meals. From this encampment we left the settlements, except for a few scattered squatters on the public lands and Indian trading establishments few and far between, and did not meet a white face for eighteen days, the time spent traveling to Edwardsburg (in southwest Cass County)....

(Mr. Edwards also wrote about some of the places they traveled through to reach Edwardsburg.)

...A large Indian settlement occupied the whole of Coldwater prairie.

From Bronson we traveled 13 miles to Sturgis prairie named after the only man then residing on it, who had been there a few

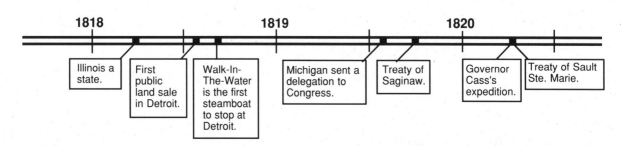

1818 — Illinois a state. | First public land sale in Detroit. | Walk-In-The-Water is the first steamboat to stop at Detroit.

1819 — Michigan sent a delegation to Congress. | Treaty of Saginaw.

1820 — Governor Cass's expedition. | Treaty of Sault Ste. Marie.

This map shows the major roads used by early settlers. Notice none of them reach the northern part of the state.

Michigan's Early Roads

Saginaw — Bay City
Grand River Road
Grand Rapids
Saginaw Road
Pontiac
Territorial Road
St. Joseph
Detroit
Ypsilanti
Chicago
Chicago Road

months. We had great difficulty in getting our teams over Hog river and marsh.

"....Three families were living on Pigeon prairie.... Part of this prairie was in a state of nature, and never looked more beautiful, coated over as it was with a covering of grass and beautiful flowers...."

From Mr. Edward's writing it is easy to see that many early towns were started in natural clearings known as prairies. Beginning a settlement in a place with few trees made it much easier for the pioneers since they would not have to spend so much time cutting down trees to get the land ready to plant crops.

Title to the Land

The Edwards family and the others they met were probably all *squatters* on public land because there was no federal land office in the western Lower Peninsula until one was moved to White Pigeon in 1831. *Squatters were people who did not buy the land where they lived.* Later that office was moved to Kalamazoo and it was through the Kalamazoo office that much of the land in western Michigan was sold.

No land in Michigan could be sold to settlers unless the land had first been given over to the federal government by the Indians through a treaty. All of the treaties did not take place at the same time. Some were for big pieces of land and some were for small pieces. Generally, the Indians did not make the treaties with complete willingness. The federal government urged or forced them

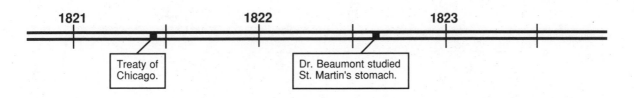

1821 · 1822 · 1823 ·

Treaty of Chicago.

Dr. Beaumont studied St. Martin's stomach.

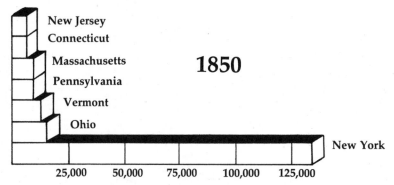

Michigan Settlers and the States They Came From

on the tribes. Sometimes the treaties were signed by Indians who had no claim to the land covered by the treaty.

Where Did They Come From?

Like the Nowlins and Edwards, many of the early settlers in Michigan were from the New England states (Connecticut, Maine, Massachusetts, New Hampshire, Rhode Island, and Vermont) or New York. Because of the Erie Canal more settlers came to Michigan from New York state than from any other.

People from these states were often known as Yankees and kept many of their Yankee ways when they moved to Michigan. Often cities in Michigan were given the same names as the places which the settlers left behind. Utica, Rochester, and Litchfield are examples.

They brought many customs too. The township system is a concept used in New England. A strong desire for education was common in New England. These settlers worked hard to begin schools in Michigan. Another idea from the New England area was a strong belief that slavery was wrong. Many of the ideas and customs these settlers brought with them helped forge and shape the way Michigan is today.

Why did they choose Michigan?

Why did the Nowlin and Edwards families choose Michigan rather than Ohio or Indiana? Before the Erie Canal opened, it was hard to travel to Michigan. It was easier for settlers to reach Ohio and Indiana as they could sail down the Ohio River. The Erie Canal offset that advantage. Probably the main reason was the best land in the two other states had already been claimed by the 1820s. Both Indiana and Ohio had much larger populations than Michigan at that time.

Still, choosing Michigan as a new home may not have been an easy choice. Several factors had kept settlers from deciding on a move to Michigan. There was bad publicity about the area which did not encourage people to move here.

Edward Tiffin produced a good example of that bad publicity when he sent surveyors to Michigan for the federal government in 1815. Their job was to see if Michigan land was fit to give to soldiers who had fought in the War of 1812. They picked a particularly poor spot to examine in the southeastern part of the Lower Peninsula. Tiffin's report said the land was quite swampy and sandy and that not one acre in a 100 or not even one in a

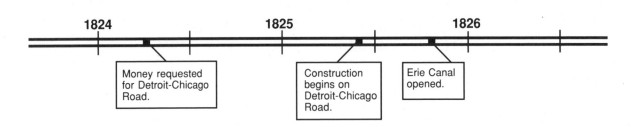

1,000 would be good for farming. Today we know most of the land was not like that at all. Abraham Edwards described some very nice land on his trip across the peninsula. But because of Tiffin's bad report, the former soldiers never had a chance to see what Michigan was really like.

A Visitor From France

Most of the people coming to Michigan at that time were Americans. There were not many foreign-born settlers at first. But Michigan did have a famous foreign visitor. A well-known French writer and historian came here in 1831. He was Alexis de Tocqueville (toak VEEL).

Tocqueville and a friend visited Detroit and then traveled north to Pontiac. With the help of an Indian guide they went on to Saginaw. There they stayed at one of the three houses in the village. The people they met spoke French, as most of Michigan outside of Detroit was still French. One of the Frenchmen had an Indian wife, as did many of the fur traders. Even in the wilderness the Indians greeted Europeans by saying hello in French. Tocqueville met a trader who sold things to the Indians. The Indians used the money they were paid by the U.S. government for their land. Tocqueville said the trader robbed the Indians because of his high prices.

Eventually Tocqueville reached Sault Ste. Marie and Mackinac Island. There he met a well-known fur trader, Magdelaine La Framboise (magd lin la fram BWAZ), who was part French and part Indian. He was impressed with her and said she was an interesting woman.

You can read more about what Alexis de Tocqueville saw and what he thought in his book *Democracy in America* published in 1835 or in *Journey to America* translated by George Lawrence, 1960.

Magdelaine la Framboise (1780-1846)

While settlers were coming to the southern part of Michigan, the rest of the territory went on much as it had for many, many years. Fur trading was still the main business activity.

Magdelaine la Framboise, a successful business woman, spoke French, English, Ottawa and Ojibwa. She owned a fine house on Mackinac Island, but she had also spent many years on the Grand River in the Lower Peninsula.

Magdelaine was born along the Grand in 1780. Her father was a French fur trader and her mother was the daughter of an Ottawa chief. When she was 14 or 15 years old, Magdelaine married another French fur trader named Joseph la Framboise. She and her husband took their canoe from the Grand River to Mackinac Island each summer to sell what they had traded from the Ottawa.

A terrible event took place in 1806. Her husband was murdered because he refused to give liquor to a man. After that tragedy, Magdelaine had to keep the business going to feed herself and her children. She even managed to send her young daughter to Montreal so she could go to school.

Her daughter did well in school and returned to Mackinac Island where she met a young American soldier, Benjamin Pierce. Magdelaine's daughter and Benjamin Pierce were married in 1816. Later, Benjamin's brother became president of the United States.

Magdelaine la Framboise was always proud of both her French and Indian backgrounds and her home still stands on Mackinac Island.

Governor Cass Works to Build Michigan

During the 18 years that Lewis Cass was governor of the Michigan Territory he did many things to help the early settlers. He urged the federal government to build better roads in Michigan.

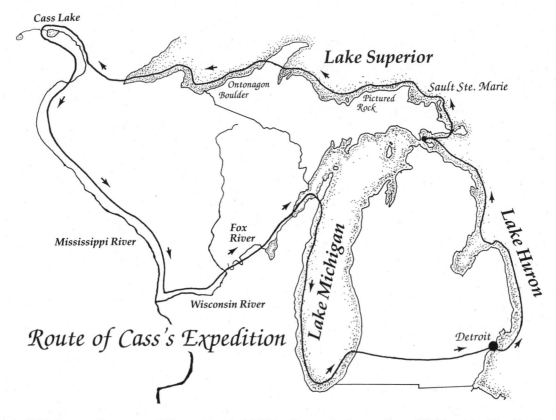

Cass Lake

Lake Superior

Ontonagon
Boulder

Pictured
Rock

Sault Ste. Marie

Mississippi River

Fox
River

Lake Michigan

Lake Huron

Wisconsin River

Route of Cass's Expedition

Detroit

In 1820 Cass and a group of 42 men traveled 4,000 miles exploring northern Michigan and the Northwest Territory.

He helped explore Michigan and the Northwest Territory and he told about all of the benefits Michigan had to offer. He also served as the Indian Superintendent. In that job he helped Michigan grow by making treaties with the Indians so the land could be surveyed and then bought by settlers.

In 1820 he headed an expedition to visit the northern part of Michigan and the Northwest Territory. His journey went almost to the beginning of the Mississippi River in Minnesota. Cass Lake is named after Governor Cass. Cass planned the trip well. He took along a map maker, a geologist to study the land, and a writer to send accounts of the trip back to the newspapers. There were 42 men in his group and altogether they travelled 4,000 miles, most of it by water.

Governor Cass planned to meet with Indians at the Soo. He had heard they were friendly with the British and he was very much against the British. At Mackinac Island about 20 soldiers joined the group for protection. When they reached the Soo, Cass went to the home of John Johnston, a fur trader. John was away, but his Indian wife Susan and his son and daughter welcomed the visitors.

Nearby was an Ojibwa village of about 200 people. A council of chiefs was held with Cass on June 16. The chiefs were not friendly. Sassaba, an Ojibwa leader, was even dressed in a British soldier's jacket. They pretended to know nothing about earlier treaties with the government. Cass wanted to build a fort at the Soo but the Indians said the government could not have any land. Finally, Cass told them point-blank that a fort would be built whether they liked it or not! Sassaba became angry, threw his war spear into the ground, and kicked away the presents Cass had brought. It looked as if there would be some real trouble and Cass was greatly outnumbered.

Sassaba went to his lodge and raised a British flag on a pole. In spite of the obvious danger, Cass strode to the lodge and tore down Sassaba's flag and threw it on the ground. He told the Indians that if they put up another flag, they would be destroyed. The Ojibwa were so amazed at the governor's behavior that they just stood there. But the Indians' anger increased.

Johnston's son, George, and his Indian mother, Susan, quickly went to the chiefs to try to cool things down. They talked to the chiefs and told them how dangerous it would be if they killed the Americans. They explained more soldiers would come to take revenge and the Ojibwa would lose in the end. Susan's speech to the Ojibwa was credited with saving Lewis Cass and his men. Later that night, the Indians signed another treaty with Cass giving up land for a fort. They kept the right to fish at the rapids and to camp on the shore.

Cass made other treaties with the tribes. Always he was acting for the United States government and not the territory or state. In 1819 he negotiated the Treaty of Saginaw. The Ojibwa gave up six million acres in the Lower Peninsula by that treaty. Three years later Cass obtained the Treaty of Chicago in which the Indians gave up most of the remaining land in the southern Lower Peninsula. It opened up a large area for the pioneer settlers. Of course, it was not good for the Native Americans living in Michigan.

The treaty process was part of a clash between two completely different cultures: the European culture which believed in private ownership of the land and used the land for farming, and the tribal culture which believed in using the land as a group and only farming enough to provide sufficient food along with hunting and fishing. Many Indians had willingly given up small amounts of land in the past but were later shocked by the American demands for such large amounts. Members of the tribes resisted the treaties but there was enough

pressure through bribes and the use of liquor to eventually get leaders to sign the papers.

The tribes did receive money for their land but it was soon spent with the traders to get supplies. The supplies were often things which the Indians had once gotten from the land themselves. Very little of the money was left to use for things which would help them in the long run. Soon Michigan would be full of settlers clamoring for farmland. One Indian leader complained that plows were driven through their wigwams before they could even leave for a new home.

Michigan was changing from a land of native tribes to a land of farmers and settlers. In 1820, Michigan had about 9,000 settlers and probably about an equal number of Native Americans. One 1837 estimate stated there were 7,700 Indians in Michigan and that the rest of the population had grown to 174,543!

Lewis Cass (1782-1866) lawyer; member of the Ohio legislature; soldier in War of 1812; Governor of the Michigan Territory 1813-31; U.S. secretary of war 1831-36; ambassador to France 1836-42; member of the U.S. Senate 1845-48 and 1849-57; 1848 Democratic nominee for president of the United States; 1858-1860 U.S. secretary of state. (Courtesty Michigan State Archives)

Lewis Cass was in charge of the affairs of Michigan for 18 years, longer than any other person. Not only was he in charge for a long period but it was an important time when Michigan was just beginning to develop. He wrote the state motto and designed the state seal.

Cass was one of the Yankees from the East. He was born in New Hampshire and went to school with Daniel Webster. When he was seven he met George Washington and shook his hand. That exciting event may have helped Cass to develop an interest in politics.

Cass' father received land in Ohio in return for his military service. In 1800 the family moved there. Soon after moving to Ohio, Lewis studied law. It was in Ohio that Lewis married his wife Elizabeth in 1806. After the War of 1812 was over, the Lewis Cass family moved to Detroit.

In 1831 President Andrew Jackson asked Cass to become secretary of war. Then Cass left Michigan to become a member of the national government for the rest of his life. He traveled overseas and was himself nominated for president in 1848. Lewis Cass did much for Michigan and his nation.

Questions

1. The Erie Canal helped many people move to Michigan. How much time could be saved by using the canal and Lake Erie to reach Detroit instead of coming from the East by road?

2. Name all of the states mentioned where early settlers came from. Which state was home to the most Michigan pioneers? What was the nickname for people from these states?

3. What is significant about the Chicago Road?

4. Why did people from the East want to move to Michigan?

5. The tribes of Michigan were pressured to give up their land through treaties with the federal government. Could settlers buy land before it was covered in a treaty? If they moved onto land and didn't buy it, what were they called? Which Indian land treaty covered the part of Michigan where you live? (Use the map on page 92.)

6. What were some of the things Lewis Cass did for Michigan?

7. Do you think the land treaties with the Michigan Indians could have been handled in some other way? Would your method provide more fairness for the Indian tribes? Explain your reasons clearly.

Chapter 6 Section 2

Forging the Landscape: Farmers Arrive!

Here are the key concepts you will find in this section:

The landscape of Michigan was changed tremendously when farmers began to cut down trees so they could plant crops.

Life on an early farm was very crude but farmers made nearly everything they needed and grew all of their own food themselves.

Early farm families only had their own muscles and that of their farm animals to help them plant and harvest crops.

Gristmills made flour from the grain and were a key part of the development of Michigan. Water power was extremely important.

Trees, Trees Everywhere!

Today much of Michigan has farms and open fields. There may be trees in the fence rows and a few to shade the farm houses. That was not what the early settlers saw when they arrived. They found a land which was as completely covered with trees as possible. These pioneers did not view a tree as a beautiful living thing which provided shade from the summer sun. They could only see the trees as enemies which kept the life-giving sun from reaching the crops they had to plant in order to feed themselves. Trees had to be cut down, burned, and removed in any way they could.

Since the time of the first settlers, the Michigan landscape has been drastically changed. Farmers forged a new view of the land by removing vast numbers of trees.

A War Against Trees

From the instant pioneer farmers set foot in Michigan, they were in a race to clear trees from their land and plant a crop which would be ready to harvest as soon as possible. Most settlers could only bring a limited amount of food with them—perhaps a few barrels of dried beans, flour or corn meal, salted pork, and maybe a cow or some pigs and chickens. Even if they had money to spend on more food, most settlements were so far away from everything that it was practically impossible to buy anything to eat.

Alexis de Tocqueville heard this comment about the pioneers from a tavern keeper in Pontiac:

"The settler takes himself to his newly acquired property.... If there happens to be a hut near, he goes to it, and receives temporary hospitality. If not, he pitches his tent in the middle of the wood which is to be his field. His first care is to cut down the nearest trees, with them he quickly builds the rude log house.... The keep of cattle costs nothing. The emigrant fastens an iron bell to their necks, and turns them into the forest. Animals thus left to themselves seldom stray far....

The greatest expense is the clearing. If the pioneer brings with him a family to help him in his first labors, the task is easy. But this is seldom the case. The emigrant is generally young, and if he has children they are small. He is therefore obliged either to supply all the

122

wants of the family himself, or to hire the services of his neighbors. It costs from four to five dollars to clear an acre.... The great difficulty is to get over the years which immediately succeed the first clearing."

Memoirs, Letters and Remains of Alexis De Tocqueville; written in 1831 published in 1862.

Clearing away an acre of trees is something which is easier said than done. And early farmers were trying to clear 40 or 80 acres of land. Often the first thing the farmer would do was *girdle* the trees. *This means they would cut off a strip of bark all the way around the tree.* When that was done to a tree, the sap would ooze out where the bark was cut away. Soon the tree would loose its leaves and die. At times corn was planted before the dead trees were cut down, just as the Indians did. Later, the dead trees were cut down and usually burned. Farmers had many more trees than could be used for lumber. Without the trees, crops would grow but the fields were still full of stumps. Stumps always got in the way of a farmer trying to plow and it was hard to remove them. They tried to burn stumps, pull stumps, and even blow them up with gunpowder!

Muscle to Do the Work

Settlers needed help to do all of the backbreaking work on the farm. Horses and oxen were used whenever possible. If they could afford them, pioneer families would bring or buy a team of oxen. (In 1830 a team of oxen cost about $45 to $55.) The early farmer liked to use oxen instead of horses because the oxen responded to voice commands. The farmers did not have to hold the reins in one hand; both hands were free to guide the plow. Oxen could survive on less grain which was often scarce. They also seemed to be more durable than horses for the hard work of plowing the rough fields in the wilderness.

Oxen were trained from the time they were young. Each was given a name and they always worked in pairs. The same oxen worked together. If one became sick or died, it was very difficult to get the other to do any work at all!

Oxen provided the muscle needed for many jobs done by early pioneers. (Courtesy Michigan State Archives)

An early settler's cabin. Most pioneers lived with only the bare essentials for housekeeping. (Courtesy Michigan State Archives)

In the 1850s horses began to replace oxen for farm work. By that time the fields were well prepared and more grain was available for horse feed.

It was common for the early farmer to bring at least one or two pigs. Pigs would eat acorns which meant the farmer did not have to get food for them, especially during the first winter. The pigs also did a helpful service—they killed rattlesnakes. Much of Michigan was swampy in those days and provided a good home for rattlesnakes.

Visit the Early Farm

What a sight it must have been to see one of those early Michigan farms. There would be a little log cabin with a wisp of smoke slowly curling up from its log and clay chimney. Two or three acres of cleared land surrounded the little log building. Corn and potato plants would be struggling to survive among the stumps and branches which were scattered all around. The clearing was also home to a few squealing pigs and the family cow. A pen for the sheep slowed down the wolves long enough for the pioneer man or woman to reach for a rifle. A stream or pond was certainly close to the cabin because a supply of fresh water was absolutely necessary.

Suppose you were curious to peek into the cabin window and see what it was like inside. That might not be an easy thing to do. Many cabins had no windows. Even if there were a window or two, few cabins had any glass for them; it was too expensive! Thin animal hides were placed over the window openings so some light could come into the room. Greased paper was also used in place of glass.

In order to see the inside of a log cabin, you would have to open the door and go inside. Don't worry about it being

124

locked. Usually the latchstring hung outside. Give it a pull and it would lift the board that held the door closed. The cabin might have a floor of split logs or it might just have dirt. More than likely the cabin had only one room.

The space between the logs was filled with mud or clay mixed with grass. Of course, that had to be replaced quite often.

The fireplace was the center of pioneer family life. It was where all the meals were cooked. It was also the only source of heat in the winter. If the pioneers were lucky enough to have Bibles or other books, fireplaces were the best sources of light for reading. Grease was made into tallow candles but they did not give off much light and were smoky.

There was not much furniture to see in pioneer log cabins, probably a split-log table, log benches, and one or two beds. Beds were made of logs and the mattress for each was held up with a webbing of rope tied across the bottom. If the family hadn't collected enough feathers from their geese or chickens, the mattress was probably filled with straw.

One item a family usually tried to bring with them from civilization was their spinning wheel. It was used to spin yarn from their own sheep's wool. That yarn would make shirts, socks, dresses, and pants for the mother, father, and all the children. Cotton was not seen too often in pioneer clothes. In fact, when the sheep herds grew large, wool was shipped east and sold for extra income.

The time of Michigan pioneers was an age of wood. Wood was used to build everything. Few cabins had any nails; the logs and beams were held together with wooden pegs. Even pitchforks were made of wood. The dishes the family ate on were made of wood too. Wood was a material which most people could make into what they needed without expensive tools.

What Did They Grow?

Pioneer farmers did not specialize in any way. They grew whatever they could and whatever they needed. Most of what they raised was used by their own families.

After the Erie Canal opened, there was a market in New York for food grown in Michigan. Wheat was one crop which could be stored and shipped on the canal. It kept well and did not spoil. It was one of Michigan's first cash crops. By selling wheat, a farmer could earn extra money to buy things at a general store.

In 1837 Michigan farmers grew about one million bushels of wheat. Michigan wheat production doubled by 1840 and was up to five million bushels in 1850. Michigan was a major supplier of the nation's wheat until after the Civil War. Then the prairies of the western states began to produce more wheat than Michigan.

The sickle was a sharp, curved knife used to harvest grain. It was later replaced by a horse-drawn threshing machine. (Art by David B. McConnell)

Harvesting the Crops

While animals could help the farmer plow the fields, harvesting was a hand operation. Most farmers cut their grain with a sickle which was a sharp, curved knife. The farmer held the stalks of grain in one hand and cut them off with the sickle held in the other. Only about one acre of grain a day could be harvested that way. Since all of the grain was ready to harvest at the same time, the amount a single person could manage to cut was very limited. In the East inventors were

Gristmills were important for early settlers. Here the grain was ground between two heavy stones and made into flour. The picture shows the Loranger mill at Greenfield Village. (Courtesy Henry Ford Museum and Greenfield Village #B-1463)

working with machines which could help farmers harvest their grain much faster; however, those machines were a rare sight in Michigan.

Gristmills Were Important

After the corn, wheat, oats, and rye were harvested, they had to be ground into flour in order to be of much use to the pioneer. Once again water played an important part in the process. The gristmills which ground the grain were all powered by water at that time. Nearly every important town was settled next to a river which could give waterpower to run the mills. Sometimes the mill was the first building put up in a new town.

Millponds were built to hold water which would go to the mill. Water from the pond flowed to a large waterwheel. It poured over the wheel and pushed it around. Inside the mill, big wooden gears transmitted the motion to a mill stone which is what actually ground the grain and turned it into a powder, the flour.

Waterpower was important not only to run the gristmills but the early factories. In addition, the rivers gave the settlers a way to travel from town to town. Boats and rafts often carried people and equipment from place to place.

Food Storage

How did the pioneer farmer manage to keep his other crops to use during the fall and winter? Refrigerators were unknown. In order to keep vegetables from rotting they were put into a "root cellar." It could be a sort of basement under the cabin or a cave dug into the side of a hill. The ground was cool enough to keep food from spoiling and yet warm enough to keep it from freezing in the winter.

Farming was Tough

Early farming was a tough life for man, woman, and child. The sons and daughters in farm families had to help do the work as soon as they were old enough. One reason parents often had a dozen or more children was that they could help keep the farm going. Children were often thought of as an asset to the pioneer farmer. As Michigan's cities grew and other jobs became available, many children who grew up on a farm could not wait to leave and find something else to do in town.

Questions

1. Why did farmers want to cut down so many trees? How did the farmers use the wood from the tress?

2. What animal did early farmers prefer to use for plowing and other work? What advantages did these animals have?

3. What was the first cash crop for Michigan farmers? What provided early settlers with material for their clothing?

4. Explain how water power helped prepare grain so it could be used as food during early pioneer times.

5. A newly married pioneer couple coming to Michigan to start a farm would have to spend money for several things. Make a list of all the things on which they might need to spend money before they could raise their first crop.

Chapter 6 Section 3

Those Frontier Days!

Here are the key concepts you will find in this section:

Michigan pioneers had to cope with malaria, cholera, and other dangerous diseases.

Wild animals, from mice to hungry bears to wolves, caused problems for Michigan pioneers.

Early settlers had to depend on their neighbors for many kinds of help.

News and letters took a long time to reach Michigan, but pioneers had many things to talk about, including building canals, new schools, and Indian uprisings.

Return to Pioneer Days?

Today people often think about pioneer days with the fond desire to go back in time and live in a log cabin, hunt in the woods, and fish beautiful, clear lakes. This may sound interesting to you too; however, be warned that life of the first settlers was not necessarily full of enjoyment.

Most pioneers indicate it was a time of hardship and trial. They had to face many problems and usually they faced them alone. Pioneers did not have modern science to help them find a solution. They had to deal with disease, insects, wild animals, floods, and droughts.

Got the Shakes Yet?

Just imagine this scene. An early settler suddenly begins to shake and tremble. Then he or she has a raging

Cabins were built with natural materials. The fireplace was made of logs and packed with clay. Window glass was expensive and scarce, so settlers used animal skins instead. (Art by David B. McConnell)

128

Native Americans seemed to be immune to ague.

Today we know it was malaria and was caused by a parasite transferred to people by the bites of mosquitoes. People might suffer from attacks everyday for months or the attacks could come every second or third day. Often the attacks were very regular, and work schedules were set up around the time when the next attack was expected. Not many people died from that kind of malaria, but it could easily put a stop to getting any work done. Sometimes farmers were so sick they couldn't feed their farm animals or plant their crops. A popular rhyme was: "Don't go to Michigan, that land of ills; The word means ague, fever, and chills."

Mosquitoes were a plague to all settlers. People often burned wood fires in and around their cabins to keep the pests away with the smoke. The insects flew in thick clouds, attacking any person or animal in range. One person said: "...They were the most troublesome of all

Early diseases caused a great deal of trouble for settlers. A person with ague would shake uncontrollably. (Art by Theresa Deeter)

fever, headache, and back pains followed with a severe chill. The crisis ends with a drenching sweat. One pioneer recalled this sort of incident: "You felt as though you had gone through some sort of collision with a threshing machine or jarring machine and came out not killed, but the next thing to it. You felt weak, as though you had run too far after something and then didn't catch it."

Is this the description of a rare disease or some sort of food poisoning? No, that was what it was like to have the ague (AY g' you). New settlers were often asked if they had yet had the ague. "Well, you will have it; everybody has it before they've been here long," was the reply given to anyone who said no to the question. Pioneers thought the disease was caused by gasses coming from the swamps. Strangely, though, Michigan's

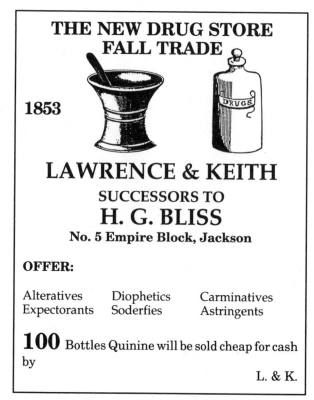

the animals that infested the woods...they would come down on you in squads and hordes, ad infinitum."

The number of mosquitoes which carried the disease probably increased when farmers cut down trees and started to clear the land. Young mosquitoes grew in wet fields and the nearby swamps. Remember, much of the Lower Peninsula was swampy at that time.

There was no cure for the malaria which distressed Michigan pioneers. They could take quinine (KWI nine) pills if they could afford them or they could make a very bitter tea from the bark of the cinchona (sin KONA) tree which contained quinine. The quinine helped keep the parasite under control in the victim.

After the swampy land was cleared and drained, the wet area used by mosquitoes for their homes was reduced. As farmers raised more cattle, the mosquitoes tended to go after the cattle instead of people. When the parasite gets into the blood of cattle, it dies and does not affect them in the same way. The invention of window screens helped to keep the mosquitoes away from people too.

A Quick Killer

The ague was a terrible nuisance, but cholera (KOL er a) was a deadly killer which took its victims rapidly. One man was playing cards and seemed to be in perfect health when he gasped, "I've got it!" His friends tried to reassure him that it was probably just an upset stomach, but he was dead before the next morning! People with cholera die from the loss of body fluids. Victims have uncontrollable vomiting and diarrhea.

The disease reached Michigan in 1832 aboard the steamship *Henry Clay*. The ship was filled with soldiers on their way to fight an Indian uprising in Wisconsin. On the fourth of July, the ship docked at Detroit and the soldiers went ashore to join in the celebration. But by the next morning, 11 soldiers had died. Then a second troop ship landed at Port Huron and the disease spread from there. Naturally, the soldiers were terrified and jumped ship to get away from the sick and to try to save themselves. In the process of running away, they spread the disease.

The newspaper at Port Huron stated:

The dead bodies of the deserters are literally strewn along the road between here and Detroit. No one dares give them (the sick soldiers) relief, not even a cup of water. A person on his way here from Detroit passed six, lying groaning with the agonies of the cholera under one tree, and saw one corpse by the roadside....

People were so scared by cholera they set up roadblocks to stop travelers from coming into their towns. At Ypsilanti the governor was even stopped and told he would be shot if he tried to go past the roadblock! In spite of all precautions, 18 people in Marshall got the disease and 11 of those died. In Detroit, Lewis Cass' daughter died, along with many others. The upper floor of the territorial capitol building was made into a hospital to treat cholera victims. Father Gabriel Richard worked so hard to help the sick that he died from exhaustion.

In 1834 cholera struck Detroit once again. During the month of August about seven percent of the population died from the disease. Many farmers were safe from cholera because they did not go into the towns very often.

At that time no one had any idea diseases such as cholera, scarlet fever, smallpox, and diphtheria were caused by germs. People did not realize that washing their hands with soap and water would slow down the spread of the disease. They did not realize that it was a bad idea for everyone to use the same drinking cup at the water pump. No one knew that flies and mosquitoes could carry diseases. If a pioneer settler could find a doctor, the cure the doctor used might easily have been worse than the disease. More often the pioneer family made their own medicines from berries, herbs, tree bark, and roots. Recipes for

130

the medicines might have been old family secrets or they could have been given to the pioneers by the Indians.

Everything Eats My Crops But Me!

The lucky pioneers survived the deadly diseases but they still had to fight to keep going. All kinds of animals made life difficult for farmers. Rabbits and deer ate the crops just as they came up in the spring. If the crops were hearty enough to overcome insects and dry weather, then blackbirds were ready to eat them before they could be harvested.

Joseph Busby from the Saginaw area tells how much trouble blackbirds were:

They would flock by the million, and it would take all our time and attention, until the corn got hard, to keep them off. Day after day, from daylight in the morning until the middle of the day, and again from two hours before sundown until dark, I have had to run up and down the field ... firing and hallooing at them to keep them from alighting.... We would build stages some distance apart, and take an empty barrel, and beat it with a stick or anything to make a noise. Only by such means could we get a crop.

Recollections of Pioneer Life in Michigan, *Michigan Pioneer Collections*, 1886, p. 126.

The people living along the Cass River were overwhelmed by a hoard of deer mice in 1853. The mice ate all the corn the settlers had managed to raise. They poured into their cabins at night looking for anything to eat. The pioneers had to protect all of their food by piling it on a table in the cabin and resting each leg of the table in a large pan of water to keep the mice from climbing up the table legs.

(Art by Charles Schafer, Michigan Department of Natural Resources)

Mr. O.H. Perry wrote, "I am so overrun with deer mice that I can hardly live in the woods. They eat the strings of my tent, my shoes, pork, hard bread, gloves, leather strings, bags, etc. and commenced last night working in my hair, and planting their cold noses on the scalp of my head!"

Bears and Wolves!

While many animals were a bother, some were downright dangerous. One winter night Mr. D. McClennand heard a great commotion from his hog pen. He raced outside in his nightshirt and saw a bear carrying off a 200-pound hog which the bear had taken from the pen!

Wolves were another big problem. They would kill farm animals and keep pioneers awake with their howling during the night. Many pioneer communities paid a bounty for each dead wolf brought to them.

(Art by Charles Schafer, Michigan Department of Natural Resources)

Wolves are much like dogs but usually larger. Young William Nowlin said he shot a wolf which was six feet from the end of its tail to the tip of its nose. Few dogs grow to that size! Wolves were all the more fearsome because they always traveled in groups or packs. Today, the only wolves known to be in Michigan are on Isle Royale, but during the early 1800s wolves were often seen in southern Michigan.

Helping Each Other

Trying to cope with so many problems caused pioneers to be drawn closer together. Good neighbors were an asset. If a pioneer family accidently let their fire go out, they had to depend on borrowing some live coals from a neighbor. Pioneers were independent in many ways. They made do with what they could make themselves. But they also needed each other. There were many things which required more than one set of hands. Building a barn is one example.

Pioneers would often come together from miles around to join each other and do a job. When they all worked to build a barn it was called a barn raising. There were also cabin raisings. Pioneers came together to husk corn, cut down trees, make quilts, and do many other projects. They called some of these activities "bees." Quilting bees allowed pioneer women to work together and talk about local news. Since many farm families lived far apart, a chance to see neighbors and socialize was an exciting event, even though everyone was working too.

After the work was finished, great quantities of food were brought out and all the people had a big meal. Many times families did not have much food to share, but there was no holding back for one of their big social events. It helped make a barn raising or a husking bee all the more exciting.

What Is For Supper?

Pioneer food was usually simple. A meal might be corn bread, called Johnny-cake, with plenty of fresh butter and sage tea. Or it might be a big platter of boiled potatoes, some venison or wild turkey, and a steaming bowl of flour gravy. It was said there was nothing left after a pioneer meal but the dishes. Hard work gave the early settlers great appetites.

Regular tea was scarce and many people had not yet developed the habit of drinking coffee. Sometimes a coffee-like drink was made from ground bread crusts.

Salt and sugar were rare items. At one time salt cost $21 a barrel in Michigan. Salt was kept in a "salt cellar" on the table. The salt cellar was replaced by the modern salt shaker. Guests were seated near the salt. It was sort of an honored seat at the table. Maple sugar replaced white sugar for making food sweet. Most pioneers made maple syrup and maple sugar each spring, just as the Indians had done for centuries.

A table set for a pioneer meal. (Art by Theresa Deeter)

132

Without refrigeration pioneers had to use special means to keep food from spoiling. Potatoes and vegetables came from the root cellar unless they were in season. Fruits like apples, peaches, and pears were often dried under the sun to preserve them. Beans, peas, and corn were dried so they could be used later. Meat and fish were preserved by drying and smoking. Smoked ham was a favorite. Fish and pork were also salted. That method of preservation used a solution of salt water to soak the meat for a long time. The meat had so much salt in it that germs could not grow and spoil the food. Of course it also tasted quite salty. Salted pork was used to flavor baked beans.

Nothing was wasted. Even grease and lard were saved and used in making tallow candles or mixed with lye from the fire ashes to make soap.

News and Gossip

When pioneer families did have the chance to see their neighbors at a "bee" or "raising," there were always many things to talk about. They might discuss the Sunday sermon given by the circuit riding preacher who had stopped last month. Or they may have given careful consideration to the upcoming election. Politics in pioneer days were often sources of heated debates. Andrew Jackson and William Harrison were two presidents considered to be heroes by many of the frontier people. Pioneers could identify with those men. They felt they were like them in many ways and that they understood the problems of the pioneer.

Also, many pioneers were concerned about the issue of slavery. There were a number of people in Michigan who were very much opposed to slavery but, on the other hand, the 1830 census listed 32 slaves living in the territory. A few small newspapers which had been started in Michigan spoke out against slavery and supported helping slaves to escape from their masters.

Perhaps there would be talk about what was happening in New England or New York. Newspapers were few and it was a novelty to receive a letter. The price of sending a letter to the East was 25 cents; however, a day's wages might be only 40 or 50 cents! Besides, it took several weeks for a letter to reach anyone.

Many New Projects

Pioneers could have also talked about the new Clinton-Kalamazoo Canal. The purpose of the canal was to make a shortcut through the Lower Peninsula by linking the Clinton and Kalamazoo Rivers. At that time it seemed no project could fail. In the 1830s people were excited about what were known as "internal improvements." The phrase meant the building of canals, railroads, and bridges. Canal building was very popular after people saw the success of the Erie Canal. Some pioneers were uncertain about the potential of the projects but most were sure they could only help Michigan to grow. The government of the Michigan territory backed the Pontiac and Detroit Railroad in 1830. Unfortunately these two examples, like many others, were never finished. They proved to be impractical and very expensive.

133

Schools in the Wilderness

Many people were awed by the building of an elementary school in Ypsilanti in 1834. The township board taxed residents to pay for the school and its teacher. Since most families had very little money, people were allowed to supply materials to build the school instead of paying taxes. Parents also had to give the school half a cord of firewood for each child they sent. Ypsilanti paid their first teacher $90 to teach for eight months! Women found jobs as early teachers. Often, it was the only paying work they could get.

In 1842 the elementary school in Detroit was made free for all students. In 1848 that city established its first high school.

Of course, some people had heard about the University of Michigania, which later became the University of Michigan. It was started in 1817, but was off to a slow start when no students showed up for classes. Its first actual classes began in 1841. There were six students and two professors. The university was supported by state government, but most of the first colleges were started by church groups.

Scary Rumors in the Woods

The year 1832 brought startling news to Michigan settlers. An Indian chief named Black Hawk led an uprising of the Sauk and Fox tribes in Western Wisconsin. Those tribes were far from Michigan but people were concerned that the Potawatomi might join Black Hawk and attack settlers in southern Michigan. Others were worried Black Hawk and his followers would come along the Chicago Road and seek British protection at Fort Malden. Black Hawk had worked with the British in the War of 1812. He had taken scalps at the River Raisin massacre and had also been at the Battle of the Thames. Many wild rumors were heard in the towns and villages of Southern Michigan.

A call was made for men to volunteer to go west and fight the Indians. Three hundred Michigan militia left Detroit in May of 1832, but only traveled as far as Jonesville. Black Hawk had already been defeated by U. S. soldiers closer to the scene.

The worst danger from the uprising was not from Black Hawk but from the soldiers sent to fight him. They were the same soldiers who brought the dreaded cholera to Michigan. The chief was captured and taken to Washington, D.C. Later, Lieutenant Jefferson Davis returned the chief to Wisconsin by way of Detroit.

The great scare that Black Hawk gave the people of Michigan caused many to think that all Indians should be sent west. Then there would be no worries about possible attacks. Settlers were so agitated they forgot they had been living for many years without any problems with the Michigan Indians.

The southern part of the Lower Peninsula had the most settlers. That fact made the Potawatomi tribe the focus

Henry R. Schoolcraft. (Courtesy Michigan State Archives)

of the plans to move the Indians. In 1838 U.S. soldiers forced about 300 members of the tribe to move to Kansas. Some of the Potawatomi escaped and started a town in Cass County. Others moved to an island on the east side of Lake St. Clair in Canadian territory. Some pioneers were on the Indians' side and helped them stay in Michigan. It was another sad time for the first Michiganians.

Let's Remember Indian History

At that time a handful of farsighted people could see that it would not be long before the Indians and their rich history would be forgotten in Michigan. One of the people was Henry R. Schoolcraft. He was hard at work to save the heritage and history of the Indians.

Schoolcraft was the map maker on the Lewis Cass expedition. During their trip he became very interested in the life of the Indians. In 1822 he was appointed Indian agent for the tribes of the Lake Superior region. He moved to Sault Ste. Marie and there he married Jane Johnston. Jane was the daughter of Susan Johnston, the Ojibwa who helped keep peace between Lewis Cass and the Indians at the Soo.

With his wife's help, Schoolcraft studied every aspect of Ojibwa life. Over the years he wrote several books about the Indians of the Great Lakes region. Some of Schoolcraft's material was used by the poet Henry Wadsworth Longfellow to write his poem "Hiawatha." From 1836 to 1841 Schoolcraft was superintendent of Indian affairs for the state of Michigan.

Dr. Beaumont performs one of many experiments with the help of Alexis St. Martin and his stomach. (Courtesy Mackinac State Historic Parks)

Schoolcraft knew his project of collecting all of the information about the Indians was beyond his own resources. In 1847 he moved to Washington, D.C., and asked the federal government to help him pay for the research. He spent 10 years there organizing his material and writing down all he learned. His books were the first serious attempt to study the life of the American Indian.

Henry Schoolcraft left behind something else for everyone in Michigan—the names of several Michigan counties. Because of his influence, Michigan has 32 counties with names related to Indian words. Think of Schoolcraft when you hear the county names of Allegan, Alpena, or Oscoda.

Dr. Beaumont and Events in the U.P.

Almost every settler coming to Michigan during the 1820s and 1830s was making a new home in the southern part of the Lower Peninsula. The Upper Peninsula was a wild and rugged land too far away for most early pioneers to consider. It was a land visited by fur traders and the soldiers stationed at Mackinac Island and the Soo. Dr. William Beaumont was one of those soldiers. He was the doctor for Fort Mackinac.

Born in New England, as were many Michigan pioneers, Dr. Beaumont arrived at Mackinac Island between 1819 and 1820. He did not know it yet, but there he would make medical history!

The American Fur Company store on the island was a busy place. There the French traders and Indians came to exchange their furs. On a spring morning in 1822, a trader named Alexis St. Martin was visiting the store when someone's shotgun accidently went off close to his body. Dr. Beaumont was called for help.

The doctor found St. Martin in serious condition. His shirt had been set on fire from the gun blast and part of his side was blown away. Some of his skin had been burned "to a crisp." Dr. Beaumont believed "any attempt to save his life entirely useless." But the doctor did what he could for the French fur trader.

The doctor was astonished that St. Martin was still alive two days after the accident. It was a very busy time for Dr. Beaumont because his wife had just given birth to their first child.

Alexis St. Martin improved very slowly. He stayed in the army hospital for several months even though he was not a soldier. For a while the local government paid the medical bills, but they decided they couldn't afford it any longer and felt St. Martin should be shipped to Montreal. Dr. Beaumont explained that such a long trip would probably kill his patient. The only thing Dr. Beaumont could figure to do was to take St. Martin to his own home.

There was one unique thing about the wound in Alexis St. Martin's side; it never healed. A flap of skin formed but it left an opening into his stomach! Suddenly Dr. Beaumont realized he could investigate what actually happened to food by looking into St. Martin's stomach while the man lay on his side. By 1825 Dr. Beaumont was doing experiments with St. Martin's cooperation.

William Beaumont continued his experiments when he was transferred to Fort Niagara in 1825 and in Wisconsin in 1829. Of course St. Martin had to be talked into going along with the doctor each time! Dr. Beaumont wrote many medical papers about what happened in St. Martin's stomach.

Alexis St. Martin's health became much better over time. He periodically left Dr. Beaumont and worked with the Hudson Bay Fur Company. He also married and eventually had 17 children!

Questions

1. How did pioneers know if they were having an attack of the ague? What is the modern name for this disease?

2. Why was the territorial capitol building used as a hospital in 1832?

3. Give four examples how wild animals caused problems for the pioneer farmers.

4. Why did early settlers look forward to barn raisings, cabin raisings, corn husking bees, or quilting bees? How did these activities help a farm family do things they could not easily do on their own?

5. What did pioneer families do so their children could go to school?

6. Michigan Indians had lost their land through treaties with the U.S. government, but many of them still lived here in the 1830s. In what way did the settlers react to the Indians of southern Michigan after the Black Hawk uprising?

7. Why did Henry Schoolcraft collect information and legends about the Indians in Michigan?

8. What was the name of the doctor who did experiments on how the human stomach works? What accident made his work possible?

7 TOWARD STATEHOOD GROWING LIKE A WEED

Chapter 7 Section 1

Becoming a State: No Simple Matter

| Here are the key concepts you will find in this section: |

The Northwest Ordinance listed three steps for becoming a state.

Stevens T. Mason became acting governor of the Michigan Territory when he was only 19. He led Michigan to statehood.

Michigan and Ohio almost went to war over the location of the border between them.

The western three-quarters of the Upper Peninsula was added to Michigan to make up for the border land lost to Ohio.

Michigan became the 26th state in the United States on January 26, 1837. It was not easy for Michigan to get its own star on the United States flag. The path to statehood had some unusual twists.

Review Early Government

Step back and review Michigan's status and how its government worked before becoming a state. At first Michigan was just an unnamed part of the Northwest Territory. During most of that time, the territorial capital was at Marietta, Ohio. Arthur St. Clair acted as governor. The territorial capital was briefly moved to Chillicothe (chil eh KOTH ee), Ohio, between 1800 and 1802. For a while, Michigan was attached to the Indiana Territory.

Congress formed Michigan into a separate territory in 1805. People here had been urging that for some time because they felt they were too far away from the center of government. The Northwest Ordinance of 1787 gave an outline of three steps in growing from a territory into a state.

Steps to Become a State

Step 1.
In the beginning a territory has no elected officials. It is governed by an appointed governor and three judges. The governor can appoint lesser officials.

Step 2.
Once there are 5,000 free adult men, an elected legislature or general assembly is formed but the governor must approve of all laws. The governor, secretary, and judges are still appointed.

Step 3.
Once there are 60,000 people in the territory, it can become a state, entering the Union equal to all the other states.

Under step one, the government worked in ways which were very different from those used now. The entire government consisted of the governor and three judges. The governor and the judges got together and wrote the laws. No one in Michigan elected those officials. They were chosen by the president of the United States. The first governor of the Michigan Territory was William Hull, the general who surrendered Detroit in the War of 1812. Lewis Cass was also governor of the territory for many years.

Step two allowed the first election. The free men of Michigan could vote for their own representatives. The representatives then chose a legislative council. In 1819 the representatives and council appointed William Woodbridge to go to the United States Congress in Washington, D.C. Since Michigan was not yet a state, Woodbridge was not allowed to vote; he could only speak his mind.

Once 60,000 people lived in a territory, it would be admitted to the United States and could form its own state government and write its own state constitution. Ohio, Indiana, and Illinois all became states before Michigan. When those states had the minimum number of people, they asked Congress to pass a law saying they could write their constitutions. The Northwest Ordinance did not really require a vote by Congress, but it became the custom.

A Surprising Change in Leadership

While Cass was governor of the territory, President Jackson appointed John T. Mason as secretary of it. Mason brought his 18-year-old son, Stevens T. Mason, to the office with him. Stevens helped his father with the work of secretary. The secretary of the territory helped the governor in many ways and sometimes took over when the governor was away from Detroit.

The older Mr. Mason thought his job was boring. He dreamed up a plan which would allow him to leave Michigan and have his son do his job. Stevens would get the salary and be able to support his mother and the rest of the family. John Mason had inherited a land grant in Texas. He wanted to go to Texas and claim his land. He also wanted to be an undercover agent for President Jackson. Texas was then part of Mexico and the President wanted it to become a part of the United States.

A Visit to the President

Before heading for Texas, Lewis Cass and the Masons went to meet President Jackson in Washington, D.C. Mr. Mason asked the President if his son could take over. Jackson really liked the young Stevens T. Mason and agreed to the unusual request. That was how Stevens T. Mason became secretary for the Michigan Territory when he was only 19. He was not old enough to vote or to even sign business contracts!

The President confided to Stevens that he wanted *him* to take control of the government in Michigan because Lewis Cass was promised the post of Secretary of War. Cass would be leaving Michigan and the President said he would not appoint another governor.

The Boy is in Charge?

After that, the pace of life quickened for Stevens in a hurry! When he came back to Detroit, there was a storm of protest over his being given the job of secretary. Members of the other political party, the Whigs, were very upset when they found that the Democratic president had appointed such a youngster to the job. A huge crowd of 2,000 gathered in Detroit to speak out against the idea of putting a "child" in charge of the territory. People wanted Stevens to be fired. But Stevens T. Mason was wise for his age. He wrote President Jackson saying the protesters were all Whigs and they were attacking the authority of the President to select the person he really wanted. Stevens also said he would always be ready to listen to the advice of older men. His strategy worked and he kept the job. But still some people mocked Stevens and called him the "Boy Governor."

Stevens T. Mason, Michigan's first governor. (Courtesy Michigan State Archives)

This article was printed in the Detroit *Journal* newspaper: "Be it remembered, ye citizens of Michigan, that General Jackson has appointed to be secretary of your Territory STEVENS THOMPSON MASON, late of Kentucky, a young gentleman who, whatever may be his amiable characteristics, will, *if he lives* to the month of October next, be twenty years of age and no more...."

Later, President Jackson reconsidered the Michigan situation and decided it would be better if he did appoint a new governor. George Porter was to be that person. Porter was a rich man from Pennsylvania. He came to Michigan to take over as governor but only stayed for short periods of time. He seemed to be bored by his duties. Stevens had many opportunities to be in charge while Porter was out of town.

Unfortunately for Porter, he *was in town* when cholera struck Detroit in 1834 and he died. But no new governor was sent from Washington.

Ready to be a State

Meanwhile, the population of Michigan was growing. Michigan had over 85,000 people in 1834, up from 31,000 in 1830. Mason requested that Congress vote to see if Michigan could write a state constitution, but Congress voted no!

Why did that happen? Didn't Congress want other states added to the Union? The trouble was Michigan's argument with the state of Ohio over the border between the two neighbors. They both claimed a small wedge of land five miles wide at the Indiana border and eight miles wide at Lake Erie.

Neighbors Fight Over Land

The small wedge was not just any piece of land. It contained the mouth of the Maumee River which flowed into Lake Erie. During the era of great canal projects there were plans to connect the Maumee River to the Ohio River and from there to the Mississippi River. People in Ohio had invested in land around the river and in the canal projects. Meanwhile, people from Michigan began to build two railroads which would end at the Maumee. Many believed the area of land would become a great center for the shipping business. They thought a great port city would grow up there. At that time both Ohio and Michigan felt their whole future depended on owning the land.

Why wasn't it clear who controlled the land between Ohio and Michigan? The Northwest Ordinance stated the northern border for Ohio was to be a line touching the south end of Lake Michigan and going east from there to Lake Erie. A border made along that line would put the mouth of the Maumee River in Michigan.

140

That was fine but when Ohio wrote its state constitution in 1803, they realized the mouth of the Maumee River would be important. They said it was to be included in Ohio even if a survey of the Northwest Ordinance line showed the river was too far north. Later, when Michigan became a territory, it used the Northwest Ordinance line as the southern border. The two descriptions overlap and Congress accepted both of them!

To make matters worse, neither side was going to give in. They were becoming serious about the issue. Each state called for its militia to march into the land, now often called the Toledo Strip. Ohio and Michigan planned to go to war with each other! Today that sounds quite funny, but both sides meant business about what they were doing. William Nowlin, the Michigan pioneer, said: "When we heard that Governor Mason had arrived at

Toledo, we wondered if we should hear the roar of his cannon. Sometimes I listened. We thought if it was still and the wind favorable, we might hear them, and we expected every day there would be a battle."

Constitution Written

On June 24, 1835, delegates representing the people of Michigan got together and wrote a state constitution. Acting Governor Stevens T. Mason felt Michigan was entitled to become a state even if Congress had said no! From that time on, Michigan acted as if it were a state and passed its own laws.

The 'Toledo War' Heats Up !

Events at the Ohio border became a comedy. Both Michigan and Ohio sent officials into the Toledo Strip to control it. Michigan passed a law called the Pains

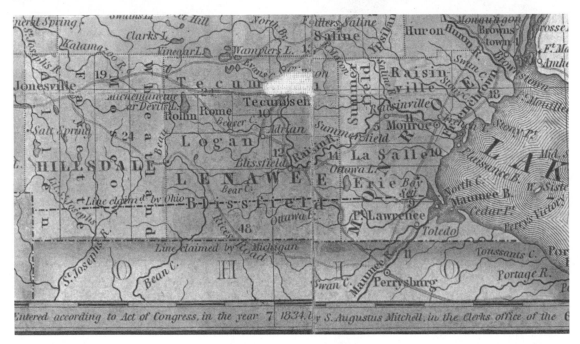

This 1834 map shows the famous strip of land claimed by both Ohio and Michigan. (Courtesy Clarke Historical Library, Central Michigan University.)

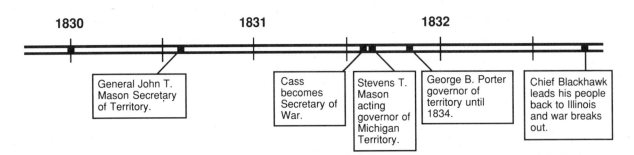

1830

1831

1832

General John T. Mason Secretary of Territory.

Cass becomes Secretary of War.

Stevens T. Mason acting governor of Michigan Territory.

George B. Porter governor of territory until 1834.

Chief Blackhawk leads his people back to Illinois and war breaks out.

Michigan patriots chased surveyors from Ohio along the disputed border during the Toledo War.

and Penalties Act, which made it illegal for anyone from Ohio to carry out any government duty in "Michigan." An Ohio judge and his guard came to the Toledo area to hold court. Michigan soldiers were sent to capture them. But the Ohioans were too smart. They held court at three o'clock in the morning and were celebrating their success by daylight.

Michigan was more victorious in another border skirmish. Several Ohio surveyors were spotted south of Adrian. A posse of Adrian citizens gave chase during the night. The next morning they found nine surveyors hiding in a log cabin. Eventually the men from Ohio gave up

and came out. But suddenly they bolted and made a mad dash to escape. The Michigan posse fired their guns over the surveyors' heads. Soon all were recaptured without injury.

Luckily, no one died during those "Toledo War" days of 1835. The most serious event took place when the deputy sheriff of Monroe County was stabbed in the side with a knife, but he recovered from his wound.

Mason Must Go!

During the "Toledo War" President Jackson decided to remove Stevens T. Mason from office. Since Michigan had

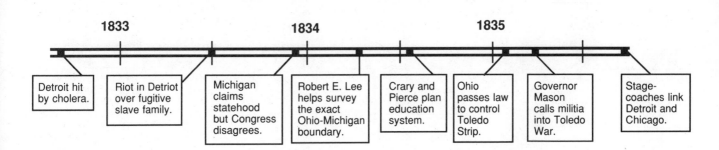

1833   1834   1835

| Detroit hit by cholera. | Riot in Detroit over fugitive slave family. | Michigan claims statehood but Congress disagrees. | Robert E. Lee helps survey the exact Ohio-Michigan boundary. | Crary and Pierce plan education system. | Ohio passes law to control Toledo Strip. | Governor Mason calls militia into Toledo War. | Stage-coaches link Detroit and Chicago. |

142

not officially become a state, he could do that. The President hoped it would help calm the situation, but it didn't.

The people in Michigan ignored the new governor sent by President Jackson. They continued to act as though they were a state. An election for the governor of Michigan was held in October and Mason won. In Michigan he was considered the governor of the *state* of Michigan, but in Washington he was considered the ex-acting governor of the Territory of Michigan!

The shaded counties on this map are named after members of President Jackson's administration. They are known as the "Cabinet Counties."

Michigan Shunned

Michigan also elected and sent two senators and a representative to Washington. People from Michigan hoped Congress would agree that Michigan did have the rights of a state and would allow Michigan's newly elected officials into Congress. Unfortunately, Congress would do no such thing.

In the matter of the border dispute, the law was on the side of Michigan, but Ohio was stronger politically. Indiana sided with Ohio because it didn't want its northern border to be changed. President Jackson knew he would need the votes of the people in those states during the next election. Since Michigan was not officially a state, its people could not vote anyway. Indiana even suggested that Ohio move its border further north so it would be even with Indiana's border!

Michigan tried to gain influence with the politicians in Washington by naming nine counties in southern Michigan after President Jackson and members of his cabinet, but it did not help. For a long time, many people in Washington seemed to have a low opinion of Michigan. When William Woodbridge arrived in Washington in 1819, he wrote that instead of accomplishing great things, it was all he could do to get people to be decent to him once they knew he came from Michigan.

A Compromise From Congress

Congress finally decided on a plan for solving the border problem. They felt the best idea would be to have Michigan trade the Toledo Strip for the western three-quarters of the Upper Peninsula. The people of Michigan were outraged. Everyone thought any land north of Saginaw Bay was a cold wasteland. The Upper Peninsula was a region of perpetual snows! The bill from Congress was called the dismemberment bill

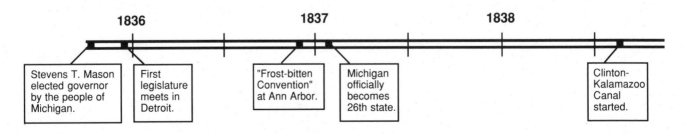

1836

1837

1838

Stevens T. Mason elected governor by the people of Michigan.

First legislature meets in Detroit.

"Frost-bitten Convention" at Ann Arbor.

Michigan officially becomes 26th state.

Clinton-Kalamazoo Canal started.

because people felt Congress was ripping Michigan apart.

Congress required that Michigan approve the Toledo Strip trade. Congress did not want to give the appearance of dealing with the unauthorized Michigan legislature, so they demanded a new group of people meet. The convention was finally held in September. The Whig political party influenced the members of the convention and they turned down the plan to trade the Toledo Strip for the western Upper Peninsula!

But slowly, Michigan's people realized they would have to go along with the compromise. There was a large sum of money involved too. The national government had a surplus of money building up from land sales. It had been decided to divide the money among all the states in January 1837. If Michigan could be an official state by then, it would share the money.

Delegates from all of the counties except Monroe and Macomb trudged into Ann Arbor on a very cold day in December 1836. They came there to decide to accept the trade set up by Congress. After two days of haggling, the delegates voted to go along with the trade and change the southern border of Michigan. Their last-minute winter meeting was known as the "Frost-bitten Convention." About four weeks later, Congress voted to let Michigan join the rest of the states. As a result of the border dispute, Michigan lost 450 square miles to Ohio and the eventual port city of Toledo but gained 9,000 square miles of the Upper Peninsula. The people of Michigan later found it was a peninsula which has some of the nation's most beautiful scenery and which is also rich in copper, iron, and timber.

Success !

At last Michigan had all the rights and responsibilities of a state. The people could vote for their local and national government officials and there wouldn't be any more meddling by the president in state matters. The people of Michigan would have a say in national affairs for the first time. Michigan had also written its first state constitution which explained how its government would work.

The Educational Oak

In the city of Marshall stood an ancient oak tree. The tree was known as the "Educational Oak." Why was that particular tree important? As the legend goes, in the year 1834, Isaac Crary and Reverend John Pierce sat under the oak and spent many long hours talking about plans for public schools in Michigan. Both men lived in Marshall. Pierce was a missionary sent into the wild west— that was Michigan. Crary was a lawyer who was very interested in seeing that children had a place to learn. That was something not very certain at the time.

Crary and Pierce wrestled with many questions. Who would be in charge of the schools? What role should state government have in the school system? And who would pay for the schools?

When Michigan wrote its first state constitution, several of the ideas developed by Crary and Pierce were included. All children would be provided with a place to go to school for at least three months a year. The expenses would be paid by the sale of the sixteenth section of each township. Money from the land sales would go into an account held by the state government and each school district would receive an equal amount. The superintendent of public instruction would be the state official in charge of all schools. The Michigan constitution was the first to actually mention such an official.

In 1836 John Pierce was given the job of being the first superintendent of public instruction in Michigan. It took some time before Michigan's schools were free. And more years passed before high schools were included in the system. But from the very beginning, the public school system in Michigan has been considered a leader in the United States. Generations of children have been educated by its methods.

144

The Educational Oak has been cut down and a statue made from the wood now stands at the Marshall Middle School.

Some Problems Continue
As a footnote to the border question, Michigan and Ohio are still not completely satisfied about the location of the boundary. A 1922 survey of the line gave Michigan control over 240 acres known as the "Lost Peninsula." The tiny peninsula in Lake Erie can only be

The Lost Peninsula

Today the border between Michigan and Ohio can still cause problems. The Lost Peninsula, a small section of southern Michigan can only be reached through Ohio.

reached by going through Ohio. More recently, the two states have been arguing over which one of them controls parts of Lake Erie. This dispute has taken place because geologists believe oil and natural gas may be found under the lake.

Even the Upper Peninsula has had its border problems. The border west of the Brule´ River was not clearly defined. At one time, until 1926, Michigan claimed a bit more of Wisconsin than it does to-day. Washington Island at the end of Green Bay was once considered within Michigan too. In 1926, however, the U.S. Supreme Court heard a case between the two states and gave Wisconsin the territory.

What happened to the "Boy Governor?"
Stevens T. Mason was reelected in 1837 and served until 1840. During his terms of office, Michigan was bustling with many activities while trying to develop itself as a new state. The population boomed to over 200,000 by 1840. Stevens had his hands full with so many things happening all at once.

In 1837 Michigan had its first railroad. There were many other plans to build canals, roads, railroads and schools.

Just as many of the projects were being started, there was a national financial crisis. To make matters even more complex, a rebellion began in Canada. During 1837 and 1838 Canada was involved in the Patriot War.

Many Canadians had become fed up with control by the British and by their own ruling class. Fighting had broken out to overthrow the Canadian government. Michigan became tangled up in the rebellion because many pioneers were on the side of those trying to overthrow the government in Canada. The Canadian revolutionaries crossed into Michigan for safety and also tried to raise volunteers to fight. There was concern they would break into the federal arsenal at Dearborn and steal weapons. The British army threatened to come into Michigan and chase down the men involved. The situation in Michigan was tense for some time.

To increase the pressure on the young governor, the Whig party opposed him nearly every chance it could. They invited Daniel Webster to visit Michigan and speak out against Mason and his policies.

Even though the young governor was busy with many projects, he fell in love for the first time. In 1838 Mason married the daughter of a New York man involved with a $5 million loan to Michigan.

Governor Mason ran for reelection on the promise to get a loan for Michigan to complete some of the internal improvements. He had been given the power to go East and borrow $5 million to pay for the projects. That was a lot of money; the entire federal budget at that time was only $20 million. The state did get the loan, but only half of the money reached Michigan before the companies which loaned it went broke. By a strange twist of the law, Michigan found itself owing $5 million plus interest after getting only $2.5 million! Governor Mason was in the middle of an impossible situation. William Woodbridge accused him of taking a bribe to get the loan in the first place. Mason was so upset he didn't even run for office again. After his last term, he and his new wife moved to New York to escape the many problems in Michigan.

In New York, Mason opened a law practice but he did not get much business. He missed the excitement of being Michigan's governor. But he felt he could not go back to the mess he had left behind. Eventually, he became depressed about his hopes for the future. After a New Year's Eve party, Stevens came down with pneumonia. His condition was not properly treated and he died. He was only 31 years old.

When news of his death reached Michigan, the people forgot about the problems with the loan and the improvement projects. They praised Stevens T. Mason for the many good things he did for the state. The people missed a "beloved friend of Michigan."

In 1848 the people of Michigan had to decide where the state capital would be permanently located. The original capital in Detroit was too far from the center of the state. Many cities went all out to lobby for the honor of being Michigan's new capital. Someone suggested Lansing as a joke because almost no town existed there. Amazingly, the vote went to Lansing because of its central location. Of course, there were few settlements in the northern part of the state at that time.

Questions

1. When did Michigan officially become a state? What year did Michigan write its constitution and begin to act as if it were a state?

2. How many people did a territory need to begin the process of becoming a state?

3. How did Stevens T. Mason become acting governor of the territory when he was only 19 years old?

4. What problem kept Michigan from becoming a state as soon as it had the minimum number of people? How did some of the politicians in Washington feel about people from Michigan?

5. At the end of the "Toledo War," compare what Michigan gained by going along with the compromise bill suggested by Congress to what Michigan lost in the process.

6. If you had been governor of the Michigan Territory at the time of the "Toledo War" explain how you would have handled the situation.

Chapter 7 Section 2

Boom and Bust

Here are the key concepts you will find in this section:

People moved to Michigan in record numbers from 1830 to 1840 and land prices rose rapidly.

It became a fad to buy land in Michigan and then hope the price would go up.

In 1837 there was a banking crisis and land prices fell. Much paper money became worthless.

In the 1840s many people from Europe began to settle in Michigan.

Beaver Island was taken over by a self-appointed king.

Michigan Fever!

The number of people coming to Michigan kept growing. Pioneers had "Michigan Fever" and wanted to move to the state. In just one day, October 7, 1834, ships brought 900 new settlers to Detroit. All kinds of wagons pulled by oxen and horses were leaving Detroit and going west and north. It was said during the summer of 1836 a wagon left Detroit every five minutes from daylight until dark. The wagons usually took the Chicago Road or Territorial Road. Between 1830 and 1840 Michigan grew faster than any other state or territory in the United States.

```
Population recorded by U.S. census:

      1810— 4,762
      1820— 8,896
      1830— 31,639
      1840— 212,267
      1850— 397,654
```

Just as the number of people increased, so did the rush for Michigan land. About the time Michigan became a state, the demand for land went wild. The Kalamazoo land office sold over 1,600,000 acres in 1836. Business was so brisk the office had to close for 18 days just so the clerks could bring the books up-to-date. Anyone who wanted to buy land had to go to one of the five federal land offices in Michigan. The others were at Detroit, Monroe, Ionia, and Flint. White Pigeon also had an office for a short time.

Kalamazoo was then just a small village and only had four hotels. It quickly overflowed with people who came to do business at the land offices. Everyone wanted rooms in the hotels and often three strangers slept in the same bed and late arrivals paid to use the floor!

Land was available for sale as soon as it had been surveyed. Each area of land was put up for auction for two weeks. During that time, people would bid against each other for the best parcels. All of the land which was not bought at the auction was sold at the minimum price of $1.25 an acre.

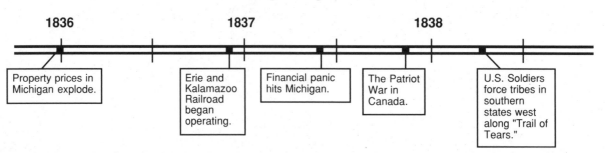

1836 — Property prices in Michigan explode.

1837 — Erie and Kalamazoo Railroad began operating.

Financial panic hits Michigan.

1838 — The Patriot War in Canada.

U.S. Soldiers force tribes in southern states west along "Trail of Tears."

The Kalamazoo land office was a center of much activity as pioneers and land speculators rushed to buy land. (Courtesy Michigan Bell an Ameritech Company)

Settlers sometimes built farms on land which had not been surveyed or even obtained from the Indian tribes. They had no deed for the land and were called squatters. When the land came up for auction, it was possible for someone else to buy it and take the farm away from them. Naturally that often caused trouble at the land office. Some squatters would threaten violence if anyone tried to buy the land where they were living. After 1830, squatters had the right to buy "their" land before the auction.

Get Rich Quick!

With so many settlers moving to Michigan, it was only natural that the price of land would go up. It became a fad in Michigan during the late 1830s to buy land with the hope of selling it at a higher price. That was known as land *speculation. Speculation is going into a risky venture where something is bought with the idea of selling it when the price goes up.* Everyone was doing it, from the very rich to those who had only a few extra dollars. For a time it seemed the price of land could only go up. That encouraged more people to get into the act. Lewis Cass made a great deal of money by selling parts of his farm, which later became downtown Detroit. Another example was the Porter farm in Detroit. It was purchased for $6,000 in 1833 and sold for $20,000 in 1835.

Land speculation was helped because it was a time of general prosperity and easy money. As the fad continued, people became rather careless; often they did not even go to see the land they were buying.

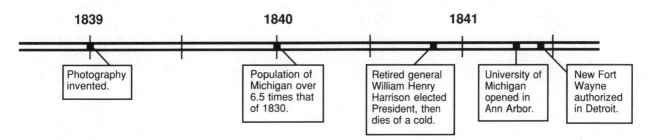

1839 — Photography invented.

1840 — Population of Michigan over 6.5 times that of 1830.

1841 — Retired general William Henry Harrison elected President, then dies of a cold.

University of Michigan opened in Ann Arbor.

New Fort Wayne authorized in Detroit.

148

It Couldn't Last Forever

The story of Antoine Campau (ahn TWAN kam POE) is a good example of such carelessness. Campau decided to invest in some land along the Grand River, even though he had not visited the site. People who missed the original rush to buy land offered to buy his. Without anyone looking the parcel over, the offers came in. The first was for $100, then $300, $500, and $800. Campau said:

"I thought if it was worth so much to them, it was worth as much to me. But finally I offered to sell. Then the value dropped, and every offer was lower than before. Finally I was offered $300, and I thought I would go down and see the place. When I got there I couldn't see it. I asked everybody where it was, and hired a friend to look it up, he could not find it, the record keeper (at the land office) could not find it, nobody could find it—it was under more than 20 feet of water."

Campau's Land Holdings

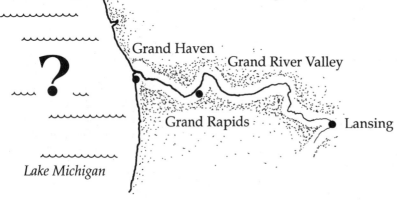

Mr. Campau had bought a parcel well out into Lake Michigan!

A Panic in 1837

In 1837 the land speculation bubble burst. The United States had a banking crisis. The time of easy money came to a quick stop. The problem started when President Jackson issued an order that after December 1836, only gold or silver could be accepted at any land office. The new order made it hard for people to buy land and the price went down, just as it did for Antoine Campau. It was a terrible blow to people who had used all of their money to buy land hoping to get rich quickly.

The time of easy money came about because laws allowed new banks to start up and to print their own money. Such a practice is unheard of now, but it was common then. The money was good as long as everyone accepted it. And everyone accepted it as long as the banks were in good financial shape. Trouble developed because there was nothing to back the paper money printed by the banks. Some banks had gold and silver in their vaults, but not enough for all of the money they printed.

Don't Put Your Money in a Wildcat Bank

The bank crisis in Michigan was worse than in some parts of the country. Since the territory was growing so fast, many new banks had started here. Michigan had passed a law which allowed any 12 landowners to start a bank if they had $50,000 and if at least $15,000 was in gold or silver. No one had been watching the situation carefully and many of the banks were just a hoax.

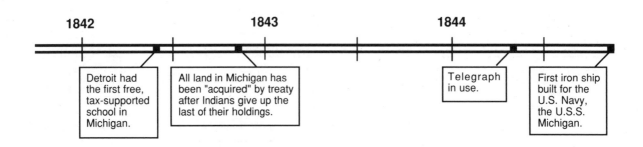

1842

1843

1844

Detroit had the first free, tax-supported school in Michigan.

All land in Michigan has been "acquired" by treaty after Indians give up the last of their holdings.

Telegraph in use.

First iron ship built for the U.S. Navy, the U.S.S. Michigan.

At the time of wildcat banks in Michigan, each could have its own paper money printed. Here are several samples. (Courtesy Clarke Historical Library, Central Michigan University.)

These banks were called *wildcat banks. A wildcat bank did not really do business as a bank. Some dishonest people decided they could get rich by having a bank office and printed money.* The money was unloaded on unsuspecting merchants.

If a banking official came to check a wildcat bank, the owners would quickly borrow gold and silver from someplace else so it would appear the bank had the required amount. As soon as the official left, the gold was immediately loaded on a wagon and returned. One bank inspector even saw a wagon pass him on the road and recognized the barrel it was carrying. The same barrel had been full of gold and silver at the bank he just visited!

Not Worth the Paper it Was Printed On

Soon farmers and merchants were reluctant to accept printed money, and if they did, it was at a discount. Discounted paper money might be worth only half its printed value. It depended on how good the bank was which printed it. Much of the paper money became completely worthless.

The bank crisis and the fall of land prices scared many people in Michigan and caused hardships because they lost their savings. The time was called the Panic of 1837.

Is it Real?

Before the panic, speculators from the East had been selling town lots to

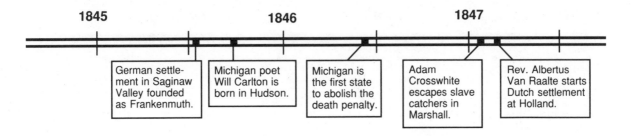

1845

1846

1847

German settlement in Saginaw Valley founded as Frankenmuth.

Michigan poet Will Carlton is born in Hudson.

Michigan is the first state to abolish the death penalty.

Adam Crosswhite escapes slave catchers in Marshall.

Rev. Albertus Van Raalte starts Dutch settlement at Holland.

150

people who were interested in moving to Michigan. That seemed reasonable; however, many of the towns did not actually exist. They were only on paper. The speculators had nice maps made which showed the town and its name. They told people what a wonderful place this or that new town would be. People thought the speculators were honest and believed them.

When the new owners moved to Michigan, they found they had a lot in a "paper city." All they saw was a thick woods. The many nice things they thought were in the city did not exist. There was no gristmill, no bank, no hotel, no school, no general store.

Ghost Towns in Michigan

Sometimes a village was begun but just didn't last. Perhaps it was not in a good location. Or some nearby town begin to attract people to it instead and too many folks moved away. The Panic of 1837 did not help. Several towns started in the late 1830s and 1840s became ghost towns. Port Sheldon, 10 miles south of Grand Haven, was such a place. Singapore, near the mouth of the Kalamazoo River on Lake Michigan, was built to be a great port city. But things turned out differently and finally all the people moved away. Not only did Singapore become a ghost town but it was eventually buried by sand dunes!

Life Goes On

The panic made life in Michigan hard for many people. But most farmers could take care of themselves and grow their own food. Because farmers were independent from the rest of the economy, the panic did not bother them as much as it did people who lived in the cities and towns.

Michigan became the home of many people from other lands. Often these immigrants only brought what they could carry. (*Harper's Weekly*, October 1891)

Even so, most towns survived. New settlers continued to come. Several counties had also been organized. In 1828 Michigan had 10 counties, but by 1836 the number had increased to 27.

Settlers From Overseas

Most of the settlers coming to Michigan during the 1830s were from New England and New York. In the 1840s the mix of settlers began to change. More started to come from Europe.

A series of problems of that time in different parts of Europe caused many people to *immigrate* or move to the United States. Significant numbers of people moved to Michigan from Germany, Ireland, Holland (or the Netherlands), and a part of England called Cornwall. Later, more people arrived from other countries.

Germans

Many of the early immigrant groups looked toward religious leaders for guidance. The Germans were no

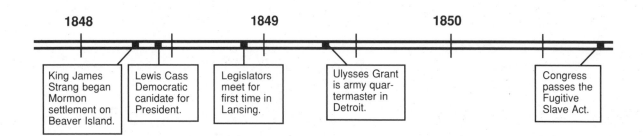

1848 — King James Strang began Mormon settlement on Beaver Island.

Lewis Cass Democratic canidate for President.

1849 — Legislators meet for first time in Lansing.

Ulysses Grant is army quartermaster in Detroit.

1850 — Congress passes the Fugitive Slave Act.

exception. Reverend Fredrich Schmid led 34 German families to mid-Michigan in 1833. The Germans began to settle the Ann Arbor area and the Saginaw River valley, forming towns like Frankenmuth. Catholic Germans started Westphalia in the central Lower Peninsula. These immigrants left Germany because of crop failures and a revolution in 1848.

The Irish

The Irish were driven out of their homeland by a potato disease in 1845. These people rented the land they farmed and could not continue to pay the rent when their crops failed. Because of that, most of the Irish were often very poor when they arrived in the United States. Since they did not have much money to start farms, a large number of Irish worked in the cities, mines, and factories. Detroit had a big Irish population for many years. In 1833, Father Bernard O'Cavanaugh helped begin the first Irish parish church in the western states.

The Dutch

The Dutch came to find religious freedom and they came in groups. The Dutch government had started a govern-

Ethnic Groups in Michigan

This map shows some of the places in Michigan where groups from other countries have settled. The modern flags of these countries are pictured. The flag of Saudi Arabia represents the many countries of people from the Mideast. Many cities also have people of African heritage. The flag of Ghana represents one of the areas in Africa where those people first lived. (Art by David B. McConnell)

ment-run church in the Netherlands and many people there disagreed with its policies. Since they could not change the government church, these people left the country. Reverend Albertus C. Van Raalte led the first Dutch settlers to America to start a "Dutch Kolonie." They first arrived in western Michigan in 1847 and started Holland, Michigan. Grand Rapids also has many people with a Dutch background as does Zeeland.

The Cornish

The Cornish came from Cornwall in southwest England. Cornwall had been a major center of copper mining but the ore was nearly gone. In the 1850s they were sought out to come to Michigan and work in the new Upper Peninsula copper mines. They moved to towns like Houghton and Eagle River. A common nickname for the Cornish which was often heard in the mines was "Cousin Jack."

A King In Michigan?

Another group came to Michigan so they could practice their religion. They were the Mormons. The leader of their group was James Jesse Strang. The Mormon communities were often attacked by others. They left Illinois in 1847 and some of them moved to Beaver Island in Lake Michigan. They hoped the isolation of the island would give them peace.

Unfortunately, it was not long before there were problems with people from Charlevoix and Mackinac. In a most unusual move, Strang had himself crowned king in 1850. He said he ruled the Kingdom of St. James. St. James is still a village on the island. By 1852 "King" Strang was elected to the Michigan legislature. There were problems within and outside the "kingdom." In 1856 James Strang was shot by one of his followers. He was taken to Wisconsin by ship where he died. Without his leadership, the members of his group left the island and scattered.

Questions

1. How much greater was the population of Michigan in 1840 than it was in 1830?

2. Where did settlers have to go to buy land? What might happen if a settler built on land which had not yet been surveyed?

3. The panic of 1837 proved that many people were either greedy or dishonest. Explain what greed and dishonesty had to do with land speculation and wildcat banks.

4. Give some reasons why people moved from Europe to Michigan.

5. Name the four main ethnic groups who came to Michigan during the 1840s and 1850s. Name one city or town which had many settlers from each of these groups.

6. Who was James Jesse Strang and where did he live in Michigan?

7. As an honest 1830s land promoter, write a list of things which would encourage settlers to buy land in your town. Mention features which were important to early pioneers.

Chapter 7 Section 3

Canals & Copper

Here are the key concepts you will find in this section:

Early development of transportation and industry went hand in hand.

State government helped to build the first railroads during the 1830s.

A copper rush took place in the Upper Peninsula during the 1840s.

In 1844 iron ore was discovered by surveyors in the Upper Peninsula.

The Soo Locks were built at Sault Ste. Marie so ships carrying copper and iron ore could go between Lake Superior and Lake Huron.

Government Goals

After the turmoil of becoming a state died down, there were two major goals for government in Michigan: development of a strong economy and a statewide transportation system. Development of industry and transportation went hand in hand. Michigan could not have profitable industries without good transportation and it could not have profitable transportation without something worth shipping.

Railroads Begin

By the late 1830s, people could see that railroads would be an important part of the future. The state government decided to add railroads to the list of projects it planned to develop. Railroads got an early start here. In 1837, Michigan had the first steam locomotive west of New York state. It was used on the Erie and Kalamazoo line. That railroad went from Toledo, which was considered to be a part of Michigan when the first work

The first trains were slow by today's standards as they traveled an average of 25 miles an hour. But they were still an important improvement in transportation. (Courtesy Michigan State Archives)

154

was started, to Adrian, Michigan. It never reached the Kalamazoo River, the intended end of the line.

Those first railroads were laughable by today's standards. During the winter men might sit on the front of the engine to sweep snow off the track. And what tracks! They were actually made of wood and just had iron strips nailed on top. The train had to stop often to pick up more wood from farmers along the line and to encourage livestock to get off the tracks. Horses often pulled the cars of the "train" while the engine was being repaired or needed elsewhere!

The grand opening of the Michigan Central from Detroit to Ypsilanti was flawed when the engine broke down on its return trip and the reliable horses had to pull Governor Mason and a trainload of officials back home. But even such crude trains were exciting to the early pioneers who had been cut off by the lack of good roads and felt isolated in the Michigan wilderness. Even the first railroads were great time-savers. The Michigan Central could take passengers or freight to Ypsilanti from Detroit in about two and a half hours. A wagon on the road would need two days for the same trip. By 1849 it was possible to take a train from Detroit and reach Chicago in a brisk 36 hours; though passengers had to take a ship across Lake Michigan to complete the trip. The cost of goods began to fall as soon as railroads reached Michigan communities. The price of salt shipped from New York state went from $15 a barrel down to $9.

Not Enough Money

Unfortunately, Michigan could not pay for all of the projects it planned. Many things, especially the canals, were never finished. Even though Michigan had a good head start with railroads, development slowed down and nearby states soon had more miles of track. The solution was for state government to get out of the railroad business. All of the state-owned railroads had been sold to private companies by 1846.

Although there were trains, stagecoaches (also know as diligences) continued to operate in Michigan until the 1860s. This one has stopped to pay its fee on a toll road. (Courtesy Michigan State Archives)

Dr. Houghton's Work

The linking of transportation and industry were especially important in the Upper Peninsula. Douglass Houghton was the person who helped to bring these two key elements together in the northern part of the state.

Houghton was invited to come to Michigan in 1830. He gave lectures in Detroit on the latest scientific wonders from the East. When he arrived he did not look like someone who would do great things for Michigan. He was just 21 years old and five feet five inches tall. He looked more like a student instead of someone who would be giving lectures. However, the talks that Houghton gave were very popular. Not only did Douglass Houghton know about chemistry and geology, but he was studying medicine too. He opened a medical office in Detroit in 1831.

A Chance to Explore

Everyone was interested in learning more about what Michigan was like and what valuable things could be found in the region. Lewis Cass had led one group to explore in 1820; then Henry Schoolcraft headed another group and Houghton was asked to go along. During the trip he found pieces of copper along Lake Superior. Remember that prehistoric Indians worked copper on Isle Royale and in the Upper Peninsula. The French and British had also found some copper and had looked for more. But during all of that time no one had yet gone to the trouble to make a scientific search for copper in Michigan.

Once Dr. Houghton returned from his trip with Schoolcraft, he spent most of his time treating patients in Detroit. He was a popular person in the city and became mayor. He also began to speculate in land and formed a partnership with two brothers, Bella and Henry Hubbard. By 1836 Dr. Houghton gave up medicine so he could concentrate on making money in the great land boom. But while he was doing all of these other things, he told many officials that there should be a complete study of Michigan's animals, plants, and minerals, including copper. He just kept thinking about that copper he had seen in the Upper Peninsula.

Search for Minerals

After Michigan became a state, Governor Mason chose Dr. Houghton to find out exactly what resources were here. Houghton was given the job of state geologist. In 1837 he began to explore every part of the state. At first Houghton and his assistants traveled all over the Lower Peninsula. They looked for things like salt springs and clay deposits which could be used to make bricks. They found material which could be used to make glass and they found deposits of coal.

In 1840 Dr. Douglass Houghton took several assistants and headed to the Upper Peninsula. They planned to really study the copper situation.

The Great Boulder

Houghton knew one place he wanted to study. He had been there before. On the Ontonagon River there was a large piece of almost pure copper, called the Ontonagon Boulder. He wanted to bring back samples from the massive copper rock. When they reached the mouth of the river, they found an Indian village. The Indians seemed friendly and greeted them in French. Houghton gave the Indians a gift of bread and tobacco. But the Indians did not want them to continue any further. They believed the copper rocks in the region to be sacred. They did not care for other people visiting their spiritual places. They especially disliked the idea of someone cutting off pieces as samples!

The chief of the Indians in the area was away, but he had told his son to stop any boats from going up the river. Dr. Houghton reminded the Indians that even though the Indians owned the land, an 1826 treaty did allow U.S. citizens to examine and remove minerals from the area.

Dr. Houghton kept trying to make his point. The Indians were just as deter-

Douglass Houghton served as Michigan's first state geologist. He lost his life when a sudden Lake Superior storm caught his boat in October 1845. (Courtesy Michigan State Archives)

mined to keep them out. Finally, the Indian leader said if they could have a barrel of pork and one of flour, Dr. Houghton could go up the river. The doctor felt that was blackmail and said he would only give them enough for their immediate needs. A deal was finally made. But Houghton's group was not sure they could really trust the Indians and kept a careful watch. The Indians probably didn't trust the Americans either and knew some of the sacred copper would disappear.

The great copper boulder was located on the west branch of the Ontonagon River about seven miles above the forks. Mr. Bella Hubbard wrote what the rock looked like:

"... one end rises about a foot above the water... It has at first appearance a very striking effect, resembling a mass of perfectly pure copper, its bright colored edges glittering among the black rocks and water.... We estimate the contents at 20 cubic feet.... One piece cut off

with our chisels measured three inches thickness pure metal, remarkably close grained and heavy."

from Bella Hubbard's *Journal* of the 1840 Houghton Expedition.

Dr. Houghton published his report on the Upper Peninsula in 1841. He talked about the Ontonagon boulder and other copper deposits and said they would be a source of wealth for the people of Michigan but he also warned future miners it would take lots of hard work, money, and patience to succeed. As soon as the report was out, miners began to trickle into the area around the Keweenaw Peninsula—that little finger of land which pokes into Lake Superior. The federal government made a land treaty with the local tribes in 1842. Then the way was clear for more mining activities.

In 1843 Michigan copper got more publicity when a Detroit businessman named Julius Eldred removed the Ontonagon Boulder after a tremendous amount of work. He took it to Detroit where he charged admission to people who wanted to see the magnificent rock. The federal government did not think Eldred had a rightful claim to the rock and decided it should become the property of the War Department, even though Eldred had spent 16 years planning to move the boulder.

Eldred had paid close attention to detail. He had negotiated trading licenses, mineral permits and paid an Indian $150 for his claims to the rock. To add insult to injury, Eldred found another mining group ready to move the rock when he got there. Deep in the woods there was no court to decide whose claim was correct. Eldred was not going home empty handed; so he paid the other group $1,365 for their interests in the great hunk of metal.

Once in Detroit, the government seized the copper boulder and sent it to Washington. The stories about Eldred's fight to keep his big rock appeared in many Eastern newspapers. The 3,708 pound Ontonagon boulder finally ended at the Smithsonian Institution where it is still on display.

The Copper Rush!

The first great mineral rush in the United States began to take place in Michigan's Upper Peninsula. More and more adventurous miners arrived. They brought their pickaxes and shovels. They expected to become wealthy by just picking up pieces of copper off the ground. While they searched, they had to swat great swarms of mosquitoes and black flies. During the winter they found themselves dangerously cut off from any source of supplies by huge snowdrifts and frozen lakes. But still thousands came, hoping to get rich.

Father Baraga, also known as the snowshoe priest, came to the Great Lakes from Yugoslavia in 1830. He began preaching to the Ojibwa in the Lower Peninsula. He moved to L'Anse in October of 1843 and spent the winter of 1844-1845 at Fort Wilkins in Copper Harbor. (Courtesy Michigan State Archives)

Angus Murdock described what it was like in his book, *Boom Copper*:

"Soft palmed clerks, whose heaviest work had been lifting ledgers and pushing quill pens, came ashore with picks slung over rounded shoulders. Tidewater Easterners arrived in fishermen's outfits....Others were ex-lawyers, ex-preachers, ex-husbands, ex-everything you can think of except expert miners."

Even though there had not been time to finish surveying the land, the federal government opened a mineral agency at Copper Harbor in 1843. There was also concern that the Indians would resent the arrival of so many miners on their sacred land. In order to be certain no trouble would take place between the miners and Indians, Fort Wilkins was built at Copper Harbor.

The fort only operated until 1846. There seemed to be little need for it and the soldiers were wanted for the war with Mexico. The fort probably did more to protect the Indians from the miners than the other way around.

The "miners" sloshed through swamps and streams looking for pieces of the red metal. Some tried setting off a couple of pounds of gunpowder to loosen copper from surrounding rock. Some dug shallow pits when they found copper on the ground to see if there were any more beneath it; however, very little real mining took place at first.

The Cliff Mine Story

John Hays helped get the first actual copper mine going. He was a druggist in Pittsburgh who wanted to have some excitement in his life. He started by spending more time in the saloons on the Keweenaw than he did tramping through the woods. In 1843 he happened to meet a man with some good claims who was out of money and tired of digging for copper. Then and there they wrote an agreement on the back of an old letter. Hays and a friend from the East would give $1,000 for a one-sixth interest in the man's claims.

John Hays, known as Old Blind Hays because of serious eye problems, was

158

The Cliff Mine was the first successful copper mine in the Upper Peninsula. It was started by John Hays, a druggist from Pittsburgh. (Courtesy Michigan State Archives)

bubbling over with excitement in his new venture. He was able to find several other people in the East to invest money in the mining partnership. At first Hays did not have much better luck than most of the other early miners. They did find about $3,000 worth of copper, but they spent $25,000 to get it. Not a very good way to get rich!

Finally a new location was chosen and they started digging a mine shaft into the side of a steep hill near Eagle River. It was in that shaft they found a piece of copper so large it had to be broken up before they could continue. Afterwards, many more large boulders and hunks of nearly pure copper were found. One old prospector said, "Most of them were bigger than my outhouse back there!" During the many years of copper mining, pieces much larger than the Ontonagon Boulder were discovered. In 1845 John Hays climbed up to the top of the hill and named the spot the "Cliff Mine." The Cliff was the first successful copper mine in the Upper Peninsula.

Surveyors often marked information on trees. For many years these "witness" trees were important in finding property boundaries. (Courtesy Marquette County Historical Society)

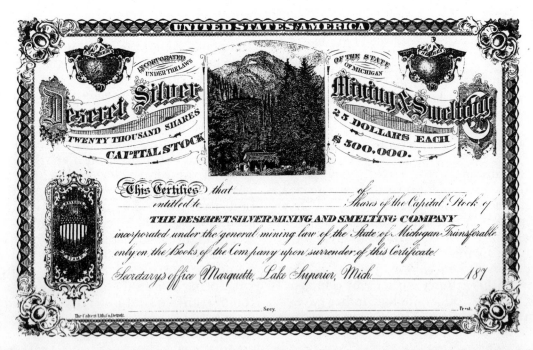

Stock shares like the one shown above were issued to investors who put money into the early mining operations.

In 1849 the mining company was able to pay money back to the people who had invested to get it started. But the investors had to put in $320,000 to make it profitable! Many of the first investors had lost hope and sold out before they ever received a cent. Soon, over 100 mining companies were digging down after copper. News of the discovery of gold in California in 1849 caused most of the remaining non-expert prospectors to leave the Michigan copper fields.

Compass Confusion

Douglass Houghton wanted to know more about the land in the Upper Peninsula. The state government had run out of money and had discontinued the state geologist's job after 1841. So Houghton went to the federal government. They were willing to have Houghton survey the township lines. A man named William Burt was assigned to be the deputy surveyor with Houghton.

Burt and his assistants were working on the township lines for Marquette county near Teal Lake. Then something most unusual happened. Jacob Houghton, Douglass's brother, gave this account:

William Burt, the discoverer of iron ore in the Upper Peninsula.

"On the morning of the 19th of September, 1844, we started to run the line south between ranges 26 and 27. As soon as we reached the hill to the south of the lake, the compassman began to notice a fluctuation... of the magnetic needle.... At length the compassman called for us all to 'come see a variation which will beat them all.' Mr. Burt called out, 'Boys, look around and see what you can find!' We all left the line, some going east, some going to the west, and all of us returned with specimens of iron ore."

William Burt was really excited, not because he thought he could become rich, but because it helped to prove how important his solar compass was. Several years before, Burt had invented a compass which used the sun to show directions. He kept saying, "How would they survey this country without my compass!"

A new billion dollar industry was born in Michigan! The discovery of iron was even more surprising than the discovery of copper because people had known the copper was there all along. No one had any idea Michigan had iron ore. Douglass Houghton had made careful studies just a few miles from the location of a 150-foot high mountain of solid iron ore and never saw a trace of it!

The Challenge of Iron Mining

It was tough to make a profit on copper but it was even harder with iron. Most of the copper was found in nearly pure form. When it wasn't pure, it often had silver in it, which made it even more valuable. It could be cut and hammered and used almost as soon as it came from the ground. Iron was different. It was not found in pure form, but was combined with other minerals. That meant each ton of iron ore contained a great deal of waste.

Members of the Jackson Mining Company found bright iron ore under the roots of this old tree. (Courtesy Michigan State Archives)

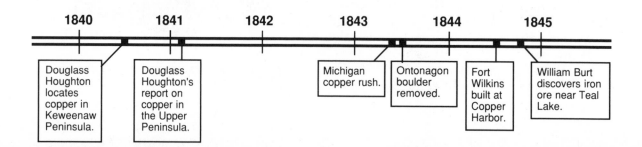

1840	1841	1842	1843	1844	1845
Douglass Houghton locates copper in Keweenaw Peninsula.	Douglass Houghton's report on copper in the Upper Peninsula.		Michigan copper rush. / Ontonagon boulder removed.	Fort Wilkins built at Copper Harbor.	William Burt discovers iron ore near Teal Lake.

They Came from Jackson

Some men from Jackson, Michigan, made the first try to mine the iron ore commercially. What was unusual about it was they originally planned to go north and find copper and silver! Philo Everett was a Jackson businessman who caught the "copper fever." He gathered with neighbors around his stove and talked of going to the Upper Peninsula and finding a fortune. The group formed the Jackson Mining Company, even though not one of them knew much about mining nor about the land where the minerals were found. In July 1845, Everett headed north with three other men. The journey took 21 days.

Philo Everett had some very good luck. At the Sault he met Tipo-Keso, an Ojibwa woman. She told the greenhorns about a mountain of mineral ore near her uncle's camp on Teal Lake. Everett and his friends went to the camp and were met by her uncle, Marji-Gesick, who entertained them. The next day Marji-Gesick led them to the area of the mountain of ore. Under the roots of a big pine tree which had fallen down they found some bright iron ore. Today the city of Negaunee is near that spot.

Samples that the Jackson men brought back with them were taken to the little village of Hodunk near Union City in Branch county. There, at a small forge, the first iron was made from Upper Peninsula iron ore.

In 1847 the Jackson Mining Company loaded assorted equipment and transported it to a place about three miles east of their mine. It was on the Carp River that they set up a forge. The purpose of the forge was to purify the iron ore and get rid of the waste materials in it. By forging the ore near the mine, the miners hoped to save money on shipping costs. But it was also expensive to run the forge.

The forge made pieces of iron about two feet long and four inches square. The pieces were stacked up until winter when they could be put on a sled and taken to Marquette harbor. Once at the harbor, they could be put aboard ships when the ice melted in the spring.

The Jackson mine proved that the Upper Peninsula had high quality iron ore and attracted the attention of people far and wide. The new Michigan Iron Industry Museum is now located at the site of that first forge on the Carp River.

The Cost of Shipping

It was the cost of shipping which ruined most miners' hopes of a profit. It cost $18-20 to ship a ton of ore to Boston and the markets on the East Coast. About that same time it only cost $15 to ship it from South America! There was not much demand for copper or iron in Detroit so most of it had to be shipped far away. A cry for better transportation began to be heard. After all, there was certainly something worth shipping from the Upper Peninsula.

Bottleneck at the Rapids

The big problem was the mile-long St. Mary's rapids. At that spot the water falls about 20 feet pouring from Lake Superior into Lake Huron. The rapids made it impossible for any ship to sail in or out of Lake Superior. Everything had to be unloaded at Sault Ste. Marie and hauled by man or beast to the other end of the rapids and reloaded onto one of the few small ships working on Lake Superior.

Most of the ships in the bigger lake had been slowly dragged around the rapids; a job which took at least several weeks. Because there were only a few ships on Lake Superior they could charge extremely high prices to haul cargoes. To make the situation worse, all the ships

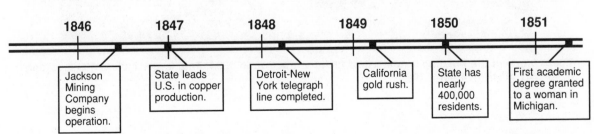

1846	1847	1848	1849	1850	1851
Jackson Mining Company begins operation.	State leads U.S. in copper production.	Detroit-New York telegraph line completed.	California gold rush.	State has nearly 400,000 residents.	First academic degree granted to a woman in Michigan.

162

stopped work for five months each year during the icy northern winter.

The answer to the problem was to build a canal and locks which could take ships around the rapids at the Soo. Just such an idea had been discussed along with other early canal projects in Michigan. But no one had been able to get the project started.

Michigan had tried to get help from the federal government for many years. The great leaders in Washington did not feel kindly to building a canal and locks in far away Michigan. In 1840, Senator Henry Clay said such a project was, "a work beyond the remotest settlement of the United States, if not the moon!"

Eventually, the resistance was overcome. An eastern newspaper publisher by the name of Horace Greeley helped to promote the idea. It was Greeley who made the famous quote, "Go west young man, go west!" He wasn't telling men to become cowboys; he was telling them to visit Michigan's copper fields! President Fillmore signed a bill in 1852 which authorized the building of the Soo locks and released 750,000 acres of federal land in Michigan. The land would be the reward to those who built the locks. The state of Michigan would operate and control the locks once they were finished.

Locks at the Soo

An unlikely group came together to build the locks and claim the 750,000 acres of land. It started with a 24-year-old weighing scales salesman, Charles Harvey. Harvey just happened to be at Sault Ste. Marie when the news arrived from Washington. He worked for the Fairbanks brothers and he knew they were interested in making investments in the area. Erastus Fairbanks was a former governor of Vermont. Harvey thought getting 750,000 acres, which is two percent of Michigan's land area, would appeal to the Fairbanks. He wrote to them immediately. The St. Mary's Falls Ship Canal Company was formed and Charles Harvey was put in charge of the work in Michigan.

These workers are building a new set of locks at the Soo in 1894. This larger lock is 800 feet long. (Courtesy Steelways Company)

Lots of politics took place in Lansing over the canal project. Some legislators thought the profits the builders would make were just too much. Other officials wanted to put so many restrictions on the project that it would have been impossible to find anyone to do the work. It was decided that everything had to be finished in two years. Perhaps two years seemed reasonable because the canal was only one mile long.

There were seven other companies who made bids to build the canal and locks. But the officials in Lansing seemed to be most impressed by the wealth of the investors in the company Harvey worked for— so they got the contract. The officials figured these people certainly had enough money to be sure the canal was built properly.

Work Underway

Charles Harvey hardly knew what he had gotten himself into. Supervising most of the work on the canal and locks fell on his shoulders— the shoulders of a scales salesman. The U.S. Army loaned Captain Augustus Canfield to help with the technical engineering details. Work started on June 4, 1853. Eventually 1,600 men came to work on the project. Unfortunately, the Soo was at least 20 days from any good source of supplies. Food and clothing had to be stored for the workers during the winters. The winters were bitter cold, sometimes reaching 30 degrees below zero!

In the winter the workers ate breakfast before daylight and went to work as soon as they could see. Many times the first thing they had to do was to find their tools which were often covered by a foot of snow during the night. Sometimes they had to chop through ice to even get to the rock they were trying to take out. They only had a 45-minute lunch break. At dark they could quit. What the workers accomplished was nothing less than a miracle under the worst conditions.

The job of building the canal was much more difficult than the company engineer had predicted. The final cost was nearly a million dollars— almost twice as much as he had estimated. In the summer of 1854, there was an outbreak of cholera at the camp and many workers died. In spite of all the problems, the canal and locks were finished five days before the deadline!

On June 18, 1855, more than a thousand people came to see if the locks would really work. Indeed, the first ship passed through without any problems. More and more ships passed through each year. By 1865, over 280,000 tons of freight shipped through in one season. The freight was mostly copper, iron ore, and grain.

Each of the two locks was 350 feet long and 70 feet wide. For many years, the size of the ships built on the Great Lakes was determined by the dimensions of the Soo Locks. The locks were made larger in 1876 and many times since. By building the Soo Locks, the people of Michigan forged a key link to the Upper Peninsula. The locks made it possible to develop the great copper and iron resources in the Upper Peninsula. All from land that was once traded for the Toledo Strip!

Questions

1. What happened to many of the projects started by Michigan's government during the early days of statehood?

2. Give two specific examples how the first railroads helped people in Michigan.

3. What is the Ontonagon Boulder? Where was it found and what happened to it?

4. Write a short paragraph about the first profitable copper mine in the Upper Peninsula. Remember to mention the three basics, who, when, and where.

5. Which of the following did Douglass Houghton do: He was the very first person to find copper in Michigan. He was the first to do a scientific study of copper in the Upper Peninsula. He was responsible for the work which eventually led to the discovery of iron ore in the Upper Peninsula. He designed the Soo Locks.

6. How long did it take to build the Soo Locks and when did they open? What did the company that built the locks get in return?

8 A STAND AGAINST SLAVERY

Chapter 8 Section 1

A Way to Freedom: The Underground Railroad

Here are the key concepts you will find in this section:

Michigan was admitted to the United States as a state which did not allow slavery.

Many people in Michigan were against slavery. They wanted to abolish or stop its practice.

Once slavery was made illegal in Canada, many escaped slaves passed through Michigan on their way there. They were often helped by members of the "Underground Railroad."

Some escaped slaves stayed in Michigan. From time to time southern slave catchers came after them.

A Question of Freedom

The 1830s through the 1860s was a time of great struggle in Michigan and the whole nation. In many ways Michigan was right in the center of the conflict. It was a conflict which put neighbor against neighbor and state against state. Finally, the strain was too much and the United States was actually ripped apart when many states left the union. What follows is the story of Michigan during that terrible time.

The idea of allowing slavery in a nation founded on the principles of individual freedom was a sort of poison which began to slowly create more and more problems for the United States. But the use of slaves had become the economic way of life in the southern states. The states which wanted slavery were afraid they would be outvoted in Congress by those who wanted it stopped. By the time Michigan was admitted as a state,

Congress was forced to balance each new state which did not allow slavery with one new state that did allow it. Arkansas was the slave state admitted about the same time as Michigan.

Michigan was a "free" state. It did not allow slavery. Earlier, the Northwest Ordinance stated that slavery was illegal in the Northwest Territory. Yet there were slaves here. Early census reports mention slaves in Michigan. Some were brought here before the time Michigan was a part of the United States. Some early slaves were Indians. Later, judges ruled that those who were slaves in slave states must continue to serve their masters if the owner moved to Michigan. The law treated slaves just like any other property— a horse, a wagon, or a plough. Slaves sold for a lot of money and were considered to be valuable.

Put yourself in the place of a slave. Slavery was not a great life. Slaves had

166

to work hard and you could be whipped if the master did not think you were doing enough work. You did not get paid for your work and you could not hope to see your children do any better. In southern states it was against the law to teach a slave how to read. Your husband, wife, or children could be sold and you might never see them again. If given the opportunity, wouldn't you want to run away and start a new life in a place where you could be free?

Some Take Action Against Injustice

Elizabeth Chandler was a young Quaker woman whose heart was open to the troubles of the slaves. Her parents had both died before she was nine years old. In 1830 with her brother and aunt, she moved west from Pennsylvania to Adrian, Michigan. She had been writing antislavery poems for a newspaper in the East since she was 18. She was the first woman writer in the United States to make the slavery issue her theme.

Elizabeth especially appealed to other women to end slavery. She wrote these lines about a slave mother losing her child:

Think of the frantic mother,
Lamenting for her child,
Til' falling lashes smother
Her cries of anguish wild!

Think of the prayers ascending,
Yet shriek'd alas! in vain,
When heart from heart is rending
Ne'er to be join'd again.

During 1832 she started the first society in Michigan whose goal was to abolish slavery. Four years later her brother helped to start the statewide Michigan Anti-Slavery Society in Ann Arbor. Members of those groups were called *abolitionists* (AB oh LISH un ists). *Abolitionists wanted to abolish or end slavery.* Unfortunately, Elizabeth died when she was only 26, some 30 years before the end of slavery.

Through Michigan—On To Freedom!

There are early accounts of slaves escaping into Michigan from Canada. But in 1834 all of that changed. In that year Canada outlawed slavery which meant slaves from the United States would be safe in Canada. Because of the strong feeling against slavery in Canada, many Canadians were willing to help escaped slaves start a new home. Also, Canada did not allow slave catchers to go after slaves there.

The Underground Line

Over the years slaves did break away from their masters and escape. Many people in northern United States realized what a cruel thing slavery was and some of them began to try to help the escaped slaves. Beginning in the late 1830s, a number of Michigan people started working in an organization called the Underground Railroad .

The Underground Railroad did not have steam engines and passenger cars. It was a loosely organized group of people who were willing to help the runaway slaves. It was called underground because it was supposed to be secret.

Railroad terms were used for the Underground Railroad. "Conductors" took the slaves in their wagons to the next house or "station." The "conductors" usually fed their "passengers" and kept them out of sight in a barn, stable, cellar or nearby woods until they could leave at night. The next "station" was generally just 15 or 20 miles away. The "conductor" would have to be sure the trip could be completed before daylight.

Many times thinly disguised newspaper ads were printed in local papers telling about a new "shipment" which would arrive at the "station."

Laura Haviland—One Woman With a Cause

Laura Haviland's friends called her "Superintendent of the Underground Railroad." She was a quiet and gentle woman who devoted her life helping others. In 1837 Laura and her husband

Laura Haviland holding a device used to restrain a slave. (Courtesy Michigan State Archives)

started the Raisin Institute, a school for orphans on the Raisin River near Adrian. It was the first Michigan school which accepted black children.

In 1845, disease took the life of Laura's husband and one of their children. With great effort Laura raised money to keep the school going, care for her six remaining children, and pay taxes on their farm.

Her work to help escaped slaves increased after her husband's death. She went to Ohio, Indiana, and Kentucky to do whatever she could. Not content to assist those who had already managed their escape, Laura actually helped slaves to make their getaway! Outraged slave owners put up a $3,000 reward for her capture.

Bravely, Laura Haviland continued. Later she served as a nurse in the Civil War and worked to help educate blacks in Kansas. She died in 1898 at the age of 90. There is a statue of Laura Haviland in front of the Adrian City Hall.

STOCKHOLDERS
OF THE UNDERGROUND
R. R. COMPANY
Hold on to Your Stock!!

The market has an upward tendency. By the express train which arrived this morning at 3 o'clock, fifteen thousand dollars worth of human merchandise, consisting of twenty-nine able-bodied men and women, fresh and sound, from the Carolina and Kentucky plantations, have arrived safe at the depot on the other side, where all our sympathising colonization friends may have an opportunity of expressing their sympathy by bringing forward donations of ploughs, &c., farming utensils, pick axes and hoes, and not old clothes; as these emigrants all can till the soil. N. B.—Stockholders don't forget, the meeting to-day at 2 o'clock at the ferry on the Canada side. All persons desiring to take stock in this prosperous company, be sure to be on hand.

Detroit, April 19, 1853.

By Order of the
BOARD OF DIRECTORS.

This handbill was distributed throughout Detroit in 1853 telling about the safe passage of 29 slaves to Canada. There was also a request for donations to help the freed slaves. (Courtesy Michigan State Archives)

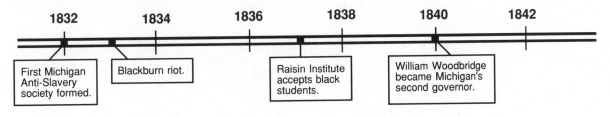

| 1832 | 1834 | 1836 | 1838 | 1840 | 1842 |

First Michigan Anti-Slavery society formed.

Blackburn riot.

Raisin Institute accepts black students.

William Woodbridge became Michigan's second governor.

A Quaker Connection

Pamela Thomas, just 23 years old, learned about escaped slaves through her husband who was a Quaker. The Quakers were a religious group who also called themselves the Society of Friends. They were against violence and slavery. The Quakers took a strong stand against slavery and they did more than just talk. Many Quakers were members of the Underground Railroad.

Pamela remembers her first feelings about her husband, Dr. N.M. Thomas, "I thought him fanatical, when he asserted, 'Slavery cannot continue to exist under our government. If it is not put down by the ballot, it will go down in blood.'" Dr. Thomas meant that if slavery couldn't be made illegal by a vote, the nation would eventually go to war.

Doctor Thomas was so well known for his antislavery feelings that escaped slaves often came to him for help at his home in Schoolcraft which is near Kalamazoo. His wife became active in helping slaves after she met an old woman who had escaped slavery in Missouri and walked to Michigan. The former slave told Pamela Thomas some of the unmentionable things women slaves had to endure from cruel masters. Afterwards, Pamela felt she must do what she could for those trying to escape.

It wasn't easy for the Thomas family. Pamela said, "They began to arrive in loads of from six to twelve. This brought much hard work to me and great expense to my husband. Often after my little ones were asleep and I thought the labor of the day over, Friend Zachariah Shugart (Quakers called each other "friend") would drive up with a load of hungry people (escaped slaves) to be fed and housed for the night."

Not all escaped slaves knew about the Underground Railroad or used its services. Their journey was a hard and dangerous one in any case. The worst part of the trip, through the southern states, was made on their own. They had a long way to go from their master's home to the first station. The escaped or fugitive slaves must have been suspicious of anyone they met.

The Routes They Used

Several routes were used by the escaping slaves. The routes went through New York, Indiana, Ohio, and Michigan.

One route was known as the "Michigan Central Line." It had the same name as the real railroad. The Central Line went from Niles and Cassopolis through Schoolcraft, Battle Creek, Parma, Jackson, Dexter, Ann Arbor, Ypsilanti, and Detroit. Most of the routes ended at Detroit, but many times the fugitive slaves crossed the river at Port Huron. From Detroit it was on to Windsor or Amherstburg in Canada. Sometimes escaped slaves were put aboard ships and taken over parts of the Great Lakes. Some sailed from Toledo or Sandusky, Ohio, to Canada. Many of the relatives of escaped slaves still live in southern Ontario.

It is very difficult to know how many escaped slaves used the Michigan route of the Underground Railroad. Since the work of the railroad was secret, few people kept any records and probably no one knew all of those who were "conductors." Some historians guess as many as 40,000 to 50,000 slaves passed through Michigan, while others think those numbers are too high.

The Feeling Was Not Unanimous

Not everyone approved of the Underground Railroad, even though most of Michigan was against slavery. From time to time people would yell and swear

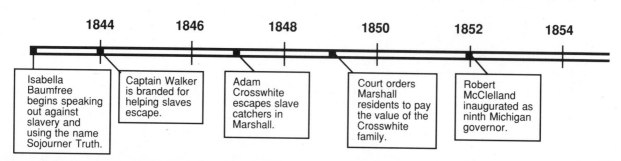

1844 — Isabella Baumfree begins speaking out against slavery and using the name Sojourner Truth.

1846 — Captain Walker is branded for helping slaves escape.

1848 — Adam Crosswhite escapes slave catchers in Marshall.

1850 — Court orders Marshall residents to pay the value of the Crosswhite family.

1852 — Robert McClelland inaugurated as ninth Michigan governor.

1854

THE UNDERGROUND RAILROAD IN MICHIGAN

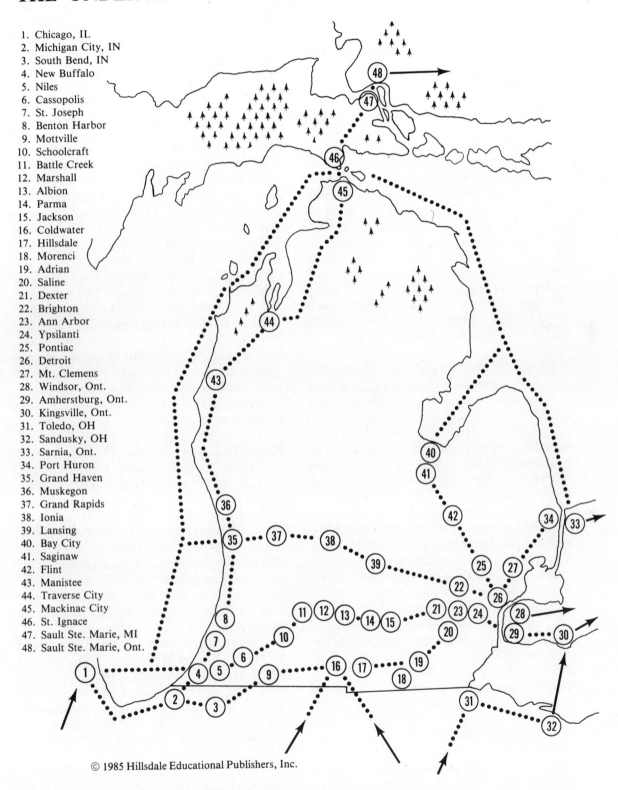

1. Chicago, IL
2. Michigan City, IN
3. South Bend, IN
4. New Buffalo
5. Niles
6. Cassopolis
7. St. Joseph
8. Benton Harbor
9. Mottville
10. Schoolcraft
11. Battle Creek
12. Marshall
13. Albion
14. Parma
15. Jackson
16. Coldwater
17. Hillsdale
18. Morenci
19. Adrian
20. Saline
21. Dexter
22. Brighton
23. Ann Arbor
24. Ypsilanti
25. Pontiac
26. Detroit
27. Mt. Clemens
28. Windsor, Ont.
29. Amherstburg, Ont.
30. Kingsville, Ont.
31. Toledo, OH
32. Sandusky, OH
33. Sarnia, Ont.
34. Port Huron
35. Grand Haven
36. Muskegon
37. Grand Rapids
38. Ionia
39. Lansing
40. Bay City
41. Saginaw
42. Flint
43. Manistee
44. Traverse City
45. Mackinac City
46. St. Ignace
47. Sault Ste. Marie, MI
48. Sault Ste. Marie, Ont.

This map shows many routes which were used by the underground railroad. Most led to the Canadian border. (Map by David B. McConnell)

at members of the Railroad— and sometimes worse things happened! The Battle Creek office of an antislavery newspaper run by Erastus Hussey was burned. In Illinois, the owner of another antislavery paper was killed by a mob! Slave owners would sue members of the Railroad who had helped their slaves to escape. If they lost in court, abolitionists often had to sell their homes and farms to raise the money.

A sailor with connections to Michigan, Captain Jonathan Walker, was helping seven slaves escape in Florida. He was caught and convicted in 1844 as a slave stealer. With a red-hot iron they branded the letters S.S. in the palm of his right hand so all who met him would know he was a slave stealer. That was just part of his punishment for helping the slaves. There is a historic monument in Muskegon, Michigan, in honor of the "Man with the Branded Hand."

A Home in Michigan—But Not Safe!

Often, however, the escapees decided it was safe to stay in Michigan. Some families remained near towns on the Underground Railroad lines. Many escaped slaves moved to Cass County. The number of black people there increased from five in 1840 to over 1,300 by 1860. In the late 1860s at least 60 percent of Michigan's blacks lived in that county.

Rutha and Thornton Blackburn escaped from Kentucky to Detroit in 1831. Two years passed, but then someone recognized Thornton and sent word to his former owner. The owner sent a slave catcher after the Blackburns.

The ex-slaves were put in jail until they could be sent south. Remember, the Northwest Ordinance said slaves would be returned to their masters in any of the original states. Many black people wanted to help the Blackburns. Rutha was smuggled out after exchanging clothes with a visitor. She was taken to Canada.

The next day a large crowd, most of whom were black people, stood in front of the jail. They knew Thornton Blackburn would soon be put aboard a steamship which would carry him back to slavery. The sheriff tried to reason with the crowd three times and get them to go home but they would not. Then, the sheriff turned and saw Thornton standing in the doorway of the jail and holding a pistol! Somehow the gun had been smuggled into the jail and Thornton had hobbled out in his leg irons. The sheriff jumped for the gun and wrestled with Thornton. The crowd held the sheriff and took Thornton away. Thornton was eventually smuggled across the Detroit River. At that time there was less sympathy in the white community. Many Detroiters were shocked by the attack on the sheriff. Thirty members of the crowd were arrested and thrown into jail. The Mayor of Detroit was so worried he asked for soldiers to help keep order. The situation did not look good for the Blackburns either. They were arrested in Canada. Michigan asked that they be sent back, but under a new law the Canadian government had the right to refuse, and it did. Finally the Blackburns were released and were able to start a new home near Toronto.

Slave Catchers In Marshall

Over the years, people in Michigan became more sympathetic with the escaped slaves. Another famous event took place at Marshall, Michigan. In 1843, Adam Crosswhite and his family ran away from Frank Giltner's Kentucky plantation because Crosswhite learned that his four children were to be sold. The Crosswhites made the tough, exhausting journey and finally settled in Marshall.

Four years later, during 1847, slave hunters came to Michigan. Their arrival made everyone nervous and the countryside was in an uproar. Crosswhite was afraid they might come after his family. He had told friends that he had a gun and would fire a warning shot if he saw any slave catchers.

On the morning of January 2, 1847, David Giltner (the son of the Kentucky plantation owner), a slave catcher named

Francis Troutman and a local deputy were pounding on Adam's door. His neighbors heard the boom of his warning shot and came running. The cry of "slave catchers!" was shouted through the streets of Marshall. Soon over 100 people surrounded the Crosswhite home.

Words and threats were yelled back and forth. Francis Troutman began to demand that people in the crowd give him their names. They were proud to tell him who they were and sometimes even told him the correct spelling. Each name was written down into a little book. Finally, the deputy sheriff, swayed by the crowd's opinion, decided he should arrest the men from Kentucky instead of the Crosswhites.

The slave catchers were charged with breaking and entering, assault and battery, and illegal possession of firearms. Everything was done strictly according to Michigan law. By the time the slave catchers could post bond and get out of jail, the Crosswhites were on their way to Canada. But the story does not end here.

A Case in the Court

The Giltners went to the federal court in Detroit. They sued the crowd from Marshall for damages. Since they had many of their names it was easy to decide whom to sue. They wanted to be paid the value of the Crosswhite family. They believed the law treated slaves just like any other property. The Giltners felt their property, the slaves, had been stolen.

July 21, 1848, was the fateful day in court. The Giltners were sure they would win. Fortunately, the jury had different ideas and would not make a verdict one way or the other. The men from Kentucky had to go home empty-handed. But they were determined to be paid for the value of their slaves.

The Giltners were neighbors of Senator Henry Clay. There was some lobbying in Washington because many believed the slave owners had been mistreated in Marshall and in court. Even some people in the North, like Lewis Cass, thought it would be better to keep peace with those in the South. These Northerners did not like slavery but felt it was more important to keep the North and the South from splitting apart.

The Verdict Hurts

Finally, the Giltners had a second trial with a United States Supreme Court judge brought to Michigan to take charge. A specially chosen jury said the Giltners should recover what the Crosswhites would have sold for in a slave auction. To keep the citizens of Marshall from having to pay, Zachariah Chandler, a prominent Michigan abolitionist, helped raise the $1,925.

The Crosswhite case and others like it received national attention. Southern slave owners began to demand their rights. Senator Henry Clay of Kentucky denounced Michigan as a "hotbed of radicals and renegades." More trouble was brewing....

She Spoke the Truth— Isabella Baumfree

Elizabeth Chandler wrote about a black woman whose child was sold as a slave. She wrote about the pain and agony but Isabella Baumfree *felt it*! Her son Peter was sold as a slave and taken to Alabama.

Isabella was born in 1797 in New York state where she was a slave. She knew the humiliation of being sold along with sheep when she was a young girl. New York passed a law which would free the slaves by 1827, though the black children would have to continue working until they were adults. Her master promised to free her a year early, but decided she was such a good worker he just couldn't do it. He said she worked more than any man because Isabella would do laundry at night and be ready to go out into the fields in the morning.

Isabella was a strong, proud, six-foot tall woman who took matters into her own hands. In 1826 she gathered up her belongings and left with her youngest

Sojourner Truth. (Courtesy Michigan State Archives)

against slavery and for the equality of women. When she began speaking, Isabella changed her name to Sojourner Truth. She said that God had sent her on a sojourn or trip for the truth. Through her travels she met many great women of that time: Susan B. Anthony, Lucretia Mott, Elizabeth Cady Stanton, Lucinda Stone, and Harriet Beecher Stowe. She wrote several songs. Here are some of the words to one:

> I am pleading for my people—
> A poor, down-trodden race,
> Who dwell in freedom's boasted land
> With no abiding place.

> I am pleading that my people
> May have their rights restored,
> For they have long been toiling
> And yet have no reward.

In the 1850s, Sojourner Truth came to Battle Creek where she began to work with the Underground Railroad. But she continued to earn her living doing housework.

During the Civil War Sojourner Truth visited the black soldiers at Detroit. On October 29, 1864, she talked with Abraham Lincoln at the White House. While in Washington, she helped at the Freedman's Hospital and worked to end discrimination on the streetcars in the city.

Sojourner Truth came home to Battle Creek in her old age and died in 1883. Born when our nation was young, Sojourner Truth saw many things during her life. She saw a new nation talk about freedom for all and lived to see a time when people began to believe in it. Her body is buried in the Battle Creek cemetery, but her spirit lives on.

daughter. A Quaker family took her in and paid her master money so he would quit bothering her.

Then, she discovered her son Peter was no longer at the old master's house. She was told the shocking news that he had been sold and taken into the deep South. It meant he would probably never be free. But Isabella was a fighter and went to court, finally winning his release.

Since New York was mostly Dutch at the time, Isabella did not learn English until she was 30 years old, but she was a powerful speaker in any language. Isabella became very religious over the years. In 1843 she started traveling throughout the North and speaking

Questions

1. What human rights struggle created conflict in Michigan and the whole nation from 1830-1865?

2. List five Michigan cities which were stations on the Michigan Central Line of the Underground Railroad.

3. Briefly tell what each of the following people did: Elizabeth Chandler, Laura Haviland, Sojourner Truth, and Erastus Hussey.

4. Write a short paragraph about the Adam Crosswhite case.

5. If you had lived in Michigan during the days of the Underground Railroad, how far would you have been willing to go to help the escaped slaves? Explain your reasons.

Chapter 8 Section 2

New Politics From the Wolverine State

Here are the key concepts you will find in this section:

Because people in Michigan and other northern states helped stop slave catchers from capturing escapees, national laws were passed to punish abolitionists who helped fugitive slaves.

The Republican party was formed in 1854 at Jackson, Michigan. This new party was against slavery and fought to change the new proslavery national laws. Abraham Lincoln was the first Republican president.

In 1859 John Brown, a radical antislavery leader, came to Detroit and asked people to lend support to his plans to give guns to slaves so they could revolt.

Lincoln's election in 1860 shocked the southern states. They began to leave the Union and formed the Confederate States of America.

Around this period, two inventors lived in Michigan. Thomas Edison lived in Port Huron and Elijah McCoy moved to Detroit.

Punish the Abolitionists

Because of the Crosswhite case and many others like it, Senator Clay from Kentucky pushed a new law through Congress in 1850. It was known as the Fugitive Slave Law. The new federal law was an outrage to many people in the North. It made it very risky for anyone to help an escaped slave. Heavy fines and penalties would be given to any member of the Underground Railroad who was caught.

Here are some sections of that law:

It shall be the duty of all marshals to obey and execute all warrants (for the arrest of escaped slaves)...should any marshal refuse...he shall, on conviction, be fined the sum of $1,000...should any fugitive escape...such marshal shall be liable for the full value...of said fugitive.

All good citizens are hereby *commanded* to aid and assist in the prompt and efficient execution of this law, whenever their services may be required....

In no trial shall the testimony of such alleged fugitive be admitted in evidence.

Any person...who shall harbor or conceal such a fugitive...shall be subject to a fine not exceeding $1,000 and imprisonment not exceeding six months....

State Laws Fight Back!

But the work of the "conductors" went on as usual and business even picked up. Some "conductors" were even free blacks, including William Lambert and George de Baptiste (bap TEEST) of Detroit.

The tempers of many in the northern states boiled over against the Fugitive Slave Law. By 1855, Michigan and several other states had passed Personal Liberty Acts. The antislavery leader Erastus Hussey introduced Michigan's version. These state laws were almost the exact opposite of the Fugitive Slave Law. Instead of fining people who helped the slaves hide, the fines were against those who chased them. Instead of keeping a slave from testifying, it was the former owner who could not testify.

Equal Treatment Still Hard to Find

In spite of the fact that many in Michigan were against slavery, they were not always ready to admit that blacks and whites were really equal. At that time only white men could vote. In 1843 a convention of Michigan blacks demanded the right to vote, saying it was their right under the U.S. Constitution.

In 1850, Michigan made a new state constitution and the issue of allowing blacks to vote was considered but not included. The new constitution went so far as to allow those whites born in other countries to vote if they said they would become citizens. Also, male Native Americans could vote if they gave up loyalty to their tribe. The issue of allowing black men to vote did go on the state ballot in 1850 but was defeated.

Trouble in the West

By the mid-1850s, the nation was losing any idea of compromise about slavery. People were either completely against slavery or completely for it. In 1854 Congress passed the Kansas-Nebraska Act. That law formed the Kansas Territory and said the people there would decide whether they wanted slavery or not.

Soon settlers from both the North and South were rushing to Kansas so they could vote their preference. Fighting began between groups who were for slavery and groups who were against it. Many people were killed and the new territory was nicknamed "Bleeding Kansas." One Kansas abolitionist took the law into his own hands. His name was John Brown. Brown took revenge for the killing of some antislavery people by killing a group of proslavery supporters. Within three years, John Brown was in Michigan trying to find backers for a bigger plan of his.

The Birth of a New Political Party

Meanwhile the two major political parties, the Whigs and the Democrats, were coming unglued. Each party became divided into groups which were proslavery or antislavery. People who were strongly antislavery were not satisfied with either party. They thought too many compromises were being made to keep the Southerners happy. Some of these people began to form new political parties which were against slavery.

In 1854 a small group gathered in a meeting house in Ripon, Wisconsin. They were thinking about starting another antislavery party. The editor of the *Detroit Tribune* also called for a meeting with people from all parties to support a new political group. On July 6, 1854, supporters poured into Jackson to organize and make a list of candidates for office. The meeting in Jackson was so large there wasn't enough room in any building to hold all of the people. They met under the oak trees on Morgan's Forty, a farm on the edge of town. The 1,500 people at the meeting decided to form the Republican party.

This plaque marks the spot where the Republican Party was organized in Jackson. (Courtesy Michigan State Archives)

They chose the name because they felt republican meant having personal freedom where each person was on an equal level. Gathered around a small table, the leaders decided the party was going to call for the repeal of the Fugitive Slave Law and the Kansas-Nebraska Act. Some delegates also wanted to call for the complete end of slavery in the entire country, but they were outvoted. The Republicans decided on a ticket of men who would run for state offices in Michigan. Kinsley Bingham was nominated to run for governor.

Not Everyone Is Excited

Though many people in Michigan were strongly against slavery, the new party was ridiculed. The *Detroit Free Press* (July 8, 1854) said the men on the Republican ticket were not qualified to

hold office and that Bingham was dishonest. The newspaper felt the Fugitive Slave Law was following the ideas in the United States Constitution, the supreme law of the land.

The editors of the *Free Press* must have been among the many who were surprised when Bingham was elected governor and the Republicans also won control of the Michigan legislature.

A Visitor Who Becomes Famous

Other Republican meetings took place around Michigan. On August 27, 1856, a tall, slender lawyer from Illinois was invited to speak at a Kalamazoo meeting. Zachariah Chandler, the

Zachariah Chandler, a powerful U.S. senator, controlled the Michigan Republican Party much of the time from 1835 to 1860. (Courtesy Michigan State Archives)

Detroit Free Press

OFFICIAL PAPER OF THE CITY

SATURDAY MORNING JULY 8, 1854

THE FUSION TICKET

The abolitionists had it their own way at Jackson, and they drove with a tight rein. They not only constructed a platform after their own notions of architecture, containing all the antislavery planks, but they made such a ticket as pleased

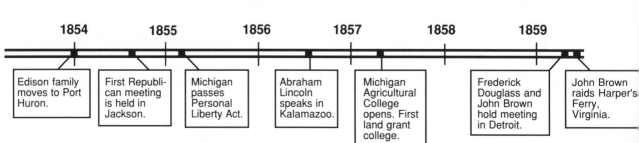

1854	1855	1856	1857	1858	1859
Edison family moves to Port Huron.	First Republican meeting is held in Jackson.	Michigan passes Personal Liberty Act.	Abraham Lincoln speaks in Kalamazoo.	Michigan Agricultural College opens. First land grant college.	Frederick Douglass and John Brown hold meeting in Detroit.	John Brown raids Harper's Ferry, Virginia.

prominent abolitionist and a Republican leader, was really quite disgusted with the fellow because he just did not speak out strongly enough against slavery. Who was the lawyer from Illinois? He was none other than Abraham Lincoln!

Republicans Have a Great Impact

The new party grew stronger and stronger. In 1857 the state legislature chose Zachariah Chandler as U.S. Senator. In 1859 another Republican was elected governor and Bingham became the other senator from Michigan. Chandler was in charge of the Republican party for most of its first 25 years and was responsible for forming many of its policies.

The Republican party had a great impact on Michigan and the United States. Up to that time, Michigan Democrats had won every election for governor except one. Then the tables turned. Michigan had all Republican governors except for three terms during the next 78 years! On the national level, the Republicans won the next 14 out of 18 elections for president. It wasn't until

1932 that the power of the Republicans began to fall in a serious way.

A Dangerous and Bloody Plan

Most abolitionists were against doing violent acts, but some were more radical. One of the most radical visited Detroit in the spring of 1859. He was John Brown, recently from Kansas.

The great black antislavery speaker Frederick Douglass came to Detroit and gave a lecture on the night of March 12, 1859. Sitting in the audience was Brown. He was an older man with a long white beard who had just helped 14 slaves reach Canada on the Underground Railroad. And Brown had a plan to free slaves— all the slaves!

Later that night, Brown, Douglass, and several other Detroiters, including William Lambert and George de Baptiste, met in the the two-story home of William Webb on East Congress Street. Brown had to be careful because the president of the United States had put up a reward of $250 for his arrest. All must have been in a hush when Brown began to tell what he was going to do. He

William Lambert, whose name can be pronounced LAN bear. (Detroit Plaindealer)

John Brown met at this house in Detroit to gain the support of abolitionists for his planned attack on Harpers Ferry. (Farmer's History of Detroit)

planned to have a group of blacks and whites go with him to the federal arsenal at Harpers Ferry, Virginia. They would overpower the guards at the arsenal and take it over. Then they would spread the word for all nearby slaves to flee their masters and come to the arsenal and take the guns and ammunition stored there. Brown's goal was to have an army of slaves march against the South. He hoped to get advice, money, and support from the people of Detroit.

Frederick Douglass immediately realized that Brown's idea was reckless and certain to fail. What would happen if the U.S. Army came after him? Others voiced some lukewarm support and said they would try to find some blacks in Canada who might want to help.

A few months later, telegraph lines all over the country were buzzing with news about an attack at Harpers Ferry on October 16. But it was a disaster. Brown and his men had no trouble in taking the arsenal, but the town's people soon surrounded it and poured in rifle fire until the regular army arrived. Soldiers under U.S. Army Colonel Robert E. Lee quickly broke down a door and captured Brown. Seventeen lives, including two of Brown's sons, had been lost.

John Brown was convicted and hanged. Here is what the December 3, 1859, *Detroit Advertiser and Tribune* said about Brown:

Some spoke harshly of the old man, but the majority expressed an undisguised sympathy for him.... He was misguided, and died for his own criminal folly...but in his own idea he gave his life for the freedom of the black slave.

The Republicans go to Washington
The nation hardly had time to recover from the shock of the raid at Harpers Ferry before it was time for the presidential election of 1860. The Republicans had nominated Abraham Lincoln. The Democrats nominated Stephen Douglas. By that time the country was already so divided that Lincoln was not even on the ballot in 10 southern states. Still, Lincoln won the election. And Austin Blair was the new Republican governor of Michigan. After the election, most people in the South were quite alarmed. The nation had a new president— a man whose name had not even been on their ballots. They had not been allowed to vote neither for nor against him! The southern states felt they had lost control of the political process.

Many states in the South were wanting to *secede* (suh SEED) from the Union. *To secede is to pull out or withdraw from some organization or group.* Before Lincoln had been sworn into office, Lewis Cass resigned his post as secretary of state because President Buchanan refused to force all the states to stay together. By February 1861, seven southern states said they were no longer a part of the United States. They even set up their own government. Soon, more states followed. Jefferson Davis, the former U.S. secretary of war became president for the new group. The group or confederation of states, called itself the Confederate States of America. The slavery issue had finally torn the country in two.

Young Thomas Edison. (Art by George Rasmussen)

Edison Grows up in Michigan

What else was taking place in Michigan during the years just before the Civil War? Two young men with inventive minds were thinking about ways to make new things.

When you get up in the middle of the night and reach for a light switch instead of a match and a kerosene lamp, you can thank Thomas Edison who grew up in Port Huron. When he was seven, Edison moved from Ohio to Port Huron with his parents. That was in 1854. His father started a feed and grain business in that city. It was in Port Huron that Thomas Edison got his start on the road to many scientific discoveries. Edison's life was shaped by events which happened in Michigan.

Thomas Edison grew up to become one of America's greatest inventors. In order to accomplish that, he had to overcome two significant problems. To begin with, he had almost no regular education. Edison started school late because of poor health. After a mere three months in a one-room school, his teacher ruled that he was too addled and confused to be taught anything. From then on, it was up to his mother to educate Tom. Soon he was reading every book in the house and doing chemistry experiments in the basement!

The other problem was Edison's hearing. By the time he had made his inventions of the light bulb, sound recording, and moving pictures he was nearly deaf.

In 1859, Port Huron was buzzing with excitement because the railroad line from Detroit was coming to town. Twelve-year-old Edison overheard some railroad officials talking about the need for a boy to sell newspapers, candy, and peanuts to the passengers. He walked up to the men and boldly asked "How would I do?" He got the job on the train to and from Detroit. The next stage of Edison's education began while he had eight hours to kill each day in Detroit waiting for the train back home. He saw a sign for the Detroit Free Library and made up his mind to read every book in the place.

After going through a few shelves of books, Edison decided to concentrate on those about science.

He discovered he couldn't do many experiments as he was away from home all day. To remedy that, he set up his lab in the corner of the baggage car.

On an August day in 1862, Edison was waiting for a train at the Mt. Clemens station. An engine was moving some freight cars toward the station when he noticed the station agent's little boy playing in the gravel— right between the tracks! Edison made a mad dash and grabbed him when the train was so close it knocked off the heel of Edison's shoe. The grateful agent offered to teach Tom all about being a telegraph operator. Edison spent many hours at Mt. Clemens learning to use the telegraph key and to read Morse code.

One night as the train was leaving Fraser, Michigan, Edison did not hear the conductor call out, "All Aboard!" Tom ran to catch the moving train. In a desperate grasp he caught hold of the handrail on the last car but didn't have the strength to pull himself up. He was dragged along behind the train as it went faster and faster. The brakeman grabbed Edison by the neck trying to save him, but his hands slipped and he got his ears instead. Edison felt something in his ears snap, and he began to grow deaf from that day on. His life was saved, but he eventually lost his hearing!

A few weeks later Edison's career on the railroad ended. The train hit some rough tracks and knocked over his chemicals. The baggage car caught fire, and the conductor had to help him put it out. The conductor was so mad at Edison that he threw him and all of his equipment off the train!

Edison continued to work as a telegraph operator with the railroad. He left Port Huron and went to his first job at Adrian. For some time he moved from city to city, but after a while Edison found work in the East. In 1869 Thomas Edison sold his first real invention which was a new type of telegraph equipment. An invention he might not have made if he hadn't been taught morse code by the station agent in Mt. Clemens. He was paid $40,000 and that money got him started with full-time research.

Today, thousands of people visit one of Edison's labs which was moved from New Jersey to Greenfield Village in Dearborn. It was in that lab he developed the light bulb.

A Well-Oiled Machine...

Thomas Edison was not the only inventor to live in Michigan. Elijah McCoy was behind the well-known phrase, "Is that the real McCoy?" Elijah McCoy was a black man, the son of slaves who had escaped to Canada on the underground railroad. After going to school in Canada, he spent five years in Scotland studying mechanical engineering.

When he was 21 years old he came to Michigan and moved to Ypsilanti, working as a fireman on Michigan Central Railroad engines. McCoy studied steam engines while he worked and soon developed ideas for improvements. His first major invention was a lubrication device for oiling moving parts on train engines. The lubricator was a great improvement over what had been used before, and was patented on July 23, 1872.

Other people quickly copied McCoy's idea, but often their lubricators did not work as well as the original. So engineers soon began asking, "Is that the real McCoy?"

During his career Elijah McCoy made 78 inventions and received 48 patents on various lubricating devices. His work was considered even more important as machines became a key part of an industrial America and those machines would not work properly unless they were well lubricated. Remember Elijah McCoy each February during Black History Month in Michigan.

Questions

1. Under the Fugitive Slave Law what kind of punishment could a person working with the Underground Railroad receive if convicted?

2. Exactly where and when did the Republican party first meet to organize and make a list of candidates for office? Why did people say the meeting was held "under the oaks?"

3. The first meeting of the Republicans called for the repeal of which two national laws? What did some people at the meeting want to do but found they were outvoted?

4. Explain what impact the Republican party had on the state of Michigan over the years.

5. If John Brown had told you about his plans to attack the government arsenal at Harpers Ferry, what advice would you have given him? Explain your reasons.

6. What was unusual about Thomas Edison's education? What did he spend his time doing while he waited for his train in Detroit? What heroic act did Edison do at Mt. Clemens?

7. Elijah McCoy was another inventor who lived in Michigan. What well-known phrase was associated with this man? What kind of things did he invent?

Chapter 8 Section 3

Michigan's Army Goes Off to War: 1861 - 1865

| *Here are the key concepts you will find in this section:* |

Once war started, Michigan's government worked rapidly to send volunteer soldiers to fight for the Union. They served with the infantry, cavalry, engineers, navy, and sharpshooters.

Soldiers from Michigan fought in many important battles, including Bull Run and Gettysburg.

Several people from Michigan became famous during the Civil War. One of the best known was George A. Custer.

No actual fighting took place in Michigan, but things were not always quiet. Detroit had two serious riots and there was a southern plot to take over the ship *U.S.S. Michigan* and free southern prisoners held on a Lake Erie island.

Michigan supplied large amounts of material to the North during the war. Seventy percent of the North's copper came from Michigan.

It Looks Like War!

At first, many in both the North and South hoped the division of the United States into two nations could take place peacefully. However, as each southern state seceded, it took over the federal forts and arsenals in its territory. President Lincoln believed this must stop. In his inaugural address he pledged to hold the property and places belonging to the government.

When Michigan's new governor, Austin Blair, was sworn in that same year, he proclaimed: "The Union must be preserved and the laws must be enforced in all parts of it at whatever cost.... Secession is a revolution, and revolution...is treason and must be treated as such...." Most people in Michigan were ready to fight to keep the southern states from leaving.

The tension between the two sides was broken when Confederate forces attacked Fort Sumter near Charleston, South Carolina. The fort was one of those belonging to the United States government. That blaze of Confederate

Austin Blair believed strongly in preserving the Union. As a result, the people of Michigan were the first to form an army to fight the Confederate forces. A statue of Blair still stands in front of the capitol building. (Courtesy Michigan State Archives)

cannon fire in the darkness of the early hours of April 12, 1861, began a great and terrible civil war.

They Were Not Ready

Neither side was prepared for war. The North had a regular army but it was not nearly large enough. President Lincoln immediately asked each state in the North to send volunteers to fight. At that time, states had a great deal more control over the army than they do today. Governor Blair was willing to send soldiers, but was not sure how to pay for the supplies and equipment which would be needed. The state had no money at that time. The governor and other state officials thought up an unusual emergency plan. They asked people to pledge their own money to back a loan. Right away the officials at the planning conference offered $23,000.

Volunteers Came

Men throughout the state were ready to fight. They felt it was their duty to preserve the Union. Each city or town formed local units and gave them distinguishing names. The Jackson Greys, Coldwater Light Artillery, Ypsilanti Light Guard, and the Manchester Union Guard were some of the units. Often, they also had their own colorful style of uniforms. All were preparing to join in a great adventure and put a stop to the southern rebellion. Each soldier was asked to serve for three months. Most people were sure the fighting would be over long before then.

Of course, very few of the new soldiers had any kind of military training. Commanding officers were usually chosen from each town's leading citizens. Governor Blair appointed the top commanders himself. Most of the units traveled to Fort Wayne in Detroit for some training. Many of the men found that practicing marches and drills was rather boring. Some complained when they did not get pie with supper!

The original group of 800 or so soldiers was given the official name "1st Michigan" and sent to Cleveland by ship. From Cleveland they traveled by train toward Washington. Many newspapers along the route exclaimed about the good appearance and fine equipment of the 1st Michigan.

At 10 o'clock on the night of May 16, 1861, the 1st Michigan marched down the streets of Washington, D.C. Abraham Lincoln is said to have remarked: "Thank God for Michigan!" He was relieved to see troops willing to serve from the western states.

Michigan Soldiers Were There in the Beginning

People still thought that the war would be over as soon as the Union troops marched south and thumped the Southerners. Richmond, Virginia, was the Union target. In July the soldiers of the 1st Michigan met the enemy near a little creek called Bull Run. It was the opportunity for which the Union forces had been waiting. A swift victory might end the rebellion.

On that hot summer day the 1st Michigan saw action with the enemy for the first time. They had to load their single shot muskets and take aim at another human being. They smelled the burnt gunpowder and heard the cries of the wounded. They faced the whistling cannon balls and the gleaming, sharp Confederate bayonets. War was not as easy as they had been led to believe.

They felt the earth vibrate with the hooves of J.E.B. Stuart's Confederate cavalry who surprised them from the rear. When the dust had settled after the day's fight, the 1st Michigan found six of their men were dead, 37 were wounded, and 70 had been captured, including their commanding officer. The dazed survivors straggled back to Washington, walking more than 60 miles in 24 hours without food or sleep. Detroit and the North were shocked. The *Detroit Free Press* said: "We are beaten; it is a defeat and a rout." It seemed certain there would be no quick Union victory. And indeed the Civil War would continue until 1865.

The Civil War was a violent and bloody conflict. This sketch shows Custer's cavalry in a skirmish at Culpepper Court House, Virginia. (Sketch by Edwin Forbes, courtesy Library of Congress)

Cavalry from Grand Rapids

Later that fall, 1,163 men joined the 2nd Michigan Volunteer Cavalry at Grand Rapids. They were one of the few units outfitted with Colt repeating rifles. Captain Russell Alger rode with the 2nd. He would become governor of Michigan after the war.

The Grand Rapids soldiers went south down the Mississippi River and were soon deep in Rebel country. During that time Governor Blair visited the soldiers and, at Captain Alger's suggestion, agreed to put Philip Sheridan in charge. Sheridan was a regular army officer who was not from Michigan. Under Sheridan's leadership the 2nd Michigan reached Booneville, Mississippi. Then, on July 1, 1862, the Confederates sent 6,000 troops to wipe out Sheridan's unit of about 800!

As soon as Sheridan realized the situation, he sent a telegram to the main Union force asking for help. But, it was too far away to come to the rescue. The Confederates were confident as they marched forward. They came in hard. Suddenly the 2nd Michigan let loose with their repeating rifles. The Southerners had never faced such a withering fire. It was hair-raising.

Sheridan then told Captain Alger to take a group of cavalry around behind the enemy and to charge in fast, yelling all the way. He did as commanded. Alger might have been the hero of the battle except, in the excitement of the charge, he rode into a tree and was knocked out! The cavalry went on without him and succeeded in driving off the Confederate soldiers. The 2nd Michigan was saved from destruction by their rifles and Sheridan's good tactics.

Trouble at Home

At home in Michigan, many people were upset with the hardships the Civil

War was causing. Lots of items were in short supply. Prices, it seemed, were always going up. Women and old men had to do work which the soldiers would have done if they had been home.

To encourage more men to join the army, a rally was planned in Detroit. The speakers were all leading Michiganians, including Lewis Cass who was now 80 years old. Eber B. Ward, one of Detroit's richest businessmen, also came to speak.

Lewis Cass supported the Civil War and spoke strongly in favor of more men volunteering to fight. (Courtesy Michigan State Archives)

After the speeches started, a few people in the crowd began to shout "Bull Run" "Bull Run." People in the North felt Bull Run was a stinging defeat and the war was becoming hopeless. Perhaps some felt Eber Ward and others were becoming rich from war profits. Also, there had been talk of forcing men to fight by drafting them. Soon the crowd became nasty. When Eber Ward tried to speak, they yelled "Kill him!" The speakers were chased into a nearby hotel. The crowd had become a mob and would have followed right on in except for the sheriff. He stopped in the doorway, pulled out his pistol and invited them to "come on."

It was a bad riot. But next March Detroit had a race riot which was much worse. On March 6, 1863, a mob came after a black man. He had been convicted of a crime and soldiers were acting as a guard, taking him from the courthouse to the jail. Along the way, the mob began to throw bricks and stones at the man and the guards. After a time of this abuse the soldiers fired their rifles into the mob. Unfortunately an innocent bystander was killed. The mob went wild and turned on the black section of town. The riot went into the night. Before it was over, 30 to 35 buildings had been set on fire and a number of blacks had fled the city by crossing the river into Canada. Afterwards, many in Detroit were ashamed of what happened.

Turned Down At First

Even though one of the reasons for the Civil War was to stop slavery, black men were not allowed to join the Union army at first. Some tried to enlist but they were turned down. It wasn't until 1863 that black units were formed in Michigan. Blacks who were living in Canada came back so they could go into the army too. The black soldiers from Michigan fought bravely. Many times they faced greater risks because some Confederates would not take black prisoners alive. By the end of the war, over 1,600 men had fought in the black units from Michigan.

Some Native Americans also served from Michigan. Many of those were in Company K, First Michigan Sharpshooters.

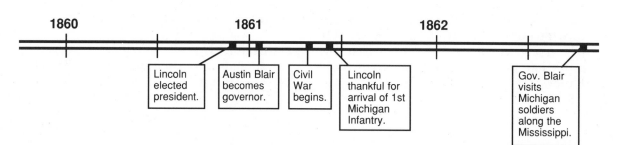

Kinchen Artis came to Michigan from Ohio. He served as a corporal in Company K, First Michigan Colored Regiment. (Courtesy Michigan State Archives)

Some Helped the South

The Civil War was a conflict which divided states, communities, and families. Even in Michigan there were those who favored the Confederate cause. Lt. Daniel Ruggles was once stationed at Fort Wilkins in the Upper Peninsula. Later he commanded a unit in the Confederate army. Emily Mason, a sister of Michigan's first governor was a close friend of the Confederate General Robert E. Lee. She worked hard to help southern soldiers in camps and in hospitals.

Helping the Sick & Wounded

The Red Cross had not been formed at the time of the Civil War. In its place, courageous and dedicated women helped in the Sanitary Commission. It was this commission that gathered food, blankets, books, and newspapers which were sent to the soldiers on the battle fields.

The more adventurous women actually went into the field as nurses. They helped with the gruesome task of aiding wounded soldiers. Julia Wheelock, Anna Etherage, Elmira Brainard, and "Michigan Bridget" Devins all worked in terrible conditions to do what they could for the wounded.

Anna Etherage was about 21 years old when the war began. She volunteered immediately in Detroit. It is hard for people today to realize what it must have been like to try to treat battlefield wounds with the crude equipment and lack of drugs during the Civil War. Women nurses were often ready and willing to run into battle to help the wounded. They had to be cool to do their work among the bursting shot and shell. Once Anna was bandaging the wounds of a soldier when he was torn to pieces by a cannonball! Many times bullets and shell fragments tore holes through her dress but somehow she was never injured. She was held in the highest regard by Union soldiers.

Elmira Brainard left Lapeer and served as a nurse with the 7th Michigan for some time. Later she worked with the Michigan Relief Association. The Association was much like the Sanitary Commission.

Besides wounds from battle, the Civil War nurses and doctors had to face a great deal of disease. For every four Michigan soldiers who died from wounds, 10 died from disease! One of Michigan's past governors, Moses Wisner, joined the army and then died of typhoid fever in 1864. One astonished soldier said, "We have lost about 30 by disease since the regiment was organized and have not lost one by the bullet."

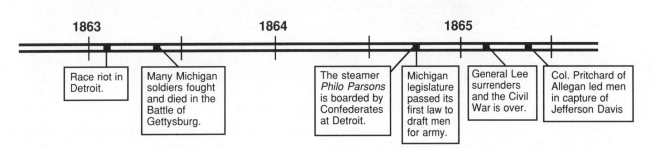

1863   1864   1865

Race riot in Detroit.

Many Michigan soldiers fought and died in the Battle of Gettysburg.

The steamer *Philo Parsons* is boarded by Confederates at Detroit.

Michigan legislature passed its first law to draft men for army.

General Lee surrenders and the Civil War is over.

Col. Pritchard of Allegan led men in capture of Jefferson Davis

186

A Most Unusual Soldier!

Not every woman involved in the war effort was a nurse. Michigan had at least one who enlisted in the army. Sara Emma Edmonds had been traveling around the country as a Bible salesman. Yes, salesman! She ran away from home in Canada and figured the only way she could earn a living was by pretending to be a man.

She was living in Michigan when the war started and she enlisted as a man. How she kept her secret is a mystery, but Sara served for two years as Franklin Thompson in the 2nd Michigan Infantry. At that time she was wounded and asked to be discharged. She was probably afraid of being discovered when she was treated. It is not clear

whether she actually got a medical discharge or left the army on her own. After the war, she wrote that she had also been a Union spy.

"Come On You Wolverines!"

George Armstrong Custer was one of the most controversial people to come out of the Civil War. He was born in Ohio and moved to Monroe, Michigan, a few years before the war began.

Custer was appointed to West Point Military Academy by Michigan Congressman John Bingham. Only three days after graduating from West Point, he found himself at the Battle of Bull Run. Almost immediately, Custer became known for his bold manner on the battlefield. He became valuable as a person who would risk anything to gather information for his commanding general. He went up in a newfangled contraption, the hydrogen-filled balloon, to watch enemy positions.

Sara Edmonds, the woman who disguised herself as a man and fought in the Union army. (Courtesy Michigan State Archives)

Custer's daring leadership in a cavalry charge led to his promotion to the rank of general. This was two days before the Battle of Gettysburg in Pennsylvania.

The battle on the rolling hills around the little village of Gettysburg was considered to be the turning point in the war. The Confederates considered it a daring advance into Union territory. At a critical moment, the Confederate cavalry planned a surprise charge into the back of the Union troops. It was at that moment when General Custer and Colonel Alger led their Michigan cavalry units out and into a countercharge against the Confederates. The Confederates did not know they were there.

Custer led his soldiers while waving his sword and shouting "Come on you Wolverines!" The cavalry charge by the two sides was an awesome affair. Six thousand Confederates commanded by J.E.B. Stuart faced 5,000 Union soldiers. The earth shook from the thousands of running horses and their thunderous noise rolled across the fields.

General George Custer, the well-known commander of a Michigan cavalry unit. (Courtesy Michigan State Archives)

Both sides claimed victory. But the result was that the Confederate's surprise attack was stopped. If it had succeeded, Gettysburg might have been a Confederates' victory instead of one for the Union side. It was probably the most important military action involving Michigan soldiers during the war.

What They Said About Him

In the years since, historians have made all kinds of comments about Custer. Much of what has been said focused on the death of Custer and all of his soldiers in the great battle with western Indians at Little Big Horn in 1876. But here are comments from two soldiers who knew him during the Civil War. James Kidd remarked:

He was not a reckless commander.... No man could have been more careful of the comfort and lives of his men. He was cautious and wary, accustomed to reconnoiter carefully.... More than once the Michigan brigade was saved from disaster by Custer's caution.

At the end of the war, General Philip Sheridan wrote to Mrs. Custer:

April 10, 1865

My Dear Madam,

I respectfully present to you the small writing table on which the conditions of surrender of the Confederate Army...were written by General Grant—and permit me to say...that there is scarcely an individual in our service who has contributed more to bring about this desirable result than your very gallant husband.

George Custer also had a younger brother. Tom Custer served in the Union army and was distinguished because he was the only soldier to receive two Congressional Medals of Honor.

George Custer and one of his other brothers owned a farm near Monroe but he spent very little time there. But many of his relatives lived in Monroe, and several men from the town died with Custer at Little Big Horn.

Secret Agents and a Dangerous Plot

No Confederate soldiers ever marched into Michigan during the war, but that was not because they didn't have plans to do so! Michigan was far away from the fighting but over 3,000 Confederate prisoners were held on Johnson Island in Lake Erie, just off the coast of Sandusky, Ohio. A plot was made by a group of Confederates to free the prisoners, give them guns, and have them attack cities along the Great Lakes. The Confederates also planned to take over the *U.S.S. Michigan*. Since the *Michigan* was the only armed American warship on the Great Lakes, it could have done much damage to shipping.

The Confederates sent Jacob Thompson as a secret agent, to Windsor, Canada. In Windsor, Thompson developed the plot and gathered others to help. There were two parts to his plan. A small group of agents were sent to Sandusky, Ohio, so they could become friendly with the officers on the *Michigan*. The warship was stationed there and it guarded the prison on Johnson Island. On a specific night, these Confederate agents would go aboard the ship with the excuse of having a party. They would give the

sailors on the *Michigan* drugged liquor and take over the ship once they had passed out.

The second part of the plan was to hijack the *Philo Parsons*, a steamship which made daily runs from Detroit stopping at Amherstburg, Canada, and the other islands near Johnson Island. Once the Southerners were in control of the *Parsons,* they would watch for a signal from the *Michigan*. When the signal was given, they would know the sailors were unconscious. The *Michigan* would be used to attack the prison and the *Parsons* would carry away the prisoners.

The action began a little after four o'clock in the afternoon of September 19, 1864. The *Philo Parsons* was in Lake Erie. A man burst into the pilot house with a pistol saying, "I am a Confederate officer. There are 30 of us, well-armed. I seize this boat and take you prisoner. You must pilot the boat as I direct you...."

Later, the *Parsons* approached the *Michigan* in the dark, looking for the signal. They waited and waited but it never came. The Canadians had kept a

The *Philo Parsons*. (Art by David McConnell)

close watch of what Jacob Thompson was up to and warned the U.S. government. Colonel Bennet Hill was a member of the Union army in charge of watching out for spies at Detroit. Colonel Hill also had an informer among the Confederate agents. Through the informer, Hill learned all about the Confederate plan. Colonel Hill had warned the *Michigan's* captain and he was ready. The *Parsons* had no cannon and they could not attack the *Michigan*. When no signal was seen, the Confederates knew something had gone wrong. They quickly sailed toward the Canadian shore where they escaped.

News of the adventure excited everyone up and down the Great Lakes. The thought of an invasion right in their backyard made the people of Michigan want to fight the South just that much more.

The Army & Michigan's Resources

The war effort increased the demand for many natural resources. The need for copper and iron went up. Copper was used to make military items from brass buttons to cannon barrels. Michigan iron went into steel for bayonets, swords, and guns. The North had been using cotton from the South but now almost all cotton supplies were cut off by the war so Michigan farmers helped by producing more wool.

The Hijacking of the *Philo Parsons*

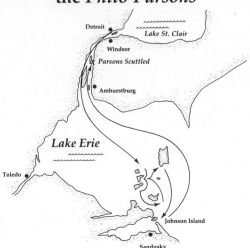

At first, it was hard to produce more with fewer workers. As a remedy, more labor-saving machinery was used in the mines, factories, and farms. Demand for new plows, reapers, mowers, and threshing machines increased.

Farmers and miners had the money to buy new equipment because the price of everything kept going up. Copper went from seventeen cents a pound to over forty-six cents. Wheat went from $0.64 to $1.84 a bushel. You can realize how expensive wheat was when you consider many people earned less than $2.00 for a day's work. Farmers, however, made more money than ever before.

Michigan provided the Union with wheat, wool, and nearly 70 percent of the copper used during the war. Manufacturing businesses increased during the war. There were nearly four times as many companies making things in 1870 as there were in 1860. It was the beginning of Michigan's change from a farm state into a manufacturing state.

The End In Sight

By 1865 there was little doubt the Union side would win the long and bloody war. The South just did not have as many men and resources as the North. General Robert E. Lee surrendered to General Ulysses S. Grant in the village of Appomattox Courthouse in April 1865. The Union army had beaten the Confederate forces. The Civil War was over and the country was united again. One soldier exclaimed, "Everyone is wild with joy. As for myself, I cannot write! I cannot talk; only my glad heart cries...." But it wasn't all over for Michigan soldiers quite yet. The Union army had not been able to find Jefferson Davis, the former Confederate president. It was Colonel Ben Pritchard of Allegan who lead the pursuit which finally captured Davis on May 11, 1865.

Shock and sorrow came over Michigan just three days after Lee's surrender when President Lincoln was shot and killed. The President was often affectionately known as Father Abraham in Michigan. Grown men were seen crying along the streets when they heard the news.

The Human Cost

Michigan soldiers came back home—the homes some had not seen for three or four years. And there were many who never came back. Over 4,100 were killed in battle or died from wounds and about 10,000 more died from disease. Michigan sent more than 90,000 men and at least one woman to fight and end the southern rebellion. All except about 5,000 had volunteered to go. Three times as many Michigan soldiers were in the infantry as were in the cavalry. Michiganians also served with the navy, engineers, artillery, and sharpshooters.

They came back to a state which had changed in many ways. Michigan was becoming an industrial state. Great demand would build up for the state's natural resources: its lumber, copper, and iron. Nature's storehouse was full and ready to be used in Michigan!

Questions

1. During the Civil War, each state had much more control over its soldiers than they have today. Give some examples to back up this fact.

2. What happened at the first battle of Bull Run? What did the *Detroit Free Press* say about the battle?

3. List three important people from Michigan who were involved in the war effort. Explain what each person did. Did some people from Michigan help the Confederate side?

4. Name what was probably the most important military action by Michigan soldiers during this war. Who was the person in charge of these troops?

5. How many Michigan soldiers fought in the Civil War? Compare how many of these died from wounds and how many died from disease?

6. What happened with the ship, *Philo Parsons*? Give details of this event. If the Confederates had been successful, how could this have caused problems in Michigan and on the Great Lakes?

9 WE TAKE FROM NATURE'S STOREHOUSE

Chapter 9 Section 1

Lumbering: Rugged People and the Smell of Sawdust

Here are the key concepts you will find in this section:

After the Civil War, Michigan became the number one lumber-producing state, because there were large amounts of white pine available to loggers.

Loggers used Michigan's rivers to float their wood to sawmills.

In the beginning, loggers used hand axes and just worked during the winter. But improved technology soon allowed them to work all year long.

No effort was made to plant new trees, to conserve the timber resources, or to stop wasteful logging practices. Now only a very few of Michigan's original pine trees are left.

Everyone Wanted Lumber!

One of Michigan's most exciting periods was the lumber era. In many ways it was like the Wild West, but there were rough and tumble loggers instead of cowboys. Soldiers came back from the Civil War battlefields. Most returned to their farms and were soon behind the plough. But some looked for work with more excitement and they found it in Michigan lumber camps.

Lumber, lumber—everyone wanted lumber after the Civil War. There was an enormous increase in the demand. It was needed to rebuild the war-damaged buildings and for new houses in fast-growing cities like Chicago. Michigan was growing fast too. The state's population increased almost 60 percent during the 1860s. For years, Maine and New York had been the leading lumbering states, but their supply of trees was shrinking.

A Land Thick with Trees

But Michigan had plenty of trees! There were vast forests which stood ready to be cut and made into boards. Several kinds of trees grew here, but the one the loggers wanted most was the white pine. It is now Michigan's state tree. The northern two-thirds of Michigan was covered by straight, majestic pines reaching well over 100 feet toward the sky. Some of the best trees reached 200 feet and were five to seven feet in diameter. These giants had been growing

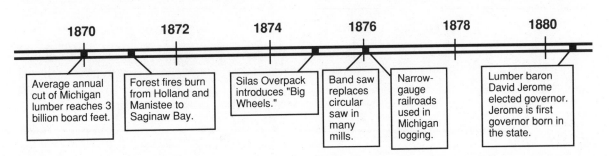

1870	1872	1874	1876	1878	1880

Average annual cut of Michigan lumber reaches 3 billion board feet.

Forest fires burn from Holland and Manistee to Saginaw Bay.

Silas Overpack introduces "Big Wheels."

Band saw replaces circular saw in many mills.

Narrow-gauge railroads used in Michigan logging.

Lumber baron David Jerome elected governor. Jerome is first governor born in the state.

These two Native Americans were cutting down huge white pines near Manistee about 1888. (Courtesy Michigan State Archives)

for 300 years. The cry of "Timberrr!" had been heard in the woods and forests since the first days of settlement. But Michigan's commercial lumbering did not start in a really big way until the 1840s and 1850s. After the Civil War it grew even faster. From 1860 to 1870 the number of workers in the lumbering industry went from about 7,000 to 20,000.

There were so many trees that many people thought it would be impossible to ever cut them all, but they were dead wrong. There is only one place where original trees were left standing in the Lower Peninsula. This is at Hartwick Pines State Park near Grayling. Many people will never have the chance to see the glory of one of these 200-foot giant white pines.

The Rivers Were Important

There were very few roads in the northern woods but Michigan's streams and rivers were just right for floating logs to the Great Lakes. Some of the great logging rivers were the Muskegon, Manistee, Au Sable, Tittabawassee, Menominee, Escanaba, and Manistique.

The biggest and finest examples of white pine were given the nickname of "cork pine" because they floated well in the water. Each spring rivers were filled with bobbing and swirling logs.

The Saginaw River Valley was the first main lumbering region and logging operations continued there until the 1900s. When lumbering was at its peak, there were 112 sawmills between Saginaw and Bay City! The other major

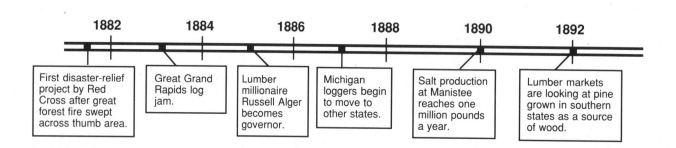

1882	1884	1886	1888	1890	1892
First disaster-relief project by Red Cross after great forest fire swept across thumb area.	Great Grand Rapids log jam.	Lumber millionaire Russell Alger becomes governor.	Michigan loggers begin to move to other states.	Salt production at Manistee reaches one million pounds a year.	Lumber markets are looking at pine grown in southern states as a source of wood.

lumber area was along the Muskegon River. Logging moved farther north and into the Upper Peninsula as the years passed. Nearly all cities and villages in the northern part of the Lower Peninsula and in the eastern end of the Upper Peninsula had their start during the lumber era.

A Winter's Work

In the earlier years, cutting and moving the trees was a winter job because it was easier to haul logs through the woods with snow or ice on the ground. The cut logs were hauled on horse-drawn or ox-drawn sleds.

Men left their families and friends and spent the winter months in the forests cutting the trees. They were called "shanty boys" because of the crude bunkhouses where they lived. Many of the loggers were immigrants. Some were from Sweden and others were born in Finland, Norway, or Canada.

The lumbering business was full of colorful people and unusual terms. Dynamite Jack, Chris Crosshaul, Cedar Root Charley, and Slabwood Johnson were just a few of the characters cutting down the pine. A shanty boy might have to "shoot a jam" or dynamite a log jam on a river. If the "shoot" did not go well, the shanty boy could find himself "taking a drink standing up," or, falling in the water. If he stayed too close to the explosion, he might go to "section 37," the place where good loggers went when they died!

A Day in the Life of a Shanty Boy

A typical day in the lumber camp began in the cold and dark before the sun was up. Teamsters drove sprinkler sleighs which held large tanks of water. The water sprinkled the sides of the trail and formed a slick coat of ice for the runners of the sleds which hauled the logs.

The camp cook, who might be a man or a woman, and the cook's helpers (cookees) began the big task of preparing breakfast. Bread, biscuits, cookies, and pies were put into the oven. Doughnuts were fried. Pancake batter was mixed and gravy put into the skillet. Gallons of

Good food and plenty of it provided the energy needed by the hard-working shanty boys who cut the lumber. The cooks along with their helpers called cookees, made meals of pork and beans, biscuits, pancakes with gravy or syrup and hot coffee on wood-burning stoves. (Courtesy Clarke Historical Library, Central Michigan University)

Lumber camps consisted of little more than crude log cabins and barns. This camp had a cook's cabin, men's cabin, barn and office. (Courtesy Michigan State Archives)

coffee and tea were brewed—all using the big woodburning stove.

The shanty boys were up and out of their bunks before daylight too. They gathered in the cookhouse and ate an enormous breakfast in silence. Talking was always forbidden while eating because of an old loggers' custom.

Once in the woods, the swampers would get the brush away from the bigger trees. The fellers used axes or long crosscut saws to cut down the trees. As soon as the mighty pines hit the ground, the swampers or limbers chopped off the small branches and buckers worked hard at sawing the trees into logs about 16 to 20 feet long.

At noon, a meal was brought out to the men. It was eaten right in the woods. The men worked until the sun started to go down. Then they heard the sound of the cook's "gabriel." The gabriel was a very long tin horn blown to bring the shanty boys back to camp. The tired, weary, and hungry men walked back ready to eat. After supper it was time to dry out their clothes and socks around the bunkhouse stove and then turn in early for a night's rest.

Time for a Story and a Shave

Saturday night was the time for relaxation and celebration because Sunday was their day off. Some shanty boys told tall tales about lumber legends such as the great Paul Bunyan and his blue ox, Babe. All loggers' tales were full of fantastic exaggeration. Paul Bunyan was just like other loggers only larger— 12 feet and 11 inches tall, weighing 888 pounds, without his socks! There were stories about other great shanty boys: Ole Olson, Whiskey Jack, and many more.

On Sunday the shanty boys had time to wash clothes and maybe have a shave or haircut. No doubt, time was taken to pick the "livestock" (bugs) out of their bedding. But the men could seldom leave camp until the end of the logging season.

The River Drive

By spring, each camp had carefully stacked thousands of logs at the rollway. The nearby rivers might have dozens of camps scattered along them.

All the logs were stamped on one end with a specific mark. The mark was like the brand used to identify cattle. Then, each lumber company could spot its own logs. But there were log "rustlers" and river thieves who pulled logs out of the river, cut the ends off and stamped them with their own log mark. When the logs arrived at the sawmill, the thieves were paid for them instead of the true owners.

The river drive was the next step in taking the logs to market. The drive was complex and dangerous. When all was ready and the water flowing fast from the spring snow melting, the logs were released. They rolled into the river with a thunderous splash! The men who worked on the river drive were called river hogs. They stood on the logs as the timber bobbed and weaved with the current. The rivers became a mass of moving logs. It took skill and luck to keep the thousands of logs moving down river. River hogs had to watch out for the beginning of logjams.

A logjam stopped everything from moving on the river. The tremendous weight of all the logs pushing down on a jam could make it seem as solid as concrete. There were several famous log

The final result of a winter spent logging was the spring log drive. One way to get the logs into the river was to use a slide like this one near the Big Manistee River. (Courtesy Michigan State Archives)

Log jams were dangerous and happened often. One of the biggest ever took place on the Grand River in 1883. When it finally broke free, it destroyed three iron railroad bridges in its path. (Courtesy Michigan State Archives)

The steam ship *Albert Soper*, and others like it, carried choice Michigan boards from sawmills to market along the Great Lakes. (Courtesy the Library of Congress)

jams. A granddaddy of all jams took place in Grand Rapids in July 1883. The whole river was blocked back for seven miles! When the jam broke free, a sea of logs, estimated at 100 million board feet, moved down the river, sweeping bridges and everything else out of its path.

At the end of the river drive millions of logs came floating into the ponds by the sawmills. There, boom companies sorted logs by looking at the log marks. Booms were a kind of floating fence and they were used to keep the logs from each logging operation separated. Sometimes the logs would be taken directly to market before they were cut by the mill. In 1873 a raft of logs 2,000 feet by 70 feet, containing about 1 million board feet, was towed from the Pere Marquette River to Chicago.

Mountains of Sawdust

What was a sawmill really like? The first ones were powered by water, much like a gristmill. By the 1870s, most mills were using steam engines to run their equipment. They were also using large circular saw blades, 50 inches or more across. The logs were pushed into the blade and one board was cut off with each pass.

A small mill was one cutting 10 million board feet or less each year. A big mill might cut four times as much wood. The John McGraw & Company mill in Bay City was just such a large mill. In that sawmill 350 men earned a living. They were paid $30 to $50 a month, about twice what a shanty boy made. They worked 11 hours a day, six days a week.

After the wood had been cut, it was placed into neat stacks to "season." The seasoned boards were less likely to warp and change their shape. Much of the finished lumber was put aboard ships and transported on the Great Lakes.

The mills ran day and night. The mill owners used their inventiveness so that nothing was wasted; any steam left over from the boilers was used to dry lumber. All the scrap wood went into the fireboxes to heat the boilers and make

The circular saw cut one board at a time which made slow work of sawing so many logs. Later it was replaced by gang saws which could cut a whole log into boards in one pass. (Courtesy Michigan State Archives)

the steam. Several mills had salt brine wells nearby and used their steam to evaporate the brine. By doing that, they also had salt to sell.

New Ways to Work Faster

Improved technology helped loggers to do the impossible task of cutting down almost all of Michigan's pine. The

Silas Overpack's invention of big wheels made it possible to haul logs in the summer when sleds could not be used. The logs were chained to the axle between the wheels and lifted off the ground. (Courtesy Michigan State Archives)

Michigan ax was developed early. It had two blades instead of one and helped the fellers do more work. In the 1870s the ax was replaced by the two-man crosscut saw. Early saws did not work well to cut thick trees because their blades became clogged with sawdust. The simple addition of shorter teeth, called raker teeth, pushed the sawdust out.

At the sawmill, circular blades were replaced by band blades, which were like a ribbon of steel. Gang saws were also introduced. Each gang saw had many blades, sometimes up to 40. In a gang saw, two or three whole logs could be sliced up in a single pass.

Big Wheels Overpack

Silas Overpack was not even in the lumber business but he was the fellow who made it possible to log the whole year round. Overpack made wagons in Manistee. One day a farmer came to him and said he was trying to clear the trees from his farm. It was a hard job to move them over the rough ground. He asked

Overpack to build him the largest set of wooden wagon wheels he could. The farmer used the wheels successfully to haul his logs. Overpack made his wheels nine to ten feet tall, and soon began to market the idea of using them to the loggers. Big wheels made in Manistee were shipped to every lumbering area in America for 50 years. Using Overpack's wheels pulled by horses or oxen, logs could be hauled over the bumpy ground in the woods without a sled. The logs were chained to the single axle and lifted up under the axle when it was hitched to the animals.

The Little Engine That Could

Rivers were the key routes used by loggers to take the wood from the forests. The more trees the shanty boys cut and the bigger the lumbering industry became, the less wood remained near any large river. The loggers had to move the logs farther and farther to reach a river.

In 1876 Winfield Scott Gerrish, a logger from Clare, Michigan, saw a small

These people are riding a train pulled by a Shay narrow gauge engine near Harbor Springs. The ease of laying tracks for this type of train opened lumber areas far from rivers. (Courtesy the Library of Congress)

narrow-gauge locomotive at the Philadelphia Exposition. Narrow-gauge trains use narrower track than trains use today. Right away he ordered a narrow-gauge train engine and had it shipped to Michigan. He built a short railroad and used it to haul logs all year and at much greater distances from the rivers.

Gerrish had some problems in using a locomotive on the flimsy tracks through the forests. Ephraim Shay came to the rescue. Shay moved to Harbor Springs, Michigan, from Ohio and was quite a

times they used their money to influence lawmakers in Lansing. Five lumber barons actually became governors. Henry Crapo, David Jerome, Josiah Begole, Russell Alger, and Aaron Bliss all served in the state's highest office.

David Ward was another of the great lumber barons. His uncle was Eber B. Ward of Detroit. David Ward began as a landlooker. It was his job to scout through the forests and find exceptional stands of pine which could be logged easily. Landlookers were usually paid a percentage of the value of the lumber which was sold.

Logmarks were registered and each county kept a file of those used in its area. Some loggers used more than one mark to identify their logs. Here are four examples used by C. F. Ruggles.

tinkerer. He decided to build a locomotive that could give better traction over the rails used by the loggers. His engines had gears on each wheel and the wheels were turned by an axle which went alongside the engine. Loggers called these little engines "side winders." The idea worked, and by the late 1880s Shay locomotives were used widely.

Lumber Barons — the Lucky Ones

The shanty boys did the hard work of cutting the trees but it was the owners of the lumber companies who frequently became rich. The wealthy owners were often known as "lumber barons." Many

It was in the landlooker's best interest to find good locations. David Ward did well and invested his earnings in timberland himself, becoming a millionaire.

Some lumbering greats started at the bottom and worked their way to the top. Charles Hackley, Perry Hannah, and Louis Sands were three who fit that description. Charles Hackley was just one of the 40 lumber millionaires living in Muskegon during the 1880s. He eventually owned railroads, ships, and much timberland outside of Michigan. Hackley worked hard to improve Muskegon and gave the city several million dollars for various projects. His house still stands in Muskegon and can be visited.

Louis Sands was born in Sweden; just as were many others in the lumbering business. He came to America trying to find a better way of life. Eventually he found work as a shanty boy in Michigan. He saved his money and finally had enough to buy his own timberland. Most of Sand's operations were near Manistee. Over the years, Sands earned a great deal of money and formed companies which provided Manistee with its electricity and gas.

The great Mr. Sands kept tight control of his camps. He was well-known for serving beans to his loggers. A song was even written about life in a Louis Sands lumber camp. Jim McGee was his foreman or "big push." Here are a few verses:

Who feeds us beans? Who feeds us tea?
Louis Sands and Jim McGee.
Who thinks that meat's a luxury ?
Louis Sands and Jim McGee.
We make the big trees fall ker-splash.
And hit the ground an awful smash!

And for the logs, who gets the cash?
Louis Sands and Jim McGee.

from *Lore of the Lumbercamps* by Earl C. Beck, University of Michigan.

Traverse City was another booming lumber town and it became the home of Perry Hannah. Hannah moved to Michigan when he was just 13 years old. He worked in the woods and became an office clerk with one of the lumber companies. He too started his own outfit, Hannah, Lay & Company. Hannah owned much land in Traverse City and also ran several other businesses.

Often lumber barons owned many different businesses which were related to timber in some way. There were factories which made wooden shingles, matches, toothpicks, and more. For many years there was a big demand for bark from hemlock trees to use in the tanning of leather. And large amounts of scrap wood were used to evaporate salt brine.

The removal of all the trees by loggers destroyed the ground cover. Without plants to hold the topsoil in place, wind and rain washed it away and the area was badly damaged by erosion. This photo shows cutover country in Clare County. (Courtesy Michigan State Archives)

Quick and Dirty

Certain lumber barons were known for their dishonest practices. Their real interest was to get the trees cut as fast as possible and they did not always care whose trees they were cutting. One technique was to go to the government land office and buy 40 acres, the smallest piece of land allowed. They would then hire loggers and tell them to "log round forty." That was understood by foremen to mean that they should cut down trees on the 40 acres and everything else nearby— 40 acres to the north, 40 acres to the south, east, and west!

Since the goal was to cut as much lumber as possible, few people paid much attention to what would happen to the land after the loggers were through and had moved on. No one took the time to replant new trees. Nor did the loggers leave enough trees standing to stop soil erosion from wind and rain. Loggers stopped paying taxes on many acres of land. Eventually, the state took the land back and some of it became Michigan state parks.

What Trees Meant to Michigan

Logging operations had a big impact on Michigan. From the end of the Civil War to 1900, the lumbering industry dominated Michigan's economy. During that time, about 160 billion board feet of pine were cut here. That was an awesome quantity of wood; it was enough to build 10 million six-room houses! Michigan produced more lumber than any other state from 1869 to 1899. The years of greatest production were the late 1880s.

The Michigan trees were called "green gold" by the loggers. The average wholesale price of 1,000 board feet of lumber was $13.00. Multiply that by the amount of wood cut, and you can see that wood worth over $2 billion was taken from Michigan forests during the peak lumbering days. It has been said that Michigan's green gold was worth more than all the gold taken from California during the same period.

Loggers and their improved technology stripped the pines from Michigan faster than any shanty boy ever thought possible. By 1905 the amount of trees cut in the Lower Peninsula had dropped drastically. Lumbering continued in the Upper Peninsula for several more years but the end was near. After the loggers were through, they left tens of thousands of acres of cutover country. There was land with stumps as far as you could see. It was land with very few trees growing, but with piles of slashings, brush, and wood waste left behind.

Stumps and Slashings as Far as You Could See

The cutover country became a problem. At first some lumber companies tried to sell it to potential farmers. Those people who tried to raise crops on the land soon discovered that it lost its minerals quickly and could not support farming.

Forest fires were a reminder of careless lumbering. With wood waste covering the land, fires burned thousands of acres and killed both people and animals. (Courtesy Michigan State Archives)

Incredible Fires!

The second problem for the cutover country was that of forest fires. The land was covered with large amounts of wood waste. When fires started, the results could be terrible. Michigan had many fires in the timberlands but two stand out. The summer of 1871 had been very dry. The country in and around Michigan was ready to go up with the smallest spark. Many people had a feeling of uneasiness for weeks. On Sunday October 8, 1871, a great fire started in Chicago and destroyed most of the city. The evening before, fires also started at several places in Wisconsin and Michigan. Some say campfires had been left by railroad workers near Escanaba. Perhaps some farmers had set fires trying to clear the slashings off their land.

The fires became so large the heat of the flames developed a wind which whipped the flames and pushed them along faster and faster. Here is what two people said about a fire near Menominee:

There was a roaring in the air and the sky was lighted up.... The smell of smoke was strong... The roaring became loud and the wind came in fierce hot gusts which fanned smoldering logs into flames.

People tried to protect themselves by going into the Menominee River.

The heat was so intense that the instant they rose out of the water, their clothes caught fire and when they inverted wooden buckets over their heads, the bottoms of the buckets would catch fire.... A bottle at the edge of the river melted and ran with a hiss into the water.

Holland, Michigan, was badly damaged by fire and so was Manistee. The fires which started in the western part of the Lower Peninsula burned across the state all the way to Lake Huron. Several towns were wiped out. Fire scorched 14,000 square miles in Michigan. Needless to say, many people died horrible deaths in the blaze.

Just 10 years later, on September 4, 1881, the thumb area of the Lower Peninsula was hit hard by another forest fire. A stiff wind picked up sparks from some fires started to clear land. Soon intense flames were racing across the thumb. People were burned trying to outrun the fire in their wagons. Others tried to escape by jumping in wells and rivers. Several villages were consumed by the fire. Four hundred people ran to the Bad Axe courthouse. It was the only brick building in town. In order to remain safe inside, the crowd had to pass buckets of water up to the roof and keep it damp.

After the fire, there was much concern for the well-being of those who had lost their homes and loved ones. That was the first disaster where the American Red Cross came to provide assistance.

Thinking it Over

Looking back at Michigan's famous lumber days, it was a time of colorful adventure. Many people became rich through logging, though most of the shanty boys spent their money without much thought for the future. Little attention was paid to the land after the trees were gone. Even though it has been nearly 100 years since logging stopped in some places, the giant trees have not returned. It may take another 100 years or more before that begins to happen.

Those Crazy Logging Words

Food, etc....

Blackjack— coffee
Morning glories— pancakes
Wanigan— a combination cookhouse and bunk house built on a raft and used during the river drive.

Jobs......

Buckers— those who cut trees into logs
Boss of the rob shop— camp clerk
Fellers— those who cut down the trees
Landlookers— those hired to find good land to log. Also called timber cruisers
River hogs— shanty boys who took the logs down the river
Scalers— those who measured the logs to decide how many board feet each contained

Swampers— those who cleared brush away
from the trees
Teamster— a wagon driver

Slang and Other Terms....
Board foot— the standard of measurement; a
piece one foot long, one foot wide and one
inch thick.
Boom— a kind of floating fence used to keep
the logs in the river separated
Boom company— a company that collected
and separated the logs at the end of a river
drive
Cutover country— land covered with stumps
after logging was finished
Daylight in the swamp— start of the work day
Livestock— body lice
Log mark— a unique mark hammered onto a
log to show ownership
River drive— floating logs down a river to the
sawmill

Rollway— the steep bank where logs were
stacked next to the river waiting for the
river drive.
Slashings— the branches, brush, and limbs left
over after logging

Tools......
Cant hook— a long pole with a sharp metal
hook on the end. They were used like
levers to move logs, especially to roll them
over.
Caulked boots— logger's boots with sharp
spikes on the bottom
Crosscut saw— a large saw, seven or eight feet
long, with handles on each end. It was used
by two loggers who pulled it back and forth.
Michigan ax— an early two sided ax
Misery whip— crosscut saw
Peavey— a pole much like a cant hook but
having a spike at the end

Questions

1. What were the years of greatest lumber production in Michigan?

2. How large were the tallest white pine trees cut by the early loggers? How long did it take for the trees to grow so big?

3. Name three of the great logging rivers used in Michigan. Tell where each one is located and into which Great Lake it empties. Why did loggers use the rivers?

4. Explain each of these logging terms: Board foot, cutover country, log mark, rollway, slashings, take a drink standing up.

5. What invention first made it possible to log the whole year round? What new idea allowed loggers to cut trees far away from rivers?

6. How did the state get much of the land which eventually became state parks and forests?

7. Explain how logging practices contributed to forest fires. Where and when were some of the worst forest fires in Michigan?

8. Design your own unique log mark and tell why you made it that way.

Chapter 9 Section 2

Copper and Iron by the Ton

> *Here are the key concepts you will find in this section:*

New discoveries of copper and the use of better mining equipment allowed Michigan to produce a large percentage of the nation's copper for many years.

Copper miners were provided with good benefits, but the work was dangerous and often in unsafe conditions.

In 1913 copper miners went on strike. The strike was long and tragic.

Railroads helped open new iron mining areas in the southern and western part of the Upper Peninsula.

Mining of both Michigan copper and iron declined over the years.

Fast Growth in Mining

Just as the lumber industry was being affected by new equipment and better ways of doing things, so were the iron and copper mines of the western Upper Peninsula. Early miners used picks and their own muscles to chip rock from beneath the ground. The story of those first mines was introduced in Chapter 7.

By the 1870s and 1880s, steam engines were compressing air to run heavy drills and hammers. Men were lowered deeper and deeper into the dark pits with contraptions called "man engines" and "man cars." Eventually, some of the mines went below 5,000 feet!

Rich, New Discoveries

Large new deposits of copper were found in the Keweenaw Peninsula near Houghton, Hancock, and Portage Lake. To make it easier to ship the copper, the lake was dredged and a canal was cut across the rest of the peninsula in 1873. When a person looks out over the canal today there is not much activity, perhaps a ship or seaplane leaving to take visitors to Isle Royale. But in the peak mining years over 1,000 ships passed along the canal each summer!

Miners working with new deposits had to have heavy equipment to crush the rock and smelters to melt and purify the metal. All of that machinery cost lots of money, but the investment was worth it. In 1871 the Calumet and Hecla, one of the newer mines near Portage Lake, produced over 10 times the amount produced by the Cliff Mine, the oldest copper mine in the Upper Peninsula.

"The most famous copper mine in the world!" is what they called the Calumet and Hecla. Just two years after it opened, it was producing 46 percent of Michigan's copper!

Many New Workers

With the great increase in mining came the need for more and more workers. The population of the mining towns

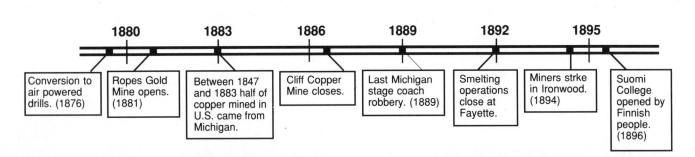

1880	1883	1886	1889	1892	1895
Conversion to air powered drills. (1876)	Ropes Gold Mine opens. (1881)	Between 1847 and 1883 half of copper mined in U.S. came from Michigan.	Cliff Copper Mine closes.	Last Michigan stage coach robbery. (1889)	Smelting operations close at Fayette.	Miners strke in Ironwood. (1894)	Suomi College opened by Finnish people. (1896)

grew rapidly. Houghton County had 88,000 people in 1910 and was the fourth largest county in Michigan! The large population and the money from mining allowed culture to reach the North Country. The city of Calumet even had its own opera house which attracted top actors from around the world.

People came from many places to work in the mines. In 1900, half of the people living in Houghton County were born in another country. Immigrants came from Canada, Cornwall (in England), Czechoslovakia, Finland, Germany, Italy, Norway, Poland, and Sweden. Large numbers arrived from Finland. They even started the only Finnish college in the United States—Suomi College (SUE owe mee). Suomi, located in Hancock, is still in business today as a two-year college.

The Cornish from Cornwall were very respected for their mining knowledge. Many of the mine captains, superintendents and shift bosses were Cornish. The Cornish also gave us the pasty (PASS tee)—a sort of meat pie made with potatoes, turnips, and onions. A pasty was the miner's "box lunch." The men carried them into the mines wrapped in newspaper.

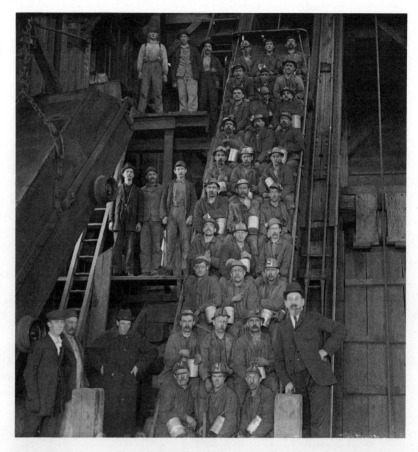

Man engines or man cars were like elevators which quickly raised and lowered workers into deep copper and iron mines. The cars were open and safety was not the greatest concern.(Courtesy MTU Archives and Copper Country Historical Collections, Michigan Technological University)

Profits Often Went Somewhere Else

Most of the profits from the lumber industry stayed in Michigan and were used to start other businesses in the state. On the other hand, most of the Michigan copper mines were owned by people in the eastern states. Because of that, a large part of the profits left Michigan and went to people in places like Boston. By 1909, the Calumet and Hecla had paid over $100 million dollars to stockholders. Just think, all of that money from mining came from the "frozen wasteland" traded for the Toledo Strip!

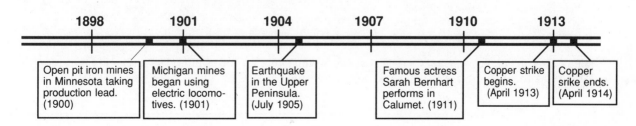

1898   1901   1904   1907   1910   1913

Open pit iron mines in Minnesota taking production lead. (1900)

Michigan mines began using electric locomotives. (1901)

Earthquake in the Upper Peninsula. (July 1905)

Famous actress Sarah Bernhart performs in Calumet. (1911)

Copper strike begins. (April 1913)

Copper srike ends. (April 1914)

Benefits for the Workers

Michigan's big copper mine owners respected their workers. They wanted to have a stable group of happy employees. Over 1,000 rental homes were built for the people who worked for the mines. Their homes were repaired free and the garbage hauled away by the company. Those workers who wanted to build their own houses could lease land for five dollars a year. The companies built schools, libraries, hospitals, and bath-houses. They also had medical and death benefits for the workers. In 1898 a local newspaper said "No mining company in the world treats its employees better than the Calumet and Hecla." In spite of these many benefits, being a miner was hard and dangerous.

But Dangerous Work !

Many miners were killed or perma-nently injured. Between 1855 and 1975, 2,000 miners died in Michigan copper mines. They were not all strong men; many young boys were given jobs in the mines. For their work they were paid half of a man's salary. Today, it is against the law to hire children in any industry.

The 1890 Report of the Mine Inspector for Houghton County listed this accident:

Accident 9.—Charles F. Carlson, John H. Sullivan, and a boy named Andrew Adamsky were at work in the...No. 4 shaft in the Osceola Mine.... They had drilled three holes...and had moved the drilling machine about 15 feet... with the intention of drilling more holes before blasting. They had with them...about eight pounds of dynamite and a full box of blasting caps. They were last seen...by a party of tram-mers (miners who load broken rock into cars and push the car to the central shaft) who left with a car of rock. An explosion occurred just as the trammers reached the shaft. What caused this explosion is not known, but it is supposed that fire dropped from a burning candle on the box of caps, which caused them to explode. An inquest was held before Justice Vivian and a verdict returned by the jury, "That the deceased parties were killed by an accidental explosion of eight pounds of dynamite and a box of blasting caps."

Mines were dangerous places. Cave-ins caused serious injuries and deaths. The timbers in this mine shaft have been partially crushed by the weight of the rock above them. (Courtesy Michigan State Archives)

A miner with a one-man drill.

Troubled Times at the Copper Mines

Changes were coming to Michigan's copper range. By 1913 a whole generation had lived in copper company houses, gone to company schools, and read books at the company library. Life was pretty good for the miners, considering the standards of the time. However, some people felt the company controlled everything; which in many ways it did.

Some miners talked about starting a union so they would only have to work eight hours a day instead of twelve. They also wanted to have a minimum wage. Miners in some western states had already started unions. Before long, Michigan copper miners started to join the Western Federation of Miners. In 1913 at least 9,000 belonged to the union.

The copper mining companies in Michigan were facing their own problems. New mines were producing copper in Montana and Arizona and doing it cheaper because they were open-pit mines working on the surface. How could the mines in Michigan compete? At that time, drill crews had two men. The mine owners felt the answer was to only have one miner work each drill.

One-Man Drill Means a Strike...

The miners were really upset over the new policy. They were afraid many men would lose their jobs. They were worried that miners might be injured and no one would know about it because each man was working alone.

July 23, 1913, a strike was called by the union against the Calumet and Hecla mine. Miners stood in picket lines around the entrances to the mine. Mine captains and supervisors crossed the picket lines because they felt they should keep working. The communities around the mines were divided by the strike. Were the miners right or wrong?

208

Governor Woodbridge Ferris sent the entire Michigan National Guard, about 2,500 men, to the Copper Country. Some people in the area sent telegrams and told the governor that the situation was desperate and that troops were needed. The sheriff did not think he could keep the peace. Closer to the truth, the company had hired professional strike breakers and there was fear they would stir up trouble with the miners.

The mine owners were stubborn and would not even talk to the striking miners about the issues. The owners blamed "outside agitators" for causing the strike. They meant the union organizers for the Western Federation of Mines.

Governor Ferris tried not to take sides. These are the thoughts which he wrote to his children after a visit to the strike area:

"The socialist press (radical newspapers in favor of the miners) in the Copper Country should be put out of business. It fans the flames of the basest (worst) and most brutal passions.

The mine owners are not angels. Too long they (the owners) have waited (to provide improved working conditions). Capital and labor should be twins— should co-operate....."

Bloodshed at Keweenaw

The situation got worse. Two miners were shot and killed. Also, 139 miners were arrested for picketing, but given a suspended sentence. The company started to throw striking miners out of their company-owned homes! Later, three strike breakers were cut down in a hail of gunfire. Then the worst event of the strike took place. As is often the case, it was the completely innocent who had to pay the price.

The Women's Auxiliary of the Western Federation union gave a Christmas party for some 600 miners' children and their mothers. The party was held on the second floor of the Italian Hall in Calumet. About halfway through the party someone shouted "Fire!" A mass of children tried to run down the stairs but the doors opened

Protesting miners during the 1913 copper strike; notice the sign which says "Something just as good. Miners ask for bread. Jim offers lead." What does lead mean here? (Courtesy MTU Archives and Copper Country Historical Collections, Michigan Technological University)

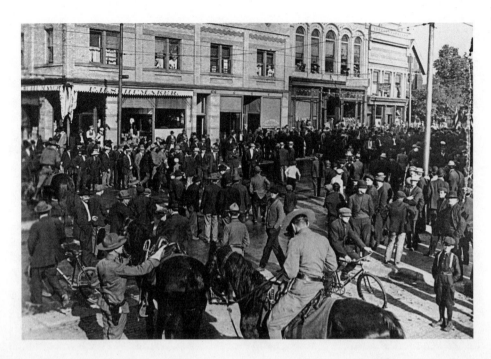

The National Guard was called in after the copper strike began. These soldiers had the unpleasant job of keeping order among the strikers. (Courtesy MTU Archives and Copper Country Historical Collections, Michigan Technological University)

toward the inside. No one could get out. Seventy-two women and children were crushed to death at the bottom of the stairs— and there never was a fire. No one ever found out who yelled the false alarm, but many people thought it was someone who was against the miners.

The Strike is Over

Finally, in April 1914, the long and tragic strike ended. The miners did not win much. An eight-hour day was the only demand met. The miners' union was broken and did not reorganize until 1943. Wages did not improve much for the copper miners; by 1919 they were paid an average of $3.76 a day, compared to $6.28 a day for iron miners. The 1913 copper strike took the spirit away from the copper industry in Michigan. Many people felt it was never quite the same afterwards.

Not Much Mining Now

Michigan copper mines have closed one by one. Today there is only a single copper mine still working in the state. It is the White Pine Mine in Ontonagon County. It too had been closed but was bought by the mine workers and reopened. About 850 people work at the mine today. The Keweenaw Peninsula still has plenty of copper, but most of it is too far below ground to mine at a profit.

Iron Mining Grows Too

Michigan iron mining began near Marquette. Later, new deposits were discovered farther south near the Menominee River. These deposits were not developed because it was impossible to take the iron ore anyplace where it could be used. Lack of a good way to move the ore to the Great Lakes stopped development of the iron range until the railroad arrived in 1878. The first railroad connected the mines to the port city of Escanaba.

In 1879 the largest known deposit of iron ore was found in the Menominee range at a place which came to be called Iron Mountain. The Chapin mine was built there.

The inside of a mine was dark and dirty. For many years miners depended only on candles for light, even while operating heavy equipment. (Courtesy Michigan State Archives)

This Mine is Wet!

The Chapin Mine had great potential but one big problem to overcome. Most of its ore was under a large swamp. Up to 3,000 gallons of water seeped into the mine each minute! To solve that problem, the owners built the largest steam-powered mine pump of its type ever constructed in America. The new pump could remove as much as four million gallons of water each day. It was given the nickname, the Cornish Pump, because it was like other pumps used in Cornwall, England. The enormous pump can still be seen by tourists.

Visit a Mine

What was it like to work in one of Michigan's mines? Charles Wright was the state official in charge of mineral statistics. This is what he saw standing in a large cavern deep inside the Chapin iron mine in 1877.

"Standing on the edge...we look downward and see here and there...the moving to and fro of the small lamps of the busy miners, whose forms are only dimly outlined by the feeble rays, making them appear more like evil spirits; an impression which is enhanced by the clanging of the drills and hammers, the heavy reports of the blasts (explosions to loosen rock), the rumbling of the skips (ore cars) moving up and down the shafts, and all these sounds echoed and re-echoed from invisible walls, pillars and roof, create in the mind an impression of awe and fear.

The Story of a Ghost Town—Fayette

Some mining companies sent their ore to steel mills along the southern Great Lakes, but a few continued to smelt their ore nearby. In order to smelt the iron ore and make pure iron, huge amounts of charcoal were used. The companies built their own furnaces to make the charcoal from hardwood trees.

The most famous operation to smelt iron and make charcoal was at Fayette on the Garden Peninsula. The Garden Peninsula was thick with the hardwoods needed for the charcoal operation. Fayette was a busy little community from 1867 until 1892. At that time the owners decided it was cheaper to ship the ore directly to steel mills in places like Gary, Indiana and Cleveland, Ohio. Fayette became a ghost town, which is now a state park and the only restored ghost town in Michigan.

More Iron Ore

Look at a map of the Upper Peninsula and you can see where the iron mines were. Each area has at least one town with "iron" in its name! The town of Iron Mountain grew up near the Chapin mine. In 1880 there were only 150 people in Iron Mountain, but by 1890 the population had jumped to 8,000. Other mines and towns started nearby. Norway, Michigan and the Norway mine are examples. Iron mines farther to the west were developed at about the same time. Around those mines grew the towns of Iron River and Crystal Falls in Iron County. (See color map page M4.)

As the railroad reached to the most western end of the Upper Peninsula, more iron ore deposits were explored.

Boomtowns sprouted up around a new iron range, the Gogebic (go GEE bik). It was the third major iron range in Michigan. Ironwood soon had 5,000 people, three newspapers, five schools, and 44 saloons! Other Gogebic Range mines were at Bessemer and Wakefield. All three of Michigan's iron ranges helped to make the state one of the leading iron ore producers from the 1880s until the early 1900s. It was then the open-pit mines were developed in Minnesota where the iron ore was near the surface.

Iron Mining Declines

These open-pit mines were much cheaper to run than the Michigan mines which were deep underground. Once the Minnesota iron mines opened, it was hard for Michigan miners to be competitive. As a result, iron mining has slowed down in Michigan. Several of the last mines closed in the 1960s and 1970s. Still, over the years, an incredible amount of iron ore has been mined in Michigan—in excess of 1 billion tons!

The wheelhouse of an iron mine. The heavy cables connect to the devices which raise and lower the miners and ore. (Courtesy Michigan State Archives)

The Copper and Iron Ranges in Michigan's Upper Peninsula

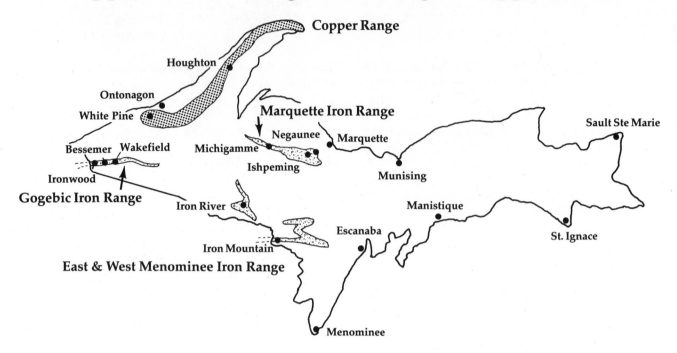

Now there are only two working iron mines—the Empire and the Tilden. Both are open-pit mines, just like the ones in Minnesota. These mines are both near Marquette and produce about 25 percent of the nation's iron ore. But, because they are expensive to operate, they may be forced to close at any time. A total of about 2,000 people work at the Empire and Tilden mines.

New Processes Help

The two open-pit mines near Marquette have been successful because they use new processes. These modern mines separate small particles of iron from powdered rock by mixing them with oil and soapy water. The iron particles float to the top with the soap bubbles. The process is called "flotation." The iron ore mined now is low grade ore and it must be concentrated before it can be used to make steel. As a part of the process, Michigan's ore is made into small pellets and baked at 2,400 degrees. These iron-ore pellets look like gray marbles. The pellets are taken by train to the ore dock at Marquette where they are poured into the holds of waiting Great Lakes freighters.

Gold in Michigan!

Copper and iron are not the only metals which have been mined in Michigan. In 1881, Julius Ropes opened a small gold mine north of Ishpeming. This mine has had its up and downs over the years. It remained closed for long periods of time. Today, the price of gold is high enough for the mine to make a profit and it is producing gold once more.

Questions

1. List all of the towns you can (mentioned in this section) which are connected with copper or iron mining in Michigan. Tell which mineral was mined at each place.

2. List three dangers which killed or injured Michigan miners. Give at least one idea which could have helped to prevent some of the deaths.

3. What caused the 1913 copper strike? In your opinion was the strike a victory for the miners or mine owners? Please give examples to support your thoughts.

4. What big problem had to be solved at the Chapin iron mine and what was done to solve it? What processes did the iron companies use at Fayette, Michigan?

5. What fact of geology makes it more expensive to operate mines in Michigan compared to those in some other places?

6. Use your imagination and the facts you have learned in this section to write a short story about a Michigan miner working underground.

Chapter 9 Section 3

A Farming Revolution: More Food for All

| Here are the key concepts you will find in this section: |

At one time, farming touched most people's lives in Michigan: 85 out of 100 people lived or worked on a farm.

At first, people farmed just to provide food for their families. During the 1860s and 1870s, farming began to change into a business.

Even by 1890 Michigan had very few good roads, so the railroads became an important way to ship food to market.

Farmers were able to grow more and more food because they had new sources of power on the farm, new farming equipment, and more available scientific information about agriculture.

Once, Most Lived on Farms

It is difficult for most young Michiganians to understand what it was like to live on a farm in the past, or even what it is like now. The reason for this is simple: only 1.5 percent of the population now earns a living by farming. Food is still very important to all of us but the golden age of agriculture is in the past. In the 1850s nearly 85 percent of Michigan's people depended on agriculture for their way of living. This section tells the story of the great growth of agriculture. More farms were started as the state's population grew. Each farmer was able to produce more food as the years passed.

The passing of the Homestead Act during the Civil War encouraged more people to try farming. That national law gave 160 acres of federal land to anyone who would build a house and live on the land for five years. In Michigan, 3 million acres were given to settlers under the Homestead Act.

How to Get the Food to Market?

It was the pioneer farmer who settled Michigan's countryside. The early farmers cleared a few acres and built a crude log cabin for shelter. The main purpose of the pioneer farm was to grow food for the family. If anything was left over, it could be sold. However, it was difficult to find someone who wanted to buy the extra food and to get the food to them.

Few Good Roads Then

Good roads are quite a recent development. Michigan only had 200 miles of paved roads as late as 1890! After the early problems created when state government went overboard trying to build canals and railroads, the constitution was changed so the state could not finance "internal improvements." Roads and highways were considered internal improvements. Therefore, state government could not build or take care of roads.

Any road work was the responsibility of the townships. Usually each farmer took care of the roads along his property. Sometimes, several farmers would get together and have a "road bee." They would all work together to fix some problem. Of course, they didn't necessarily have the right equipment to do road work. As a result of that approach, most roads were in poor condition.

Only 50 years after travelers were frustrated with terrible road conditions like these, Michigan had some of the best highways in the nation. (Courtesy Henry Ford Museum and Greenfield Village #833.80028)

Take the example of a certain wooden bridge over the Muskegon River. It had been built by John Fleming. Fleming felt he had done his duty to build the bridge in the first place, so he did nothing to keep it repaired. Neither did anyone else. In 1903, along came William Conn and his wife in their buggy. When they were halfway across the bridge, it collapsed! Down went the Conns. Down went their buggy. And down went their horses into eight feet of water! Everyone just shrugged their shoulders and shook their heads. What could they do?

More attention was given to better roads because new laws were passed. In 1893 counties were allowed to vote on whether to tax their citizens and hire professionals to take care of road work. Bicycles became quite popular about 1900. One bicycle rider was Horatio "Good Roads" Earle. He helped to get a constitutional amendment passed in 1905 so a state highway department could be formed.

Everyone Used Trains!

Farmers began producing extra food long before roads were improved. But farmers couldn't get their products to other communities without a lot of difficulty. With the development of the railroad, however, a farmer's goods could be easily shipped. Railroads were the first means of transportation which allowed farmers to reach many markets.

From the 1840s through the early 1900s, railroads tied together communities throughout the state. The lack of good roads meant that a train was almost the only way to travel between many places in Michigan, unless a Great Lakes ship was available.

Between 1860 and 1870 the amount of track in Michigan doubled, reaching over 1,600 miles. The early railroads followed the settlement of the state. The first lines were built in the south and, as time passed, new lines went farther north. It wasn't until the 1880s that railroads reached Mackinac City. Michigan state

Early railroads are best known for carrying passengers, but they were vital to farmers too. Their products could now be shipped to customers across the country. (Courtesy Michigan State University Archives and Historical Collections)

government promoted the building of new tracks by giving land to the railroad companies. Cities that did not have railroads were often desperate to attract one. Many times communities raised money to help pay for the building of a line to their location. By the 1890s more than 90 percent of the nation's freight and passengers were being moved by railroads.

Farming Becomes a Business

The ability to transport food by rail helped to change farming. So did the greater demand for food caused by the Civil War. Many farmers went off to fight and the ones left behind had to produce extra food for the soldiers and their families. But, farmers made good profits because of the high prices during the war. Farming was becoming a business. No longer was it just a way to grow food for each farmer's family. As a result, farmers had their profits to spend for better equipment and many new farm inventions became available.

New Machines Are a Big Help

It became common to see farmers using new machines—planters, reapers, and threshers—which had all been invented to make their work easier. In the United States, the number of reapers sold each year increased from 20,000 in 1860 to 60,000 in 1880. John Deere invented a better steel plow. Others decided even more work could be done if several plows were connected together.

Some Farm Machines

Planter—(also called a drill) a machine to make a small hole in the ground and drop a seed into the hole and cover it afterwards
Reaper—a machine to cut wheat, oats, or other grain
Harvester—a machine which cut and bundled grain
Thresher—a machine to separate grain from the stalk
Traction Engine—an early steam-powered tractor

The new farm machines were still pulled by horses but they allowed a farmer to do more than ever before.

Better Power Sources

First, the farmer used his own muscles; then he harnessed the ox. After the 1850s the oxen began to be replaced by horses as it was easier for the farmers to care for them. In the 1870s steam started to provide power for the farm. The traction engine was developed by taking a small railroad locomotive and replacing its wheels with bigger ones which would move the machine over the soil.

The traction engines burned coal or wood and were used to power various farm activities. They became very popular to run circular saws and threshing equipment. Professional threshing crews went from farm to farm during the harvesting season, bringing their traction engine with them. But it was usually pulled by a team of horses! The overweight steam monsters couldn't quite handle the soft, muddy farm fields. They worked just fine when they stayed in one place and had other equipment connected to them by a long, wide leather belt.

Other ideas were used to get more work with less effort. Small wooden and steel windmills were popular for pumping water for use in the farmhouse and for the farm animals. Today it is a rare sight to find a farm which still has a windmill.

About 1900, farmers began to buy smaller portable gasoline engines. After the invention of the electric light bulb, these engines were used to run electric generators. With their use the lucky farmer could have electric lights in the house and barn. No more kerosene lamps! Unfortunately, the home electric plants were expensive and many farmers couldn't afford one. It was a long time before electricity was available to most farms. Even in 1920, only eight out of every 100 Michigan farms had electric power.

At Last—The Horse is Replaced

Could the gasoline engine be used to power a machine which might replace

Windmills were used to pump water from wells. Wind power made it easier to water livestock, do laundry, and cook. (Courtesy Grand Rapids Public Library-Michigan Room)

the horse? Today we know that machine as the tractor. But many years of experiments were needed to take the bugs out of the concept. As late as 1920, Michigan farmers still used over 600,000 horses to pull their equipment. By 1940 only about half as many horses were used.

It is Always Changing!

The element of change is always a part of the farmer's life. Prices for crops and livestock go up and down. The demand for each type of crop is not always the same. In 1928 a Michigan farmer could get the high price of $5.00 for a bushel of white beans, but the 1932 price was only $0.63. Before the 1920s, large amounts of oats were raised to feed farm horses. As more farmers used tractors instead of horses, there was little need for oats. In 1880 Michigan was the third highest wool producer in the nation. Later, other materials were used to make clothes and wool production dropped. For many years Michigan was a leading wheat grower. That changed when settlers moved onto the western plains states and discovered it was much easier to grow wheat there.

The Educated Farmer

Education was a powerful force in helping farmers. Early farmers used folk wisdom and followed advice about plant-ing each of their crops during different phases of the moon. As scientific knowledge increased, many farmers realized they could learn how to do things better. The *Michigan Farmer* was first printed in 1843. Farmers eagerly read it and other magazines about agriculture.

Soon there was a strong demand for a Michigan college which would teach young farmers the best techniques. When Michigan Agricultural College opened in East Lansing in 1857, there was nothing else like it in the nation. It had an experimental farm and each student had to spend four hours working on the farm everyday. New ideas began to come from the college. One of the professors, Dr. Kedzie, experimented with growing sugar beets in Michigan. It was not long before sugar beets became a major crop.

A Great Woman Farmer!

Not all Michigan farmers were men. Sarah Van Hoosen Jones used her knowledge and education to run the family farm in Rochester. In 1921 Sarah received a Ph.D. in animal genetics. At college she learned how to breed better cattle. Many of her animals were award winners at state and county fairs. Officials came to her farm from other countries to purchase cattle for their own herds. She made

A wood or coal fire gave steam tractors their power. In the 1880s they began to replace horses for some farm work. This engine is connected to a threshing machine. (Courtesy Michigan State Archives)

One of the many Michigan farms during the late 1800s. (Courtesy Michigan State Archives)

many contributions to agriculture in Michigan.

Farmers United—The Grange

Farmers depended on railroads to take their produce to market. After a while, some began to complain that the railroads were charging too much. They believed the railroad companies made secret agreements to keep their prices high. Alone, each farmer knew there was very little that could be accomplished by complaining. In the 1870s some farmers got the idea of forming an organization so they could work together and make their ideas heard. This organization became known as the Grange.

In 1872 the Grange began to organize in Michigan and it grew very fast. By 1875 there were organizations in 600 Michigan towns. The Grange worked to elect politicians who stood for farm issues. It also promoted the idea of farm cooperatives. In a cooperative the members unite as one group to buy or sell. In that way, the farmers tried to get better prices for their crops and to buy seed, fertilizer, and farm equipment at lower prices. Several farm cooperatives still exist today.

Specialized Farming

The pioneer farmers grew and raised many things on their farms because they needed a bit of everything to get along. They wanted cows to give milk and butter. They also wanted chickens to lay eggs and some sheep to provide wool for their clothes. As farming became more of a business, Michigan farmers began to specialize. Farmers realized that some land was better suited to certain activities.

Celery

In the late 1800s, Kalamazoo became widely famous as the celery capital of America. Celery was not really eaten very much as a vegetable until it was developed in Michigan. Two Scotch immigrants brought celery seeds to the area in the 1850s. Later, Dutch farmers started

An ad from the December 12, 1886 *Detroit Sunday Tribune*. The grocery shop was on Michigan Avenue and sold items by the box, bottle and barrel (bbl). Several kinds of cigars and tea are mentioned.

growing celery in quantity. Kalamazoo had just the right kind of wet, swampy soil. Growing celery takes a lot of hard work. It is a vegetable crop that requires a lot of labor and many farm children spent long hours helping in the celery fields.

In the early days Kalamazoo went a little nuts over celery. It was made into sodas at the drugstore; there was also celery soup and celery soap, celery chewing gum and even Celerytone— a medicine which was supposed to improve your love life!

Michigan Mint

Michigan is a source for the flavor used in chewing gum and toothpaste. Peppermint is another Michigan crop. Albert M. Todd started a company to extract the mint's oil and helped Michigan become the leading producer. In 1900, ninety percent of the world's supply was grown within 75 miles of Kalamazoo! Much mint was also grown near St. Johns, Michigan. Michigan no longer leads in the production of celery or peppermint. Most of the celery land was used for homes and buildings as Kalamazoo grew, and a disease killed much of Michigan's peppermint. Today, Michigan is third among the states in the amount of celery grown and fourth in the amount of mint.

A Sweet Harvest—Sugar

Many Michigan grocery stores sell sugar which is grown right here. This sugar is not made from sugarcane but from sugar beets. They are the same kind of sugar beets which Dr. Kedzie helped farmers grow in 1888. The Saginaw River Valley has the right kind of soil for these beets and is the "Sugar Bowl" of Michigan. Tuscola County is the leading sugar-producing county.

Each fall, hundreds of trucks full of sugar beets come to one of the main processing plants at Sebewaing. The beets are unloaded into enormous piles until they are needed in the plant. Each acre yields about 20 tons of beets. Twenty tons of sugar beets is enough to make over 5,000 pounds of sugar.

The Nation's Bean Pot

Besides producing sugar beets, the Saginaw Valley is known as the nation's "bean pot." The counties around Saginaw Bay grow about 35 percent of the edible dry beans in the country. That is over 700 million pounds of beans a year! Included are white navy beans and red kidney beans.

The Fruit Belt

Many Michigan farmers specialize in growing fruit. Michigan's fruit belt is in the Lower Peninsula along the coast of Lake Michigan. This part of the state is perfect for fruit because Lake Michigan moderates the weather. Cool fall breezes blowing from the west are warmed when they pass over the water. The water then cools warm air during the early spring. Otherwise, the warm air might cause the fruit trees to blossom too soon and be damaged by a late frost.

Apples, peaches, plums, sweet cherries, and tart cherries all come mostly from this part of the state, although they are grown elsewhere in Michigan too. The Traverse City area is well known for producing red tart cherries. Michigan is the largest producer of red tart cherries in the United States. Michigan ranks about third in the amount of apples, plums, and sweet cherries grown.

We Are Tops!

Michigan leads the nation in the production of blueberries, pickling cucumbers, navy beans, red tart cherries, and eastern soft white winter wheat. However, Michigan agriculture is about things other than food. Michigan produces more Christmas trees than any other state. Also, Michigan ranks second in the bedding plant market. Bedding plants are small plants sold to farmers and gardeners so they don't have to start them from seeds. In addition, Michigan has an expanding wine industry.

A Few Do the Work of Many

The golden age of agriculture ended, not because Michigan stopped growing large quantities of food. Rather, it was because it became possible for only a few people to grow all the food needed.

Farming in Michigan reached its peak between 1910 and 1920. At that time, slightly more than half of all land in Michigan was used for farms. Now only about 32 percent of the land is needed for agriculture.

Such a change was possible because of a revolution in farming methods. Farmers have new sources of power, better machines, and better kinds of plants and animals. There is modern transportation to move the food to market. The farmers

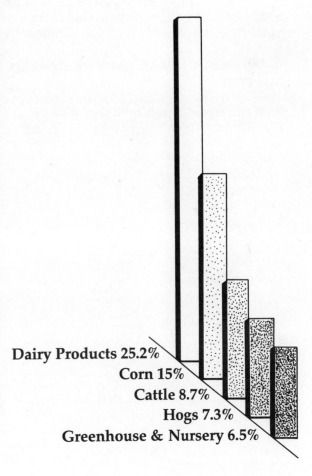

Dairy Products 25.2%
Corn 15%
Cattle 8.7%
Hogs 7.3%
Greenhouse & Nursery 6.5%

A breakdown of Michigan's top five agriculture product groups. Source: Michigan Agriculture Statistics 1988 by Michigan Agricultural Statistics Service, Lansing, Michigan.

have scientific information and educational opportunities to help them know the best ways to farm. Today, Michigan's farmers produce over $3 billion worth of food each year.

Questions

1. Why was the development of good roads and other forms of transportation important to the development of farming?

2. What was the first type of transportation which helped the farmers get their produce to markets?

3. Why were early roads not kept in good condition? What happened in the late 1800s and early 1900s that led to road improvements?

4. How did a college help start sugar beets as a Michigan crop?

5. In the late 1800s Michigan was the #1 producer of two rather unusual agricultural products. Today the state is third and fourth. What are the two products? List two agricultural products in which Michigan currently leads the nation.

6. Which part of Michigan concentrates on growing fruit? Why does fruit do well in this area?

7. Write a paragraph telling how farming has changed in Michigan since the 1860s. Use at least three examples in your answer.

Chapter 9 Section 4

Fishing On the Great Lakes

Here are the key concepts you will find in this section:

The Great Lakes were full of large and delicious fish when the pioneers arrived. By the late 1800s, Michigan had a growing fishing industry.

In the early 1900s, the industry was already declining. Too many fish had been caught in too short a time.

The sea lamprey spread through the Great Lakes between the 1920s and 1940s. They killed millions of fish and the fishing industry almost disappeared.

In the 1960s, methods were found to control the lamprey. New sports fish were planted in the Great Lakes, but pollution made some fish unsafe to eat.

Recently, there have been conflicts between Native Americans who fish commercially and people interested in sports fishing.

A Wonderful Source of Food

For many centuries the waters of the Great Lakes provided fish for Michigan's Native Americans. Fish was important in their diet. For as long as anyone could remember, Indians had been fishing the rapids at the Soo. Using a long pole and a scoop net, an Indian in a canoe could bring in as many as 500 whitefish in two hours!

When the first European explorers and missionaries arrived in Michigan, they marveled at the quality and size of the fish they saw. There were huge numbers of fish in the Great Lakes and it was easy to catch all anyone needed. After the settlers came, it was natural they would fish in the Lakes too.

Fishing is a Business

It was not long before pioneer settlers began fishing to make a profit. That was the beginning of commercial fishing in Michigan. They sold their fish to those who lived in the nearby villages. Detroit became a fishing center. As Michigan's population became larger, the demand for fresh fish increased. More men and some women caught fish to sell.

Whitefish was the favorite kind of fish. On the average, about half of the catch was whitefish. One member of the 1820 Lewis Cass expedition said

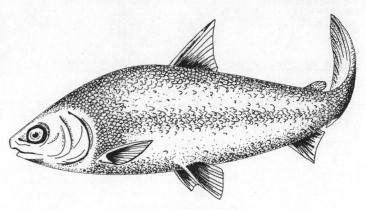

Whitefish are said to be one of the most delicious of all Great Lakes fish. They often grew to 20 pounds, and were easy to catch. Now they are much harder to find. (Art by David B. McConnell)

Hamel used a Mackinac boat similar to these. (Courtesy the Library of Congress)

whitefish was, "in the universal estimation the finest fish that swims. The meat is as white as the breast of a partridge; and the bones are less numerous and larger than in a shad. I never tasted anything...to equal it."

One problem was how to keep the fish fresh long enough to get them to market. No method of refrigeration had been invented yet and fish didn't stay fresh long after they were caught. Fresh fish could only be sold in places very close to the fishing ports. Indians had been smoking and drying fish to preserve them and that method also worked for the commercial fishermen. Fish could also be mixed with salt and packed in barrels. The trouble with salted or smoked fish was they didn't taste as good as they did when they were fresh.

Railroads Help the Fishing Industry Expand

Better transportation helped the fishing industry as it did farming. As railroads connected all parts of the state, it was possible to ship fish to market in a day or two. Large amounts of fish were taken by train to Detroit, Chicago, Milwaukee, and Cleveland. By the 1880s some railroads started to use cars cooled with ice to keep the fish fresh.

Fishing boats began to go farther north on Lakes Huron and Michigan. By the time of the 1870s and 1880s, commercial fishing boats were going out of Bay City, Alpena, Cheboygan, Les Cheneaux Islands, Mackinac Island, Traverse City, Petoskey, Charlevoix, Leland, Ludington, Muskegon, Menominee, Munising, and many other places. Especially busy were those ports on Lake Michigan. The fishing industry was growing quite rapidly and in some northern counties it was the largest industry. In others it was second or third after logging and farming.

One Fisherman's Story

In June 1886, Anthony Hamel and his crew of four were fishing in a sailboat near the Les Cheneaux Islands (northeast of Mackinac Island). He was using a kind of trap net. It was a difficult job to set that kind of net and the crew had spent the entire day putting just one net into the water and fastening it down. They probably couldn't have finished getting even one net down, except they had lots of daylight.

The next morning they wanted to check the net. There was no wind so they had to row the big sailboat out to the spot where they placed it. They were disappointed when they arrived because they didn't think there were any fish in the net. Concerned that something had gone wrong, the men decided to bring the net up to take a look. Then they had a real

surprise. When they started to move the net, it seemed to be alive with fish. There were thousands of them! They brought in so many fish they were afraid the boat might sink. Hamel and his helpers had to go to shore and return for the rest. Altogether they caught 6,300 pounds of whitefish from one net!

More and More are Caught— Perhaps Too Many!

Lake Michigan catch in selected years:	
1872	7,500,000 pounds
1875	12,000,000 pounds
1880	23,000,000 pounds
1908	47,000,000 pounds
1911	23,000,000 pounds

New technology was changing the fishing industry about the same time it was changing the lumbering industry. Steam-powered boats were replacing sail boats and steam-powered equipment was pulling in larger and larger fish nets. The steam-powered boats allowed the fishermen to go father away from shore and to fish even on days when there was no wind. The number of these new boats used on Lake Michigan almost tripled between 1880 and 1885! In 1885 there were over 1,400 fishing boats, of all kinds, on Lake Michigan alone.

Many of the fishing boats used gill nets. Gill nets look like tennis nets and catch fish by the gills when they try to backup and get out. This kind of net hangs in the water like a curtain.

The use of gill nets tends to kill many fish. They can suffocate even while in the water because they can't use their gills to take in oxygen. Since the fish are usually dead when they are pulled into the boat, they can't be thrown back to grow to full size. In spite of this, many fishermen used gill nets on the Great Lakes. Their main reason for doing so was that gill nets were less expensive and easier to use.

Men and boys repairing fish nets in 1906. The nets were rolled onto the racks and holes were repaired as they were found. (Courtesy the Library of Congress)

They Forgot About Conservation

The Great Lakes had always been so full of fish that no one ever thought fishing in these big lakes would have to slow down. That was the same way most people felt about Michigan's forests. They were so big and so full of trees people thought it would take forever to cut all the trees down. We know that wasn't true. By the 1880s some fishermen noticed they were not catching as many whitefish as before. They were not sure why. Some even started to use gill nets with smaller openings so they could capture smaller fish. They began to blame the lumbering industry. They said the river drives disturbed the fish while they were breeding in the rivers. They said too much sawdust and waste were dumped into the Lakes. Others noted that the great forest fires allowed millions of tons of soil to wash away into rivers and streams. Perhaps that hurt fish breeding too.

To help the fish population increase, state and federal governments put millions of baby whitefish into the Great Lakes starting in 1875. But it did not help. Each year the number of whitefish caught was a little less than the year before. Each individual fisherman reacted to the problem by trying to catch more fish so he could earn a living. One kind of fish, the grayling, completely disappeared from the Great Lakes. It was last found in 1936.

Great Lakes fishing was definitely on the decline. In Lake Michigan, 1908 was the peak year. Only three years later the amount of fish caught was less than half as much. Overfishing, catching young fish, poor logging practices, and pollution led to the decline.

If rules had been enforced to control fishing before so many fish had been caught, maybe the problems would not have been so great. It was hard though to enforce fishing laws because the Great Lakes are controlled by several states, along with the United States government and Canada. The state of Michigan only controls parts of four of the Great Lakes. It was impossible to get everyone to cooperate. They did try. Over 20 meetings were held starting in 1883, but it was just too difficult to design any rules which were agreeable with everyone. Finally in 1955, long after the damage had been done, the United States and Canada formed the Great Lakes Fishery Commission to solve problems relating to fishing in the Lakes.

A New Killer— The Sea Lamprey!

To make matters worse, a new villain came into the picture during the 1920s. It was the sea lamprey. The lamprey is a creature that once lived only in the oceans. A full-grown lamprey reaches a length of 14 to 30 inches. It has a long snake-like body with a gray-green color. Its skin is smooth and scaleless with seven gill openings along each side. Anyone who has seen a lamprey will not easily forget its mouth. It is a round opening with many sharp teeth in a circle. The tongue is rough and sharp and can cut through the side of a fish. Lampreys use their mouths as suction cups and attach onto fish; then slowly kill them by feeding on their blood. Because they feed in this way, they are called parasites.

Sea lampreys had been in Lake Ontario for a long time, but in the 1920s they began to be found in Lake Erie. Scientists are not certain how they got around Niagara Falls, but many believe they must have attached themselves to the bottoms of ships coming through the Welland Canal. Once again, human activity helped damage the Great Lakes. The lampreys spread through the Great Lakes. By 1947 they were found near Isle Royale.

Fishing crews found the disgusting lampreys attached to every kind of fish, but the lampreys especially went after the smooth, scaleless lake trout. It was not long before it was hard to find any

Some kinds of Great Lakes fish must always be restocked by adding more from hatcheries. Here a DNR employee holds a hose which is releasing thousands of small Grayling from a tank truck. (Courtesy David Kenyon, Michigan Department of Natural Resources)

trout at all. Commercial fishing on the Great Lakes was in trouble from the 1940s to the 1960s.

Scientists in the U.S. and Canada were busy studying the sea lamprey, hoping to find a weakness they could use to eliminate it. They knew that lampreys, like salmon and some other fish, went up rivers each spring to spawn. After spawning, the adults die. The lamprey eggs hatch and the little lamprey larvae burrow into the riverbed and stay there for four to seventeen years. During that time, the lamprey transforms into its parasitic phase. When it emerges, it is ready to attach itself to fish and feed on them. Every lamprey can kill 40 pounds of fish in its lifetime.

The sea lamprey punctures the skin of the fish with its sharp, rasp-like tongue and sucks the blood from its victim. This is the only part of the fish it eats. After a while the fish dies and the lamprey moves on.

How Can They be Stopped?

Most scientists felt the best time to try to control lampreys was while they lived in the rivers. But, they were not sure how to do it. Some tried to build barriers in the rivers to catch the small lamprey. Others tried to add electricity to the barriers. Of course the biggest problem was how to stop the lamprey without injuring other fish. Many researchers tried to find chemicals that would kill lampreys but not fish. In 1958, after experimenting with over 6,000 different chemicals, workers at the U.S. Fish and Wildlife Service finally found something that might do the job. It was called TFM.

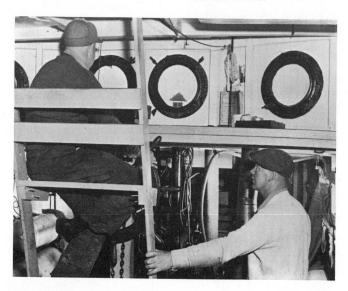

These sailors are inside a Great Lakes fishing boat. This type was often seen in the 1940s and 1950s. (Courtesy Michigan State Archives)

Tests were made and TFM did kill lampreys without hurting fish. Soon a vast program was started to treat all the rivers going into the Great Lakes with TFM. Because so many were involved, it was decided to first concentrate on Lake Superior since fewer lampreys had been found there.

The use of the chemical to kill lampreys has been successful. More edible fish are now found in the Great Lakes. However, the fight against the lampreys cannot stop. Rivers must be treated again and again. Scientists continue to develop other ways which will control lampreys without the use of chemicals.

Because the sea lamprey had killed many of the bigger fish, the population of alewives exploded. Then disease and overcrowding caused them to die by the millions. Many beaches were littered with dead alewives. (Courtesy David Kenyon, Michigan Department of Natural Resources)

Nature's Balance Upset— Too Many Alewives

The quantity of fish caught in the Great Lakes began to increase as the number of lampreys declined. Unfortunately, the quality of fish did not improve. There were few of the prized whitefish and even fewer trout. The fishing boats brought in large amounts of a new fish. It was the alewife, a small sardine-like fish. Catching alewives is good if you are working for a pet food company, but no one wants to serve them for dinner!

Alewives too became a problem in the Great Lakes. Sometimes they died for some mysterious reason and washed onto the beaches. It was common to see thousands of dead and rotting alewives on Michigan beaches in the 1960s. Once again, units of government went to work to find a solution for the problem. Scientists realized the natural balance in the Great Lakes was totally upset. Normally, lake trout would eat the alewives before their numbers increased.

Michigan decided to try a new idea to control alewives and to build up the fishing industry in the Great Lakes. Starting in 1966 they added two new kinds of salmon to the Great Lakes. Almost a million four-to six-inch coho and chinook salmon were brought in from the West Coast and "planted" in Lake Michigan and Lake Superior. The coho and chinook grew rapidly, sometimes reaching 20 inches in a single summer.

The Sports Fishing Boom

The salmon brought a change to the fishing industry. They were considered game fish and fun to catch. Many people along Michigan's shores bought big fishing cruisers and earned good money by taking people into the Great Lakes to fish. It is not unusual for a group of people to pay $300 to charter a fishing boat for one afternoon.

The sports fishing industry boomed, although it was not long until conflicts took place between the sports fishing people and the commercial fishing

The introduction of salmon in the Great Lakes has led to a boom in sports fishing. The salmon also eat alewives and control the population of those fish. (Courtesy Michigan Travel Bureau)

operators. Which group should have the right to catch the fish? The owners of the sports fishing boats believed the commercial fishing boats were catching too many of the good game fish.

Fishing Rights by Treaty

A third group interested in fishing became entangled in the confusion during the 1970s. That group was Michigan's Native Americans. Of the 60,000 or so Indians in Michigan, about 200 earn their living by fishing commercially. The Indians were given the right to fish by the federal government in many land treaties. Their rights were not just in Michigan but in other states too. Sports fishing people were concerned that Indians were still using gill nets. They said the Native Americans were taking too many fish and killing young fish in their gill nets.

The state government also had some arguments against the way the Indians were fishing. They felt the state had the right to say how everyone should fish since the government pays to have new fish added to the Lakes each year. So many fish are taken from the Lakes that new ones must be added constantly. A recent survey showed that in one year over 855,000 coho and chinook salmon were caught by sports fishermen, just in the state's Lake Michigan waters!

The question about Indian fishing rights finally ended up in federal court. In 1979, Judge Noel P. Fox decided the Ojibwa tribe living in the Upper Peninsula had unlimited fishing rights because of their treaty with the national government. It was a matter between the federal government and the Indians. The state really did not have any control over the rights listed in the treaty.

After the court decision was announced, many sports fishermen became very angry. There were fights and arguments with Indian fishermen. Some nets and other fishing equipment were damaged.

Since that time, Michigan's Department of Natural Resources has been working to set up an agreement with Michigan's tribes to set some limits on what can be caught and where. Many parts of the Lakes have been divided into fishing zones and complex rules control fishing in each zone.

Commercial Fishing Forced to Change

Meanwhile, the Department of Natural Resources told all other commercial fishermen they had to stop using gill nets by 1974. These commercial operations had to switch to trap nets. This is a more expensive type of net and requires the use of a bigger boat and a larger crew. It costs about $100,000 to supply each boat with trap nets. About 400 fishermen went out of business rather than make the change.

There are many problems which must be solved between the three groups who are interested in fishing in the Great Lakes. Cases may still go to court and the results of court cases in one state may affect others. It will probably take many years before a good solution is found that will keep everyone happy.

The Pollution Problem

Problems in the Great Lakes seem to be coming like so many falling dominoes. All the Lakes are seriously affected by pollution. Sometimes there are signs at beaches warning people not to eat any fish caught nearby. Many kinds of poisonous and cancer-causing chemicals have been found in some Great Lakes fish at certain places.

Researchers say these chemicals come from many different sources. Sometimes an industry may give off poisonous by-products like mercury. The by-products contaminate a stream which flows into the Great Lakes and the pollution is spread over a long distance. Another poison is lead. It comes from

---

PUBLIC HEALTH ADVISORY

The Michigan Departments of Public Health, Agriculture, and Natural Resources have since 1970 issued health advisories regarding the consumption of fish taken from certain waters of the State. The full advisory was revised in December, 1981 and is reprinted here. The advisory will also appear in the 1982 Michigan Fishing Guide. Some sport fish contain chemical contaminants. Although scientists are uncertain about the long term effects from eating these fish, the Department of Public Health recommends that guidelines below be followed.

CERTAIN GREAT LAKES FISH*

should *NOT BE EATEN* by *women* who are pregnant, nursing or who expect to bear children and by *children*. Others should *EAT NO MORE* than *ONE MEAL PER WEEK*.

Lake Michigan - carp, catfish, salmon, trout. In addition, whitefish in the southern half.

Lake Huron - in the southern half, muskellunge, salmon, trout; and in Saginaw Bay carp and catfish.

Lake Superior - lake trout.

Lake St. Clair, St. Clair River & Detroit River - muskellunge

Lake Erie - in the western portion carp, catfish and muskellunge

*This advisory applies to tributary lakes and streams into which these species migrate as well as the open waters of the Great Lakes.

It should be noted that, if fish are eaten, the level of most contaminants of concern can be reduced by skinning, filleting and trimming away fatty portions of the belly and dorsal areas and by cooking methods such as broiling and baking on a rack.

This 1982 warning was posted by the Department of Natural Resources. It shows the concern by scientists that certain fish were contaminated and eating too many could be unhealthy.

---

lead gasoline used in cars and trucks and is washed out of the air. Pesticides which have been banned still show up in fish. DDT is one example. That kind of pesticide lasts a long time in the environment. Other types of pollution come from burning coal in the many power plants around the Lakes. Coal contains very small amounts of poisonous chemicals such as cadmium and uranium. But so much coal is burned that the small amounts begin to add up and can cause trouble when they are washed out of the air by rain.

Acid rain is mostly formed from the small amount of sulfur in coal and oil. These fuels are usually burned to generate power. Acid rain does not effect the Great Lakes too much, but it does cause trouble in smaller lakes in the Upper Peninsula and nearby Ontario. In some lakes the acid rain injures young fish and can also damage the trees and plants.

Canada and all of the states touching the Great Lakes now have strict controls over wastes going into the Lakes. In 1986 the governors of eight states signed a toxic waste agreement. But, many of the problems are hard to correct. Some kinds of pollution remain in the sediment at the bottom of the Lakes for years.

Many fish from the Great Lakes are safe to eat, or could only cause you harm if you ate lots of them. Fish which eat other fish tend to have more poisons in their bodies. Older fish often have more poisons than younger fish because they have been exposed for a longer time. And finally, fish caught near large cities, industrial areas, or near other sources of pollution are usually less safe to eat.

Human activities have caused numerous problems for the Great Lakes in the last 150 years. People working closely together have been able to solve or reduce some of the problems, but it will take thoughtful use of the Great Lakes and the rivers and streams which empty into them to finally help the Lakes to recover from the damage. Everyone must help.

Questions

1. What kind of fish was the favorite of early fishermen? Tell why.

2. Explain how the sea lamprey hurt fishing on the Great Lakes.

3. Use the headings in this section to help you divide the history of commercial fishing on the Great Lakes into eight or nine stages. List these stages.

4. List all of the ways human activities have harmed fishing on the Great Lakes.

5. Give your own ideas how early commercial fishing should have used conservation to help fishing remain a healthy industry on the Great Lakes.

10 THE FOCUS CHANGES
FROM FARM TO FACTORY

Chapter 10 Section 1

We Made It Here - Cereal, Stoves, and Cigars

Here are the key concepts you will find in this section:

Cold breakfast cereal was invented by Dr. John Kellogg in Battle Creek.

Before the automobile, many other things were made in Detroit: railroad cars, cigars, and medicine are just three examples.

Grand Rapids became the furniture-making capital of the United States.

Dr. William Upjohn developed a new way to make pills in Kalamazoo.

Michigan's prehistoric salt deposits were used by Herbert Dow to make chemicals in Midland.

A New Food Idea—Breakfast Cereal

Travel to a foreign country and ask for corn flakes and they usually know what you want. Think about it— Michigan was the place where an internationally known food was first developed! Today, cold breakfast cereals are a regular part of many peoples' diets. They wouldn't know how to start the day without them.

Just imagine, before the 1890s cold breakfast cereals were unknown. It was Dr. John Harvey Kellogg who first thought of the concept, but he wasn't interested in actually starting a breakfast food company. Dr. Kellogg was more excited about health foods and a healthy diet. He believed in

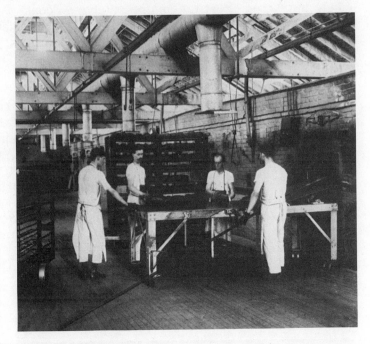

In this early Post factory ingredients for Grape-Nuts were baked in loaves and then ground into nuggets. The workers here are taking the loaves out of the ovens to cool. (Courtesy Michigan State Archives)

eating less meat, coffee, and sugar and more whole grains, fruit, and vegetables.

Dr. Kellogg was in charge of a large sanitarium in Battle Creek. The sanitarium was much like a hospital; patients came to rest and improve their health by using a better diet and exercise. Many well-known men and women came to the sanitarium. J.C. Penney was one.

What Dr. Kellogg wanted was an appealing food which was made from grain. He wanted something which he could give to patients and they could also take home when they left. He invented granola in 1876. The sanitarium did make and sell foods. A mail-order business was started and large amounts of granola (two tons a week in 1889), a coffee substitute made from roasted grains, and many other health foods were sold.

A Patient Profits

Charles Post was a patient at the sanitarium in 1891. He became very interested in the unusual foods served there. Within four years Post developed a coffee substitute called Postum. It was similar to one of Dr. Kellogg's. Charles Post marketed Postum aggressively which helped his business grow and become very profitable. Before long he added his first cereal, Grape-Nuts. So the Post Company became the first cereal company in Michigan.

What happened to Dr. Kellogg, the man with the original cereal ideas? He was involved in running the sanitarium and working with religious missionary activities. Dr. John Harvey Kellogg had a brother, Will. It was Will Kellogg who wanted to make the cereals widely known through national advertising. But the doctor felt it would not be correct to use his name in advertising, as he already was being ridiculed by the medical profession about his ideas on food.

Better Late Than Never

Finally, Will Kellogg couldn't stand to see all of the opportunities in cereal go to others. In 1906 he started a company on his own— the Battle Creek Toasted Corn Flake Company. His company made and marketed corn flakes. It started in a big old barn-like building. At the same time Charles Post sat in a magnificent office and earned a million dollars a year. The idea of making a food into flakes was unique and had not yet been copied by others. Before long though, Kellogg pulled ahead of the competition.

Unfortunately, the relationship between the two Kellogg brothers became quite unfriendly. They fought each other in court over which one could use the Kellogg name. And Will Kellogg won.

There were others who thought they could make breakfast food too. The city of Battle Creek saw a burst of 42 different cereal companies formed in the early 1900s. New products sprouted like weeds. Malta-Vita and Try-A-Bita were just two of the new names. Most of the companies and their cereals didn't last long. Even the Post company was bought by General Foods. Today, Kelloggs, General Foods, and Ralston Purina have thousands of workers still making cereal in Battle Creek. These companies make Michigan the "breakfast food state."

Products to Help the Farmer

Breakfast cereal wasn't the only thing being made in Battle Creek in the 1890s and 1900s. It was already well known that the city made more steam traction engines and threshing machines than any other city in America.

Several other places in Michigan also made farm-related products. J.G. Gross and Brothers made windmills in Saline. George Dodge was making about 1,200 plows a year in Kalamazoo. The D.M.

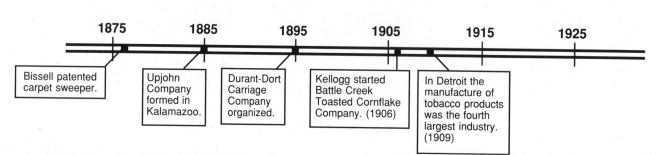

1875	1885	1895	1905	1915	1925

Bissell patented carpet sweeper.

Upjohn Company formed in Kalamazoo.

Durant-Dort Carriage Company organized.

Kellogg started Battle Creek Toasted Cornflake Company. (1906)

In Detroit the manufacture of tobacco products was the fourth largest industry. (1909)

One of the many cartoons about companies who imitated Kellogg and Post. Battle Creek boomed with cereal manufactures. W.K. Kellogg enjoyed the cartoon and used it in his advertising.

Ferry & Company didn't make equipment, but its product was essential to farming. During the 1880s it was one of the nation's largest seed companies. Each year 500 train carloads of seed left the company's warehouse in Detroit.

Not Health Foods— But Delicious

Two Detroit citizens were helping their neighbors enjoy life by making candy and soda pop. Fred Sanders opened his first candy store in 1875. He is also given credit for developing the ice cream soda. As early as 1866 James Vernor began putting his ginger ale in bottles.

The Vehicle City

Northwest of Detroit is Flint. Visitors to Flint were welcomed at the edge of the town by arches over the street saying "Flint-Vehicle City." But that was before the time of automobiles. What could the sign mean? People in Flint said "We put the world on Wheels," but it was wagon wheels they were talking about.

Several wealthy lumber families had used their money to start wagon and buggy factories in Flint. Josiah Begole started the first in 1882, just before he became governor. Begole was involved in the logging business and owned one of Flint's largest sawmills.

Making Corn Flakes Today

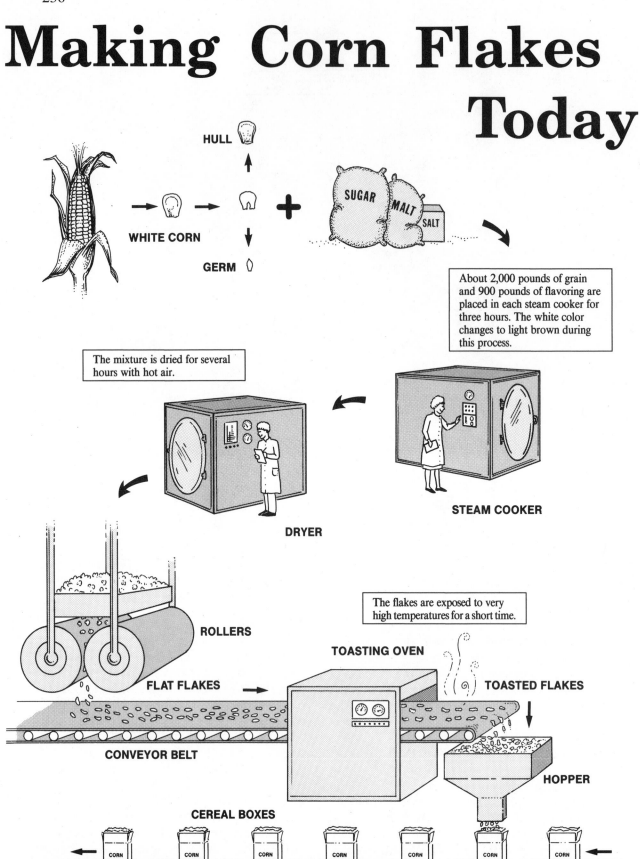

HULL

WHITE CORN

GERM

SUGAR MALT SALT

About 2,000 pounds of grain and 900 pounds of flavoring are placed in each steam cooker for three hours. The white color changes to light brown during this process.

The mixture is dried for several hours with hot air.

STEAM COOKER

DRYER

ROLLERS

FLAT FLAKES

The flakes are exposed to very high temperatures for a short time.

TOASTING OVEN

TOASTED FLAKES

CONVEYOR BELT

HOPPER

CEREAL BOXES

CORN FLAKES

CONVEYOR BELT

The wagon business really got going when William "Billy" Durant borrowed $2,000 to buy the patented design for a buggy from the Coldwater Road Cart Company. He started his company in 1886. A man named Dallas Dort joined him in 1895 and they formed the Durant-Dort Carriage company. Their company made both two-wheeled and four-wheeled buggies. Business thrived and by 1900 Durant and Dort were selling 100,000 buggies a year. And that is how Flint put the world on wheels!

Cigars and Tobacco

Ask where cigars are made, and almost no one will think of Michigan; but 100 years ago they did indeed! Even though very little tobacco has been grown in Michigan, the state was a leading producer of tobacco products. In the 1880s, 10 percent of the nation's smoking tobacco products were manufactured in Detroit alone. Michigan was also high on the list of smokeless tobacco production. Governor John Bagley's Mayflower chewing tobacco made him a millionaire.

Cigars were a popular item 100 years ago, and many cities had cigar factories. Often women took the tobacco leaves and rolled the cigars by hand. Ann Arbor had a dozen cigar factories. Grand Rapids had 50 cigar factories in 1889. By the 1940s, cigar making slowly disappeared throughout the state.

The Furniture Capital

While some women were rolling cigars in Grand Rapids, their husbands may have been at work in one of the many furniture factories in that city. Even in the 1830s a few people were making furniture in Grand Rapids carpenter shops. They used wood from the maple and other hardwood trees in the area. As the furniture industry grew, it changed from a few men working in a small shop into hundreds working in large factories. Grand Rapids had a good supply of wood and water power from its river, but natural resources alone did not provide the reason why the city became the furniture capital of the United States.

Outstanding people and ideas in combination with water power and a source of wood made Grand Rapids the furniture capital. In 1863, C. C. Comstock decided to work hard at selling his furniture outside of Michigan. He used the new invention of photography to make pictures of his furniture and hired sales people to go around the country and contact customers. Many furniture makers took displays to the 1893 Columbian Exposition in Chicago. The Exposition was like a world's fair, and many people saw the furniture. Perhaps more than anything else, it was the clever use of advertising, promotion, and a supply of skilled workers that made Grand Rapids the furniture capital.

Railroads were very important to the furniture business, just as they had been to other industries. They allowed shipments to be made far away. The Berkey and Gay furniture company was soon shipping furniture to the big cities in the East. The Berkey and Gay factory became the largest in Grand Rapids and covered several city blocks.

Growth, Decline and Change

Furniture made in Grand Rapids became known across the nation and was sold in Europe and South America. By 1901 it was said that Grand Rapids had 17 furniture factories where 15,000 different designs were made, and 6,000 people were employed. Businesses always face change just as farmers do. Unfortunately for Grand Rapids, the making of household furniture had hard times in the 1920s. Competing companies in the southeastern states did not have to pay their workers as much and could sell their products at lower prices. The giant, Berkey and Gay, had to close its factory in 1929. Only a small amount of this type of furniture is still made in Grand Rapids.

The markets for furniture have changed and the people who make furniture have had to change too. Today

A Grand Rapids furniture factory about 1900. (Courtesy Michigan State Archives)

the area around Grand Rapids is best known for office furniture. The large Steelcase Company and American Seating Company have replaced Berkey and Gay. In nearby Zeeland, the Herman Miller company also makes office furniture, as does Shaw Walker in Muskegon. Together these companies ship 40 percent of all office furniture made in the United States. So Grand Rapids is still a furniture capital— but the kind of furniture has changed!

The Bissell Carpet Sweeper

Whack! Whack! Whack! Each spring and fall, millions of women around the country dragged their carpets outside and beat them with brooms to get out the dust and dirt. It was a traditional chore that no one looked forward to doing. In the days before vacuum cleaners, Melville Bissell invented a carpet sweeper which could clean carpets without so much trouble. He developed a little push sweeper with rotating brushes. The first Bissell sweepers were made over the Bissell crockery shop.

These four turn-of-the-century Bissell workers look like they are ready to step out of the past and tell about their jobs in the factory. (Courtesy Grand Rapids Public Library-Michigan Room)

It was not long before Mr. Bissell realized he had a product which was in great demand. The Bissell Carpet Sweeper Company was making 1,000 sweepers a day in 1893. Not only was it sold in the United States but England as well. Mrs. Bissell was involved in the business too. By 1900 she was president of the company.

The First Detroit Cars Used Rails

Train cars and Detroit went together long before gasoline cars rolled down the streets. In the early 1890s about 9,000 people worked in Detroit building railroad cars. Roughly 25 percent of Detroit's manufacturing output was in cars that went on tracks. These cars were produced by the Michigan Car Company, the Peninsular Car Company, and the Pullman Palace Car company.

Stoves for Cooking and Heating

New developments not only brought time-saving Bissell sweepers into homes, but new metal stoves too. Gone were the days of cooking in the pioneer fireplace. Each kitchen could have a cast-iron stove which burned wood or coal. Many Michigan companies made that kind of stove.

Making stoves and furnaces was the third largest Detroit industry in 1904. Jeremiah Dwyer got the stove business off to a "hot start" in Detroit when he opened the first company in 1861. Before long, advertisements for the Peninsular Stove Company, the Detroit Stove Works, and the Michigan Stove Company could be found in the magazines of the day.

The Michigan Stove Company delighted visitors at the 1893 Chicago Columbian Exposition with its huge wooden model of an iron kitchen stove that was 25 feet tall! Later the model was moved to the Michigan State

240

The Michigan Stove Company's giant stove model was a Detroit landmark for many years and a symbol of the city's early industries. (Courtesy Michigan State Archives)

Fairgrounds in Detroit where millions of people can remember seeing the "Big Stove."

The Detroit stove makers had a ready source of iron to build their stoves. Eber Brock Ward's Eureka Iron Company covered over 2,000 acres of land in Wyandotte, south of Detroit. Ward's huge factory complex was supplied with Michigan iron ore brought in by his own ships and produced with charcoal from his own lumber holdings.

But stove manufacturing went beyond Detroit. The Kalamazoo Stove Company used a clever slogan in its national ads: "A Kalamazoo Direct To You." The Round Oak Stove Works of Dowagiac made a popular stove used for heating. Forty tons of iron were used every day by the company's 350 workers.

Medicine From Kalamazoo

Kalamazoo would soon be known for more than stoves. The new Kalamazoo industry began with a young doctor who drove in his horse-drawn buggy to visit patients. His name was William Upjohn. Dr. Upjohn was concerned about the pills he was giving patients. Some of them seemed "as hard as bullets" and he didn't think they could possibly dissolve in the patient's system.

Upjohn began to experiment with ways to make better pills. He was successful and patented his ideas in 1885. Soon, three other Upjohn brothers joined him in the pill business. Things went fairly well and by 1900 Upjohn pills were sold as far away as Egypt. The company had 60 employees; still, Upjohn found it hard to make a steady profit.

About 1908 it was discovered that a common laboratory chemical was an excellent laxative. Upjohn made samples and sent them to every doctor in the United States. Sales really took off; 20 million pills were sold in the first year and 45 million the next. Over the years, the Upjohn Company has grown larger and larger. Today it is a major employer in the Kalamazoo area.

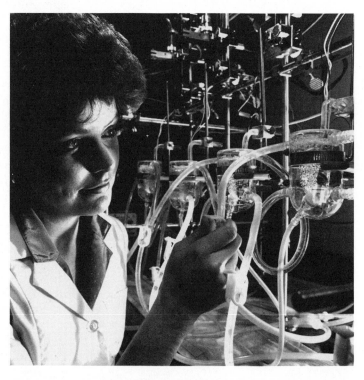

The Upjohn Company first built its business on pills which dissolved easily. Today Upjohn is a major center of medical research. (Courtesy Upjohn Company)

The wooden tower in this old photo was a well which reached down and brought up the liquid brine found near Midland. The building was the beginning of the Dow Chemical Company which used the brine to make bromine. (Courtesy Michigan State Archives)

Herbert Dow— What Can I Make From Brine?

Across the state in Midland, Herbert Dow was also thinking about chemicals. He was interested in salt brine which had been found at Midland and other parts of Michigan. Most of the Lower Peninsula has a thick layer of salt under it. In some places the salt has dissolved in underground water and formed brine.

When Herbert Dow was a college senior, someone gave him a bottle of brine. He used the school's chemistry lab to study what it contained. Like most brine, there were small amounts of chemicals besides salt. The brine also had calcium, magnesium, and bromine (BRO meen).

A few Michigan sawmills had been burning their wood scraps to make salt by evaporating brine. Usually no one cared about the other chemicals and threw them away. Herbert Dow thought nothing should be wasted. He began to wonder if there could be a use for the other chemicals and an easier way to collect them.

Bromine attracted his attention first. It is a dark red liquid which is a close chemical relative to chlorine, with a similar smell. Bromine easily evaporates at room temperature. It can be used to make other chemicals. The brine at Midland had more bromine than most.

In 1890 Dow arrived in town and viewed the scattered crude wooden towers of the brine wells. He was ready to use a new idea to try to get the bromine out of the brine. His idea was to blow air through the brine instead of heating and evaporating it.

Many problems had to be solved before he was successful. At times it looked as if he would have to give up. Success did come after much hard work.

Today the Dow Chemical Company has a huge complex in Midland. They are a leader in the chemical industry. This photo shows a large bubble of Saran Wrap in one step of its manufacture. (Courtesy Dow Chemical Company)

Making useful products from brine had become Dow's whole life. By the time he died in 1930, his company's first small wooden building had changed into one of the greatest industrial plants in the world. Today Dow Chemical makes hundreds of products. A well-known example is Saran Wrap; it contains chlorine which can also be produced from brine.

Michigan Had Many Industries

The examples given in this section are only a few of the many industries which developed in Michigan. There are several others which are not mentioned and many of the ones which are listed also operated in other Michigan cities. Paper was made in Kalamazoo, and there were also large drug companies in Detroit. It is easy to see the state had a diversified background in making numerous products. There had been a great increase in the number of factory workers between 1860 and 1890. Michigan was becoming a major industrial state. More and more people were leaving the farm and making their homes in the city. The skills needed were changing, and the problems the state faced were also changing.

Questions

1. Who started the first company to make breakfast cereal in Michigan? Which Michigan city has three cereal companies today?

2. Which Michigan city was associated with Vernor's ginger ale, Sander's candy, and cigars? In 1904, what was the third most valuable product being made there?

3. What type of vehicles first made the city of Flint famous?

4. What combination of factors helped make Grand Rapids the furniture capital of the United States during the late 1800s?

5. What underground resource contained the chemicals Herbert Dow used? Name one product made by the Dow Chemical company today.

6. Design and draw a time line on a sheet of paper going from 1860 to 1960. Label the time line with three products listed in this section. Make the time line so you can include as much of the following information as possible: when each product was first made, when its production was greatest, when it was last made, and how many were made or how many workers were employed.

Chapter 10 Section 2

In the Factories —
The Worker's Viewpoint

Here are the key concepts you will find in this section:

Wages were very low 100 years ago.

Most employees worked 11 or 12 hours, six days a week.

There were only a few unions or organizations for workers and they were not as stong as they are today.

In 1885 there was a big strike at the sawmills around Saginaw and Bay City.

Wages and Hours Have Changed

Once it was common to hear people say, "Another day, another dollar." It is hard to realize it now, but they were serious. That is exactly what they were paid for a day's work about 1900—one dollar!

Working conditions and wages were much different in the past. Brick workers in Grand Rapids demanded $1.25 a day in 1897, but they did not get the raise. In 1899 cigar makers were paid $1.00 for every 1,000 cigars they rolled by hand! Most people worked an 11-hour or 12-hour day and it was not unusual to work six days a week. Overtime pay was unheard of at that time. Many factories had machines without safety guards for moving belts and pulleys which could catch a worker's arm or clothing, causing a terrible accident. However, viewpoints were different then. Most people, even other workers, felt if someone had an accident the person was probably careless.

It is true prices were also much lower long ago. Rent for a house was generally between $5.60 and $7.60 a month. Men's suits cost between $8.00 and $12.00 and sirloin steak was about $.10 a pound according to ads in the 1886 *Detroit Tribune.*

Children in the Factories

Along with men and women, many children also had to work because their parents needed the extra money to help make ends meet. The children stood side by side with adult workers in the factories and did the same jobs, but they did not get the same pay. In Michigan furniture factories around 1910, boys between 14 and 16 years old were paid $.89 a day and girls $.75 a day. By that time, adult workers were usually paid $2.00 a day.

Most people did not see anything wrong with children working. The majority of teenagers did not go to high school since there were few free public high schools. Not until the 1870s and 1880s did it become common to find high

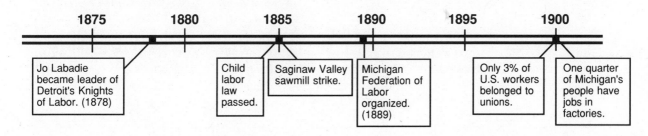

| 1875 | 1880 | 1885 | 1890 | 1895 | 1900 |

Jo Labadie became leader of Detroit's Knights of Labor. (1878)

Child labor law passed.

Saginaw Valley sawmill strike.

Michigan Federation of Labor organized. (1889)

Only 3% of U.S. workers belonged to unions.

One quarter of Michigan's people have jobs in factories.

244

In the 1800s and early 1900s it was normal for children to work in factories. Between 1885 and 1915, the minimum age of child workers was raised from 10 to 15. (Courtesy Western Michigan University Archives and Regional History Collections, Kalamazoo, MI)

worked for the same reason then that they do today—so the family could have more money or because they had to support themselves. The 1891 Michigan Bureau of Labor and Industrial Statistics *Annual Report* included these comments from women workers:

"My father and mother are both invalids. I support them."

"I have 10 children to support."

"I am working in the men's clothing factory in Detroit. This firm starts work at 7:30 in the morning and stops at 5:30 in the evening, and closes down at noon on Saturday."

"I am working in a hotel. Men get three times as much as women for the same work."

Some Workers Organize

Workers complained about the long hours and low wages, but there were no effective unions to help them. If a worker complained to the factory owner, he or she might be fired. Owners and bosses were not necessarily trying to be mean to their employees, but no owner could stay in business if the company paid higher wages than the competition.

There were a few workers' associations. During the 1860s and 1870s the Knights of Labor became popular with Michigan workers. This group was run like a club or lodge with a password and secret handshake. The aim of the group was to have an eight-hour workday and higher wages. Any worker could join, except lawyers, bankers, gamblers, and

schools in most towns. Often people felt working in a factory was good training for children.

Before 1885, there was no minimum age at all for factory workers. In 1885 workers had to be 10 years old and in 1893 it was raised to 14 years old.

Women in the Factories

In 1910 women held 25 percent of all jobs, not including the work they did at home and on the farm. Many women

Women have worked in industry for years. In 1910 Diamond Crystal Salt employees packed salt in paper cans at St. Clair. (Courtesy Michigan State Archives)

responsible for collecting information about wages, safety, and accidents. In the 1890s that bureau began to inspect all factories in the state once a year to make sure they had fire escapes, that their boilers and elevators were safe, and that machines had safety guards.

The Great Sawmill Strike

By the summer of 1885, before the 10-hour law had gone into effect, the Saginaw-Bay City area had a bitter strike of sawmill workers. The employees wanted to work the new 10-hour day for the same amount of money they were currently earning. Their slogan was "Ten hours or no sawdust!" The sawmill owners thought

barkeepers. Officials in many cities were members of the Knights too. The Knights of Labor felt the best way to improve conditions was to change the laws. In order to do that, members ran for the Michigan legislature. Thirty-eight were successfully elected in 1886.

Joseph Labadie became the leader of the Detroit branch of the Knights of Labor in 1878. He was someone right from the pages of Michigan history, as he was part Indian and part French. Labadie was unusual for a labor leader because he was a poet and journalist, but he loved people!

Thomas Barry of Saginaw was another leader in the Knights of Labor and a member of the Michigan legislature. In 1885 he helped see that a state law was passed limiting the workday to 10 hours.

Changes began to take place in state government about the same time. Michigan started a Bureau of Labor in 1883. For the first time government was

Jo Labadie organized the Knights of Labor which worked to improve life for workers by changing government policies. (Courtesy Michigan State Archives)

the employees should work 11 hours for what they were being paid. They came up with their own saying: "Eleven hours a day or no flour on the table." The workers were not timid about their demands. A thousand men took two barges from Bay City and went up the river to Saginaw. They stopped at each sawmill they passed and closed it down.

The workers felt they were right and they were united. For several weeks they stayed off the job. But how were they going to feed their families? Few of them had any savings. The Knights of Labor tried to help the strikers by passing out food given to them by sympathetic store owners. But the handouts were not enough to last for very long. After eight or nine weeks, most of the men were back at work. They had to swallow their pride and accept pay cuts when the 10-hour law went into effect.

No Strong Unions Yet!

The Knights of Labor began to lose power by the late 1880s. Members who were highly skilled felt they were the aristocrats of labor and resented members who had few skills. Some people also gave the Knights part of the blame for a terrible railroad strike riot in Chicago that took place in 1886. Many people were killed in the riot, and the publicity did not help the organization. As the Knights began to fade away, Joseph Labadie became a leader in a new group called the American Federation of Labor or AFL.

The Knights of Labor and the AFL were the beginning of the labor movement in Michigan. It took many more years before Michigan had any strong unions. In the meantime, people's attitudes had to become more positive toward unions and the workers had to become more organized.

An early Michigan strike took place in the sawmills of the Saginaw Valley. Workers struck over hours and pay. They closed the mills for about two months, but were not very successful in getting their demands.

Questions

1. What were the wages for an adult worker in a Michigan furniture factory in 1910? What were boys and girls paid in the same factories?

2. What argument might factory owners use when workers asked for more money?

3. What method did the Knights of Labor feel was the best way to improve working conditions? What did members do to accomplish this goal?

4. Give at least one example of how women were not treated fairly in their jobs at this time.

5. How did the Knights of Labor help workers in the 1885 sawmill strike?

6. In your opinion how were families, children, and education affected when many children had to work in factories? Write a short paragraph explaining your thoughts and include facts from this chapter.

Chapter 10 Section 3

Time for Reform:
Who Was Potato Pingree ?

Here are the key concepts you will find in this section:

In the 1880s and 1890s some leaders in Michigan began to realize democracy was not working very well. The rich and powerful had much control over city and state government, but the average person had little say in what happened.

Hazen Pingree became mayor of Detroit and later governor of Michigan. Even though he was rich, he wanted to see everyone have a fair deal in government.

The nation was in a bad economic slowdown starting in 1893 and Pingree wanted to help the poor grow their own food. He let them start gardens on land which belonged to the city of Detroit.

Pingree was an early leader in making needed reforms in state government. This was not easy for him and he lost many old friends.

Democracy Was Not Working Well

As you study American history you will learn about a time called the "Progressive Era." During that time some leaders realized democracy in the country was not working as well as it should. They saw certain rich and powerful people using the system for their own selfish advantage. There was bribery and vote buying in state government. The average person seemed to have little say. Democracy had gotten out of tune.

Josiah Begole was governor in the 1880s and he said, "A large class of our citizens,...have no one whose special duty it is to investigate their condition and report what legislation is necessary for the protection of their interests. I refer to the laboring classes."

In 1893, Governor John Rich removed the secretary of state, the state treasurer, and the state land commissioner from office because these three men had agreed to report false vote tallies for a statewide vote.

Powerful Companies Have Control

Throughout the state, large companies influenced government officials with their money and power. In the words of Hazen Pingree, railroads were said to be "among the grossest offenders in tax dodging." Five Michigan governors had tried to have the taxes on railroads increased but the railroads were so powerful all of them failed!

As mayor, Hazen Pingree made giant steps in reforming Detroit's government. (Courtesy Michigan State Archives)

In the cities some companies had *monopolies* on important services. *A company had a monopoly if it was the only one to provide that service in a city and, because of this, they could set any price they wanted.* Companies providing electricity, gas, telephones, and streetcar services were all monopolies.

There were other abuses too. At that time U.S. senators were not elected by the voters, but instead were chosen by the state legislature. That method allowed powerful people to have control over who filled the important position of senator.

In Michigan, one of those who wanted to get democracy back in tune was Hazen Pingree. He was ahead of his time in many ways. The real Progressive movement did not start nationwide until after Pingree's death in 1901.

Pingree Hears About Michigan in Prison!

Hazen Pingree was born in Maine. He was a soldier in the Civil War during which he was taken prisoner. While he was in a Confederate prison, he heard other soldiers tell about the opportunities Michigan had to offer. When the war was over, he came to Michigan and began to make shoes. In 1866 he started a shoe factory with Charles Smith in Detroit. The shoe business was very good and by 1890 the company of Pingree and Smith was selling $1 million worth of shoes each year.

Pingree Surprises Many

In 1889 several wealthy Detroit business people were looking for someone to run against the Democratic mayor. They wanted to see changes in city government— but probably not exactly what Pingree did. He was elected and was the type of person who felt people should get their money's worth; which is probably why he did so well with his shoe business.

He suddenly realized the people of Detroit were receiving a bad deal in many ways. He found the electric company bribing city officials. He learned the gas company charged twice as much in Detroit as it did in other cities. He also found that Detroit had a streetcar company which only used run-down horse-drawn cars instead of the nice new electric ones used in most cities. He found valuable downtown lots were given special property tax breaks, and that factory owners were not charged as much property tax as home owners.

Pingree was a shock to the people who had helped elect him. He brought the owners of the electric and gas companies to his office and demanded changes. The first thing the gas company did was to offer him a $50,000 bribe to leave them alone! Eventually he did get the company to lower its prices. The electric company flatly refused to lower its rates. Pingree took direct action against the company by having the city build and

250

run its own electric plant. Electricity from the city plant cost about one-quarter what the private company charged! The average citizen loved what Pingree was doing, but his old friends gave him a cold shoulder. They stopped talking to him and didn't invite him to their homes.

Gardens for the Poor

A depression or business slowdown hit the United States very hard in 1893. It was called the "Panic of 93." Many people in Michigan lost their jobs when business slowed down. About 25,000 people were out of work in Detroit. That was one tenth of the population then. Crowds of men stood around city hall just waiting for news about work.

One of Hazen Pingree's projects for the poor was opening up city-owned property to be used for gardens. Pingree is shown here inspecting one of those gardens. (Courtesy Michigan State Archives)

Hazen Pingree searched for ways to help those who were having hard times. He offered to let the poor in Detroit use empty city land so they could grow their own potatoes and vegetables. He held an auction and sold his favorite horse to get money for the seeds. News about what Hazen Pingree did was in newspapers across the country and he was given the nickname "Potato Pingree." The wealthy people laughed at Pingree's new nickname but he was a hero to the poor people who needed the food.

Hazen Pingree was reelected mayor of Detroit three more times. He had several successes but felt state government made it difficult for him to correct many of the things which he believed should be changed. He tried to run for governor twice but was blocked by the political party leaders.

Pingree for Governor

Then the political bosses of the Republican party decided to change their strategy toward Pingree. They were looking for a way to get him out of Detroit. The 1896 governor's election was just such an opportunity! If Pingree's name were on the ballot for governor, they knew his popularity would help other Republicans be elected. They were especially interested in being sure the presidential nominee, William McKinley, received many votes from Michigan.

Pingree thought being governor would help his reform program and he agreed to run. The party leaders had an ace up their sleeves as they knew the conservative members of the state senate would slow down any new ideas coming from Pingree. There was not much chance any of them would be made law.

Pingree won the election and became Michigan's 24th governor. But Hazen Pingree had a plan of his own to surprise the political leaders who wanted him out of Detroit. He would continue to be mayor and hold both offices at the same time! And that is exactly what he did for about three months. Then the Michigan Supreme Court ruled it was against Michigan's constitution for him to be a mayor and governor at the same time. He would have to give up one or the other. Pingree remained governor and was reelected in 1898.

It Wasn't Easy In Lansing

It was rough for Pingree in Lansing. He had a hard time trying to pass new laws. He fought hard to see that railroads paid their fair share of taxes. A bill for that purpose eventually passed, but not until just after Pingree left office. After his second two-year term as governor, Hazen Pingree was tired and bitter about political life. His wife was shocked by all of the controversy and didn't want to go out into public.

Hazen Pingree left office to go hunting in Africa. On his way home he became sick and died at the age of 60. The entire state of Michigan was saddened by his death. Even some of his enemies admired him for his courage and efforts to tackle so many difficult problems. He was a leader with new ideas to improve state and national government. Others would later use those ideas. His work in Michigan shows the type of sacrifice that is sometimes required of men and women in public office. It shows how much courage is needed to change the system against the wishes of powerful opposition.

A Woman Writes About Politics

Hazen Pingree was not the only person to notice the rich had used government to get special privileges. Marion Marsh Todd was a woman who spoke out and wrote about the abuses she saw. Marion moved to Michigan as a young girl and grew up in Eaton Rapids. Marion Todd did not run for political office as Hazen Pingree did. She used a different approach to attack the important political issues of the day. Her weapon against the powerful and unscrupulous was the written word. Between 1886 and 1902 she wrote five books on political subjects.

In one book, Marion Todd showed how the railroads misused their power by charging high prices and paying too little in taxes.

In another book, Todd wrote about the laws the United States had passed to protect American industry from foreign competition. At that time products made in other countries had a large tax, called a tariff, added to them when they were sold here. The idea behind the laws was to increase the costs of products not made in America. But Todd said such laws only helped the rich American factory owners sell their products at even higher prices. It was her opinion that those laws were written only to help the rich people.

Marion Todd knew about such matters not only from her experiences in Michigan but from her travels as well. She was well-educated having gone to law school in California and she also worked on a newspaper in Chicago.

Cheated!

Big businesses do good things in our communities and provide us with many excellent products. But in the past there were times when that was not always true. A concentration of power in a single person or group often leads to unfair treatment of others.

Charlotte Kawbawgam, whose Indian name meant Laughing Whitefish, fought big business and won her right to shares in the Jackson iron mine. (Courtesy Michigan State Archives)

252

An example of that is the case of Charlotte Kawbawgam, whose Indian name was Laughing Whitefish. Charlotte was the daughter of Marji-Gesick. It was Marji-Gesick who helped Philo Everett find the place to start the Jackson iron mine. Marji-Gesick was given shares of stock in the mining company as payment for his help. After her father died, Charlotte wanted the shares. The mining company had made a great deal of money from the discovery, but they refused her the stock. They came up with the poor argument that since her mother and father were not married in a church and did not have a marriage license they were not legally married. And so she was not the legitimate child of her father.

Charlotte Kawbawgam was determined to have fair treatment and obtain the stock. She sued the mining company in court. Finally the case reached the Michigan Supreme Court. In 1883 the Court ruled she could inherit the stock. That court case was a first for Indian rights. The court said that just because Indian customs were different, it did not mean her parents were not married.

Questions

1. Who had much control over state government in the 1880s and 1890s?

2. According to former Michigan governor Josiah Begole, what group of people had no one to speak for them and no one to look after their interests?

3. List the changes Hazen Pingree made while he was mayor of Detroit and governor of Michigan.

4. Why was Hazen Pingree given the nickname of "Potato Pingree?" What very unusual thing did Pingree try to do after he was elected governor of Michigan?

5. In your opinion, how was the case of Charlotte Kawbawgam an example of a powerful company trying to take something away from an average person?

Chapter 10 Section 4

Great Lakes Ships and Cargoes

Here are the key concepts you will find in this section:

Until the 1920s, ships were an important way for people to travel in the Great Lakes region.

Great Lakes freighters have developed from small sailing ships to modern diesel-powered giants over 1,000 feet long carrying 60,000 tons of cargo.

A great race took place in 1901 between two passenger ships on Lake Erie.

Great Lakes ships continue to be an important way to move certain kinds of cargo but passenger use has fallen considerably. Cars, trains, and planes compete with ships today.

In November 1913, a terrible storm hit the Great Lakes causing 12 ships to sink and 251 sailors to drown. It continues to be an unlucky month on the Great Lakes because the Edmund Fitzgerald also sank during a November 1975 storm.

From the Very First

The vast, blue waters of the Great Lakes have been a transportation route for Michigan people since the time of the Indians in their birchbark canoes. As Michigan grew up, the Lakes became more important. La Salle tried to carry the first cargo on his little sailing ship the *Griffon*. Today huge freighters over 1,000 feet long and carrying up to 60,000 tons of cargo slice through the cold waters. Few ships carry passengers now, but that wasn't always so. At one time many passenger ships also crossed the Lakes.

In 1860 there were 138 side-wheelers, 197 propeller ships and over 1,100 sailboats carrying people, products and raw material on the Great Lakes.

How Great Lakes Ships Changed

What happened during the time between the early sail boats and today's freighters which are 1,000 feet in length? At first, wind was used to power ships because it was free and the only power source available. Sails made with hun-dreds of yards of canvass continued to push ships long after steam engines came into use. The peak year for commercial sailing ships on the Great Lakes was 1873 when over 1,500 were in operation. Sailing ships were used less frequently as the years went by until the last ones made their final voyages in the 1930s.

Early sailing ships carried people and cargo, but by 1850 most passengers traveled in steam-powered vessels. The steamships could stay on schedule without worrying how the wind was blowing.

The *Walk-in-the-Water*, carrying 29 passengers, was the first steamship to reach Michigan. The ship was 135 feet long and had a paddle wheel on each side. Ships built like the *Walk-in-the-Water* were called side-wheelers. The first ship to have a propeller on the Great Lakes was the *Vandalia* in 1841. Side-wheelers, however, remained popular for a long time. Some of the largest passenger ships on the Lakes used side wheels and operated as late as 1950. The biggest of that type of ship was the *Greater*

Early sailing schooners carried all kinds of cargos on the Lakes. This ship is shown in dry dock so that the bottom or hull can be repaired. (Courtesy MTU Archives and Copper Country Historical Collections, Michigan Technological University)

Detroit and it could carry over 2,000 passengers and was 535 feet long.

Where Were the People Going?

Where did the passenger ships travel? In general, they went to and from Buffalo, Cleveland, Detroit, Port Huron, and on to ports around Lake Huron and Lake Michigan, finally reaching Milwaukee and Chicago. Others passed through the Soo Locks to Marquette, Duluth, and other ports on Lake Superior. The early 1900s were great years for passenger travel on the Lakes. Large and fast "night boats" linked Detroit, Buffalo, and Cleveland with overnight service.

Famous Travelers

In the 1880s and 1890s the passenger ships were built with luxury in mind. Famous people often traveled on such ships. The waters around Michigan hosted at least three great authors— Charles Dickens, Herman Melville and Mark Twain. Dickens made a voyage on Lake Erie. In the summer of 1840 Melville

The *Greater Buffalo,* an awesome sight, was one of the two largest side-wheel ships ever built. It and the *Greater Detroit* each had more than 1,500 berths or beds. They sailed between Detroit and Buffalo. (Courtesy Dossin Great Lakes Museum)

sailed west from Buffalo to Chicago and was caught in a storm on Lake Erie that "threw travelers from their berths and horses across the deck." His trip took a week and cost him ten dollars. Mark Twain took the luxurious *North West* from Mackinac to Duluth.

A Great Race!

One of the most exciting events in Great Lakes history took place on Lake Erie in 1901. A Detroit newspaper article listed the fastest ships on the Lakes, but forgot to mention the new *Tashmoo.* The owner of the *Tashmoo* was quite upset at that mistake. He said the *Tashmoo* was the fastest ship on the Lakes and offered $1,000 to any ship which could beat her.

Well, Thomas Newman just knew his *City of Erie* was the fastest ship on the Lakes! The *Erie* was a little longer and almost twice as heavy. It was a "night boat" and sailed to ports on Lake Erie. The *Tashmoo* was an excursion ship which carried passengers on short trips

from Detroit to Port Huron and resorts like Boblo. She was owned by a Michigan company and the *Erie* by an Ohio company. The rivalry between the two states made prospects of a race even more exciting. A 94-mile course was chosen on Lake Erie.

On June 4, 1901, thousands lined up along the route to watch. The owners of the *Tashmoo* had beefed-up her steam engine just for the race. The chief engineer on the *City of Erie* was thinking ahead too. He had hundreds of pounds of crushed ice brought aboard in case his engines started to overheat.

Boom! The starting cannon fired and the ships were off. The engines on both ships were wide open and the decks shook with the power. Soon the *Tashmoo* was two lengths ahead and looked like a winner. However, it was too soon to count the money. In another 30 miles the two ships were neck and neck. And worse was to come for the *Tashmoo;* the beefed-up engine was overheating. The captain had to slow down.

Passengers boarding two steamers docked at Port Huron. Rivalry between competing ships led to races such as the one between the *Tashmoo* and the *City of Erie*. (Courtesy the Library of Congress)

The smiles of those aboard the *Erie* were getting bigger and bigger as it pulled farther and farther ahead. But the Erie began to have its own trouble— a spring broke on a valve. A young sailor had to sit on the steaming valve to keep it closed. On the other hand, the *Tashmoo* was speeding up. A couple of miles from the finish line the *Tashmoo* had almost caught up! But strain as it might, the Michigan ship lost by 45 seconds— The *City of Erie* was the winner!

Fewer People On Ships Today

As more roads and highways were built, cars took people where they wanted to go. By the 1920s and 1930s passenger traffic was fading away.

People still use ships to reach a few places, mostly islands in the Lakes. Ships take passengers to Boblo, Isle Royale, and Mackinac Island each summer. You can still take your car across Lake Michigan on a ferry from Ludington.

The use of ships has never been a perfect way to travel on the Great Lakes because they are filled with ice during the winter. Great Lakes ports are closed several months each year.

Ships & Freight

Besides carrying passengers, ships were the trucks of the 1800s and early 1900s. If a machine needed to be sent to Alpena or Muskegon, it would usually be taken by ship. That kind of cargo was called package freight. There were also bulk cargoes. Bulk cargoes are such things as lumber, wheat, iron ore, or coal. Bulk cargo, except for lumber, is normally poured into the hold of the ship.

Michigan's natural resources became important bulk cargoes for the freighters. Ships carried copper from the Keweenaw Peninsula and iron ore from Escanaba and Marquette. Cut lumber was loaded in Ludington, Bay City, and other ports. After the Civil War, Michigan produced more iron, more copper, and more lumber. The increase made business very good for bulk cargo ships.

This picture was taken about 1900 as two ships passed through the Poe Lock at Sault Ste. Marie. The ship on the right follows the design introduced by the *R. J. Hackett.* (Courtesy the Library of Congress)

A Unique Design for the Lakes

Early sailboats often carried bulk cargo but they were not really built for it. In 1869 Eli Peck built something new. His style became the pattern of Great Lakes freighters for the next 100 years! The trend-setting ship was named the *R.J. Hackett.* Its engine had been put all the way back in the stern. To make its hold as large as possible, the sailors' quarters and pilothouse were as near the front as possible. The middle of the ship was almost the same level as the dock so cargo could be poured right into the hold. The *R.J. Hackett* could carry 1,200 tons of iron ore.

Like all other early ships the freighters were built of wood. The first one to be made of iron, the *Onoko,* was launched in 1882 and it could carry over 2,100 tons—much more than any other freighter at that time.

Freighters Become Larger

Each new freighter was a little longer and bigger than the one before. There were limits, however. Anyone who built ships for the Great Lakes had to keep one fact in mind: the ships could not be any bigger than the locks at Sault Ste. Marie or those in the Welland Canal between Lake Erie and Lake Ontario. If they were, the ships could not travel between these places and they could not go into some of the Great Lakes. A larger lock was built at the Soo in 1881 and an even larger one was finished in 1896. Expansion has continued ever since. The Welland Canal, which is made up of a whole series of locks, was enlarged in 1887. The locks at the Welland Canal are the most spectacular on the Great Lakes. These locks are set up like a giant staircase and they bring ships around Niagara Falls.

Development of the Great Lakes Freighters

1869   the *Hackett* — 211 feet long
1882   the *Onoko* — 282 feet long
1895   Great Lakes freighters 400 feet long were being built
1906   freighters reached 600 feet
1971   the *Roger Blough* — 858 feet long and carrying 45,000 tons of cargo
1972   the *Stewart Cort* was built with a 1,000-foot hull that could carry 51,000 tons of iron ore

Faster Ways to Unload

People worked on better and faster ways to get the bulk cargoes out of the ships. Every hour spent on loading and unloading was an hour the ship could have been sailing. The more trips a ship makes in a season, the greater the profit. At first, bulk cargo had to be brought out of the ship in wheelbarrows. Later, large mechanical scoops went into the hold through open doors called hatches.

Today, most ships can unload themselves. A conveyor in the bottom of the hold brings the bulk cargo up to a crane which moves it over the side of the ship. The ability to bring raw materials right next to a factory is quite useful.

What About Now?

Freighters, about 300 of them, still haul millions of tons of bulk cargo on the Great Lakes. Almost 30 percent of the cargo is iron ore— the biggest percentage of all cargo shipped. The U.S. Steel Corporation owns more freighters than anyone on the Great Lakes. Its 44 ships carry iron ore to its steel mills. Most of the iron ore no longer comes from Michigan, but from Minnesota, and is taken to steel mills in Indiana, Illinois or Ohio. Michigan does ship a large amount of limestone which is about 20 percent of the bulk cargo carried. Another important item is cement, which is also about 20 percent of the total. A large cement plant is located at Alpena. Coal is another cargo shipped on the Lakes. It is mined in southern Illinois and West Virginia, then brought to Great Lakes ports by train. From there it is taken by ship to power plants and factories located along the Lakes.

Why We Still Need Ships

Since trains and trucks can now reach most mines and ports, why are

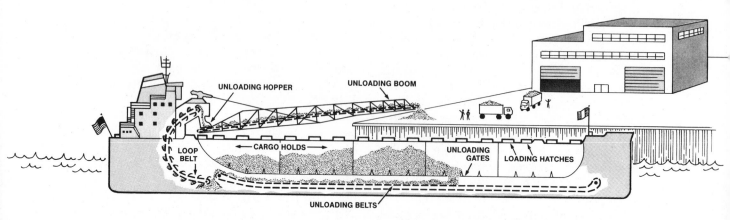

A modern self-unloading freighter. The bulk cargo is brought from the hold using conveyor belts and scoops. Then it travels over the side on the unloading boom. (Art by Theresa Deeter)

This lock on the Welland Canal is closing behind a ship as it heads toward Lake Ontario. The canal was built to move traffic around Niagara Falls and raises or lowers ships 326 feet. (Courtesy David B. McConnell)

ships still used to carry bulk cargo on the Great Lakes? The answer is a matter of economics; it is cheaper and easier to use large ships. Ships can move larger cargoes with less energy than any other method. If the steel mills near Chicago needed 15 million tons of iron ore each year, it would take 300 trips by modern freighters to bring it from the port of Duluth. If the ore were shipped by train, it would require over 2,300 trips with trains of 100 cars each. If trucks had to be used, it would take at least 600,000 trips!

In addition to the Great Lakes freighters or "lakers," ships from over seas can also now reach Michigan and the Great Lakes. These ocean-going ships, called "salties" because they sail on salt water, use the St. Lawrence River which connects the Great Lakes with the Atlantic Ocean.

A Link to the Ocean

For a long time it was impossible for ships to reach the Great Lakes from the Atlantic Ocean because of the waterfalls and rapids along the way. The Welland Canal and other systems of locks were built to go around those difficulties. Together the St. Lawrence River and the locks are known as the St. Lawrence Seaway. The Seaway was officially finished in 1959. It was a big project and Canada worked with the United States on the Seaway. Over 22,000 workers were needed to build it. In the process of forging this link between the Atlantic Ocean and the Great Lakes, they dug up 210 million yards of earth and used 6 million yards of concrete. As many as 3,000 ships have used the Seaway in a single year; though not as many use it today as they once did. One reason for the decline is that the largest Lake freighters are too big to pass through the Seaway locks since they can only allow ships up to 730 feet in length.

The partnership of the United States and Canada in building the St. Lawrence Seaway is only one example of how the two countries work together concerning the Great Lakes. In 1871 they signed a treaty allowing ships from either country

260

Shipwrecks and Accidents

Danger has always lurked on the Great Lakes. Over the years, 6,000 ships have sunk or been destroyed! Terrible storms have flooded sailboats and steamers alike. Ships have caught fire. Others have smashed against rocks or reefs. Some have even run into each other because of fog or mixed-up signals.

November— High Winds and Waves

November is an unlucky month for sailing the Great Lakes. As the winds turn cold, many bad storms have suddenly caught captains by surprise. Year after year at least one ship sank in the Lakes during October or November storms. But few sailors were prepared for what nature handed them in November 1913. It turned into one of the greatest storms in Great Lakes history!

Most captains didn't pay attention to the storm-warning flags. They had much work to do and several cargoes to ship before the end of the season. The storm was coming from Minnesota and moving toward the east. It crossed Lake Superior with snow and winds gusting 40 miles an hour. Captains gritted their teeth and gripped their wheels as their ships rose and fell with the waves. They knew their business and felt they would enjoy another Thanksgiving with their families. But two captains were wrong; their ships sank in Lake Superior. The worst was yet to come. On Sunday, the ninth of November, all sailors on Lake Huron should have said their prayers as few ships on that lake would survive. The storm became frantic; winds were 90 miles an hour and the waves 40 feet high! Captain Lyons on the freighter *Sheadle* was in Lake Huron near Harbor Beach and remembered what it was like.

"In about four hours the wind had come up from 25 to 75 miles an hour.... The bell rang for supper at 5:45 P.M.... when a gigantic sea mounted our stern (a large wave washed over the back of the ship)... sending torrents of water through the passage ways... breaking the windows... washing our provisions out of the refrigerator... The supper was swept off the tables and all the dishes smashed.... Volumes of water came down on the engine through the upper skylights, and at times there were from four to six feet of water in the cabin.

From a letter and narrative given to K.T. Lyons by his father the captain of the *Sheadle*.

The waves covered the deck of the *Sheadle* with "a solid mass of blue water!" Amazingly, the *Sheadle* made it through the storm and reached its destination on November 12th. Her crew was lucky.

In the November 1913 storm 12 ships sank with the loss of all the crews. Experts believe 251 sailors died. Altogether 57 ships were damaged as a result of the bad weather.

The raging storm which sank the *Edmund Fitzgerald* pounded one of its life boats and badly damaged it. (Courtesy Nancy Hanatyk)

The *Stewart J. Cort* as it passes Detroit on its first voyage. The ship is 1,000 feet long and 105 feet wide. It carries 51,500 tons and can travel at 16.5 miles per hour. Amazingly, the *Cort* can unload in less than three hours. (Courtesy Bethlehem Steel Corporation)

The Edmund Fitzgerald

In another November, years later, sailors again faced a great storm. The 729-foot *Edmund Fitzgerald* left Duluth with a load of 25,116 tons of iron ore pellets in 1975. At first, it was sunny. But the following evening, Lake Superior was in a nasty mood. The captain of the *Fitzgerald* radioed the *Arthur M. Anderson* to keep an eye on them because the *Fitzgerald's* radar was not working.

It was snowing and dark as the waves grew larger. The Anderson's captain frequently looked for the *Fitzgerald* in his radar. At 7:25 P.M., he glanced at the radar screen and was shocked to find the *Fitzgerald* gone. He tried the radio but there was no answer. That was because the *Edmund Fitzgerald* was at the bottom of Lake Superior under 529 feet of water, broken in two pieces! Her whole crew of 29 drowned and no one would ever know exactly what had happened. The *Edmund Fitzgerald* was the most recent, but probably will not be the last, ship to have a tragic end on the Great Lakes.

Visit a Shipwreck!

Today many people enjoy scuba diving to see the remains of shipwrecks in the Great Lakes. There are four underwater preserves in Michigan located near Alpena, Mackinaw City, Munising, and off Huron County. Since 1980, state law has protected wrecks in Michigan's boundaries. Divers cannot damage the wrecks or take anything back with them. It is hoped the wrecks will still be there for future generations of divers to see.

Imports and Exports on the Lakes

The Great Lakes and the ships which travel on them continue to be important to Michigan. The state has 30 ports where lakers and oceangoing ships can load and unload cargo. Detroit, Escanaba, Rogers City, and Stoneport handle the most cargo by weight, usually 10 million tons or more each year. Some ports ship out far more than they receive; Rogers City and Stoneport are examples. These ports are next to large limestone quarries. Detroit, Marysville, and Muskegon receive much more than they send.

Certain ports specialize in *imports*, and others in *exports*. *Imports are products from another country which are shipped to the United States and sold. Exports are items from the United States which are taken to other countries and sold.* Saginaw is an important port for the overseas export of edible dry beans. Many products are imported and exported through Detroit. A foreign ship at Detroit may unload olive oil and wine and return with a cargo of military tanks.

Shipping History Still Alive

The history of ships and sailors is still alive in Michigan. There are several opportunities to learn more about Great Lakes shipping. Belle Isle in the Detroit River is the home of the fascinating Dossin Great Lakes Museum. One of the fancy rooms from the passenger ship *City of Detroit III* has been rebuilt in the museum. The Lake Michigan Maritime Museum is in South Haven. There visitors can see a commercial fishing tug and a boat used in the U.S. Life Saving Service. Visitors can learn about the 500 ships built in the Saginaw-Bay City area at the Museum of the Great Lakes in Bay City.

Tourists can step back in time and go aboard at least four other historic ships. The large passenger steamer *Keewatin* is at Saugatuck and the old freighter *S.S. Valley Camp* is at Sault Ste. Marie. The replica of the *Welcome* rides in Mackinaw City's harbor and looks as if it could set sail with supplies for British soldiers at any time. The oldest Great Lakes ship still in existence is the *Alvin Clark* at Menominee. The ship sank in 1864 and was raised and restored. Those who are interested in seeing the

The ice breaker *Mackinaw* is 290 feet long. She has three propellers, one in the bow and two in the stern. The bow propeller sucks water from under the ice, allowing the ship to break through. (Courtesy U.S. Coast Guard)

modern icebreaker *Mackinac* can stop at her home base in Cheboygan. A replica of the *Madeline,* an old 55-foot sailing ship, can be seen at Traverse City. Also in Traverse City is the Great Lakes Maritime Institute. Young men and women who are interested in training to work on Great Lakes freighters can study at the institute.

As we look to the future, there remain some questions about Great Lakes shipping. Should new, larger Soo Locks be built for the bigger freighters? Should Coast Guard ice breakers be used to clear paths through the winter ice so ships can operate in the winter? But no matter what happens, Michigan and the Great Lakes will always be linked together as one— both part of a vital transportation system. Michigan industries enjoy an advantage because they can be connected to world markets by water routes. And anyone, young or old, can have the advantage of watching the ships sail by!

Questions

1. Compare the number of commercial ships that used the Great Lakes in 1860 to the number on the Lakes today. Give two reasons why there are fewer ships today.

2. Give some specific examples to show how the Great Lakes ships became larger, longer, and had greater ability to carry cargo or passengers.

3. Explain why ships are still useful to carry bulk cargo on the Great Lakes. Name three important bulk cargoes.

4. What is the St. Lawrence Seaway and what does it allow ships to do?

5. Explain why experienced Great Lakes sailors were not completely surprised that the Edmund Fitzgerald sank during a November storm.

6. Pick one of the museums or other places where you can learn more about Great Lakes ships and tell why you would like to visit this place and what you would like to learn there.

7. Design your own time line for this section. Include what you think are the most significant events about shipping on the Great Lakes.

11 WE PUT THE WORLD ON WHEELS—*FORGING AMERICA*

Chapter 11 Section 1

From Quadricycles to Corporations

> **Here are the key concepts you will find in this section:**

In 1896 Charles King and Henry Ford built two of the first cars in Detroit.

Ransom Olds started Michigan's first car company in 1897. Within a few years Buick, Cadillac, Ford and Packard were also making cars here.

Michigan has been a leader in car manufacturing since the 1900s.

Henry Ford's goal was to make a sturdy car which anyone could afford. That car was the Model T.

In 1908 William Durant from Flint started General Motors and began buying many car companies.

A New Way to Travel

In the 1890s young people were attracted to the automobile. That new invention was just as exciting to them as the personal computer is today. The first cars had just appeared in the United States. Young and old alike watched in wonder as little engines sputtered to life using gasoline for fuel. A gasoline engine attached to a wagon made an automobile— at least something slightly similar to a car! Though at that point there was uncertainty as to the best method to power a horseless carriage. Fredrick Forsyth of Bay City even invented a spring-powered wind-up car! Others were working hard to make steam-powered and electric cars. Ransom Olds built a steam-powered car in 1887. He drove it down a Lansing street before daylight so he would not be embarrassed if it broke down.

Several people in Detroit were very interested in cars. One was Charles King. When he heard that America's first automobile race was going to be in Chicago, he couldn't wait to go. At the race six fragile cars struggled to start. It took one car a whole hour to get going. Boys had fun throwing snowballs at the drivers as they chugged along the streets. King was thrilled to be a passenger in one of the racers. Later, the two drivers for the car passed out from cold and exhaustion, allowing King to take over. Coated with mud and oil, King came in second—four of the six cars had given up! What was the average speed of the race? Only seven miles an hour.

Detroit's First Cars

On an early spring night in 1896 Charles King finished building his very own car. He went around downtown Detroit to show off what he had made. But he waited until after 11 P.M. so he would not scare horses or people! King was a good machinist and inventor; he even made parts for another person who was trying to build a little car of his own— Henry Ford.

In 1902 primitive cars replaced horses at the Grosse Pointe race track. The daring winner finished the five-mile course in 10 minutes and 51 seconds. (Courtesy Library of Congress)

Ford finished his car in June and it was called the quadricycle because it used four bicycle wheels and quad means four. Ford had been so excited he did not realize the car was wider than the door of the shed where he worked. He had to knock out some bricks so it could fit through the doorway.

All those who saw the little cars King and Ford had built thought they were

Henry Ford started down the road to automotive history in this small Detroit workshop where he built his first car. Today the workshop has been rebuilt on the grounds of Greenfield Village. (Courtesy Henry Ford Museum and Greenfield Village #833.67782)

266

interesting—nice toys to use for a spin around the park and most people had no idea horseless carriages would actually become a major kind of transportation. While these men were continuing their experimenting, someone else was ready to go into production. That person was Ransom Olds.

Michigan's First Car Company

Olds had worked several years at building steam and gasoline engines in Lansing. With his experience he was able to start the first Michigan automobile company in 1897. His Olds Motor Works began to make cars in Detroit.

Then disaster struck! In 1901 the building burned. The only thing saved was one experimental car. In order to stay in business he had no choice but to build *that* model since all his other designs were destroyed. Olds also began a trend in car production when he realized

Ransom Olds, the first really successful car maker in Michigan, and his best-selling model. (Courtesy Michigan State Archives)

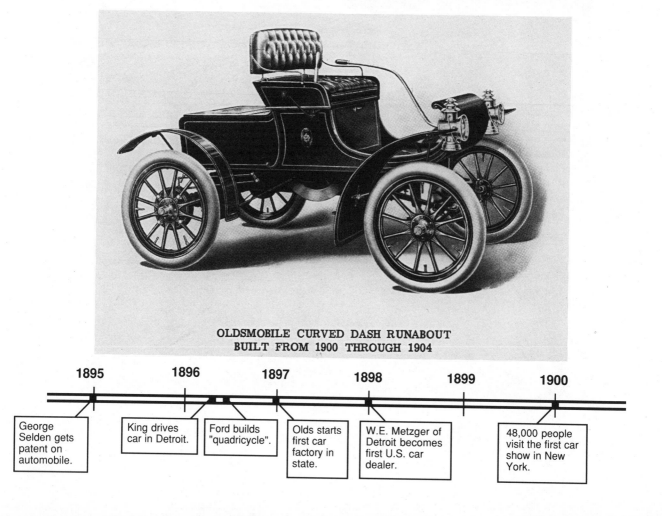

OLDSMOBILE CURVED DASH RUNABOUT
BUILT FROM 1900 THROUGH 1904

1895   **1896**   **1897**   **1898**   **1899**   **1900**

George Selden gets patent on automobile.

King drives car in Detroit.

Ford builds "quadricycle".

Olds starts first car factory in state.

W.E. Metzger of Detroit becomes first U.S. car dealer.

48,000 people visit the first car show in New York.

he would have to order all of the parts for his car from other suppliers. He no longer had a factory where he could make them himself; he would just put the parts together which they sent him. That was the first major example of *out-sourcing, the process where companies buy parts from other manufacturers.* Olds decided to move his assembly operation to Lansing.

The fire turned out to be a blessing for Ransom Olds as the design he was forced to use was a great success. He built 425 cars the first year. That model was called the curved-dash Olds and because it was so popular, the song *In My Merry Oldsmobile* was written about it. The reason many people bought the Olds car was that it only cost $650. That was still a large amount in those times, but much less than the cost of other cars. The next year Oldsmobile production reached 2,000.

Many New Companies Begin

What happened to Ford and King? Charles King kept his interest in cars but earned a living making engines for small boats because there was a good market for them. Henry Ford was working in one of Thomas Edison's power plants. Meanwhile, he used every spare minute to develop new automobile ideas. Then he decided to quit his job at the power plant and he started a company to make cars. It failed. He tried again but failed once more. It was then he looked for others who would join him in a third try.

His efforts became easier after Olds sold 2,000 cars, for suddenly people could see there was a profit in making them. In

Henry Ford seated on an experimental tractor. Ford spent years on tractor designs in the hope of making life easier for the farmer. (Courtesy Henry Ford Museum and Greenfield Village #833.63072)

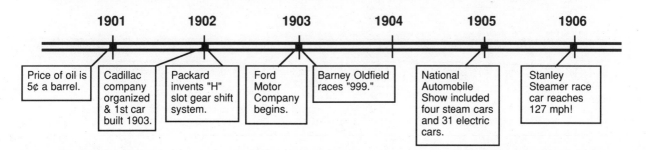

1901	1902	1903	1904	1905	1906

Price of oil is 5¢ a barrel.

Cadillac company organized & 1st car built 1903.

Packard invents "H" slot gear shift system.

Ford Motor Company begins.

Barney Oldfield races "999."

National Automobile Show included four steam cars and 31 electric cars.

Stanley Steamer race car reaches 127 mph!

1903 Henry Ford got his wish. He found people willing to put up money to start yet another company.

Thus, the Ford Motor Company was created. Henry had the title of chief engineer. He was joined by coal dealer Alex Malcomson and some of his employees, including James Couzens. Couzens had to scrape and borrow every dollar he could find to have enough money to join the company. Others who invested in the new business included John and Horace Dodge. Their own company would be making the engines and parts for the Fords.

During 1902 and 1903 people were starting small automobile companies left and right. Almost everyone thought they could succeed. The founders of these businesses usually had experience in some kind of manufacturing or metal working.

A good example was David Buick who had been making bathroom fixtures. He borrowed money and started his own company in 1903.

Henry Leland, at age 61, seemed too old to be interested in a newfangled contraption like the automobile, but he went into the business anyway. Cadillac was his company. At one time Leland had worked for Olds.

The year 1903 not only saw the start of Ford, Buick, and Cadillac, but also the beginning of the Packard Company in Detroit. Henry Joy, whose father James had made a fortune in railroads, was impressed with a new Packard he saw. He was so impressed, he bought the company. The Packard was first made in Warren, Ohio, but Henry Joy moved the company to Detroit.

These are only a few examples of the new car companies in Michigan. Of course, companies were in other states and other countries too. But Ransom Olds' early success helped Michigan become a leader in making cars. In just a few years there were over 1,000 car companies in this country. It was much like the beginning of the personal computer industry when many electronics companies started operation in basements and garages.

Michigan Became the Leader

What factors helped Michigan become the leader in the automobile industry? As you can see, there were several people experimenting with cars here. That was a plus because they often helped each other. There were also people with money willing to invest in the new idea. Those who invested money in the new companies were given stock in the companies and became part owners. They were called stockholders. Money was needed for a building, for advertising, for parts and materials, and to pay workers who would put the cars together. Several who had made money in lumbering or mining helped start Cadillac, Oldsmobile, and other car companies. Also, Michigan had many skilled workers who could use tools and make parts for cars. At that time Michigan did not have any strong unions or strict labor laws which might have forced young companies to start in another place. In addition, Michigan had many of the raw materials needed for early cars. Iron, copper, and wood were all close by. All of these things helped make Michigan the leader in an exciting new business.

Early Car Racing

With so many new companies making cars, how could anyone stay out in front? The early car makers used racing as a way to get publicity and to prove to the public their cars would hold up.

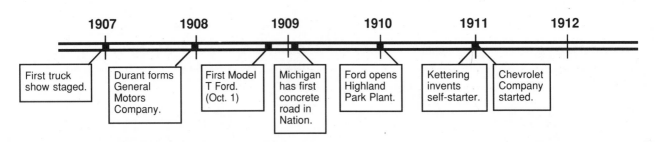

1907 — First truck show staged.

1908 — Durant forms General Motors Company.

First Model T Ford. (Oct. 1)

1909 — Michigan has first concrete road in Nation.

1910 — Ford opens Highland Park Plant.

1911 — Kettering invents self-starter.

Chevrolet Company started.

1912

Racing was a real challenge at a time when some cars might not come back from a trip around the block!

Henry Ford decided he should try racing too; and when he built a race car he really built a race car! It was named the *999* after the fastest train in the country. The car was a brute. It had four cylinders, each seven inches across.

Ford had created a monster. He said: "The roar ... alone was enough to half kill a man. There was only one seat. One life to a car was enough.... We let it out at full speed. I cannot quite describe the sensation. Going over Niagara Falls would have been but a pastime after a ride...."

Henry Ford and his assistant, Tom Cooper, drove the car on the track at Grosse Pointe but were afraid to actually use it in a race with other cars. They found a bicycle racer named Barney Oldfield to drive. People said Oldfield would do anything once. There was one small problem to overcome; they had to teach him how to drive! Cooper and Ford were worried about Oldfield but he said to them: "Well, this chariot may kill me.... I may as well be dead as dead broke."

The race took place on October 25, 1902, at Grosse Pointe. The 999 blasted off and in four laps left the other cars in its dust. Oldfield set a new American speed record—nearly 60 miles an hour. Cars had come a long way since that first race in Chicago only seven years before. Henry Ford always said he owed his success to Barney Oldfield.

Years later, Henry Ford poses with his race car *999*. Sitting quietly, the car does not seem so dangerous, but we can't hear the roar of its engine! (Courtesy Henry Ford Museum and Greenfield Village #188.21670)

Should Cars Be Expensive Or Cheap?

Some of the stockholders in the Ford company wanted to make an expensive car. They knew there was a good profit margin in a car that sold for $3,000 or $4,000— about the same price as a new house in those days! But Henry Ford had the idea that what the country needed was a nice cheap car which anyone could buy. After all, Ransom Olds had done well with his curved-dash Olds. Luckily for Ford, Olds had a fight with his stockholders and quit Oldsmobile in 1904.

A Villain Prepares to Strike!

While Henry Ford worked on his design, a villain slipped onto the scene. A shrewd lawyer had set a trap for all the new car companies. He was George Selden. Back in 1879 he had the wisdom to see that it might be possible to build a horseless carriage using an engine burning a fuel like gasoline, and he applied for a patent. However, he never actually built a car. Realizing that such a patent was not worth much in 1879, he used delaying tactics so it was not granted until 1895.

Because he owned a patent on the concept of the automobile, Selden went to the companies making cars and said he wanted a part of their profits— or he would take them to court. It was a shock to the car makers. Several companies joined together to negotiate with Selden. In a strange twist they decided to join him and form an association to control the manufacture of cars. They created a monopoly, called the Association of Licensed Automobile Manufacturers.

But Ford refused to cooperate. He said the Selden patent was based on an out-of-date design. The Association said they would sue Ford; they would sue anyone who bought a Ford car; they would sue everybody! That worried many people who were thinking about buying a Ford car. The Ford Motor Company, almost alone, fought against the Association. It was a tough situation for a company that had only $595 in cash after its first month in business.

Ford and the Association of Licensed Automobile Manufacturers went to court. Only after six years was the judge ready to decide. He said the patent was good! Everyone was astonished, even the members of the Association. Quickly most of the other car makers joined the Association. General Motors paid $1,000,000 for the cars it had already sold! But not Henry Ford. An appeal was made to a higher court. Two more years passed. In 1911 the second court said the patent only covered cars with the same kind of engine used in Selden's design, and no one used that kind anymore! Ford had won at last. It had been a very expensive fight but it had also given the Ford company good publicity.

A Ford For Everyone

In the meantime, some early Ford stockholders left the company, and then Henry Ford finally convinced the others

People who bought early cars bravely faced many problems— including being sued by the monopoly that owned the Selden patent. (*Country Life*, May 1904)

to let him make an inexpensive car. That car was the Model T and it was introduced in 1908.

The Model T was designed for the conditions at that time. It could go over bad roads and even drive across fields. It was not fast but most people found it impossible to drive over 40 miles an hour on the bumpy dirt roads which existed. The first mile of concrete highway wasn't poured until 1909. The Model T was built very simply so it could be fixed by the average person if it broke down, and it did break down often. It had other advantages. Farmers found the Model T was handy for jobs. They would jack up the back, take off a tire and attach a pulley to the wheel and power a saw or electric generator.

Most families gave a name to their Fords, just as they had to their horse.

"What's your car called?"
"It's Elizabeth Ford"
"You mean you've got a tin Lizzie!"

Tin Lizzie became a popular name for the Model T.

At first the Model T cost about what other low-priced cars did; but Henry Ford made it his personal goal to keep lowering the price. In 1908 the new model sold for $850. By 1916 the price was down to $360 and to $290 in 1926. The last year for the Model T was 1927, and by the time production ended, 15 million had been sold. That was more cars than any other model except the Volkswagen "Beetle."

The Model T was once the most popular car in America. (Courtesy Henry Ford Museum and Greenfield Village #833.4502)

This chart compares the number of Fords sold with Buick and Oldsmobile. Buick was another very popular car. Almost all of the Fords were Model Ts and 1925 was the best year for Model T sales. Oldsmobile lost its early lead and soon fell far behind.

	FORD	BUICK	OLDSMOBILE
1908	6,398	8,820	1,055
1909	10,607	14,606	1,690
1910	18,604	20,758	1,425
1911	34,528	18,844	1,271
1912	78,440	26,796	1,155
1913	168,220	29,722	1,175
1914	248,307	42,803	2,254
1915	308,213	60,662	7,696
1916	500,000	90,925	10,263
......			
1925	2,024,254	201,572	34,811

William (Billy) Durant began the General Motors Company. (Courtesy Michigan State Archives)

From Carriages to General Motors

In Flint, William Durant and Dallas Dort had one of the country's largest companies making carriages. Durant was a farsighted person; he realized the future belonged to the horseless carriage. He knew he must go into that new field or his business would fade away. He heard that David Buick's car company was in financial trouble in 1904; so Durant bought it.

Henry Ford and many of the other automobile pioneers were mostly interested in the mechanical aspects of cars. Durant was different. He spent most of his time thinking about finances and company organization.

By 1908 the Buick had become the largest selling car in the United States. Durant began to use his profits to buy other car companies. He planned on a grand scale and established General Motors as the master corporation. GM then began to buy dozens of other companies making cars and car parts. Some of the most important ones were Oldsmobile, Cadillac, Oakland (which became Pontiac), Champion Spark Plug, and Fisher Body Corporation. Even Henry Ford agreed to sell, but Durant found he could not borrow enough money for the deal.

General Motors went deep into debt borrowing to buy the companies Durant wanted. In order to get the money, Durant made some unsound arrangements with bankers. He had to give them control of the company to get his loans. The bankers were worried because Durant was buying so many outfits. So in 1910 they threw him out.

Down But Not Out.....

Durant was not beaten by this major setback. He became friends with the Swiss racing car drivers Louis and Gaston Chevrolet. In 1911 Louis Chevrolet and Durant started the Chevrolet Company. Durant wanted to make the Chevy a low-priced car to compete with Ford's Model T. Their 1916 model was called the "490" because it sold for $490. Eventually the low-priced Chevrolet built in Flint became a serious threat to the Model T.

Using the money he made from selling Chevrolets, William Durant bought enough General Motors stock to take control away from the bankers in 1915. Chevrolet soon became a part of GM too.

Once Ford and General Motors were both well established, they began a competition which still continues. These two large companies had many advantages over the smaller car companies. Today they are the largest American car companies.

In 20 years the auto industry had grown up. It was not a passing fad. It was a major part of Michigan's economy. By 1914 almost 78 percent of the nation's cars were made here and they had a value of nearly $400 million. Thousands of men and women worked in the state's auto plants. The attraction of these good jobs brought more people to the state each year.

Questions

1. What did Henry Ford call his first car and in what year did he build it? Did Henry Ford invent the automobile?

2. What was the first company formed in Michigan to manufacture cars and who started it? This company was later moved to which city?

3. List four factors that helped Michigan become a leader in making cars.

4. Write a short explanation about the importance to the early car industry of each of the following: Selden patent, "999," Model T, Louis Chevrolet.

5. Who started General Motors? Why does GM have so many divisions like Buick, Chevrolet, and Fisher Body?

6. Imagine that you lived in 1900 and you wanted to start a company to make cars. Choose a name for your new car. List the important things you would need to begin your company. Select a Michigan city for the location of your factory and tell why you made this selection.

Chapter 11 Section 2

Ford, Durant, Olds, and Others Help the Auto Industry Grow

Here are the key concepts you will find in this section:

Henry Ford was a leader in the auto industry and was responsible for some dramatic new ideas. The moving assembly line and doubling workers' wages were two of them.

The Ford company built the River Rouge plant in Dearborn. This was the largest industrial complex in the world. Nearly everything needed for a car or truck could be made there.

Ford stuck to the Model T for 19 years, but people became restless for newer cars. General Motors stepped in and became the number one car company. It stressed better styling, modern research and nice colors.

The Chrysler company was started in 1924 and soon became the third largest American auto company.

In the Factory— Making the Cars

What did new workers see when they appeared for the first time at a car factory? It must have been a bewildering experience. Take the Ford Highland Park plant as an example. It had thousands of people producing cars. Workers were scurrying back and forth gathering parts going this way and that. Some workers put engines together in one place and others put the body together in another. Much of the car body and parts of the wheels were made of wood in those early days. When the engine was finished, it was put on a cart and pushed over to the body. Then the crew worked to install it. Making cars was not very efficient then.

Henry Ford was about to change all of that. The Ford company received so many orders for the Model T they could not produce them fast enough. In 1913, Ford and his engineers realized they had to develop a new process. A unique idea came to them. Could parts be brought to the workers instead of the workers gathering up the parts? Henry Ford said, "Save ten steps a day for each of 12,000 employees, and you have saved 50 miles of wasted motion and misspent energy."

The Assembly Line is Born!

That simple idea was a new concept in manufacturing. It was called the moving assembly line. Every car would be assembled in a continuous process. Each worker stood in one place and the necessary parts came by on a moving belt. Careful studies were made of what each person was doing. They found out how long it took to put on a bolt or to tighten a screw. A worker might just place a nut on a bolt. The next worker would tighten the nut, and so on. The new process really worked. Before the moving assembly line, it took 12.5 hours to put each car together. After the assembly line, the time was cut to 1.5 hours. It also meant that workers with fewer skills could do almost any job.

Many auto engineers from other companies were allowed to visit the Ford factory and see how the assembly line worked. One person said, "It was so simple and logical, so easy to comprehend.... It

Better ways of making cars developed quickly. The top picture shows automobile workers before the moving assembly line, while the bottom picture shows an assembly line of the 1920s. (both pictures Courtesy Michigan State Archives)

spread like wildfire." The year after the assembly line went into operation, the Ford company was making 42 percent of all the cars in the United States. Ford engineers including William Knudsen from Denmark kept working to make the assembly line even better. While other car companies tried to please customers with more powerful engines and better features, Ford only made the Model T.

He continued to spend every second trying to figure out ways to save time and cut expenses.

Workers Don't Stay Long

Ford was pleased with the success of his Model T and the new moving assembly line, but there were problems to face. There were many workers who did not like the assembly line. To meet their

276

quotas they often had to work without any breaks..."no allowance was made for lunch, toilet time, or tool sharpening." It had always been difficult to keep workers, but the problem became worse. In 1913 the Ford company planned to give a Christmas bonus to each man who had been there three years. The managers were shocked to find only 640 qualified, out of 15,000 employees! Ford was spending a fortune to train thousands of new workers who only stayed a short time.

jobs in 1913, and they immediately rushed to Detroit. By 2 A.M. the next morning, men were standing outside the Highland Park plant in the snow and cold wind. They waited to see if they could get one of the five-dollar jobs. By the time it was light, the startled office workers saw 10,000 faces looking in through windows. They put up "No Hiring" signs but that did not stop the people from coming. In a few days there were 15,000 people outside the plant. After the unemployed waited several days without getting jobs,

---

54   *MOTOR AGE*   January 8, 1914

Ford Company to Divide $10,000,000 Among Employes

Profit-Sharing Plan Announced Whereby Minimum Wage for Males Is Advanced from $2.34 to $5 a Day—Hours Decreased from 9 to 8 Daily

SECRETARY OF COMMERCE REDFIELD PRAISES FORD'S GENEROSITY

Washington, D. C., Jan. 6—Special telegram—A "social advance" and a "recognition of the value of a man in industry," were Secretary of Commerce Redfield's characterizations today of the Ford Motor Co.'s plan to distribute $10,000,000 to its employes.

The Five Dollar Day

In January 1914, Henry Ford decided to offer nearly double the going wage. Ford workers would earn $5.00 a day! At the same time the workday was shortened from nine hours to eight. The new wage was a complex arrangement. The basic wage stayed the same except workers got $2.66 in profit sharing. But that only applied to men, not women.

The response was amazing. Headlines across the country had FIVE DOLLAR DAY! in big letters. Other business leaders were not pleased with the idea of trying to match those wages. One said, "the most foolish thing ever attempted..." and another cried "it would mean the ruin of all business in this country." Ford later said the five dollar day was "one of the finest cost-cutting moves we ever made."

News of Ford's high wages started a wave of people migrating to Michigan. There were many people without good

they became violent. They threw bricks and shoved the Ford workers as they tried to go inside the plant. As a last resort, the police were called and fire hoses were used to spray the crowd. With their clothes icy and frozen the unfortunate people had no choice but to go home. It was a sad side effect of a good idea.

In spite of the better wages, not everyone was excited about Ford's new ideas. This is what the wife of one Ford employee wrote to Henry Ford. "The system you have is a slave driver! ...My husband has come home and thrown himself down and won't eat his supper—so done out! Can't it be remedied? ...That $5 a day is a blessing — a bigger one than you know, but oh they earn it."

More Efficiency & Lower Costs

The management at the Ford company kept working to make cars more efficiently. That was Henry Ford's goal.

Ford thought it was silly to have the Model T available in several different colors, and then wait to see which one a customer ordered. He said people could have the Model T in any color they wanted "as long as it was black." In his search for ways to save every penny, Henry Ford began to think about a factory where he could do more than just assemble cars. He wanted to make the steel, the glass, and everything else which was used.

He sent real estate agents to look along the River Rouge, south of Detroit. He dreamed of a huge plant where ships could bring iron ore, coal, and limestone. Raw materials would go in one end of the factory and completed cars, tractors and trucks would roll out the other.

Trouble With the Stockholders

Henry Ford was often called a visionary. He saw so far into the future that most people did not understand the wisdom of what he was trying to achieve. Almost as soon as Henry Ford talked about plans for the new factory, he had trouble with some of his partners, the Dodge brothers. Such a large project would be expensive, and the Dodges wanted the extra profits divided up among those owning stock in the company. The Ford Motor Company had saved over $50 million. The Dodges had a special reason they needed the money. They had just started their own company to make cars and were competing with Ford! In fact, by 1917 the Dodge Brothers Company was ranked fourth in production.

Since Henry Ford owned more than half of the stock, he controlled what the company did, even though there were seven other partners. He declared the new plant would be built and that was all there was to it. John and Horace Dodge decided to fight. They went to court to force the Ford company to divide the profits. A famous trial took place in Detroit. Once again Henry Ford was deeply involved in a legal problem. He resented others trying to tell him how he should

The Dodge brothers took money they earned from Ford and began to make cars themselves. (Courtesy Michigan State Archives)

run the company, but the judge said that $19 million must be split among the stockholders.

After Ford lost that case, he decided he wanted to get rid of the other stockholders. Negotiations took place so Henry Ford could buy the stock of the Dodge brothers, James Couzens, and the others. Ford borrowed money to make the final settlement of over $100 million. All of the investors made huge profits. For example, James Couzens received over $29 million.

That was how Henry Ford came to own the entire Ford Motor Company. One historian said: "Never had one man controlled completely an organization the size of the Ford Motor Company.... Ford wielded industrial power such as no man had ever possessed before!"

A Super Factory to be Built— The Rouge Plant

With the trial over, the great factory could be completed. Construction had started during World War I on 2,000 acres of land along the River Rouge in Dearborn. By 1924 things were in full swing at the Rouge plant. In that single year 141 ships came up to its docks. An army of 75,000 busy workers arrived each day. Ford planned to make 500,000 tons

raw iron ore into a finished tractor. The Rouge plant was one of the largest industrial complexes in the world— a city in itself. It had 93 buildings with 330 acres of windows. There were 93 miles of railroad track. It took a crew of 5,000 people just to keep everything clean and they used 86 tons of soap each month to do it! The mighty Rouge plant continues to be an important part of the Ford Motor Company today.

A part of the huge Ford factory on the River Rouge. Ships can bring raw materials directly to the plant. (Courtesy Ford Motor Company)

of steel at the Rouge and by 1926 furnaces were melting iron ore into a white-hot mass and steel production had begun. Ford tractors were made there too. The process was amazing. It only took a little more than 28 hours to change

General Motors Passes Ford

While Ford was spending all of his energy on ways to make the Model T for less money, other companies were paying more attention to what people wanted in a car. Times had changed. As more and more roads were paved, people wanted cars which could travel 50 or 60 miles an hour. Women wanted cars with style and nice colors— not black.

There were efforts to make changes at the company, but as Henry Ford grew older he seemed to be a different person. It was hard for anyone to change his mind and those who tried often lost their jobs. His power was absolute. He tended to let a few ruthless men run the company. Good workers and managers left Ford and went to GM. They helped to develop the Chevrolet. In the 1920s Henry's son Edsel was made president; however, that made little difference. Henry stayed in control. Edsel tried to talk his father into making a more modern car.

In 1927 Henry Ford finally listened to Edsel and replaced the Model T with the Model A. The Model A was a much better car and had good sales. But Ford had waited too long. After 1930, GM became the largest car company and Ford has been in second place ever since. Although in 1987 Ford did make more money than GM.

The GM Approach

General Motors used a different approach than Ford. Much of GM's success was due to the management of its new president Alfred Sloan. Sloan placed his emphasis on research and styling. General Motors began the idea of bringing out new models each year. That was quite different than Ford's having the same model for 19 years!

Charles Kettering was one of GM's leading scientists. He developed the electric starter for cars. In the early days all cars were started with a crank. When the engine caught, many people were injured and some killed by the spinning crank. Kettering also worked to improve gasoline. Early gas caused engines to have a heavy knock. Kettering and those in his lab made the first "ethyl" gasoline.

Besides striving to build better cars, Alfred Sloan and Charles Kettering co-founded a cancer research center which is still famous for its work.

Another early leader at General Motors was Charles Mott. In 1926 Mott started a foundation which has given millions of dollars to many worthy causes over the years.

In the late 1920s the entire nation was eager to see what Ford would do to replace the out-of-date Model T.

As the Model T became out-of-date, the Chevrolet became a popular GM model. (Courtesy Chevrolet Motor Division, General Motors Company)

As president of GM, Alfred Sloan led the company into the top sales position. (Courtesy Michigan State Archives)

The huge General Motors headquarters building which was designed by Albert Kahn. (Courtesy Michigan State Archives)

End of an Era

During an economic slowdown in 1920, William Durant lost control of General Motors once again. He started other car companies but never had as much success. But Durant's luck was much better in the stock market and his wealth increased. He predicted economic trouble coming in 1929 and even spoke with President Herbert Hoover about it. Unfortunately for the auto pioneer, he tried to hold up the price of some stocks in the great stock market crash of 1929. Durant lost almost everything. By the 1940s the founder of General Motors, a man who was once so busy he had appointments at 1:30 A.M., was working in a bowling alley and selling hamburgers to GM workers.

The two great pioneers of the auto industry, William Durant and Henry Ford, both died in 1947, just a few weeks apart.

The Dream of Walter Chrysler

Behind GM and Ford, the third largest car company in the United States is Chrysler. The company was started long after Ford and GM. It made its first car at a time when many early car companies were going out of business. The company is named for Walter Chrysler.

Chrysler did not even begin working in the auto industry but was an employee in a factory producing locomotives and train cars. There he became an expert in working with metal. In 1911 he switched jobs and started at Buick. After only five years, he was considered to be so important that his salary was a fantastic $500,000!

In 1920 a disagreement caused Chrysler to leave Buick, but by 1924 he had taken over two other car companies which were having trouble. Soon these companies were building cars with Chrysler's name on them! His company rapidly increased sales and eventually bought Dodge Brothers.

Olds Fades From the Scene

And what happened to Ransom Olds, the founder of the first car company in Michigan? He left Oldsmobile and started another company in 1904 called REO.

The REO name came from his initials. REO made cars and trucks in Lansing. After 1907 Olds was not very active in the company and spent his time traveling and boating. Ransom Olds faded away from the auto industry. He died in 1950. Even his mansion in Lansing was torn down to make room for a freeway.

Michigan's car industry has changed from the time of Fredrick Forsyth's spring-powered wind-up car! All of the top three American car companies are based in Michigan. Michigan auto pioneers indeed forged a new industry. Manufacturing cars has joined the historical list of major economic activities taking place in Michigan, along with fur trapping, farming, fishing, mining, and logging. What will be our next new industry? Only the future will show us.

Questions

1. Why did the Ford Motor Company install the moving assembly line in its factories? Explain what the assembly line is.

2. Why did Henry Ford want to double the wages of his workers in 1914? What problem was he trying to solve?

3. What great project did Ford build in Dearborn, Michigan, and what was its purpose?

4. Briefly explain how the approach used by General Motors was different than that used by Ford for making and selling cars in the 1920s.

5. Who started the third largest American car company? Was it started before or after most others?

6. Do you think the moving assembly line has helped American industry? Do you think the assembly line has made life better or worse for American workers? Explain your answers.

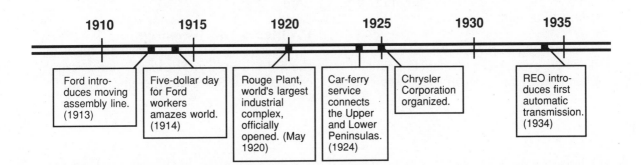

1910   1915   1920   1925   1930   1935

Ford introduces moving assembly line. (1913)

Five-dollar day for Ford workers amazes world. (1914)

Rouge Plant, world's largest industrial complex, officially opened. (May 1920)

Car-ferry service connects the Upper and Lower Peninsulas. (1924)

Chrysler Corporation organized.

REO introduces first automatic transmission. (1934)

Chapter 11 Section 3

Life Just Isn't the Same ....
...........Changes in Society

Here are the key concepts you will find in this section:

The car was the first improvement in personal transportation in centuries and it affected daily life in many ways.

Cars made in Michigan, especially Model Ts, were the focus of many jokes and sometimes even songs.

Michigan not only led the nation in the development of cars but also in other ideas related to cars. The first mile of concrete highway is one example.

The growth of the auto industry brought thousands of new jobs to Michigan cities. Detroit and Flint grew the most from the car industry but eventually factories making cars and car parts were scattered across the state.

The high wages paid to auto workers attracted thousands of people to Michigan and helped change the ethnic makeup of Michigan's population.

It Will Never Be Like That Again

Life in Michigan, the United States, and indeed the whole world was never quite the same after the first car chugged down the road. As one auto pioneer said, "The automobile is the first improvement in individual transportation in centuries." That is something to think about. Cars touched almost every part of life. Popular culture was affected by cars. People talked about cars. People joked about cars and people even sang about cars.

The Model T seemed to have a good share of fun poked at it. There were little books full of nothing but Ford jokes. Here is a sample:

A car dealer asked an old customer if he would like to buy a speedometer.

"Can I sell you a speedometer?"
"I don't use one. When my Ford is running five miles an hour, the fender rattles; at twelve miles an hour, my teeth rattle; and at fifteen miles an hour the transmission drops out!"

On the Old Back Seat of the Henry Ford and *The Little Ford Rambled Right Along* were popular tunes. The last song cleverly told of an average fellow in his Model T and how he stole away the sweetheart from the guy in an expensive car when it ran out of gas.

Farmers could go to town in their Model Ts in minutes instead of spending hours in a horse-drawn wagon. Blacksmiths wondered where their business went. Some began to sell gasoline and fix cars which had broken down. The blacksmith's shop became the gas station!

Problems and Blessings

Michigan was right in the thick of the auto industry. The car brought many changes and Michigan people were indi-

It wasn't long before people realized cars brought problems along with benefits. Now they had to put up with noise, accidents, and traffic. (Courtesy Michigan State Archives)

rectly responsible. Henry Ford dreamed of everyone having a car but he probably never dreamed about expressways and cloverleaf interchanges.

Such a large number of cars was both good and bad. Owning a car meant the freedom to travel when and where a person wanted, but everyone owning a car meant traffic jams, parking problems, and noise. Fifty people died in Detroit auto accidents in 1915 and two years later the number rocketed to 148. Not that the police weren't busy trying; they gave out 30,000 tickets that year. To control the chaos of cars, Detroit policeman William Potts invented the well-known red, yellow, and green traffic light in 1920. Michigan had another milestone when the first white center line was painted down the middle of River Road near Trenton. An additional first for Michigan was the nation's first mile of concrete highway on Woodward Avenue in Detroit.

People Travel, See, and Learn

Cars affected culture in others ways too. Once people could travel easily, they were more mobile. Country lifestyles and city lifestyles began to mingle. City people

visited the country. Farmers climbed into their tin lizzies and took a drive to see the bright lights of the city. People could see and do things they could only dream about doing before automobiles. The auto industry established the eight-hour day and the five-day work week. That gave workers more free time, thus more time for leisure activities.

One of the leisure activities was traveling around the country in a new car. It was considered to be a great event when the whole family piled into the car and went for a Sunday afternoon drive. It wasn't long before families used their cars for camping. That caused tourist cabins to be built along the main roads so families on long trips would have places to stay overnight.

Help For the Early Drivers

Longer trips, however, were adventures. Most roads were dirt and not marked. Motorists needed help with all the problems they faced, and in 1916 the Detroit Automobile Club was started. William Bachman was in charge of the club's Signs and Road Posting Committee. He worked hard to be sure routes were marked for tourists. Bachman often

284

Early drivers had few good maps or signs to guide them. (Courtesy Clarke Historical Library, Central Michigan University)

took buckets of paint and put colored rings on utility poles to guide drivers. By 1920 the club had marked out 1,500 miles of roads and William Bachman had earned the nickname, "Father of Modern Highway Marking."

Meanwhile, the Detroit Automobile club changed its name to AAA Michigan. The AAAs stand for American Automobile Association. In 1919 AAA began the school safety patrol program and in 1922 they started emergency road service.

Michigan was also a pioneer in building roadside parks with picnic tables. The first roadside park in the United States was near Saranac in Ionia county. Allan Williams built those first tables from old wooden guard rails. The idea caught on and roadside tables became a symbol of Michigan's hospitality to tourists.

The Model T had both good points and bad points for the adventurous

pioneer drivers. It was good at going though mud, but going down steep hills was another thing entirely. The Model T had no second gear to use when going downhill and it did not have much of a brake system either! But the resourceful driver had a solution for any situation. When a pioneer driver looked down a long hill, he or she would find a small-sized tree. The tree was quickly cut down and tied to the back bumper of the Model T. It dragged behind to slow down the car!

The driver had to remember to check the gas as there was no gauge. The tank was under the front seat, so the car was parked and out jumped the front seat passengers. The seat was lifted up and a measuring stick lowered into the tank. In only a few minutes the driver had certain knowledge of the fuel supply.

Now You'll Need a License

It was not long before state and local governments were involved in motoring. They wanted people to license their cars and to take out driving licenses. The first state car licenses were issued in 1905. Those Michigan license plates were leather; however, by 1910 metal ones were introduced. Before 1919 anyone who felt capable of handling a car could crank it up and go. But lawmakers were concerned about wild soldiers coming home after World War I. They decided to license all drivers. There was no renewal date for early licenses. Detroit had its own driver's license requirements. The first woman to receive a Detroit license was Marie Comstock in 1900. Michigan did not require any driver testing until 1938.

Cars Bring New Jobs to Michigan

Jobs, jobs, and more jobs were brought to Michigan by the car companies. Since the beginning of the auto industry, 315 different makes of cars have been manufactured in the state and over half of these were made in Detroit. All of

that activity brought many changes. In 1900, Detroit had 15,900 people making a living in machine shops and metal working operations. Within 15 years just one auto company, Ford Motor, had over 18,000 people working in Detroit. More and more cars were made each year and the leading companies grew rapidly. By 1927 Ford and General Motors were two of the ten largest companies in the United States.

Auto Cities Become Boom Towns

At one time or another, cars have been made in 50 Michigan cities. Jackson, Kalamazoo, Grand Rapids, and Pontiac each had several car factories, but Detroit and Flint became major centers of car production. The population of these two cities exploded after 1900. By 1910 Detroit had doubled its population. In another ten years it more than doubled again! So, Detroit with its 900,000 plus population had moved from the tenth largest U.S. city to the fourth. In the process, the city of Detroit expanded its boundaries. It grew from 23 square miles

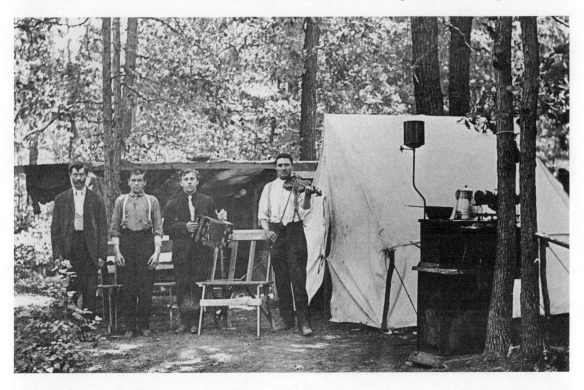

About 1909, so many new auto workers were needed in Flint that they had to live in tents until houses could be built. (Courtesy The _Flint Journal_)

to 139 square miles by 1927 and completely surrounded the smaller city of Highland Park and the Polish community of Hamtramck. There were so many people who flocked to work in Flint that they often had to live in tents until homes could be built. One Flint auto worker had all of his living room furniture in his tent, including the piano!

Workers From Many Lands

Many of the new employees had just arrived from other countries. During the early 1900s, large numbers of Italians, Poles and others from southern and eastern Europe made a new home in Michigan. Many of these new Americans settled in the large cities hoping to find jobs in the growing car factories, and they did. In 1914 over 70 percent of the workers at Ford were born outside of the U.S. They came from 22 different countries. To keep the situation in the factories from becoming too confusing, the foreign workers were given classes in how to speak and read English.

Workers were also coming from the southern states. Auto wages were very good; men and women were eager to join the work force. In 1927 the average farm family earned only $548 a year. Meanwhile, Ford company workers got about $1,500 a year. It is no wonder people left farms and moved to the big cities of Michigan.

Large numbers of blacks also moved north to Michigan with hopes of finding a better living. In 1910 there were 17,115 black people living in the state. That rose quickly to 60,082 by 1920 and by 1930 the number had nearly tripled again to 169,000. In many cities blacks could not expect to find much of a job. Often they were only allowed to be waiters, maids, elevator operators or train porters, but in the auto plants there was more opportunity. Blacks were engineers, punch-press operators, tool makers, riveters, and welders. Even so, they did not usually have the best jobs in the car factories. A large percentage had to work in the hot, sweaty foundries filling molds with liq-

More and more Michiganians found work in auto factories. This is a shift change at the Ford Highland Park plant about 1920. (Courtesy Michigan State Archives)

uid metal. As for living conditions, blacks and other minorities had to exist in cramped and substandard housing. At that time it was very unusual for the different races and ethnic groups to live together.

Cities Grow Up and Up

With so many new people moving to Michigan, the cities developed rapidly. New buildings went up in Detroit each year. Skyscrapers were towering above the cars far below— the cars which made all of it possible. In 1920 General Motors opened a large new headquarters building in downtown Detroit. Albert Kahn, a well-known Michigan architect, was chosen to design it. When it was finished, it was the largest office building in the world.

Eight years later, Kahn designed another Detroit landmark, the Fisher building. Located across the street from the GM headquarters, the building was named after the seven Fisher brothers who started the Fisher Body division of GM. For many years the building has been famous as the home of the Fisher Theater and radio station WJR, who broadcast from the "golden tower of the Fisher Building."

Albert Kahn had a long association with auto companies. He designed many factories in the Detroit area. The first car factory he planned was for the Packard Company in 1903. His factory buildings introduced a new style which was much more open and had many more windows. Kahn's designs shaped the way factories were built for over 40 years.

Not Just Detroit

At one time Michigan had many companies making cars and trucks around the state. Some were very small and only made a few cars. The Deal Company in Jonesville is one example. It was only in business from 1908 to 1911. Others were much larger and more important. REO was one of those. It made cars and then trucks in Lansing until 1976. REO was the second company started by Ransom Olds. There was also the Checker Cab Company in Kalamazoo. Checker was famous for making taxicabs until 1982. Now all of those companies have faded from the scene.

Businesses making parts for cars also spread across the state. Even though the workers at Ford Rouge plant made a complete car, truck, or tractor directly from raw materials, most companies did not do that. They bought steering wheels from one company and axles from another, while their engines came from a third. The companies making these other parts were, and still are, in many Michigan cities and towns.

As the early companies earned more money, they usually bought the smaller outfits which made parts for them. General Motors, Ford, and Chrysler now have dozens of divisions which make parts for their cars and trucks

Saginaw Steering Gear is an example of a small auto parts company which grew and then became part of one of the large auto companies. It made a patented steering gear which was used in Buick cars.

Albert Kahn, a world famous architect who was well known for his designs of factories, including many automobile plants in Michigan. (Courtesy Michigan State Archives)

288

Within a few years Buick bought the company and later GM bought Buick. By the 1980s that GM division had grown to the point where it had 18,000 employees.

General Motors also has many people working on research and testing. Their large technical center in Warren has about 24,000 employees. GM test drives its cars at a 4,000-acre proving ground just outside Milford. The proving ground which has about 80 miles of roads was set up to test every kind of driving condition possible.

Henry Ford deliberately tried to spread factories into the country. He believed it would be helpful for farmers to have another source of income when they were not working in their fields. Ford wanted most of the small factories to use water power from nearby rivers. The first was an old mill at Northville. Later, Ford built factories at Nankin Mills, Plymouth, and Waterford. Larger plants were set up at Flat Rock and Ypsilanti, both on the Huron River.

Ford also bought iron mines and logging camps in the Upper Peninsula. The lumber was loaded on Ford ships and taken across the Great Lakes to the Rouge plant to be used for cars and trucks. Iron Mountain was a center of Ford operations for years. The city of Kingsford is named after the local Ford executive who helped plan the work in the Upper Peninsula.

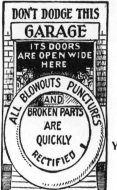
An interesting ad from the September 28, 1916 *Centreville Observer*. (Courtesy the Library of Michigan)

In less than 100 years the car industry has changed Michigan in many ways. It brought new jobs and new people to fill those jobs. Cars have changed our way of life, culture and travel too. They have even given people things to laugh and sing about as well.

Here are several of the large plants making parts for General Motors; each one has 2,000 or more workers. This chart shows how the production of cars and the parts to make them has spread across Michigan:

Bay City	Chevrolet engine parts
Constantine	transmissions
Grand Blanc	Fisher Body
Grand Rapids	Fisher Body
Kalamazoo	Fisher Body
Lake Orion	new assembly plant
Lansing	Oldsmobile assembly and Fisher Body
Livonia	Chevrolet and Fisher Body plants
Pontiac	Fisher Body, Pontiac assembly, GMC truck and coach
Three Rivers	transmissions
Willow Run	warehouses for cars and parts
Ypsilanti	GM assembly and transmissions

Questions

1. Why do you think so many jokes were made about the Model T?

2. List six Michigan cities where cars or car parts have been made or are made today.

3. Who designed the Fisher Building and the General Motors headquarters building in Detroit?

4. How was the ethnic makeup of Michigan changed by the people looking for jobs in the car factories? Give a specific comparison of wages which was responsible for attracting so many people to work in the auto industry in 1927.

5. In your opinion, how has the auto industry affected the town or city where you live?

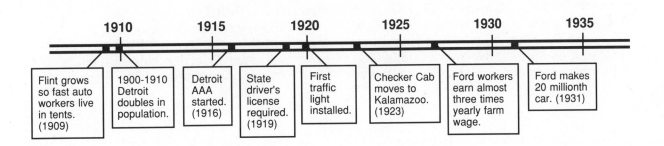

12 AN AWESOME WAR AND AFTERWARDS —

WORLD WAR I

Chapter 12 Section 1

From the Plow to the Gun

Here are the key concepts you will find in this section:

Two Michiganians, Rebecca Shelley and Henry Ford, joined the peace movement and worked to stop the war before the U.S. became involved.

Once the U.S. joined the war, Michigan factories made huge amounts of war supplies including ships and planes.

During this time many Michigan people with a German background were often mistreated. German names were changed and there were strong anti-German feelings.

The government built Camp Custer, a very large military base, near Battle Creek, and built Selfridge Field, a military air base, near Mt. Clemens.

During the fall and winter of 1918-1919 there was a terrible flu epidemic and many soldiers and civilians died in Michigan.

In 1918 a large group of Michigan soldiers had to go to northern Russia where they eventually fought the communist revolutionaries.

From Peace to War

Michigan saw the year 1914 begin in a quiet way as farmers throughout the state plowed their fields and planted their crops. Life was good and there was reasonable prosperity. At first, few people really noticed the disturbing news reports from Europe. There had been an assassination in some tiny country and a war had started. Almost everyone thought it was not our problem and we should keep to ourselves.

The war in Europe quickly grew in size. Soon it was of awesome proportions. In 1915 the French army had 1.3 million casualties and the Germans 848,000! A number of Americans felt Germany was the aggressor. But there were some who were not supportive of England either. There were still bitter feelings left from the time of the Revolutionary War and it did not help matters that England, just 50 years ago, had given assistance to the Confederate side during the Civil War. To confuse the issue even more, Michigan also had many citizens of German descent. It was hard for people to choose one side or the other.

Should We Help?

The countries at war soon ran short of ammunition and supplies. England and France started to order war materials from American companies. Many busi-

THE MARSHALL WEEKLY NEWS-STATES

MARSHALL, MICHIGAN, FRIDAY, JULY 31, 1914.

RUSSIA'S STAND MAKES GREATEST WAR OF HISTORY INEVITABLE

MARENGO 'SINK HOLE' DRIED UP BY NEW DREDGING

KARLE IS ACQUITT

ALL EUROPE IS PREPARING FOR DEATH STRUGGLE

ARRESTED FOR MURDER OF SEVEN YEARS AGO

BELGRADE SHELLED BY THE AUSTRIAN FLEETS

July 1914 newspaper headlines tell of trouble ahead in Europe as World War I begins. (Courtesy Michigan State Archives)

ness people welcomed the orders and hired new workers. But one of Michigan's most important businessmen, Henry Ford, was defiantly against the idea. He said, "I hate war because war is murder, desolation, and destruction." He remarked he would rather burn his factory than supply materials for war.

Ford printed his antiwar thoughts in the Ford company newspaper. Ford's top executive, James Couzens, had English parents and he thought Ford should make supplies for England. Finally Ford wrote an article for the paper that upset Couzens so he instructed the newspaper employees to take it out. Then he told Henry Ford what he had done.

Ford snapped back, "You can't stop anything. It's going to stay in."

"All right. Then I quit," was Couzens' reply.

"Better think it over, Jim," advised Ford.

"I have. I'm through."

James Couzens kept his word and left his important job with the Ford Motor Company.

Stop the Fighting!

Ford had a talk with a Detroit Free Press reporter and told him he was ready to finance a "world-wide campaign for universal peace." That got big headlines in the newspapers. It wasn't long before people were at Ford's doorstep to see just what he would do.

Rebecca Shelley from Battle Creek came to see Ford. Shelley was a young woman with a strong faith and she believed the war could be stopped if important people would meet and talk things out. On Ford's behalf, his assistant told Shelley to get positive statements from foreign officials saying they would agree to peace talks.

Shelley was a brave woman. Even though she was only 28 years old, she traveled to New York City and in her quiet but forceful way asked to see Count von Bernstorff, the German ambassador. Count von Bernstorff was the highest German official in the United States.

She wrote a letter to her father on October 11, 1915, telling about their meeting. Shelley said the ambassador basically agreed that the war should be

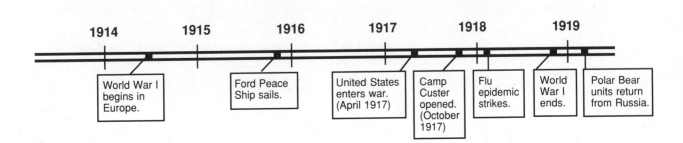

1914 — World War I begins in Europe.

1915 — Ford Peace Ship sails.

1917 — United States enters war. (April 1917)

1917 — Camp Custer opened. (October 1917)

1918 — Flu epidemic strikes.

1919 — World War I ends.

1919 — Polar Bear units return from Russia.

Rebecca Shelley (Courtesy Bentley Historical Library, University of Michigan)

realized diplomats must be very careful and she still considered the interview a success. Then in November 1915 Rosika Schwimmer, a Hungarian woman interested in the peace movement, had several meetings with Ford. She had met with some European leaders who wanted to stop the fighting. Rosika encouraged Ford to continue his peace efforts. After these meetings, Henry Ford made plans to go to New York and talk with other leaders of the peace movement.

A Peace Ship

During the New York conference, someone mentioned the idea of taking a ship to Europe with pacifists. Ford jumped at the idea. They would sail in a "peace ship" immediately! But immediately was too soon. Some of the people wanted to make careful plans first, but not Ford. By that evening he had chartered a Swedish ship for the trip to Europe from New York. Invitations went to famous and influential people asking them to come on the peace ship; however, few people seemed very thrilled about the idea and nearly everyone turned Ford down, including President Wilson and

stopped, but he only said that off the record; officially he could not make the statement she wanted. At any rate, she

Ford's Peace Ship leaves New York harbor in 1915. (Courtesy Henry Ford Museum and Greenfield Village #636)

World War I fighter planes are being built in this Fisher Body plant. (Courtesy Clarke Historical Library, Central Michigan University)

In another part of the plant women are glueing sections of wood used in the wings. (Courtesy Bentley Historical Library, University of Michigan)

Thomas Edison. One of his friends said, "Mr. Ford's heart is bigger than his head...." Mrs. Ford then realized the peace ship was probably a bad idea and tried to stop Henry from going. Henry Ford did not comprehend the planning such a project would need, and being firmly convinced of the rightness of the cause, forged ahead.

There were only 100 *pacifists (people opposed to war or the use of force)* who went with Ford. Rebecca Shelley and Rosika Schwimmer were aboard, plus a mob of reporters. They left for Europe in December 1915. On the trip Ford became quite sick and was not in condition to do much. Once they arrived in Europe no one in any position to stop the war would even see them. After a few days in Europe, Henry Ford and his friends took another ship back to America.

The failure of the peace ship and the ridicule Ford received hurt his feelings very much. But many people were sympathetic. One New York newspaper said, "...he at least TRIED."

The War Goes on

As the war continued, the people of the United States were shocked by Ger-man activities. They used submarines to sink ships, including passenger liners. They used poison gas on the battlefield and there were incidents of German spies in the U.S. trying to stop shipments of war supplies to England. Finally, on April 6, 1917, Congress declared war on Germany.

Rebecca Shelley continued to oppose the war, but Ford changed his mind. He was now convinced only a show of strength could end the fighting.

Michigan Industry Joins the Fight

Workers in the auto plants made a variety of equipment for the war effort. Buick, Cadillac, Ford, Lincoln and Packard produced about 30,000 airplane engines. The 4,500 employees of the Fisher Body plant in Detroit turned out 1,600 fighter planes, 5 bombers and 400 training planes. Realize that fewer than 1,000 planes had been made in the entire country before 1916! Women in Grand Rapids worked on fabric parts for airplanes at the Hayes-Ionia company and others made plane parts at Wilson Body in Bay City. Altogether nearly 20 percent of all the World War I military planes were made in Michigan. Surprisingly, the

Ford Motor Company built 60 ships. These submarine chasers were assembled at the River Rouge plant. Many Model T trucks and ambulances went overseas with U.S. soldiers. Detroit alone had $750 million in war contracts.

Everyone Helps

Michigan farmers were asked to grow more food than ever before. Large amounts were needed to feed not only our own soldiers but to help feed the French and English too. Food production went up 25 percent even though many men had to leave the farms and join the army. Often women did much of the farm work. To conserve food, people were urged to have "meatless days" and "wheatless days."

Women entered important jobs both at home and in the war. Nurses provided vital assistance for the troops. Women worked in factories and on farms. They delivered ice to people in the cities for their iceboxes. They were railroad engineers and streetcar conductors. They did their work well and were proud of what they accomplished but most of their jobs were considered temporary. Nearly all of the women workers were replaced by men after the war was over. Often the women were reluctant to leave but they were given little choice in the matter.

Things German Are Not Popular

Quickly, everyone in Michigan became enthusiastic and ready to fight. Even though Germans were the largest ethnic group in Michigan, there was much anti-German feeling. The German language was dropped in schools. The town of Berlin near Grand Rapids changed its name to Marne and the Germania elementary school in Saginaw became the Lincoln elementary school.

Michigan Men and Women to War

Even before the United States entered the war, some Michigan men had already joined the Canadian army. By the time the war ended, 135,485 Michigan men served in our armed forces.

The federal government started plans to train all of these men and women. A huge army installation was built near Battle Creek. It was called Camp Custer and General Custer's widow even came to the opening ceremonies. Ten thousand acres of farmland were bought. The people of Battle Creek were amazed by the 4,000 train carloads of materials that

A group of World War I nurses from Michigan. (Courtesy Michigan State Archives)

The idea of going to fight in Europe may have sounded exciting but Michigan soldiers soon discovered the horrors of war. (Courtesy Michigan State Archives)

arrived for the camp and the 8,000 carpenters needed to do the work. When it was completed, Camp Custer had over 2,000 buildings in all. Included was a hospital and a large power plant. The camp was ready in only six months! Some said that nothing like it was ever built in America before! During the war 50,000 soldiers trained at Camp Custer.

Others trained at Selfridge Field, a new air base near Mt. Clemens. It was Michigan's first military air base. The land for the base was given to the government by the president of the Packard company. One of the soldiers at Selfridge was Eddie Rickenbacker. He already had a connection with Michigan, because he was a well-known race car driver. Rickenbacker be-

came famous during the war. He shot down 26 enemy planes, more than any other flyer with the U.S. forces. Rickenbacker's family, like many other Americans, came from Germany.

Part of the base hospital at Camp Custer near Battle Creek. (Courtesy Michigan State Archives)

A Killer at Home—The Flu

During January 1918 the U.S. had a severe coal shortage. Coal was the most important fuel at that time and the crisis caused a lot of hardship. Businesses which were not involved in making war supplies had to close for a week to save coal.

The next fall, Michigan people were feeling relief because after nearly 18 months the war was almost over. Then tragedy struck. One of the worst worldwide flu epidemics ever known took place. It was called Spanish influenza and it spread very quickly.

The doctors at Camp Custer were taking precautions to protect the soldiers. They were told, "There is nothing to worry about." Then on September 29 the first man came down with the flu. The sick soldier was quickly separated from the rest, but that did not help. In only three days 2,500 men were sick and seven had died. By October 9, over 6,000 were sick at the camp and 94 had died. Before the epidemic was over, 573 soldiers left Camp Custer in simple pine coffins!

If the flu could kill strong young soldiers so fast, what did it do to everyone else? Cities all over Michigan reported so many deaths that after a time the newspapers stopped printing the numbers. Over 500 died in Battle Creek, over 600 in Kalamazoo, and over 3,800 in Detroit.

The flu epidemic was a very sad way to end a time which had already seen terrible killing and bloodshed. Some 5,000 Michigan soldiers died in the war and another 15,000 were wounded. Some of the wounded had been exposed to poison gas and never completely recovered.

Our Soldiers in the Soviet Union!

Although the war was over, some 5,000 Michigan families could not see their sons and husbands yet. In one of the most unusual aspects of the war, a large group of Michigan troops had been sent to the cold frozen land of northern Russia. Many of the men had trained at Camp Custer and their group was known as the Polar Bears. Their orders were to fight the communist forces who were trying to form the Soviet Union. Their official mission had been to protect military supplies the United States had sent to the Russian government, but a revolution started in that country. The Russian government was fighting the communist revolutionaries and the

World War I soldiers at Camp Custer. (Courtesy Michigan State Archives)

Michigan soldiers were caught in the middle.

The survivors of the Russian mission came back to Michigan in 1919. In White Chapel Cemetery in Troy stands a stark white polar bear monument. Many of those who did not live to see their home state again are buried beneath that monument.

World War I changed Michigan. Michigan was no longer a quiet farming state. It had some of the largest factories in the nation. It also had a well-trained work force for it had become an industrial state. The soldiers had been introduced to cars, tanks, planes, and radios during the fighting. Many of them found life on a farm too dull. They were more excited about life in a busy city. Michigan's transportation and communications systems would change rapidly after the war.

Questions

1. Who was Rebecca Shelley and what did she have to do with World War I?

2. Why do you think Henry Ford's peace ship project was a failure?

3. Give some examples that show how large Camp Custer was.

4. What famous American flyer trained near Mt. Clemens?

5. What event in Michigan caused many deaths just as World War I was ending?

6. Suppose your family had come to Michigan from Germany. What do you think some of your reactions would have been during World War I?

298

Chapter 12 Section 2

Rum Runners, Gangsters, and the 1920s

Here are the key concepts you will find in this section:

Michigan, and then the nation, voted to stop the sale of alcoholic beverages. Immediately people began to make their own liquor and criminals started selling it.

The area from Ecorse to Port Huron became a central point for smuggling liquor from Canada to the United States.

Gangs were able to operate in some areas with little interference from the police. There was corruption in local government and often officials did not go after those violating prohibition.

Major Michigan cities faced poor racial relations in the 1920s. Housing for black people was not good but they were not allowed to move into white neighborhoods.

Several well-known authors, including Ernest Hemingway, had Michigan connections in the 1920s.

After the War — Changes at Home

In Michigan there were abundant jobs making war supplies, but when the war ended, the government stopped production. Without the need for airplanes and guns, large numbers of workers found themselves without jobs. It took two or three years for the economy to start moving ahead again. Some of the people tried to make money at the illegal job of selling outlawed liquor.

In 1916 a new state constitution outlawed the manufacture and sale of alcoholic beverages. That law went into effect on May 1, 1918, a few months before the war was over. From that point on Michigan was to be "dry."

Reformers, called prohibitionists or temperance advocates, had been trying to prohibit the sale of liquor for nearly 100 years. Drunkenness caused many broken families and much poverty. In 1915 Henry Leland, the president of the Cadillac Motor Company, invited the evangelist Billy Sunday to visit Detroit

VOTE "DRY" FOR US

(Courtesy Michigan State Archives)

THE CENTREVILLE OBSERVER.

VOL. XXVII, NO. 2.   CENTREVILLE, MICHIGAN, THURSDAY, SEPTEMBER 21, 1916.   WHOLE NO. 1,357.

THE RECRUITING STATION OF THE FUTURE DRUNKARD

GRANGE FAIR.

Everything in Readiness for the Big Grange Fair to be Held Here Sept. 26, 27, 28, 29 and 30.

The entire county is looking forward to the Grange Fair to be held at this place next week. The officers have provided ample entertainment for all and they promise something doing all the time. The Grange has the fair in charge and the success of the fair last year is a guarantee for this year. Below we print the official program for each day:

WEDNESDAY, SEPT. 27.
Being School Day the sports will be all of athletics.
Pageane—some school, good prize.
Relay Race — open to all, cup or trophy.
Basket Ball—girls, ball.
Soccer Ball—boys, ball.
Base ball—boys, cup or trophy.

THURSDAY, SEPT. 28.
Two aeroplane flights.
Two balloon ascensions with double parachute drop.
Free-for-all race.
Basket ball game.
Base ball game — Constantine vs. Three Rivers.
The Polarro Bros. in their comic Trick House exhibition.
Being Republican Day noted speakers will be present.

FRIDAY, SEPT. 29.
Two aeroplane flights.
Two balloon ascensions with double

Probate Court.

Proceedings in the probate court for the week ending Sept. 16, 1916.
Estate of Martha G. Andrews, deceased. Final account allowed.
Estate of John R. Williams, deceased. Petition for appointment of administrator filed, order for hearing entered.
Estate of John R. Byrd, deceased. Final account allowed, executrix discharged.
Estate of Eliza M. Whitman, mentally incompetent. Annual account allowed.
Estate of Sarah A. McClellan, deceased. Commissioners' warrant and report filed.
Estate of Charles B. Wyman, deceased. Bond filed, letters issued.
Estate of Thomas J. Jones, deceased. Petition for allowance of final administration account and for final distribution filed, order for hearing entered.
Estate of Mary Ann Millen, deceased. Petition for appointment of administrator filed, order for hearing entered.
Estate of Walter W. and Beryl Z. Mandigo; minors. Annual account of guardian allowed.
Estate of Stephen O. Black, deceased. Order appointing special administrator entered, bond filed, letters of special administration issued.
Estate of Margaret Hartman, deceased. Petition for license to sell real estate filed, order for hearing entered.
Estate of Charles B. Wyman, de-

Before prohibition there was a strong drive against saloons and drinking.

and speak against the evils of alcohol. Billy Sunday came and stayed for 11 weeks. He spoke to a total of more than 1 million people. In 1916 prohibition passed in a statewide vote. However, prohibition eventually caused some big problems of its own.

The Effects of Prohibition

Just before Michigan's law went into effect, those who liked to drink rushed out and bought all the liquor they could find. When those supplies started to go down, gangsters began to bring truckloads from Ohio. Liquor was still legal there. The Purple Gang and other criminals saw it was possible to make big profits selling liquor to those who wanted it. While that was going on in Michigan, the nation voted to have national prohibition. The U.S. law went into effect in January 1920.

The wilderness of the Upper Peninsula was another place where prohibition was not very popular. In that rough and tumble land, when miners and loggers wanted a drink no one was going

to stop them! They felt they were "north of the law." There were plenty of towns with someone running a still and making moonshine. The thick woods of the Upper Peninsula had many places to hide an illegal still. People usually knew that "so and so" was delivering quart jars of liquor hidden under a wagonload of firewood.

Rum Runners Across the River

The Detroit River has a good view of the Canadian liquor distiller Hiram Walker. With a supply of alcoholic beverages so close to Michigan, it did not take gangs of "rum runners" long to start bringing Canadian liquor and beer across the border. They used fast speedboats and could make the trip in only a couple of minutes. Cars or trucks waited for the boats on the Michigan side and helpers quickly transferred the liquor. Then the vehicles roared off.

The beginning of prohibition made the 100-mile Michigan-Canadian border, from Ecorse to Port Huron, a battleground between law officers and smugglers. It

In April 1929 a *Detroit News* photographer hidden in a warehouse caught these rum runners unloading suitcases of liquor from a boat along the Detroit River. (Courtesy The *Detroit News*)

has been estimated that 85 percent of all the liquor smuggled into the United States from Canada passed through that area—perhaps as much as 500,000 cases a month. To stop the smugglers, the government used the U.S. Customs Service, the Immigration Service, Federal Prohibition Agency, and the Coast Guard—a total of 250 officers. The Coast Guard patrolled the Detroit and St. Clair rivers with three large patrol boats and several speedboats. The Michigan State Police and Detroit Police Department assisted. To make it easier for rum runners, railroad engineers were often bribed to sound their whistles as a warning when a government patrol boat was coming.

Moonshine, Bribes, and Illegal Bars

Illegal liquor was made throughout Michigan, not just in the Upper Peninsula. Stills were hidden in the basements

During prohibition police raided this illegal still in Jackson County. (Courtesy Michigan State Archives)

of homes, in barns, or in old warehouses. When shifts changed at the big auto factories, people waited nearby in cars to sell liquor to the workers. All of that activity provided the gangs with loads of cash.

They used some of the money to bribe the police and members of the sheriff's department to look the other way and not report what was going on. Judges were bribed to give short sentences.

Bullets Fly

Criminal activity and violence usually go hand in hand. And the Metro area was practically a shooting gallery. In 1925 as many as 53 bodies were recovered from the Detroit River which had become a convenient dumping place for victims.

Citizens wondered why the local government did not take strong action to arrest the gangsters. In 1930 many people were convinced the mayor of Detroit and other important officials were taking bribes. A citizens group worked to recall the mayor and have him replaced. The recall election was to be held on July 21, 1930. That month became known as "bloody July" as gang killings reached a new peak with 10 murders.

Murder at the Hotel

Jerry Buckley was a popular Detroit radio announcer who had attacked the lawless situation. He spoke out against gangsters and corrupt officials. Just before the recall election, Buckley lashed out at the mayor and said he should be thrown out of office. Then on election day Buckley broadcast the results; by midnight he was able to tell his listeners the vote had gone against the mayor and he was out.

The radio announcer Jerry Buckley (Art by George Rasmussen)

Once his program was over, Jerry Buckley went to a downtown hotel to wait for someone who had promised him a "hot" news tip. At 1 A.M. he was sitting in the hotel lobby when three men approached. Suddenly the strangers pulled pistols and blazed away. The furniture splintered and Buckley was riddled with 11 bullets.

Detroit went into shock. Over 100,000 people came to the funeral. The public demanded swift action from the police. But corruption continued. The police did a poor job of investigating the murder. Two policemen who had found a good lead were transferred off the case and the police commissioner went on vacation.

While citizens remained outraged, the killings continued. The lawlessness would last until prohibition was discontinued in 1933. Prohibition was an idea that did not work.

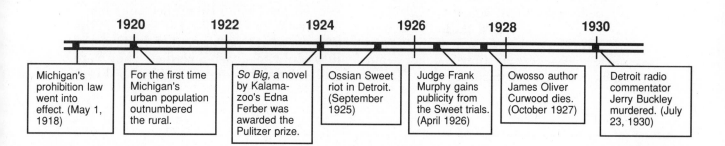

1920	1922	1924	1926	1928	1930

Michigan's prohibition law went into effect. (May 1, 1918)

For the first time Michigan's urban population outnumbered the rural.

So Big, a novel by Kalamazoo's Edna Ferber was awarded the Pulitzer prize.

Ossian Sweet riot in Detroit. (September 1925)

Judge Frank Murphy gains publicity from the Sweet trials. (April 1926)

Owosso author James Oliver Curwood dies. (October 1927)

Detroit radio commentator Jerry Buckley murdered. (July 23, 1930)

302

Racial Violence

Those were violent years in other ways too. The Ku Klux Klan (KKK), an organization against Blacks, Jews, and Catholics, was active after World War I. Its members used terror against black people who came to Michigan to find better jobs during the war. The KKK members were ready to attack blacks for

Dr. Ossian Sweet. (Art by George Rasmussen)

any reason, no matter how trivial. Tension developed between the races. In the 1920s the black population of Detroit increased from 41,000 to 120,000. It was extremely difficult for all of the black people to find housing. The lack of housing caused a sad event to take place.

Dr. Ossian Sweet was a young man who had completed medical school and had even continued his studies of medicine in Vienna and Paris. The 31-year-old doctor had returned to Detroit and finally found a nice house for his family. But there were problems.

The trouble with the Sweet's home was its location—in an all white neighborhood. Almost the minute they moved in, the Sweets received nasty phone calls. The next day a crowd gathered across the street in a school yard. They had no sense of fairness as they did not want black people in their part of town. It did

not matter that Ossian Sweet, a well-educated man, could not find a decent home anywhere else.

Dr. Sweet and his wife Gladys were scared to death by the angry people outside. Dr. Sweet asked his brother and six friends to stay with them. They came and they brought guns too. Six police officers were there to keep the crowd under control and two more officers arrived to direct traffic. The Sweets remained indoors and tried to be calm.

About 8:00 P.M. people started throwing rocks at the house and the police didn't stop them. Dr. Sweet jumped up and looked outside. He reeled back in shock when he saw about 700 angry people surrounding his home. By that time, window glass was crashing as rocks rained in from every direction.

Suddenly, another brother pulled up in a car and made a mad dash for the house. Dr. Sweet swung open the front door so he could get inside. At that instant the mob surged toward the house. Bang, bang, bang.... several shots were fired from the upstairs of the Sweet home. The ugly mob scattered; but a man who had been smoking his pipe on a friend's porch across the street lay dead. He had apparently been hit by a bullet fired from Ossian Sweet's house.

Only then did the police spring into action. They rushed into the home and arrested everyone inside for murder. The Sweets were held for trial. To help in their defense, the National Association for the Advancement of Colored People (NAACP) hired the nationally famous lawyer, Clarence Darrow.

A Famous Trial

The judge at the Sweet's trial was Frank Murphy. Many people said the trial would be the end of his career because it would be an impossible situation. Darrow talked for hours in a sweaty, packed courtroom. He argued that someone else may have shot the victim so the Sweets would be blamed. For days the jury could not reach a verdict. They were so divided they shouted and threw things

Part of a 1924 *Detroit Times* cartoon about Judge Frank Murphy.

at each other. Finally, Judge Murphy declared a hung jury and asked for a second trial.

In the second trial, Darrow based his case on the fact that white people would have the right to defend themselves in their home and that the Sweets had the same right. At that trial Henry Sweet admitted he was one of those who shot at the crowd, but he said he fired in self defense. Clarence Darrow spoke about the issue of racial prejudice. He said, "This great state and this great city... must face this problem and face it squarely." As a result of the second trial, the jury said the Sweets were not guilty. Frank Murphy was given high marks for conducting a fair trial. The Ossian Sweet incident was a needless negative mark against Detroit.

Best Sellers From Michigan

While some people spent their time in the illegal liquor trade, others tried something more useful and read books written by Michigan authors.

Edna Ferber was a woman author born in Kalamazoo. During the 1920s she wrote some of her best-known stories including *So Big*, *Show Boat*, and *Cimarron*. Ferber's *So Big* was very popular and won a Pulitzer prize.

James Oliver Curwood's exciting adventure stories, similar to those of Jack London, were of the rugged life in Alaska. His writings included *The Alaskan*, *The Gold Snare*, and *Valley of the Silent Men*. Curwood lived in Owosso and his studio was constructed to look like a castle. Tourists still visit Owosso to see "Curwood's Castle." James Oliver Curwood died suddenly from the flu in 1927.

Edgar A. Guest's short poems usually provided his readers with a smile or a chuckle. He was often called the "Poet of the Plain People." For many years a new poem by Guest appeared each day in the Detroit Free Press. His poem *Home* begins with the well-known line: "It takes a heap o' livin' in a house t' make it home."

Ty Cobb was a famous base-stealing Detroit Tigers player when Ring Lardner wrote about him in his story, *Tyrus: The Greatest of 'Em All*. Lardner's work had a sort of cynical humor to it. Some other stories written by Lardner about that time were: *Bib Ballads*, *Gullible's Travels*, and *The Big Town*. Lardner was born in Niles but had moved to Chicago by the time he did most of his writing.

Ernest Hemingway did not live in Michigan. He grew up in Oak Park near the city of Chicago. But he spent much time at his family's summer home at Walloon Lake not far from Petoskey. He enjoyed his time there and used Michigan settings in several stories. An Upper Peninsula setting was used in his book, *The Big Two-Hearted River*.

The author Ring Lardner. (Courtesy Michigan State Archives)

Oliver Curwood's studio in Owosso known as Curwood's Castle. (Courtesy Michigan Travel Bureau)

During the 1920s, Michigan grew rapidly and took on a new character. It had its greatest percentage of population increase in those 10 years. For the first time, more people lived in the cities than on the farms. The growing cities required more government services—more streets, roads, and schools. That growth brought problems. For instance, the racial troubles between whites and blacks became more intense. Prohibition gave criminals a source of easy cash and they used it to bribe officials. Some parts of government were corrupt, but citizens took action to clean them up. In spite of problems, there were bright spots. Most people had good jobs and decent incomes. Michigan authors delighted the country and gained national recognition.

Questions

1. What was prohibition and when was it in effect in Michigan?

2. List some positive and negative ways in which prohibition affected Michigan.

3. What geographical feature made the area between Ecorse and Port Huron a center for rum runners smuggling illegal liquor?

4. Put yourself in the place of Dr. Ossian Sweet in 1925 and describe what your thoughts and feelings would have been when a mob surrounded your home.

5. Select two of the stories mentioned in this section written by authors with a Michigan connection and tell why you might like to read them.

6. How could railroad engineers, gangsters, judges, and other people justify breaking the prohibition law?

Chapter 12 Section 3

Modernizing Michigan

Here are the key concepts you will find in this section:

Michigan women fought for and won the right to vote in 1918.

Mary Doe, Lucinda Stone, and Anna Howard Shaw are Michigan women who worked hard for women's voting rights.

Michigan was a leader among the states making early passenger airplanes.

In 1920 Michigan had one of the first radio stations in the nation. Many radio firsts came from Michigan stations. The Lone Ranger program was developed by station WXYZ.

Private companies built the Ambassador Bridge and the Detroit-Windsor Tunnel in the late 1920s. Today these are the busiest links between the United States and Canada.

At Last Women Could Vote

The 1920s saw the people of Michigan become more modern in their thinking. They showed this by granting women the right to vote for the first time. In 1918 the state constitution was changed to give women voting privileges. Michigan was two years ahead of the nation in that respect; the U.S. Constitution was changed in 1920.

It had been a tough fight to get these changes. Men were often against voting rights for women. They had a variety of reasons. Some men thought women could not comprehend the issues during elections. Some religious leaders thought if women voted, there would be more divorce and the family unit would fall apart. Saloon owners and those who made liquor were against women voting too. They thought if women voted, they would help pass prohibition.

It Was a Long Struggle

Women had worked hard for a long time to have voting rights. Suffrage is another name for voting rights, and the phrase "women's suffrage" was used often. The issue had been up for a state-wide vote several times, but it always failed to pass. In 1912 Governor Chase Osborn backed women's suffrage. It came close to passing that time, losing by only 800 votes.

The Women's Equal Suffrage Society often had a large tent at the state fair. A banner on the tent read: "The law says criminals, idiots, insane, children, and WOMEN cannot vote." Women felt they were no better than those groups since they were also denied the vote.

Some of the Leaders

Lucinda Stone and Mary Doe worked for women's suffrage in the 1800s. Mary Doe was president of the Michigan Equal Suffrage Association. That particular group allowed men to join, and Michigan Governor Josiah Begole was once its vice president.

Another Michigan woman who led in the fight for equal rights was Anna Howard Shaw. At the high school in her hometown of Big Rapids is a memorial to her. Anna had struggled since the 1880s to help women have equal rights. She once said, "Around me I saw women overworked and underpaid...not because

This was the headquarters for women's suffrage at the Michigan state fair grounds. They urged men to allow them the right to vote. (Courtesy Michigan State Archives)

their work was inferior but because they were women... and with all my heart I joined the crusade for equal rights." In 1904 she replaced Susan B. Anthony as president of the National American Women Suffrage Association. Anna Shaw died in 1919. She did not live quite long enough to see her dream of voting rights for all American women come true. In 1920, for the first time, any woman could vote in the presidential election.

Suffrage for women was a great step forward. Since that time, women have not only been actively voting, but running for elected office. In Michigan they have been on city councils, university boards, the state supreme court, and been elected to the office of lieutenant governor. Today, the League of Women Voters and similar organizations continue what earlier groups started long ago. The League provides educational materials on important election issues.

New Possibilities

People experienced two new thrilling possibilities in the 1920s. They could sit by their "wireless" or radio and hear another person's voice coming from hundreds of miles away. The second great thrill was commercial aviation. People could buy a ticket and fly from city to city in a commercial airplane as the countryside glided by beneath them. And Michigan was a leader in both of those new fields.

Airliners From Michigan

Who developed one of those first airliners? None other than Michigan's Henry Ford! But the airliner story began with another man, William Stout. Stout started a company in Detroit to make an all-metal passenger-carrying airplane. The all-metal design was quite unique because most planes were made of wood and canvas. William Stout was a leader in his field as Ford had been in his.

Ford and Stout got together when they first talked about the possible location for a new landing field. It would be one of the first in Michigan. Henry Ford offered some land in Dearborn and by the next day tractors were clearing it. That airport was near the present location of Greenfield Village and Henry Ford Museum in Dearborn.

Henry and Edsel Ford eventually bought Stout's company. Stout continued to work with Ford engineers to build a new design. They wanted a plane which was superior to all others. They planned

308

William Stout speaking at the Grand Rapids Public Airport. (Courtesy Grand Rapids Public Library- Michigan Room)

to give it three motors, so if something went wrong with one engine, the other two would keep the plane in the air. Engine failure was a big worry to passengers long ago because it happened often. The completed plane was called the tri-motor.

The tri-motor built by Ford and Stout was the largest commercial plane made in the United States at that time. Its wings spanned 70 feet. It could fly at 100 miles an hour or better and carry 14 passengers plus some freight.

Soon the tri-motors were sold to several airlines and to the army and navy. Starting in 1926, Ford planes carried the U.S. mail between Detroit, Chicago, and Cleveland. In 1929 Admiral Richard E. Byrd flew a Ford tri-motor plane on his expedition over the South Pole.

A Hero Born in Michigan

In 1927, Charles Lindbergh crossed the Atlantic Ocean alone in his single-engine plane, *The Spirit of St. Louis.* Instantly Lindbergh was a worldwide hero. People in Detroit were especially proud because Lindbergh had been born in the city and his mother was a science teacher at Cass Technical High School.

Once Lindbergh was back in the United States, he flew his plane on a tour around the country. Two of his first stops were at Dearborn and Grand Rapids. While at Dearborn he took Henry Ford for a ride—the first passenger to fly in the famous plane after its return. Ford then asked Lindbergh if he would manage the airplane factory; although Lindbergh turned him down, they did remain friends.

Charles Lindbergh. (Courtesy Michigan State Archives)

POWER POWER POWER

CUT ANY ENGINE ON A FORD PLANE
AND YOU STILL HAVE PLENTY OF POWER

PILOTS undergoing training on Ford Tri-motors at the Ford Airport at Dearborn soon learn what it means to have a plane that will carry on with a dead engine.

For their course includes the cutting of any engine, by the chief pilot, in a steep climb, in a sharply banked turn. They learn from actual experience that there is no time when a Ford plane can't be brought to horizontal flight when an engine suddenly dies.

Another thing about this power. With three engines working the power load with the 5-AT is 10.6 pounds. There's the power to pull you out of a small field—to climb quickly over obstructions. It helps the pilot out of those slight mistakes in judgment where only a world of power will carry the plane through safely. Even with only two engines you have more power for your load than many a plane possesses. The power load then is only 15.9. Still plenty of margin, plenty of reserve.

More than half the accidents in commercial aviation, according to the Department of Commerce, are attributable to the pilot. But how often is the real reason the fact the plane wouldn't come through as the pilot expected, because the sheer, brute power he needed wasn't available?

In the Ford Tri-motor there's all the power you need or want. Even with one engine dead. Safe flying starts with power—dependable, uninterrupted power and plenty of it. The Stout Metal Airplane Company, Division of Ford Motor Company, Dearborn, Michigan.

FORD TRI-MOTOR
5-AT

Span 77 ft. 10 ins. Maximum speed, 133 M.P.H. Maximum radius of action (standard equipped) 5 to 6 hours. Ceiling, 18,000 ft. Weight empty, 7500 lbs. Disposable load, 6000 lbs. Power load, 3 engines, 10.6 lbs. per H.P.; 2 engines, 15.9. Cabin accommodates 14 passengers, pilot and mechanic. Construction: ALL-METAL *throughout, exposed surfaces Alclad alloy. Power: 3 Pratt & Whitney Wasps, totaling 1275 H.P. Price, complete with standard equipment including instruments, seats, toilet, etc., fly-away Dearborn, $55,000. (Prices and specifications subject to change without notice.)*

310

In the late 1920s Ford had 1,600 workers making trimotor planes, but the operation was really one big experiment. It had never made much money. When the Great Depression (a business slowdown) hit the country in the 1930s, Ford closed the airplane part of his business. But the trimotors did not die easily. They were well-made, and a few of them were still flying as late as the 1970s.

Radio—Sound from a Box

In the early 1920s the thrill of a new invention, the radio, was sweeping the country. Once again, Michigan people were involved in important developments. James Scripps was the founder of the *Detroit News.* He had been interested in wireless experiments since 1901 when he received a message from Thomas "Wireless" Clark sent from two blocks away. In 1920 Scripps believed it was time for his newspaper to become involved in radio. The *News* bought a puny 20-watt radio transmitter and put it in a corner of the sports department. The small transmitter could be heard about 100 miles away, but only under the best conditions. That was one of the first radio stations in the country.

Radio Firsts From Michigan

The first public broadcast from the *News* station was in August 1920 when the election results were sent out over the air. There were probably not more than 300 people with radio sets near enough to hear it!

For those listeners it was not just a matter of clicking on a switch and sitting back in an easy chair. Fifteen or twenty feet of wire had to be strung up to use as an antenna. The radio itself might not be much more than a coil of wire on an oatmeal box connected to a crystal of silicon or a piece of pencil lead. The operator listened through a set of earphones or a

borrowed telephone receiver. Usually it was difficult to make out the broadcast through a steady background of static.

Better equipment, however, was on the way for both the stations and listeners. In the meantime the *News* station had been assigned the call letters WWJ. They were broadcasting boxing fights and symphony concerts. Another newspaper, the *Detroit Free Press,* started a station of its own in 1922.

WWJ broadcast one of the first football games in 1924 when the University of Michigan's coach, Fielding Yost, gave the station permission since the game had been sold out long ahead of time. Announcer Ty Tyson made the historic play by play report. Tyson was at the microphone again when the first Detroit Tigers game was broadcast in 1927.

From Our Studios— The Lone Ranger

In 1930 a third station, WXYZ, began in Detroit. Unfortunately, it wasn't long before the two owners found they were losing money fast. While they wondered what they should do, one of them

A girl listening to an early radio about 1921. (Courtesy Michigan State Archives)

remembered his days in the theater. He knew they always made money with a good western. Soon the station's staff was talking over ideas for a new program based on a hero from the wild west. "I see him as a sort of lone operator....He could even be a former Texas Ranger." Then someone shouted, "There's his name! The Lone Ranger." From 1932 until 1954, live radio stories about the masked man on his white horse were sent across the nation from Detroit. Brace Beemer was well known for his role as the Lone Ranger on radio from 1941 to 1954.

It must have been fun to work in radio during those early days. All kinds of sound effects were made right in the studio— galloping horses, thunder, and gunshots. But the listeners might have been puzzled if they could have seen Tonto. Bald-headed John Todd, who was not an Indian, but wore glasses and dressed in a business suit, read his lines!

Other great radio drama came from WXYZ. In 1936, the *Green Hornet* took to the air and in 1939 *Challenge of the Yukon* began. That program later became *Sergeant Preston of the Yukon.*

The broadcast room of Michigan radio station WWJ in 1931. The announcer is at the left and the other people are making different sound effects for their radio program. Can you tell what sounds each man is making? (Courtesy Michigan State Archives)

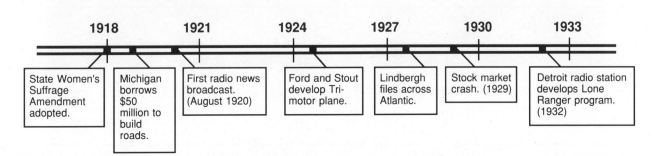

1918	1921	1924	1927	1930	1933

State Women's Suffrage Amendment adopted.

Michigan borrows $50 million to build roads.

First radio news broadcast. (August 1920)

Ford and Stout develop Tri-motor plane.

Lindbergh files across Atlantic.

Stock market crash. (1929)

Detroit radio station develops Lone Ranger program. (1932)

One radio broadcaster recalled, "Detroit was a hot spot in 1938. Radio stations WWJ, WJR, and WXYZ all had drama shows, and as an actor you could work at two or three of them each week."

Better Roads and Bridges

Michigan was becoming physically modern, too. In 1919 the state borrowed $50 million to build new highways. Over 1,000 miles of new roads were being finished each year.

Soon Michigan would also be connected to Canada and drivers could zip between the two countries. Before 1929 the only way to reach Canada was by ferry across one of the three rivers which separate Michigan from Ontario. Or it was possible to take a train and use the Port Huron railroad tunnel. Joseph Bower decided to do something to make a better link between Michigan and Canada. He formed the Detroit International Bridge Company and raised money to build a bridge between Detroit and Windsor.

In 1927 work was started. The bridge's two steel towers soared 263 feet above the Detroit River. Only a few months before the bridge was to be finished, engineers discovered something

A crew pouring concrete for one of Michigan's first highways. (Courtesy Michigan State Archives)

The Blue Water Bridge between Port Huron and Sarnia, Ontario. (Courtesy East Michigan Tourist Association)

wrong with the 19-inch diameter cable being used. All of the heavy cable which held up the roadway had to be replaced. In spite of that delay, the bridge was finished in a little over two years. It opened in 1929 and was the longest suspension bridge in the world when it was completed. It was named the Ambassador Bridge as a note of goodwill between the two countries.

Now, about 5 million cars go across the bridge each year and Detroit is the busiest crossing place between the United States and Canada.

First International Car Tunnel

The Ambassador Bridge does not handle all of the traffic across the 1,850 foot-wide Detroit River. Soon after work started on the bridge, a tunnel was being bored under the river by another private company. The Detroit-Windsor Tunnel opened in 1930 and was the world's first automobile tunnel between two countries. The tunnel is still being used and carries about as many cars and trucks as the Ambassador Bridge.

Other bridges from Michigan to Canada were built later. The 8,021 foot Blue Water Bridge from Port Huron, Michigan, to Sarnia, Ontario, was finished in 1938. The International bridge which begins at Sault Ste. Marie and passes over the St. Mary's River was not completed until the 1960s.

Questions

1. Give two reasons why some men did not want women to be able to vote. Did Michigan allow women to have voting rights before the United States Constitution was changed?

2. Name two women and two men from Michigan who backed women's suffrage.

3. What safety feature did a trimotor plane have which helped early airline passengers feel safe?

4. What kind of businesses started the first radio stations in Michigan?

5. Name the two countries and two cities the Ambassador Bridge connects. Who owns this bridge?

6. In your opinion which of the modern changes that took place in Michigan during the 1920s was the most important and why?

13 BLEAK TIMES LEAD TO ANOTHER WAR -
1930s & 1940s

Chapter 13 Section 1

Michigan Bends Under the Depression

Here are the key concepts you will find in this section:

Late in 1929 a severe economic depression, or business slowdown, hit the country.

Michigan businesses had quick declines in sales. They could not afford to keep all of their workers on their payrolls, so many people lost their jobs.

Nearly 200 Michigan banks closed and their customers lost much of their savings. Due to a lack of money, people lost their homes and farms in tax sales and bank foreclosures.

Father Charles Coughlin (KOG lin) of Royal Oak had a popular radio program during the 1930s. But he made many radical statements and was ordered by the Pope to stop broadcasting.

James Couzens and Frank Murphy were two Michigan men with government positions who tried to help those in need.

Thousands of Michigan citizens were given jobs by the WPA and CCC federal programs.

The Good Times End

Life was going well in 1929, very well indeed. Or so it seemed. It was also the year Michigan auto pioneer William Durant went to talk with President Hoover. Durant recognized some government policies he thought could hurt the stock market. That possibility worried him. The stock market had gone up and up. It seemed an easy way to make money. Millions of people had bought stocks even though the stock prices were much higher than they had ever been before. Investors thought stocks would just continue to go up. But in October 1929 they suddenly went down! The value of investments fell so much in one day people said the stock market had crashed.

Stock market investors felt rich one day and then were shocked to see their money gone the next. To make things worse, many banks had also invested their customers' savings in the stock market. They lost money too. When people came to withdraw their savings, they were often told the bank could not pay. That increased their fears. Suddenly crowds of people swarmed to the banks

316

EIGHT-DAY HOLIDAY FOR ALL BANKS IN MICHIGAN

 DETROIT TIMES EXTRA

330 YEAR. NO. 137   DETROIT, MICHIGAN, TUESDAY, FEBRUARY 14, 1933   24 PAGES   THREE CENTS

Proclamation Closing Banks to Protect State

Whereas, in view of the acute financial emergency now existing in the city of Detroit and throughout the state of Michigan, I deem it necessary in the public interest and for the preservation of the public peace, health and safety, and for the equal safeguarding without preference of the rights of all depositors in the banks and trust companies of this state and at the request of the Michigan Bankers' Association and the Detroit Clearing House and after consultation with the banking authorities, both national and state, with representatives of the United States Treasury Department, the Banking Department of the State of Michigan, the Federal Reserve Bank, the Reconstruction Finance Corporation, and with the United States Secretary of Commerce, I hereby proclaim the days from Tuesday, February 14th, 1933, to Tuesday, February 21st, 1933, both dates inclusive, to be public holidays during which time all banks, trust companies and other financial institutions conducting a banking or trust business within the state of Michigan shall not be opened for the transaction of banking or trust business, the same to be recognized, classed and treated and have the same effect in respect to such banks, trust companies and other financial institutions as other legal holidays under the laws of this state, provided that it shall not affect the making or execution of agreements or instruments in writing or interfere with judicial proceedings. Dated this 14th day of February, 1933, 1:32 a. m.

WILLIAM A. COMSTOCK, Governor of the State of Michigan.

ERNIE SCHAAF SUCCUMBS | *STATEMENTS BY OFFICIALS* | UNION GUARDIAN TRUST CO.

and wanted their money. Of course, it was impossible for so many people to be paid in cash all at once. Banks use the depositors' money to make loans; it does not just sit in their vaults. Many banks could not come up with enough cash and they had to close. By 1932 nearly 200 Michigan banks had gone out of business. There were many depositors who never did get all of their money and some didn't get any at all.

Less Business and Fewer Jobs

The stock market crash and the bank closings were a shock to everyone. Afterwards, people simply did not have money to buy things; it was as if someone had turned off the "switch" to the economy. Michigan business was tied closely to the automobile industry. For example, in Genesee County half of the working people had jobs with General Motors. In the United States there were almost 4.5 million cars sold in 1929, but car sales fell rapidly. In 1930 less than 3 million were sold and by 1931 sales were less than 2 million.

It was not possible for companies to keep everyone working after such a big decline in sales. As a result, many employees lost their jobs. The Ford Rouge plant had 98,337 workers in 1929. By 1933 there were only 28,915. That was just the tip of the iceberg. Business was bad for all of the companies making parts for cars, for those making tires, and many others. The need for Michigan's raw materials fell sharply. The production of Michigan copper was cut in half after 1930. In 1932 shipments of Michigan iron ore fell to less than one-tenth of the previous year. As many as 63 percent of those living in the mining counties had to go on *welfare. Welfare refers to the government programs which provide assistance to families so they can have the necessary essentials of food, clothing and a place to live.*

Everyone cut back and no one bought anything that was not absolutely essential. All big manufacturing towns were in trouble, whether it was Kalamazoo with its paper mills, Grand Rapids with its furniture companies, or Battle Creek with its cereal companies. In Grand Rapids over 34,000 people needed welfare aid by 1932. In Lansing only one-third of the workers who had jobs in 1929 continued to work in 1930. It was not just a business slowdown. It wasn't just a recession. It was a depression—the Great Depression!

There had been depressions or "panics" in the past; 1893 was one example. But never before the Great Depression were so many people living in the cities. Michigan's urban population had really grown, and the city people could not get food from the family farms.

People Lose Their Homes and Farms

As the depression continued, it became especially difficult for people who were buying their homes or farms. They ran out of money to pay the loans. Banks foreclosed and took the property. To get back their money, the banks sold the properties to someone else. There was also the problem of property taxes. Those taxes paid the costs of local government and schools. Michigan had a law then which affected property with overdue taxes. If the taxes had not been paid for the last 26 months, the law permitted the government to auction the property to the highest bidder. Large numbers of people were thrown out of their own homes and off their farms because of bank foreclosures or property tax sales. In 1933 the U.S. Census Bureau estimated Michigan had the highest rate of unpaid property taxes of any state in the nation!

Of course, those who lost their homes and possessions were bitter and angry. Was it their fault the banks closed and they could not get money they had saved for their taxes?

One of the worst years of the depression was 1933. Farmers across the country were ready to revolt. At a tax sale in Montcalm County that January, about 150 farmers picketed. They threatened those who had come to bid. When each item was auctioned off, no one offered more than a few cents. A grand piano was sold for four cents and a hay loader for eleven cents. After everything had been sold, the purchasers gave the things back to the owner, who was very relieved and grateful.

Government Was in Bad Shape Too

The cities and schools became desperate due to the lack of property tax

In the Depression years a group of unemployed workers rode to Lansing carrying a banner with the words "the army of the unemployed." They wanted people to help them fight starvation. (Courtesy Michigan State Archives)

318

income. Grand Rapids and Detroit ran out of money to pay teachers and city workers. In 1933 Detroit printed about $42 million of paper IOUs called *scrip*. *Scrip was a replacement for money and it looked something like real paper money too.* Stores that accepted the scrip were paid back by the city when real money was available again.

Millions Listen to Father Coughlin

In such bleak times nearly everyone looked for a new leader who might help. Father Charles Coughlin became popular for his radio talk shows. He was the parish priest at the Shrine of the Little Flower church in Royal Oak. He was excited about the new field of radio broadcasting, and he felt speaking over the radio would be a great way to reach people. He did not limit himself to sermons, but commented on the problems of the depression, society, politics, and business matters too. He often spoke against banks and big business.

In the early 1930s roughly 30 million Americans tuned to his program, "Golden Hour of the Little Flower." He was so popular in 1934 the post office reported Father Coughlin received more mail than any single person in the entire country! There were more than letters of support; many envelopes contained money. Before long, Father Coughlin had large sums at his disposal.

Even CBS radio network carried his program. Some of what Father Coughlin had to say made sense, especially at first. For example, he warned about the dangers of communism. And there was a real communist threat. Some communists had taken part in a hunger march against the Ford Company in 1932. There was a fight with police in Dearborn and four marchers were killed and 50 or 60 more wounded. The fascists or pro-Nazi groups were active in Michigan too. Both groups wanted to use violence to take power.

When Franklin Roosevelt first ran for president, Father Coughlin supported him all the way. But once Roosevelt was elected, Coughlin changed his mind. Coughlin said we needed more than a New Deal; the country needed a "new deck." He did not think President Roosevelt was making enough changes. Coughlin said, "Democracy is doomed. It is either fascism or communism." The fascists or Nazis were gaining power in Germany and Coughlin's speech was taken to mean he approved of Hitler's actions. His programs became more anti-business; he also attacked blacks and Jews. The Catholic church tried to stop Coughlin's radio broadcasts. In the meantime, CBS had dropped his program, but Coughlin formed his own radio network.

Father Coughlin had become an embarrassment to his own church. Finally, in 1942 the Pope gave direct orders to keep Coughlin from speaking in public, and his radio program ended.

Father Coughlin appearing before a hearing in Washington D.C. (Courtesy Michigan State Archives)

James Couzens— a Good Citizen

James Couzens left the Ford Motor Company and was ready to spend his time doing things to make Michigan a better place to live.

His first new job was as police commissioner for Detroit. Starting in 1916, Couzens spent three years working to stop crime in the city. He attacked the gangsters who controlled some of the city's officials, and he was even thrown in jail for contempt of court in the process! Mayor Oscar B. Marx told him he was the most unpopular man in the city. Couzens decided he would try for the mayor's job and find out just how unpopular he was. Couzens was better liked than Marx thought as he won the election! Couzens served as mayor from 1919 to 1923. During his term, he was able to finish Mayor Hazen S. Pingree's dream of having a city-owned streetcar system.

Then he was appointed by the governor to finish the U.S. Senate term of Truman Newberry who had resigned. While in the senate, he faced a tough fight with Andrew Mellon, the Secretary of the Treasury. Couzens had been critical of Mellon and Mellon fought back. He investigated Couzens for not paying enough income tax when he sold his Ford stock. Andrew Mellon told Couzens he owed the government a staggering $10 million. In the famous trial which followed, it was discovered Couzens had already paid more than was required.

James Couzens at his desk. (Courtesy Michigan State Archives)

Instead of being relieved that his money was safe in the bank, Couzens amazed everyone by giving the $10 million to help needy children.

During the depression, President Hoover was against spending any money to help those out of work. As a counterattack, Couzens made a famous speech in which he said: "We spend hundreds of millions of dollars on the army and navy in an attempt to guarantee security from outside attack. Why is it any less logical or sensible to spend the taxpayers' own money on our people, to maintain security within the country?" James Couzens kept his job in the United States Senate until he died in 1936.

What Could be Done?

In the first three years of the depression, the reaction of those in Michigan government was often the same as those in charge of national agencies. It was difficult to believe the situation was as bad as it was. The general view in the 1920s was that government should not interfere in business problems. So, few wanted to start interfering. Michigan Governor Wilbur Brucker told President Hoover, "The people of Michigan will take care of their own problem."

For awhile, most cities thought the churches, the Salvation Army, and other private organizations could help all the needy. Besides, the common opinion about accepting welfare was different then. It was not considered honorable to take it, and those in need would only ask for help when they were completely desperate. In spite of that, 640,000 of Michigan's some 4,900,000 people were on welfare in 1933.

Grand Rapids, Muskegon, Flint, and Saginaw started public relief programs to help those without jobs. In Detroit, Frank Murphy, mayor since 1931, tried to start city garden projects and public housing. The city, however, was very short of money.

Democrats Were Voted In

In November 1932 the people of Michigan were tired of the depression,

A Depression era class which helped women learn how to sew so they could make clothes for themselves and their families. (Courtesy Michigan State Archives)

and with no solution in sight, they changed leadership and elected a Democratic governor, William Comstock. He was only the third Democratic governor of Michigan since the Civil War. In that same election they voted for Franklin Roosevelt for president. That was the first time since 1852 that a Democratic presidential candidate had received Michigan's vote!

Governor Comstock began the state sales tax to raise money for state government. Three cents were collected on each dollar of sales. The new tax was very unpopular, and there were rumors the governor was using the money to build a large mansion for himself. Of course the rumors were not true. The reason for the passage of the state sales tax was to cut the property tax. Many homeowners complained they could not pay their property taxes and were afraid they would lose their homes. The state also changed its laws so people could have more time to pay overdue property taxes.

Once Roosevelt was in office, the federal government started a number of programs to help the jobless. The new idea was to create jobs and pay the workers with federal money. The Works Progress Administration, or WPA, hired people to do what they could do best. It hired writers to write books and articles. It hired artists to paint and draw. Many Michigan post offices had paintings done inside their lobbies by WPA artists. Some of these murals can still be seen in the post offices of Caro, Frankfort, Howell, Iron Mountain, Marquette, Paw Paw, and Plymouth. Other WPA projects included hiring carpenters to build public buildings and workers to repair roads and highways. In 1938, Michigan had over 200,000 people in WPA jobs, more than at any other time. Another Roosevelt program which had much impact on Michigan was the Civilian Conservation Corps, or CCC. That program began in 1933 and lasted until 1942. During the depression, thousands of young men had no jobs. The CCC was designed to give them something productive to do. Nearly 100,000 worked in the Michigan CCC camps while the program was in operation.

Young men, most of them between 17 and 28 years old, could join for one year. They were supposed to be from families who were on welfare. Each "C" was paid $30.00 a month, but $25.00 of

The CCC provided jobs for many young men in the 1930s. The men in the top picture are having a lunch break in the field and those in the bottom picture are working on a construction project. (Both photos courtesy Michigan State Archives)

322

that went to his family. At that time, privates in the U.S. Army only made $18.00 a month. Besides their pay, the members of the CCC had a clean place to sleep, hot meals, clothes to wear, and the opportunity to join educational programs. Some CCC camps were set up for unemployed army veterans of World War I.

They lived in camps in the northern part of the state. It was not fun and games for these fellows. The camps were usually placed under the direction of an army officer and run much like an army camp. The "Cs" often complained about having to do calisthenics at 6 A.M., especially when it was outside in the winter snow. In spite of all the hard work, most of those who joined felt lucky to be a part of the CCC program.

Men in the CCC fought forest fires, built trails, roads, campgrounds, parks, and planted trees— almost 500 million of them! They worked in the new Isle Royale National Park, Seney National Wildlife Refuge, and many other places. Some of the pine forests we see in northern Michigan today were planted by the CCC on cut-over land which was left barren by the loggers.

When there was free time, the Cs liked to go to the nearest town and see a movie. The 1930s were the Golden Age of movies, and nearly every town had one or more movie theaters. It was a special thrill to see the newsreels telling about Michigan's 'hot' sports teams. The Detroit Tigers won the World Series in 1934, 1935, and again in 1940. The Lions were in the football news when they became the National Football League (NFL) champs in 1935. The Red Wings were champions too. They won the Stanley Cup in 1936 and 1937. Joe Louis from Detroit won the heavyweight boxing championship in 1937. The next year (1938) all of America was proud of Louis when he knocked out Germany's Max Schmeling. Eddie Tolan won the 100-and 200-yard dashes in the 1932 Los Angeles Olympic Games. He was the first black to win two gold medals in the same Olympics.

Joe Louis— Boxing Champion and American Hero

"Joe had more than fighting greatness—he was great as a man, a national hero, and as a citizen of these United

Joe Louis, the famous boxer from Michigan, talking to a group of children. (Courtesy Michigan State Archives)

States," said Wilfrid Diamond, a biographer.

His complete name was Joe Louis Barrow, and he was born May 13, 1914 on a farm in Alabama. He came with his family to Michigan in 1926. His teen-age years were spent in Detroit, and he learned his boxing skills there. Even after he became famous, his connection to Michigan was strong. He lived in Detroit part of each year; he contributed to local charities and he worked with the young people.

In 1937 Joe Louis won the world's heavyweight boxing championship. He became known as the "Brown Bomber" by sportswriters and boxing fans. The name was appropriate because he was black and a tough fighter. He followed faithfully the advice of his trainer to always fight clean and on the level. Louis successfully defended his title 25 times between 1937 and 1948, which was more than any other heavyweight champion. In 1949 he retired from boxing undefeated.

During his boxing career he earned $4,600,000, but by mid-1950, he found there was not a cent left. Besides, he owed the U.S. government more than $1,000,000 in back taxes. His finances had not been handled wisely. He tried to make a comeback and fought two more fights, but lost. In 1952 he quit boxing for the last time.

In 1978 Detroit named its new sports arena in his honor. Louis was a beacon of hope for other blacks and a champion admired and respected by all Americans. He died April 11, 1981, and was buried in Arlington Cemetery near Washington, D.C.

An Outstanding Michiganian

Frank Murphy was one of Michigan's great individuals. He held practically every government position: judge, mayor, governor, attorney general of the United States, member of the U.S. Supreme Court, and more. Frank Murphy's grandparents came from Ireland. He was born in Harbor Beach, Michigan, in 1890.

Murphy studied law at the University of Michigan. After graduation, he joined the army and went to France for a short time during World War I.

Murphy was first noticed by the public while he was the judge at the Ossian Sweet trial in 1925. He kept that explosive situation under control and carried out a fair trial. When the mayor of Detroit was recalled for corruption in 1930, Murphy decided to run for that office and was elected. As mayor of Detroit, he received more national attention for his programs to help the poor. Among other things, Murphy allowed homeless families to move into empty city warehouses and homeless men into empty auto factories.

Murphy worked to help elect Franklin Roosevelt president in 1932. After his victory, Roosevelt appointed Murphy as governor-general of the Philippine Islands. In 1936 Roosevelt was up for reelection, and he was worried that Father Coughlin would be a problem in Michigan. Coughlin in his popular radio program was speaking out against the President. Murphy was asked by Roosevelt to return to Michigan and run for governor. President Roosevelt felt Murphy was popular in the state and if Murphy were on the ballot, it would help Roosevelt's own chances. So, Murphy came back and became Michigan's first Catholic governor.

Even before Murphy took office, there was trouble waiting for him. The great auto workers' sit-down strike had started in Flint. The workers had taken control of the General Motors factories and they refused to leave. In January 1937 Murphy sent the National Guard to Flint to keep the situation under control. Even though many people wanted him to use the Guard to throw the workers out of the auto plants, Murphy believed it would not be the right thing to do. He did use his influence to win a settlement between General Motors and the strikers.

While he was governor, Murphy began Michigan's liberal unemployment insurance law and he started civil ser-

324

Frank Murphy. (Courtesy Michigan State Archives)

Frances moved to Michigan from England in 1910. She first worked with children involved with the Wayne County courts. Later, she helped start Children's Village. The Village had several cottages where children who were under the court's protection could live together. Each cottage had a housemother to guide the small group of children living in it. With understanding and love from Frances, the children learned how to get along with each other and work together so they could be productive parents when they grew up.

She believed children from broken homes needed to be in a situation which was as much like a real home as possible. Frances Knight was a pioneer in the "family plan" of child care. She was invited to a White House Conference On Child Care by President Roosevelt. In 1948 Frances Knight retired to her home at Mullet Lake. Her methods for the care and treatment of children were internationally known and copied by many others.

vice for state employees. Before civil service, government workers were given their jobs solely on the basis of the political party they supported. In spite of his popularity, Michigan's many Republican voters caused him to lose his bid for reelection in 1938.

After Murphy's 1938 defeat, President Roosevelt appointed him as U.S. Attorney General. After about a year in that office, he was nominated to be a member of the U.S. Supreme Court. He held that very important position until he died in 1949.

Frances Knight and Her Special Family.

The depression years were hard for everyone, but imagine what it was like for orphans and little children from broken homes. Frances Knight's mission in life was to help those children.

In summary, the 1930s got off to a bad start with a terrible business slowdown. Problems of the homeless and jobless were difficult to solve. After several years, the government started programs to help the needy and people began to work together. Times were still hard but there was more hope for the future.

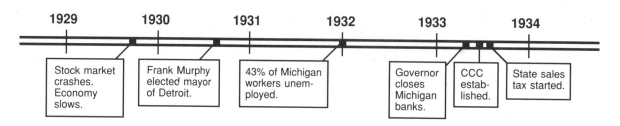

1929 — Stock market crashes. Economy slows.
1930 — Frank Murphy elected mayor of Detroit.
1931 — 43% of Michigan workers unemployed.
1932
1933 — Governor closes Michigan banks. CCC established.
1934 — State sales tax started.

Questions

1. Explain how people in Michigan were affected by the decline in car sales during the early 1930s. Along with your explanation, mention how many lost their jobs at the Ford Rouge plant and the percentage of people working for GM in Genesse County.

2. Why do you think so many people listened to what Father Coughlin had to say?

3. Why were many young men excited about being in the CCC even though they had to do lots of hard work?

4. How many Michiganians worked in WPA jobs during 1938? How many worked in the Michigan CCC from 1933 until 1942? Give one example of a project done by each of these two groups which can still be seen in Michigan today.

5. What did the senator from Michigan, James Couzens, say about spending money to help the needy during the depression?

6. Do you feel that Frank Murphy was a fair and understanding person? Give two reasons why you feel this way.

7. Who helped start Children's Village during the 1930s? What was the goal of this woman?

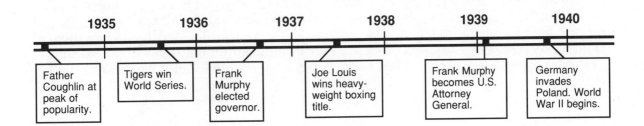

Chapter 13 Section 2

Unions: A New Friend at the Factory

Here are the key concepts you will find in this section:

Labor unions were not very effective in Michigan before 1936 because they usually did not speak for all the workers at a company.

The United Auto Workers, or UAW, became an independent union in 1936.

Three brothers of the Reuther (ROO-ther) family helped build the UAW into a strong and democratic union.

After a successful 44-day strike against General Motors in Flint, the UAW won the right to represent workers in GM, the world's largest company.

Thousands of Michigan workers joined unions after the strike in Flint. Unions became an important way to protect workers' rights for fair pay and safe working conditions.

The Depression & Troubled Workers

A period of great unrest among industrial workers in Michigan and the world developed in the 1930s. Companies had a hard time making profits, so they put pressure on their employees to do more with no increase in pay. Many workers thought *unions* could help them. *Unions are organizations of laborers formed to improve their working conditions and wages. They bargain as a unit with the management of the company where the members work.* Some joined the unions, but many were afraid to join. The idea of unions was not popular with all the people, especially those who did not work in factories.

Unions Were Weak

There were labor unions in Michigan before the 1930s, but they were not very effective. They were not effective mainly because of the division between *skilled workers* and *unskilled workers.* *Skilled workers were those whose work required considerable training. Skilled workers might be electricians, metal workers, or designers. Unskilled workers did less complex jobs such as unloading parts and cleaning the factories.* Often skilled workers belonged to a labor organization but the unskilled workers did not. If the unskilled workers decided to go on strike and stop working, it was not difficult for the company to hire new workers. On the other hand, if the skilled workers went on strike, they had only limited bargaining power as there were fewer of them in each factory.

Michigan had a tradition of being an "open shop" state. *Open shop means all workers can be given jobs in the factory if they qualify to be hired. A "closed shop" is one where every worker must belong to a union and it usually must be the same union.* It is difficult to have an effective labor organization in an open shop as no single union acts for all of the workers.

The years 1936 and 1937 were turning points for unions in Michigan. At that time the United Auto Workers (UAW)

Working conditions in most factories were dirty, cold, and noisy during the 1920s and 1930s. (Courtesy Michigan State Archives)

union broke away from the American Federation of Labor or AFL. The UAW went on to become a powerful union in the auto industry. Many people worked hard to make that happen, but three brothers were key leaders in the movement. They were Walter, Roy, and Victor Reuther.

The Reuther Brothers

The Reuther family had a long history of being politically active, even before they moved from Germany to the United States. Many generations of Reuthers considered injustice to be immoral. They left their home country in the 1880s when life there was becoming more centered on the military. Their father believed in doing things to help people. His work with labor unions was the major interest in his life. Their

father, like Henry Ford, was against World War I. But, because the Reuthers were German, the door of their house in West Virginia was painted yellow and they received threats.

Walter Reuther moved to Michigan in 1927 so he could earn more money. His wage in West Virginia was only 42 cents an hour. He wanted to work at Ford Motor, but because he was so young it took lots of persistence to get an interview. He spent three hours arguing with the guard at the gate before he was let in. He was hired though, and soon earned $1.05 an hour. Such good wages attracted many other people to come to Michigan too. Walter Reuther not only worked at Ford, but he managed to complete his high school education.

Walter became friends with some communist and socialist workers. His association with them caused him to lose his job.

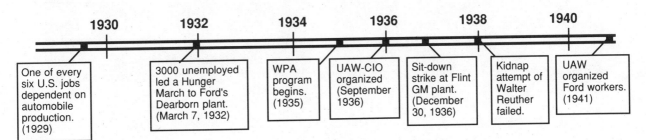

1930 1932 1934 1936 1938 1940

One of every six U.S. jobs dependent on automobile production. (1929)

3000 unemployed led a Hunger March to Ford's Dearborn plant. (March 7, 1932)

WPA program begins. (1935)

UAW-CIO organized (September 1936)

Sit-down strike at Flint GM plant. (December 30, 1936)

Kidnap attempt of Walter Reuther failed.

UAW organized Ford workers. (1941)

Making Cars In the Soviet Union

The Russian Revolution had ended, and the communists had recently formed the Soviet Union. They asked Ford to sell them the necessary equipment so Soviet workers could build Model A cars. At that time the Soviet Union had very few factories or trained workers. Ford made a contract with the Soviets to help them start a large auto factory in their country. Walter Reuther knew one of the Ford workers who was in charge of the project in the Soviet Union. Walter and his younger brother Victor were also hired to work in the Soviet Union.

Their work in the Soviet Union started in 1933, and they spent nearly two years there. The two Reuther brothers found there were problems with the communist life and the government. For one thing, the food provided for the workers was not good. They ate lots of cabbage soup and black bread. There was no butter most of the time, little fresh meat, and no fresh fruit at all. They each lost 20 pounds! Other things were different too. They saw some foreign workers taken away by the Soviet police because they said things against the Soviet government. The Reuthers returned to Detroit in the fall of 1935. Their travels and working experiences in the Soviet Union had been very interesting, but they were glad to arrive back in the United States.

Changes on the way

President Roosevelt's policies and some new laws made it easier for unions in the 1930s. The laws gave workers the right to join a union of their own choice with some protection against being fired by their boss. Before that, companies often sent "stool pigeons" to union meetings so they could find out who was joining. Not long after, the new members would find they no longer had a job! That kind of policy kept union membership down. Many workers were afraid they would lose their jobs if they dared to join.

The 5,000 workers at Kelsey-Hayes Wheel Company had been complaining of a "speed-up." *A speed-up was when the bosses at a factory increased the speed of the assembly line, and all the workers had to do their jobs faster or the parts would go by unfinished.* The speed-up at Kelsey-Hayes had caused a woman worker to pass out from exhaustion.

A worker at another plant told of a speed-up. His job was to grind off the rough edges of car bodies after they were welded together. In 1928 he did eight bodies a day and was paid $1.00 an hour. The depression forced companies to squeeze every ounce of work from employees, and by 1932 he did 32 car bodies a day and his wage fell to 35 cents an hour! That example shows what was happening in most factories and why workers were upset. Anyone who did not like the job could quit. Each company knew there were thousands of people who did not have jobs and most would be glad to work under even such bad conditions.

Immediately the Reuther brothers became involved in union activities. Walter and Victor led a strike at Kelsey-Hayes in 1936. It was a tough strike and the management was not very interested in talking with the union until Ford Motor put pressure on the company. Ford needed Kelsey-Hayes parts in a hurry. The strike was successful. The union won a minimum wage, which was the same for both men and women, and a slower pace for the assembly line.

An important strategy for the union was to find a plant which made crucial car parts that were in short supply. Then the union would try to get a strike started in that plant. They knew this would pressure the management to talk with them and not stall for time. A long strike was hard for the union members because they had no income while the strike was going on.

The Great Sit-Down Strike

The major strike of those early UAW years took place at the end of 1936. It was at the General Motors Fisher Body plants in Flint. There had been worker unrest at Fisher Body for some time. Some of the employees noticed that important equipment was being moved out of the factory. General Motors was planning ahead. They wanted to keep production going elsewhere if a strike took place in Flint.

Suddenly on December 30, 1936, workers stopped and sat down in the plant. They wouldn't leave to go home and they blocked the doors to prevent equipment from being taken out by the company. The workers said they were tired of speed-ups, low wages, poor working conditions and little job security. The sit-down strike was a fairly new idea. In that way the strikers were protected from a police attack and it stopped the company from hiring new workers to keep the plant running. The sit-down also increased the power of the union because only part of the workers belonged when the strike started. If the others had been able to go to their jobs, they might have felt they had to, and the factory would have remained open.

Workers in Fisher Body plant #2 chanted this slogan during the strike:

"When they tie a can to a union man,
Sit down, Sit down.
When they give him the sack they'll take him back
Sit down, Sit down.
When the speed-up comes just twiddle your thumbs,
Sit down, Sit down.
When the boss won't talk, don't take a walk,
Sit down, Sit down."

Strikers Face Problems

General Motors went to court so they could open the plants. The judge said the workers had no right to stay in the facto-

Factory owners and workers often clashed during early strikes. (Courtesy Michigan State Archives)

ries and the police could throw them out. Then the union received a tip that the judge was a big GM stockholder. They discovered he owned over $200,000 worth of company stock and was really trying to protect his own investment. State and federal government officials believed the judge could not issue such an order under the circumstances.

The union had its hands full helping the strikers. They formed picket lines outside the plants. Many of those marching up and down the picket lines were wives of the strikers. The union prepared food for the strikers and took it to the plants each day. There were over 1,000 strikers sitting in two buildings who needed to be fed and soon there would be more. Sometimes the company guards let them in with the food and sometimes they did not. They rounded up warm clothes for the strikers because the company turned off the heat and it was cold outside.

General Motors was becoming desperate. Other workers were joining the strike. The GM Cadillac plant in Detroit was on strike, and so were other factories across the country. By the middle of January, 112,000 of the company's 150,000 production workers had quit working!

The company wanted to get the strikers out of its buildings. They urged the police to go in after them even though the court order had been thrown out. On January 11, 1937, they took action. The police fired tear gas at the pickets and into the Fisher Body plant #2. The union members were ready. They used inner tubes to make large sling-shots on the roof. The slingshots hurled car door hinges down on the police. When the police came closer, the strikers turned on the fire hoses and sprayed them with cold water.

The police backed off to regroup. When they came back, they were sprayed with water and struck by hinges again. That time when the police pulled back, they decided they had suffered enough abuse and began to shoot at the pickets. Thirteen strikers were seriously wounded.

Meanwhile, the strikers turned over cars near the plant and blocked the street. Back came the police for a third time with more tear gas. It seemed as though the coughing and choking pickets would have to give up because of the gas, but the wind changed direction and blew the gas back toward the police. The police retreated again but kept shooting tear

Members of the Michigan National Guard in Flint during the famous sit-down strike. (Courtesy Michigan State Archives)

gas at the factory until late at night. The entire series of police attacks at plant #2 came to be known as the "Battle of the Running Bulls." Bulls was an old slang word for police.

The Governor Comes to Help

The next day Governor Frank Murphy came to Flint determined to calm things down. He ordered 3,000 National Guard soldiers to Flint. They came with all their battle gear and bayonets on their rifles. The governor was concerned about the police attacks against the union forces at Fisher Body and about the number of union supporters coming to Flint from all over Michigan and the Midwest.

Governor Murphy immediately brought leaders from both sides to his office in Lansing. Days of haggling took place between the governor, GM management, and union negotiators. The month of January passed and tension was high in Flint. Then on February 1, the union was able to get the Chevrolet engine plant in Flint to strike. That was the only factory making engines for all the Chevrolet cars around the country and Chevrolet was GM's best selling car.

The situation was grim for everyone. The governor was receiving a great deal of pressure to use the Guard to go into the factories and get the strikers out. Many people did not agree that strikers should be allowed to break the law and take over factories. A new judge issued an order to the strikers. If they were not out of the plants in two days they would be fined $15 million! And all picketing must stop too. The union sent a message to the governor that they would stay in the buildings and die there if the police or soldiers came after them.

Victory for the Union

As the sit-down strike dragged on day after day, the federal government became worried. National leaders were afraid the strike might become a revolution with much bloodshed. President Roosevelt sent messages to Governor Murphy and others urging them to solve the situation. Finally on February 11,1937,after 44 days, General Motors said the company would give in. The United Auto Workers won the right to represent GM workers who wanted to join that union. The union also had the right to go into the GM plants and ask workers to join. Wages were increased too. The strikers were joyous and the city of Flint breathed a sigh of relief.

Sit-Downs Popular

Within a month there was a sit-down at Chrysler and after about 30 days, the 17,000 strikers won the same kind of deal GM workers had. Ford Motor was the only big auto company to keep the UAW union out.

After the success of the sit-down in Flint, there was an epidemic of sit-down strikes throughout Michigan. At least 130 companies were closed by strikes. Workers went on strike everywhere. In Detroit, workers sat down in four hotels, twelve laundries, twelve clothing stores, three department stores, five trucking companies, nine lumberyards and assorted cigar factories. Some members of the National Guard even had a sit-down when they weren't paid for their duty in Flint! Each day the Detroit newspapers listed the places closed by sit-down strikes. The courts finally ruled in 1939 that sit-down strikes were illegal.

In the wave of strikes, many workers managed to win the right to join unions and some pay increases. Enthusiasm for unions was high and their membership grew rapidly. Even so, there were plenty of problems to face. Communists and gangsters tried to take over unions for their own benefit. The Reuther brothers, and other labor leaders, fought again and again to keep them out. Some union members did not like the idea of being beaten-up by police. They wanted to carry guns and shoot back. Of course, responsible union leaders knew that was wrong and would be a disaster for the union cause.

Danger in the Dark

Those were dangerous times for many people involved in union activity. Early union organizers had to be brave. In 1938 the Reuthers were at a birthday party when there was a knock at the door. Two armed thugs burst in and tried to kidnap Walter. One of the wives threw a jar of pickles at the thugs and another fellow jumped out the second floor window and ran for help. Walter was hit over the head with a lamp but not badly hurt. When the gunmen heard people coming, they decided to leave. Then there was a murder attempt in April 1948 when a shot was fired through the kitchen window at Walter Reuther. Luckily, he managed to survive but with serious injuries. In 1949 there was a similar attempt on Victor Reuther's life. He was shot while reading the newspaper in his home. No one was ever caught for any of these attacks.

Ford Fights the Union

The Ford company took a long time to unionize. Henry Ford was very old and Edsel Ford had health problems. A man named Harry Bennett seemed to control most of what the company did. He ruled the company with an iron hand and did not mind how he kept control. In the spring of 1937, the UAW tried to pass out pamphlets to Ford workers when the shifts changed.

Walter Reuther and several union leaders were present. They were having their pictures taken by news reporters on an overpass going to the Ford Rouge plant. Suddenly about 35 Ford men who worked for Harry Bennett viciously attacked and beat the union leaders. They didn't seem to mind that the reporters took their pictures while they hit and kicked the union men. When a group of about 50 women union organizers arrived, they tried to help the men and they too were attacked. One of the union men later died from his injuries. That incident at Ford was called the "Battle of the Overpass."

Ford continued to resist the union until government pressure was put on the company in the early 1940s. Ford lost an important defense contract with the federal government because relations with its workers were so bad. After a mass walkout of Ford employees in 1941, the company gave in and accepted the UAW. The union was then secure in Michigan, and its powerful presence had a great impact on the state. Walter

The "Battle of the Overpass." Seconds after this photo was taken, Ford guards on the left attacked and beat Walter Reuther and other union members. (Courtesy Michigan State Archives)

Reuther became president of the UAW in 1946. A great many Michigan workers have joined the UAW and assorted other unions since the 1930s. Michigan has become known as a strong union state.

Questions

1. Explain why workers were upset by speed-ups and other conditions in the auto plants during the depression.

2. Name the three brothers who helped build the United Auto Workers union.

3. Before the United Auto Workers union became powerful, what often happened to Michigan auto workers who tried to join a union?

4. Who was involved in the "Battle of the Running Bulls" and where did that event take place?

5. What did Michigan Governor Frank Murphy do to keep the peace during the Flint sit-down strike?

6. Which big auto company was last to allow a union to represent its workers? What year did this take place?

7. Do you think the actions of the Michigan union leaders during the 1930s were good? Should they have tried to start unions here? Write your opinion and give any examples you can to back it up.

8. As a Ford executive, how would you have dealt with the union?

Chapter 13 Section 3

Tension and Triumph in Democracy's Arsenal: World War II

Here are the key concepts you will find in this section:

Arthur Vandenberg, a senator from Michigan, warned the country to stay out of any new war in Europe.

President Roosevelt appointed several Michiganians to important government jobs.

The Japanese attack at Pearl Harbor worried the military that the Soo Locks might be a target too.

During World War II Michigan led the other states in production of war materials. Everything from bombers to penicillin was made here.

Overcrowding and other changes helped cause tension between blacks and whites in Detroit. A serious race riot took place in 1943.

The war opened many opportunities for women and minorities. They were allowed to work in better jobs and fly military planes.

In 1943 the Republican party held an important meeting on Mackinac Island. There they decided to support the formation of the United Nations.

Better Jobs But Worries of War

The grim days of the Depression had begun to fade away like a bad dream. The 1940s brought better business conditions to the state. But another war started in Europe when Germany invaded Poland and France. War was certainly a concern, but Michigan companies were pleased with their new orders for war supplies. The new jobs and higher pay helped offset the worries that the United States might become involved in the European war.

Speaking Out

Charles Lindbergh, the famous Michigan-born flyer, and Arthur Vandenberg, U.S. Senator and former Grand Rapids newspaper editor, spoke out against the U.S. entering the war. They felt our country should not worry about Europe, no matter what happened there. Arthur Vandenberg was a key leader who worked to keep the country isolated. His view was that the Atlantic and Pacific Oceans would stop any enemy from reaching us. The oceans would be giant moats to keep out invaders.

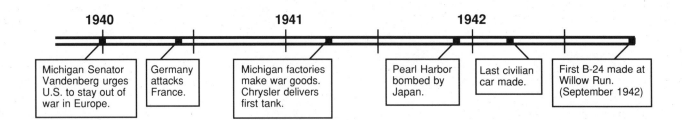

1940	1941	1942

Michigan Senator Vandenberg urges U.S. to stay out of war in Europe.

Germany attacks France.

Michigan factories make war goods. Chrysler delivers first tank.

Pearl Harbor bombed by Japan.

Last civilian car made.

First B-24 made at Willow Run. (September 1942)

In spite of what Lindbergh and Vandenberg said, the United States started military preparations in case we had to fight. In 1940 the Congress passed a law drafting young men for military service. The following year Congress passed the Lend-Lease Act. That act allowed the U.S. government to loan military supplies to friendly nations. Senator Vandenberg was strongly against both new laws.

From Michigan to Washington

President Franklin Roosevelt appointed several Michiganians to important positions. Frank Murphy was on the U.S. Supreme Court. Harold Smith was the Director of the Budget. William Knudsen left General Motors to became Director of Industrial Production. And the former owner of the *Sault Ste. Marie Evening News*, Frank Knox, was Secretary of the Navy.

Surprise Attack!

On a Sunday afternoon, December 7, 1941, America was jolted when 432 Japanese planes bombed our navy at Pearl Harbor in the Hawaiian Islands. Michigan sailors like Jim Green were there. He was lucky to survive the attack even though he was in gun turret No. 4 of the battleship *Arizona*. The *Arizona* sank when almost two million pounds of its ammunition blew up and 1,177 of Jim's shipmates lost their lives. With nearly half of our navy destroyed, we had no choice; the United States had to fight.

The Soo Locks in the Upper Peninsula were considered a very important transportation link. There was an immediate fear that enemy bombers might be able to reach Sault Ste. Marie. Consequently, that area became one of the most heavily guarded places in the nation. Over 7,000 soldiers stood by

Excitement at the beginning of World War II among Detroit draftees ready to head for military bases. (Courtesy Michigan State Archives)

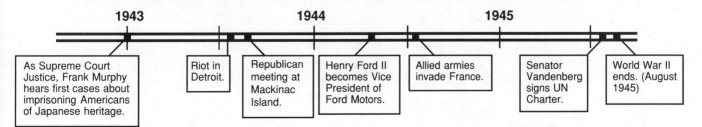

1943

1944

1945

As Supreme Court Justice, Frank Murphy hears first cases about imprisoning Americans of Japanese heritage.

Riot in Detroit.

Republican meeting at Mackinac Island.

Henry Ford II becomes Vice President of Ford Motors.

Allied armies invade France.

Senator Vandenberg signs UN Charter.

World War II ends. (August 1945)

anti-aircraft guns. Searchlights and radar scanned the sky for approaching planes. American fighter planes were also on standby at northern Michigan airfields. In 1943 a larger lock, the MacArthur, was added at the Soo.

After the surprise attack at Pearl Harbor, the entire nation was paranoid. People thought it was possible for enemy planes or spies to show up anyplace. There was a special fear that people with Japanese heritage might be spies. Thousands of American citizens on the West Coast who had Japanese ancestors were taken from their homes and moved into places similar to prison camps. It was then Michigan's Frank Murphy condemned such action as racism. Unfortunately, he was one of only a few who spoke out against the treatment of Japanese-Americans.

Switching from Cars to Tanks

There was a rush to reorganize factories for war. William Knudsen, the Director of Industrial Production, knew most of the leaders of Michigan's auto industry and he went to them when he needed help with war production. He asked the president of Chrysler if the company would build a factory to make tanks for the army. His response was, "Yes. Where can I see one of these tanks?" The leaders of Michigan industry were willing, but often had much to learn.

All kinds of materials were soon in short supply including workers for the factories. Over 600,000 young men and women from Michigan joined the armed forces. The federal government began to ration food, gasoline, tires, and many other items. The last civilian car was made in February 1942. Michigan's factories became a national asset as they were used to make all kinds of military supplies. They turned out an amazing number of war related products— everything from parts for the atomic bomb to mint oil used in chewing gum for the soldiers and milkweed pod filler for life jackets.

Made in Michigan

The shipyards in Bay City made submarine chasers and destroyer escorts. In Midland, a new Dow product, Saran Wrap, was used to package military supplies so they would not be damaged by salt water when taken overseas by ship. Kellogg of Battle Creek made K rations for soldiers in combat. Thousands of school children gathered milkweed pods for the life jackets which were made in Petoskey. Saginaw Steering Gear made over three hundred thousand .50 caliber machine guns and other products. Cannons weighing 40,000 pounds each were made in Pontiac for the navy; Lansing's REO company made army trucks and in Kalamazoo the Upjohn Company made sulfa drugs and the new drug penicillin for soldiers wounded in battle.

The Kalamazoo Stove Company switched from stoves to armor plate. The Packard company made engines for the navy's PT boats. Amphibious tanks were turned out in Kalamazoo, and workers in Cadillac made landing craft. Gliders used for the invasion of France were made in Grand Rapids and Iron Mountain. Most of the state's war production took place in the Lower Peninsula, but the Upper Peninsula increased output of its valuable copper and iron ore. The mines once again were very busy. Ford made the gliders in Iron Mountain. That factory became the largest glider plant in the country and over 4,000 were made there.

Farmers sold everything they could possibly grow and food production increased. The demand for food was so great that everyone who had any land was encouraged to start a garden. These little plots were known as "Victory Gardens" and Michigan's new part-time farmers raised more than 500,000 tons of extra food in 1943.

Michigan was among the top states in production of war materials. The state earned the title, "Arsenal of Democracy." Over a period of six years, the auto industry sold $50 billion of war equipment. Out of those sales, 39 percent was for

A senior citizen working in his victory garden. (Courtesy Michigan State Archives)

Three Big War Factories

Michigan's industrial know-how was used to build three spectacular operations. They were the Chrysler Tank Arsenal in Warren, the Fisher Body tank factory in Grand Blanc, and the biggest of all, the Willow Run bomber plant near Ypsilanti.

Chrysler made over 25,000 tanks during the war. Another 16,300 tanks were built at the Grand Blanc plant.

Willow Run was built in the middle of farms and fields near Ypsilanti. The federal government spent $100 million on the building and the Ford Motor Company ran the operation. Ford managers thought their modern production line ideas could make bombers faster and better than the aircraft companies. The goal was "a bomber an hour," even though the aircraft companies could only make one a day!

When the Willow Run plant was finished, it was one of the largest factories in the world. Its assembly line was more than a mile long. Eventually 42,000 people worked at the plant and about one-third were women. Next to the factory a large air field was built. Willow Run began to make B-24 bombers in

airplanes and aircraft parts; 30 percent was for military cars and trucks, and 13 percent was for tanks. Michigan made many of the same types of things it did during World War I, but we were in that war for only 18 months. The U.S. was involved in World War II much longer and the amount of materials made here was much greater.

A Chrysler tank coming off the assembly line at the beginning of World War II. This design soon became obsolete. (Courtesy Michigan State Archives)

The famous Willow Run bomber plant during World War II. (Courtesy Michigan State Archives)

September 1942. At first, the workers could not come close to the schedule. Some government officials nicknamed the plant "Willit Run?" By the time the war ended, however, the plant had turned out over 8,000 B-24s and almost reached the goal of one plane an hour. Part of a Michigan-made B-24 has become an important display at the impressive state museum in Lansing.

Henry Ford II Takes Over

During World War II, Edsel Ford died. The Ford company had dozens of key war contracts in addition to running the Willow Run plant. The government was worried the company would be disorganized. Henry Ford was old and had suffered two strokes. The government did not have confidence in the rest of the management. Federal officials contacted Edsel's son, 26-year-old Henry Ford II who was training with the navy. He was released from his duties so he could take charge of the company and keep it running smoothly. The FBI helped him get information on the ruffians Harry Bennett had working in the plants. It was a difficult time for young Henry II as

he had to fight for control of the huge organization and struggle to put modern managers in charge of production.

Problems on the Home Front

Working at Willow Run was not easy for most of the employees because the plant was miles away from the cities where they lived. Gasoline was rationed and drivers could only have four gallons a week. To force drivers to conserve gas, the government set the speed limit at 35 miles an hour! Getting to work was usually a long, slow process. Ride sharing was encouraged and most workers had alternate days when they drove or rode with friends.

Michigan's factories needed thousands upon thousands of workers. The possibility of high-paying jobs attracted new workers, especially from southern states. Sometimes as many as 500 people arrived each day at Ypsilanti to find a job at Willow Run. Before they could start work, they had to find a place to live and that wasn't easy. If they were lucky, they could rent a room and stay with a family who lived near the plant. Often the new workers built shacks covered with tar

Thomas Danahey explaining the need for better housing to members of the Detroit Board of Commerce. (Courtesy The *Detroit News*)

paper. Local health officials found people living with improper sewer facilities and forced them to move. The government did build army-type barracks, some for single men and some for single women, but housing remained a big problem throughout the war.

As people moved during the war, Michigan's population shifted toward the areas around big cities. Urban counties grew rapidly. Macomb County grew 32 percent and Washtenaw County 21 percent. On the other hand, several northern counties lost people. The populations of Baraga, Crawford, Kalkaska, and Keweenaw counties shrank by about 30 percent or more.

Housing Was A Big Problem

Overcrowding was a big problem for the war workers and their families in the cities. Tempers often became short. People wondered where they were going to live. Husbands and wives were upset because they were crowded into older and smaller houses with other families. There wasn't enough privacy. Housing was especially poor for black people. It was still *segregated* in most places. *Segregation is the separation of people by their race.* As the war continued, more and more blacks found jobs in Michigan. The black population in the state rose from 216,000 in 1940 to 452,000 by 1950. Nearly all of the new black families had to squeeze into the same run-down neighborhoods where blacks were allowed to live before the war. Not much had changed in the 15 years since the Ossian Sweet incident.

Racial Troubles

Out of desperation, a new housing project was started in Detroit for blacks. But some whites objected because it was in their neighborhood. Members of both races put considerable pressure on the federal government and the city council. While work was still underway, the federal government named the project for Sojourner Truth. Because she was a black antislavery leader, that angered the nearby white neighborhood even more.

Hundreds of whites and blacks stood on sidewalks near the construction yelling insults at each other. The blacks felt their right to have decent housing was being attacked; and it was.

A reporter from *Life* magazine asked one black man why he was there and he said, "The Army is going to take me to fight for democracy, but I'd just as soon fight for democracy right here. Here we are fighting for ourselves."

In the spring of 1942, the day finally came for the first families to move in. The 14-block area was surrounded by Michigan State Troops. One stood every 50 feet and each was armed with a rifle and bayonet. Over 1,000 state and city police also patrolled the area closely. Luckily, no major riot took place and after several days the crowds around the housing project left.

Detroit is Dynamite!

But tension between whites and blacks kept building and was coming close to the breaking point. A reporter for *Life* magazine wrote in 1942 "Detroit is dynamite" and it "can blow up Hitler or it can blow up the U.S." To add to the tension, there had been conflicts among black and white workers at several war factories.

Then it happened. On a warm Sunday afternoon, June 20, 1943, about 100,000 people had gone to Belle Isle to relax. That evening large crowds jammed the bridge pouring back to Detroit. Fighting broke out between the two races. Groups left that area and traveled to other parts of the city, still steamed up after punching at each other. White people made up rumors that blacks had attacked a white woman and blacks said a black woman and baby had been thrown off the bridge by whites. Both stories were untrue.

A car burning during the 1943 Detroit riot. (Courtesy Michigan State Archives)

Groups of young white men attacked blacks and threw them off street cars. Similar groups of young black men attacked whites and broke into stores. A riot had begun!

Rioting and Bloodshed

The mayor knew it was more than the police could handle. First he asked the governor for help, but the State Troops had no way to travel to Detroit and the Michigan National Guard was a part of the army fighting overseas. The governor asked that soldiers from nearby bases help stop the rioting, but the commanding officer said the governor would have to declare *martial law*. Governor Kelley thought that was going too far. *Martial law is an emergency statement from the governor or president that basic legal rights have been suspended and the military has been given control. When martial law is in effect, people can be arrested without the normal legal procedures.*

The rioting continued on Monday while officials from both state and federal government argued over the proper procedure. Finally, at 9:30 P.M. truckloads of military police roared into downtown Detroit and cleared 10,000 rioters out of

Cadillac Square—without firing a shot. The rioters knew the soldiers meant business and by midnight the streets were clear and quiet. President Roosevelt ordered 4,000 soldiers to stay in Detroit until the situation calmed down.

The riot was a great tragedy. Thirty-four people were killed and 675 more were hurt in the fighting. Over 100 fires were set and many buildings badly damaged. A lesson should be learned from the 1943 Detroit riot as it showed the terrible things that happen when different groups do not cooperate and try to live peacefully with each other.

Women at Work

In spite of the problems at the home front, the war allowed minorities and women to show what they were capable of doing. Women workers swarmed into war plants. About one-third of the workers in the factories were women. At first, employers did not like the idea of hiring women because they didn't think they could handle the work. But they desperately needed workers and they just couldn't find enough men. Those in charge soon found out that women usually did better work and were sick and absent less than men in the same factory! During the war women earned more money than ever before. For the first time many of them had the chance to quit being maids and waitresses and have jobs where their other talents and abilities really counted.

Unions took notice of the thousands of women industrial workers. The UAW hired Mildred Jeffrey to come to Michigan and take charge of its newly formed Women's Bureau.

Still, it would be some time until women workers were truly equal to men in the eyes of employers and unions. After the war most women left their industrial jobs or had to take work with less pay. For example, women had to wait until the 1970s to be accepted again as workers for the Detroit Department of

Women from Michigan flew fighters and bombers from the factories to air bases around the world. These pilots are members of the WASPS. (Courtesy USAF Photographic Collection, National Air & Space Museum, Smithsonian Institution)

342

Transportation even though many of them worked as street car operators or conductors in the war years.

She Can Fly Bombers Too!

Women did more to help win the war than make the bombers; some flew them too. Faye Wolf of Grand Rapids joined the Women Air Force Service Pilots (WASP). The women pilots flew new planes from Willow Run and other factories to air force bases in the United States and Europe. They took the place of regular air force pilots who were needed in combat. Even though no enemy planes shot at the women pilots, the work was dangerous. Some women were killed in training accidents and others crashed because of mechanical trouble with their planes.

Tuskegee Airmen

As with housing, the military was also segregated during World War II. When blacks wanted to fight for their country they had to do it in their own all-black units. About 200 black men from Michigan trained at the Tuskegee Institute in Alabama so they could be pilots. Among the group was Coleman Young who later became mayor of Detroit. The Tuskegee airmen flew fighter planes and later bombers. One of the units was stationed at Michigan's Selfridge Field for a short time in 1944. The fighter pilots saw action with the enemy in Europe and even shot down one of the dreaded German jet fighter planes. But it was not until 1948 that President Truman ended separation of the races in the army, navy, air force and marines.

Today Detroit is the home of the National Museum of the Tuskegee Airmen. The museum is located inside Detroit's historic Fort Wayne, and first opened in 1987.

POWs in Michigan

Michigan soldiers trained at Camp Custer in World War II just as they had during World War I. But they weren't the only soldiers there. German and Italian prisoners of war were kept there too. Five Michigan CCC camps had also

Soldiers on practice maneuvers in northern Michigan. (Courtesy Michigan State Archives)

been turned into prisoner of war or POW camps.

Because it was so difficult to find workers, Michigan's fruit farmers asked the government to bring POWs here to help harvest apples, cherries, grapes, and peaches. Imagine the surprise of some people when they saw prisoners of war at work picking fruit in Michigan orchards. Usually one American soldier guarded a small group of ten POWs when they worked for the farmers. During the war years, between 4,000 and 5,000 enemy soldiers were held in Michigan.

Michiganians adjusted to all kinds of war-time activities. Military planes flew overhead and trucks full of soldiers went on training maneuvers. War games and other practice exercises took place in the woods and fields of Michigan's north country.

Danger Falls from the Sky!

When the war began, people thought anything might happen; but as time passed, they came to feel Michigan was safe from enemy attack. No one believed the Japanese or Germans would be able to bomb Grand Rapids or Detroit. But they were wrong! The Japanese began a fantastic plan to send bombs to the United States carried by balloons. The balloons were released in Japan and floated on wind currents which took them along the line of 45° north latitude. Each balloon carried several small bombs designed to start fires and scare people. The balloons had clocks which dropped the bombs at the time estimated they would be over the United States.

Shocked and confused civilians found two of these bombs in Michigan. One landed near Grand Rapids and the other near Detroit. Neither of these exploded but it was possible the Japanese bombs caused some forest fires in the Upper Peninsula. Several forest fires were started in western states by that kind of device. Apparently no other damage was done in Michigan. The discovery of the Japanese balloon bombs was kept very secret by the military. The government

felt civilians might panic if they knew enemy bombs could reach the United States.

The United Nations Question

As the war continued, American confidence started to increase. After only two years, plans were started for what would happen after it was over. In the summer of 1943, Senator Arthur Vandenberg opened an important meeting of Republican party leaders on Mackinac Island. The *Detroit News* said the meeting was "the most important political party meeting to be held in Michigan since that which gave birth to the Republican party...."

The purpose of the meeting was to decide if the Republicans would support a United Nations organization after the war. Remember, Senator Vandenberg was very much against allowing the United States to get mixed up in events overseas. The attack at Pearl Harbor had changed his mind. He realized that in a time of long-range airplanes, the country was not safe from enemy attack and the best solution was to stop trouble before it got out-of-hand. However, there were many Republicans who did not see things that way. They had not changed their minds at all.

There was great concern the party would split in two. After many hours of argument and late night meetings, the Republicans decided they would support the idea of a United Nations and everyone was convinced to stick together. The meeting was a success. Arthur Vandenberg promoted the idea that both political parties needed to work together when forming foreign policy. He felt American relations with other countries were too important to be a political football.

Even though Vandenberg was a Republican, Democratic Presidents Roosevelt and Truman consulted him often on foreign affairs. After the war, Senator Vandenberg was a leader in forming the United Nations. He helped write its charter. Vandenberg also worked to set up the North Atlantic Treaty Organization, or NATO, so the free European countries and the United States could fight against communism and hopefully prevent another world war. Senator Vandenberg saw that the United States was part of a global community. What happened in other countries did effect our country too.

Peace Returns

By 1945 the fighting around the world was coming to a close. Soldiers and sailors were looking forward to the time when they could return home. People knew peace was on the way when the first new car the nation had seen in three years rolled off the Ford assembly line in July 1945. Germany and then Japan surrendered. Hundreds of thousands of people jammed the streets of every Michigan city to celebrate once they heard the war had ended.

People everywhere were ready to begin living normal lives once more. They were ready to get married, start families, and buy all of the things they couldn't while the war was on. The demand for new cars was tremendous. It was the beginning of a long boom in Michigan's economy which lasted for nearly 20 years.

Senator Vandenberg getting ready to board an airplane at Grand Rapids. (Courtesy Grand Rapids Public Library-Michigan Room)

Questions

1. How did William Knudsen's job in Washington help bring war-related work to Michigan's auto industry?

2. What do you think was the most important war-related product made in Michigan during World War II? Explain your reasons.

3. What sort of things did people in the Upper Peninsula make or produce to help with the war effort?

4. What war work was done at Willow Run?

5. Explain some of the problems poor housing conditions caused in Michigan during the war.

6. Why did it take the army so long to send soldiers to help stop the 1943 Detroit riot?

7. What happened at the Republican meeting on Mackinac Island in 1943?

8. Could riots occur again in Michigan? Why or why not?

14 MICHIGAN AS WE SEE IT TODAY

Chapter 14 Section 1

Settling Down: Colleges, Homes, and Highways - the 1950s

Here are the key concepts you will find in this section:

The return of a large number of people from the military after World War II affected Michigan. Colleges grew rapidly. There were many new homes built just outside major cities.

In 1948 a man who grew up in Owosso, Michigan, ran for president of the United States. In the same year, G. Mennen Williams was elected governor of Michigan. His terms in office began a new period of strength for the Democratic party in Michigan.

Ralph Bunche (bunch), who was born in Michigan, won the Nobel Peace Prize in 1950.

The car became a necessary way to travel. Shopping malls developed away from downtown areas. The state was connected with a large new interstate highway system.

In 1957 the two peninsulas of Michigan were finally connected by the Mackinac Bridge. It was a major achievement in the development of the state.

Coming Home !

Over 600,000 Michigan servicemen and women were scattered all around the world when World War II ended. Some sat in the smoking ruins of European cities and wondered what they would do when they got back home. What jobs did they want to have? Would there even be any jobs to have? Should they start college? Would they be able to find places of their own or would they need to stay with their parents?

In anticipation of so many young people returning to the United States, the federal government worked hard to

have a smooth transition to peacetime. Congress passed the law known as the *G.I. Bill of Rights*. It gave several important benefits to veterans— those who had been in the military. The bill included money to go to college, loans to buy homes, and even start their own businesses.

Boom Times at Colleges

There was a rush of students arriving at Michigan's colleges and universities. Take Michigan State College as an example. When the war began, there were 6,356 students on the East Lansing campus. In 1946 the college was swamped

Military style quonset huts used after World War II as temporary housing at Michigan State University. (Courtesy Michigan State University Archives and Historical Collections)

with 8,500 veterans and 9,000 more enrolled the next year. The college had to scurry to find classrooms and housing for so many new students. Over 100 war surplus buildings known as quonset huts were erected. New professors were hired and many of them had to live in some of the smaller quonset huts too. It was almost as if they had never left the army!

Michigan State College grew and grew. It joined the Big Ten athletic conference in 1949. By 1955 the word "college" no longer seemed accurate because it was much too big. The name was officially changed to Michigan State University.

Enrollment at other Michigan colleges and universities increased too. In 1947 the state began to give money to community colleges and that was a big factor in getting more of them started. Eventually, there were 29 community colleges in the state.

Dewey for President

The 1948 national election was an exciting time for many Michigan college students and others. That was the first time many veterans had the opportunity to vote for president. Their interest in that particular election was sparked because the Republican nominee Thomas E. Dewey had lived in Michigan. He grew up in Owosso and was a graduate of the University of Michigan.

Dewey went to law school in New York state and remained there afterwards. By 1948 he had twice been elected

Thomas Dewey- the man from Owosso who ran for president against Harry Truman. (Courtesy Bentley Historical Library, University of Michigan)

348

governor of that state. It was generally thought that Dewey would beat President Harry Truman. But Truman surprised many and won the election.

Soapy Williams

In 1948 Michigan was a strong Republican state and had been so for nearly 90 years. There was a saying that Democrats were as rare in Michigan as alligators, and they enjoyed about the same social standing. In spite of that, a young lawyer named G. Mennen Williams decided to run for governor as a Democrat. Labor unions supported Williams and he won the election.

G. Mennen Williams had a rather unusual nickname, "Soapy." His mother's family owned the Mennen Company which made soap and shaving cream. He got his nickname because of that connection. Williams could almost always be spotted by his other trademark, a green polka dot bow tie. Nearly every photograph of Soapy Williams shows him wearing a bow tie.

Williams ran for and won the position of governor six times. That is more times than any other person has been elected governor in Michigan. A later

governor, William Milliken, actually held the office for more years because his terms were increased to four years instead of the two-year terms Williams had.

While G. Mennen Williams was in office he had to face several problems. Probably the most difficult developed in 1959. At that time Michigan had no income tax and relied on a three percent sales tax for the money needed to run government programs. A crisis hit the state that year because the sales tax receipts were down due to a slow economy. The state government was in the embarrassing position of not being able to pay its employees. A "payless payday" happened on May 9, 1959, and was covered by national television news programs that evening. As a result, Michigan got much bad publicity.

Governor Williams wanted to pass a state income tax but the Republicans refused to vote for it. In 1967, seven years after Williams left office, Michigan did pass a one percent income tax.

Governor Williams helped to begin a trend toward the control of Michigan's government by the Democratic party. Even though the Democrats did not always control the office of governor, for

Hesper Jackson stands on the left as he talks with Governor G. Mennen Williams. (Courtesy Michigan State Archives)

349

many years they had the majority in the state house and senate.

G. Mennen Williams kept serving his state after he left the governor's office. He was a member of the state Supreme Court from 1970 to 1986. Williams died in 1988 and was buried on Mackinac Island.

A Nobel Prize Winner

Another event in the news in the late 1940s was the division of Palestine to form the new state of Israel. That produced a major conflict and was the first big problem handled by the United Nations.

Michigan-born Ralph Bunche (bunch) was a member of the UN team sent to that area to help solve the difficulties between the Arab and Jewish people. As settlements were being worked out in 1948, one of the team members was assassinated. Bunche then became the leading negotiator. For his work with that tough problem, he was awarded the Nobel Peace Prize in 1950. Bunche was the first black person to receive that award. He was also the first black to hold a top job at the State Department. The grandson of an American slave, Ralph Bunche was born in Detroit in 1904. Until his death in 1971, he tried through his work and writings to improve race relations throughout the world.

Ralph Bunche—Nobel peace prize winner. (Courtesy Bentley Historical Library, University of Michigan)

Growth of the Suburbs

During the war years many young people waited to get married. After the war ended, their attitudes changed and there was a rush to get married and start families. Next, the young couples wanted to find places of their own and they built thousands of new homes.

Most new homes were built in the *suburbs* around the larger cities. *A suburb is a smaller community at the edge of a larger city.* The demand for new houses away from downtown was caused partly by the location of new factories which were also in the suburbs. Between 1947 and 1955, Ford, Chrysler, and General Motors built 20 new factories in the Detroit area. None were within the city limits.

Suburbs around major cities mushroomed. The city of Warren is a classic example. Its population grew more than 100 times between 1950 and 1960. Harper Woods became about 20 times as big in 1960 as 1940. Allen Park and Garden City were 10 times larger after the same number of years. Livonia's population increased over seven times. East Detroit and Roseville were roughly five times larger by 1960. Detroit was surrounded by a mass of smaller suburbs which ran into and surrounded other towns and cities. The same boom in suburbs happened around other cities too. Grand Rapids saw East Grand Rapids and Wyoming grow rapidly. East Lansing multiplied its population by five times from 1940 to 1960.

The whole state grew during the 1950s. By 1960 it had 22.8 percent more people than 10 years before. Michigan was the third fastest growing state in the country! Only California and Florida were growing faster.

Shopping Mall Invented

As more people lived away from the downtown shopping areas, a new trend started and it was born in Michigan. The first shopping mall in the United States was called Northland and it was built in 1954 by the J.L. Hudson company. A large

Michigan and the nation had a housing boom following World War II. (Courtesy Bentley Historical Library, University of Michigan)

parcel of land was cleared near the growing suburb of Southfield and all the stores were built together under one roof. Shoppers could drive to one place and visit all the stores. The idea which started at Northland quickly spread across the nation. Within 20 years nearly every major city had its own malls.

But malls were not seen as a great thing by everyone. The malls took business away from downtown stores and within a few years many cities had only a few stores left in their central business districts. Their downtowns were decaying and crime was increasing. The movement of so many people away from the cities and into the suburbs was another reason for problems in Michigan's large cities.

Building Highways

When the homes and businesses fanned out from the center of the cities, better roads were needed. It became necessary to drive a car to shop, go to church, or get to work. City planners realized they had to offer another way to reach places because the streets were jammed with cars during rush hours. Expressways with several lanes going in each direction were built around the state's larger cities. The first expressway in Detroit was the John Lodge which opened in 1950.

Over the next 25 years, more than 265 miles of expressways linked the suburbs around Detroit. The area had one of the most extensive expressway networks in the country. These expressways made it easier for people to leave the cities to work and shop elsewhere.

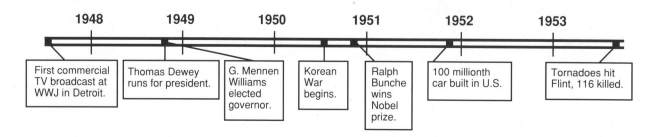

1948	1949	1950	1951	1952	1953
First commercial TV broadcast at WWJ in Detroit.	Thomas Dewey runs for president.	G. Mennen Williams elected governor.	Korean War begins.	Ralph Bunche wins Nobel prize.	100 millionth car built in U.S.	Tornadoes hit Flint, 116 killed.

In 1956 the government started a major program to built interstate highways between all large cities. Ninety percent of the cost of building the roads was paid by the federal government. Several interstates connect Michigan with nearby states. Interstate roads are labeled with the prefix "I." I-94, I-96, and I-75 became Michigan's most important interstates. The first two highways run east and west and I-75 goes north and south.

Interstate 94 goes from Detroit through Chicago and on to the state of Montana. Its construction was started in 1942 and was finished in 1971.

Interstate 96 goes from Muskegon to Detroit and it is north of I-94. It was begun in 1957 and completed in 1977.

Interstate 75 is Michigan's most important tourist highway. Travelers going north on vacation from the Detroit area can reach the Mackinac Bridge in about five to six hours. Interstate 75 stretches from Miami, Florida to Sault Ste. Marie. Work on I-75 began in 1953 and the route was done in 1973. Michigan now has about 1,150 miles of interstate roadways and only a few miles of the system remain unfinished.

Some states charge people a fee to use their expressways. Such roads are called toll roads. The people of Michigan felt more visitors and tourists would come into the state if a charge was not made. Before long, the Michigan expressways became known as freeways. Drivers in Michigan only have to pay to use major bridges or car ferries.

Roadblock Between the Peninsulas

Although the new highways planned for Michigan would be a great improvement, motorists still needed a solution for the roadblock they found at the Straits of Mackinac. There was no way to drive

Beginning in the 1950s many new highways were built in Michigan. The new roads changed the face of the cities. Large areas which had been homes and offices were replaced by miles of concrete. (Both photos courtesy Michigan State Archives)

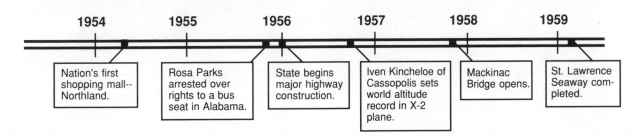

1954	1955	1956	1957	1958	1959
Nation's first shopping mall-- Northland.	Rosa Parks arrested over rights to a bus seat in Alabama.	State begins major highway construction.	Iven Kincheloe of Cassopolis sets world altitude record in X-2 plane.	Mackinac Bridge opens.	St. Lawrence Seaway completed.

352

from one side to the other. Nearly five miles of water lay in their path. A bridge was needed, but such a long bridge almost seemed a fantasy.

Today Michigan's two peninsulas are connected by the mighty Mackinac Bridge. The bridge crosses the point where the great inland seas of Lake Huron and Lake Michigan meet. It is hard for people to think of such a bridge as an extremely risky idea. But before the project was started, it seemed one big gamble. Could such a long bridge be built? Would the rock under the water hold up the bridge? How could the costs be paid? Those were big questions which had to be answered.

Would it work? Sometimes winds at the Straits of Mackinac measure 60 to 70 miles an hour. In 1940 a long bridge in the state of Washington was blown down by wind. During the cold winter months huge piles of ice stack up around the Straits. Could ice damage a bridge?

There had been discussions about a bridge at Mackinac for several years. In 1950 a state law was passed that formed a Mackinac Bridge Authority. That was taken as a a good sign by many people. But the official in charge of state highways was against the idea. There were simply too many risks. Besides, since 1923 the state of Michigan had operated five ferries which carried cars across the Straits of Mackinac. Wasn't that good enough?

There were, however, several problems with the ferry system. It took about an hour to get a car on board and across the Straits. That was when there was no waiting. Each year during deer hunting season long lines formed in Mackinaw City. So many hunters wanted to go to the Upper Peninsula that lines could be 20 miles long and it might take 24 hours before drivers could get across! Some gas stations put in 50-foot hoses so they could fill up cars while they were waiting their

Before the Mackinac Bridge was built at the Straits of Mackinac, there were some terrific traffic tie-ups. (Courtesy Michigan State Archives)

353

The Mackinac car ferry *City of Petoskey*. (Courtesy Michigan Department of Transportation)

turn to get on a ferry. A bridge would be much faster. The ships were also slowed or stopped by ice in the winter. Most people felt a bridge would help tie the Upper Peninsula and Lower Peninsula together and actually make the two parts into one state.

While plans for a bridge remained uncertain, the state purchased a new $5 million ferry, the *Vacationland*. And when asked to vote money for bridge plans, the state legislature only allowed $1.00 in the budget! The highway department and state government were not interested in spending their money to build a bridge at Mackinac.

People who really wanted a bridge had to find ways to work around those problems. They had to find engineers, geologists, and financial backers who would help them. Designers were needed who would work for nothing or close to it— at least until ways were found to pay for the project.

Bridge Ideas Take Shape

After years of waiting, things began to come together in 1953. The Korean War was over and material needed for such a large construction project would soon be available. The 250,000 Michigan men and women fighting in Korea would be home. The Bridge Authority also had developed a way to pay for the bridge. It would sell bonds to large banks and insurance companies and pay them between four and five percent interest. The interest payments would be paid from the money charged to cross the bridge. The building of the bridge would not cost the state government any money. But the legislature did say it would pay for upkeep and repairs.

Dr. David Steinman (STINE man) was hired to be the official engineer who would design the bridge. He was an expert in understanding how wind affects bridges. The main part of the bridge was going to be held, or suspended, from two

The Mackinac Bridge under construction on a winter day. (Courtesy Grand Rapids Public Library-Michigan Room)

heavy cables; therefore, it was called a suspension bridge. One of Dr. Steinman's ideas was to leave the inside two lanes unpaved. Those lanes would only be covered with a metal grate. Cars could still drive over them but the wind could pass through the openings and keep the bridge from swaying.

Over 2,000 construction workers moved to the Straits and began the huge project in 1954. Much of the work was quite dangerous. Most of the men worked while hanging from the two main cables high above the water. During the time the bridge was being built, five workers were killed in accidents. Finally it was completed. The Mackinac Bridge opened November 1, 1957. Governor G. Mennen Williams and members of the hard-working Bridge Authority went across in the first cars.

In the years since there has been an annual average of nearly 2 million cars and trucks across the bridge. The bridge has made it much easier for people and products to reach one peninsula from the other. By 1986 the bonds were paid off and the Bridge Authority was no longer in debt. Meanwhile, the car ferries were sold and taken to other places.

Railroad Ferry at the Soo

Obviously, trains cannot use the bridge. A railroad car ferry shuffled train cars back and forth across the Straits of Mackinac for 74 years. The ship was called the *Chief Wawatam*. The *Chief* operated until 1984. The operations stopped because not enough railroad cars were being moved across the Straits and it cost too much to continue operations. Since 1984 the *Chief* has been tied up at its dock in Mackinaw City waiting for someone to find a use for her. Some people are hoping money can be found to make the *Chief Wawatam* into a floating museum.

Mackinac Bridge Facts....

At 8,614 feet it is the longest suspension bridge in the world when measured from anchorage to anchorage. [The anchorages are the large concrete blocks which hold the ends of the suspension cables.] There has been confusion about the ranking of the Mackinac Bridge because the distance between its towers is less than those on the Golden Gate Bridge in San Francisco and New York's Verrezano-Narrows Bridge.

Two main towers hold up the bridge with wire cable. The towers are 552 feet above the water and rest on the rock floor over 200 feet below the water.

Greatest height of the road above water is 192 feet.

33,000 miles of steel wire were used to make the cables holding up the roadway of the bridge—more than enough to go around the world. The finished cable is a bit more than 24 inches across.

2,500 workers built the bridge but there were 7,500 others helping to provide materials. In addition, 350 engineers worked on the designs.

The plans required 85,000 blueprints.

440,000 cubic yards of concrete went into the base and supports.

It is designed to stand winds greater than 600 miles per hour.

The cost was $100 million— more than the Golden Gate Bridge and the George Washington bridges combined.

Each Labor Day the bridge is open to people who wish to walk across. Over 40,000 have walked across in a single day.

Questions

1. Why did Michigan's colleges and universities grow so much after World War II?

2. Was Thomas Dewey actually living in Michigan when he ran for President? Did most people think he had a good chance to win the election?

3. How many times was G. Mennen Williams elected governor of Michigan? Did that set a record for the most times a Michigan governor has been elected? What was Governor Williams' nickname?

4. Who was the first black person to win a Nobel Peace Prize? What outstanding work did that person do?

5. What is special about the Northland shopping mall?

6. Name three forces that began during the 1950s to cause downtown areas to decay. Write your own opinion whether the downtown areas of cities should have been protected from those developments. Explain your ideas.

7. List Michigan's three most important interstate highways. Which Michigan cities does each connect?

8. How did people travel between Michigan's two peninsulas before the Mackinac Bridge was finished? What problems did that method have?

9. List three facts about the Mackinac Bridge which interest you.

Chapter 14 Section 2

Going in New Directions Under New Stresses— 1960s

| Here are the key concepts you will find in this section: |

Michigan was caught up in the struggle of equal rights for black people in the 1960s. Two well-known black leaders, Rosa Parks and Malcolm X, lived in Michigan.

Another destructive riot hit Detroit in 1967. Many people were killed; eventually, the National Guard and Army were called in to take control of the city.

In the early 1960s many in Michigan felt our state constitution could be improved. A new constitution was developed and approved by a close vote in 1963.

The Vietnam War affected Michigan. Over 300,000 men and women from the state were involved in the war.

Michigan people played an important part in the space program. They participated in the voyage to the moon and space shuttle missions.

The first nuclear power plants in Michigan opened in the 1960s, but one soon had a serious malfunction and was closed.

Changes Come Quickly

There have always been times of change, but in the 1960s changes seemed to come faster and to be more radical. It was a time of major shake-ups in society. Blacks fought for their civil rights along with other ethnic minorities and women. Michigan made a new state constitution in 1961. That brought many changes too. Right in the middle of it all was the Vietnam War which caused a split between older and younger people.

"Mother of the Civil Rights Movement"

The years from the mid-1950s to the 1960s were an awakening time about equal rights for blacks. Blacks all over the country had been treated unfairly in a number of ways. Rosa Parks, a black woman, was coming home from work in Montgomery, Alabama. She got on a city bus and sat down, weary after a long working day. When white riders boarded the bus, the driver told her to leave her seat and stand in the back. She wouldn't do it and she was arrested for her refusal. Rosa Parks' action earned her the title of "Mother of the Civil Rights Movement."

That protest by just one woman started a citywide boycott by black people of the entire bus system. That was the beginning of a movement for black *civil rights. Civil rights are the basic rights people have that protect them against discriminatory or unequal action by the government or other individuals.* The movement was much like the movement for workers' rights to join unions 20 years earlier. Martin Luther King, Jr. became a leader of the black people during the bus boycott.

In 1957, less than two years after the bus incident, Rosa Parks moved to Detroit. Her friends and relatives were worried about her safety if she stayed in

358

Rosa Parks. (Art by George Rasmussen)

Montgomery. Rosa has remained in Detroit, and in her honor a street has been named after her.

Malcolm X

Different black people had different ideas about how to change things. Many felt nonviolent protests were the best way, but others believed that anything should be used if it got the job done. Malcolm Little, who had changed his name to Malcolm X, fit into the second group. He believed in militant methods. He grew up in Lansing, Michigan. During his years in Lansing his family was treated badly by some white people. They even burned his family's home. Malcolm X became a leader in the Black Muslim movement but in 1965 he was shot and killed.

King in Detroit

Martin Luther King, Jr., was a Baptist minister and he strongly believed nothing positive would happen in the long run if blacks used violence to gain their

Dr. Martin Luther King, Jr., led the "Walk to Freedom" march in Detroit 1963. King is to the right and just behind the police official.

rights. On the 20th anniversary of the 1943 Detroit riot, King led a march through Detroit with 125,000 people who believed in equal rights for blacks. The march ended at Cobo Hall where King gave a speech which was a warm-up for the speech he gave two months later in Washington, D.C. In the Washington speech he told of his dream of "...that day when all of God's children...will be able to join hands and sing in the words of the old Negro spiritual, 'Free at last! Free at last! Thank God Almighty, we are free at last!'"

It Started with a Raid

Leaders among blacks and whites were trying to work together but there were many problems and sometimes much tension. Even so, Detroit was thought to be a model city— better than most. That was until late on a Saturday night in July 1967. On July 23, Detroit police raided an illegal bar in a black neighborhood. It was hot and muggy when the police broke into the bar and found 85 people drinking and gambling. The police were not well prepared to take so many people to jail and a large crowd gathered outside while police waited for paddy wagons. Just as the last police car pulled away, the crowd started to throw bottles and bricks. By 5 A.M. the police were getting calls that a riot had begun! By 7 A.M. the National Guard was notified but they were all at summer practice in Grayling— a five-hour drive away.

Hundreds and then thousands of people took to the streets. Many began to break into stores and steal. The looters were both black and white. The riot was not just blacks against whites. Some white store owners shot white looters and black businesses were burned by blacks. Other blacks came out into the streets to protect the mostly white firemen. Rioters were setting fires throughout the city. Snipers were shooting at firemen as they tried to put out the fires.

Governor Romney and the mayor of Detroit asked President Lyndon Johnson to send 5,000 soldiers to stop the riot.

These burned-out buildings are silent reminders of the violence and destruction from the 1967 riot in Detroit. (Courtesy Michigan State Archives)

360

But it took a long time to get the help; just as it had in 1943. After 22 hours of arguing with federal officials, they gave their approval.

Nine days later the situation finally quieted down. The Detroit riot of 1967 was over but the waste was tremendous. Forty-three people had been killed and 700 injured. There were 7,000 arrested. Property damage was about $50 million. Some entire city blocks had been burned as a result of the 1,680 fires which were set.

Governor Romney at his desk signing a bill into law. (Courtesy Office of the Governor)

New Constitution Needed

Improvements in civil rights were taking place in Michigan before the Detroit riot. Provisions safeguarding civil rights had been added to a new state constitution in 1963. A push for a new constitution started after the payless payday for state workers in 1959. Many people felt a number of Michigan's problems were related to the out-of-date constitution written in 1908. The state constitution is the basic set of laws which govern the state. In a way it is like the rule book for state government.

In April 1961, a statewide vote was taken to decide if there should be a meeting to prepare a new, modern constitution. The vote was favorable and in September another election was held for the 144 delegates who would write the new constitution.

A number of outstanding individuals were delegates to the convention. There were presidents of universities and business leaders. George Romney, the president of American Motors, was named second in charge of the convention. There were several black delegates including Richard Austin and Coleman Young. Later, Romney was elected governor of Michigan; Austin became secretary of state, and Young became the first black mayor of Detroit.

After several months of talks in Lansing, the delegates decided on some important changes for the new constitution. They included a prohibition against discrimination on the basis of religion, race, color, and national origin. To backup that provision, a state Civil Rights Commission was set up. The office of governor was strengthened by changing the term to four years instead of two. The governor and lieutenant governor would now run together as a team and be from the same political party. There had been times in the past when the governor and lieutenant governor had been from different parties. That created some unusual problems. Elections for

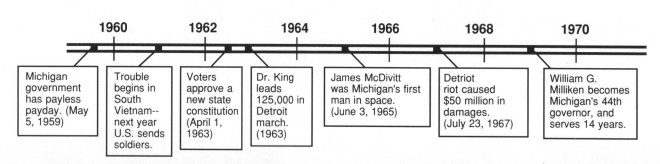

1960	1962	1964	1966	1968	1970
Michigan government has payless payday. (May 5, 1959)	Trouble begins in South Vietnam--next year U.S. sends soldiers.	Voters approve a new state constitution (April 1, 1963)	Dr. King leads 125,000 in Detroit march. (1963)	James McDivitt was Michigan's first man in space. (June 3, 1965)	Detriot riot caused $50 million in damages. (July 23, 1967)	William G. Milliken becomes Michigan's 44th governor, and serves 14 years.

Nearly everyone got into the act to support the Michigan constitutional convention or Con-Con. (Courtesy Michigan State Archives)

governor were moved so they are not held in the same year as the presidential elections. Also, the highway commissioner was no longer to be an elected office. Over 130 state government agencies were streamlined into 20 main departments.

Much of the work on the new constitution went smoothly but there were some terrific arguments. By the time their work was finished, many delegates who were liberal Democrats and conservative Republicans decided they would vote against the changes. The voters of Michigan had to decide on April 1, 1963, if they would accept the new constitution. It was close and passed by only 7,000 votes. But over the years, most authorities have felt the 1963 constitution has been a good one.

Success from Songs

In spite of the problems in Detroit, it was the birthplace of Motown Industries, one of the most successful black businesses in the United States. Motown was

begun as a record company by Berry Gordy in 1959. The business started by Gordy grew and soon had annual sales of $50 million. Motown is a contraction of the words "motor town," a nickname for Detroit.

Gordy grew up in Detroit and tried to be a boxer for a short time. He became interested in music and opened a record store but it went out of business in 1955. Gordy started working for the Ford Motor Company but a friend, William "Smokey" Robinson, Jr., told him he should start his own record company. So, with $700 in borrowed money, Motown began in a rented house.

Good things started to happen for Motown with the release of Smokey Robinson's 1960 gold record, "Shop Around." Other top songs included "I Heard It Through the Grape Vine" by Marvin Gaye.

The Motown sound of the 1960s was best known by the songs of the Supremes. Diana Ross, Mary Wilson, and

The Hitsville museum which holds the history of the "Motown Sound." (Courtesy Metropolitan Detroit Convention & Visitors Bureau)

Florence Ballard were the three young black women in that singing trio. Even though the Supremes were quite young, the group was a tremendous success. Record sales from the Supremes exceeded 12 million copies, second only to the Beatles!

Stevie Wonder was another Motown musician. He was born in Saginaw in 1950 but moved to Detroit. Wonder, blind since birth, has a great musical talent. When he was just nine years old he spent hours hanging around the Motown studios. He played every instrument he could get his hands on and earned the nickname "little boy wonder." Stevie Wonder writes his own songs with the aid of a tape recorder and braille music sheets. His success continues. He was awarded an Oscar for the music and lyrics of *I Just Called To Say I Love You.*

The Motown organization faced major changes in the 1970s. Diana Ross left the Supremes in 1970 to go on her own. Stevie Wonder also left for a time. In 1972 Berry Gordy decided to go into the movie business too. He then moved the Motown operation to Los Angeles.

Aretha Franklin. (Courtesy Metropolitan Detroit Convention & Visitors Bureau)

Today the original Motown building still stands and is named Hitsville U.S.A. Esther Gordy Edwards, sister and once business associate of Berry Gordy, Jr., has turned the building into the Motown Historical Museum. It is a showcase for the golden years of music produced in Detroit.

War in Asia—Vietnam

Meanwhile, events in southeast Asia were creeping up on the United States. American soldiers had been sent to Vietnam by President Eisenhower and more were sent by President Kennedy. Though the small country was a long way from Michigan, the fighting there began to affect people in the state. Communities were shocked by the deaths of soldiers from their towns— young men they had known.

By the late 1960s there was widespread belief that the Unites States was not handling the war properly. College students were upset at the thought of being sent to Vietnam to fight in a war in which they did not believe.

Students at the University of Michigan in Ann Arbor were particularly active against the war. One of the students was Tom Hayden from Royal Oak. Hayden was active in promoting a radical group called the Students for a Democratic Society or SDS. Years later, Hayden gained fame when he married actress Jane Fonda and became active in California politics.

The Vietnam War even affected one Michigan governor's chances to become president. Governor George Romney was interested in running for the nation's highest office but his campaign fell apart after he made the statement that he had been "brainwashed" by government officials concerning Vietnam. What Romney said was probably true about many other people but they didn't want to admit it. After he made the statement, his leader-

A Vietnam War protest by students at Michigan State University. (Courtesy Michigan State University Archives and Historical Collections)

ship abilities were questioned by national television and newspaper commentators.

Many college campuses had antiwar protests by students. The bigger universities saw thousands of students gathering and marching. In one memorable march, students from Michigan State University filled Michigan Avenue for blocks and marched the four or five miles to the state capitol building in Lansing. There they were met by a somewhat worried Governor William Milliken.

The Vietnam War was a conflict where war was never actually declared. Even so, it was the longest military action in which the United States has ever been involved. During that time, 367,000 men and women from Michigan served in Asia.

Effects Continue

To many soldiers and medical personnel, the war seemed hopeless and continued without any real victories. The grueling jungle fighting left some soldiers scarred psychologically. The violence they witnessed affected them and a few continued to react violently once back in civilian life. At one point, 1,200 of the 5,500 inmates in Michigan State Prison near Jackson, had served in Vietnam. The second largest chapter of the organization of Vietnam Veterans of America was made up of those serving time in the prison .

Ripples from Vietnam kept touching Michigan. After the communists took over South Vietnam, refugees poured out of the country. A number of the people eventually came to Michigan to make a new home. Thoa Nguyen (toe whin) and his family spent five long years trying to get to the United States. Finally in 1980, the family received help from a church organization and were brought together in Grand Rapids.

Michiganians in Outer Space

Though the 1960s had much bad news, Americans were eager to learn the latest progress in our program to explore outer space. The excitement was no greater anywhere than in Michigan. No spaceships were ever launched from Michigan but the state had a number of people involved in the space program.

Roger Chaffee from Grand Rapids was one of the first. He was selected for the astronaut training program in 1963. Chaffee became a member of the Apollo team and was preparing to go into space.

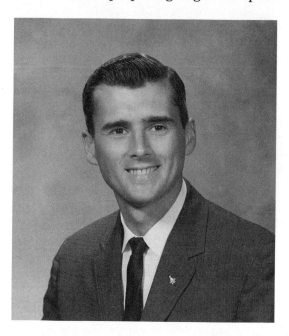

Michigan astronaut Roger Chaffee lost his life training for a space launch. (Courtesy NASA)

In 1967 he was one of three astronauts in a test launch when the space capsule suddenly caught fire. The fire was fierce because of the pure oxygen provided for the men to breathe. Before anyone could help the astronauts out of the capsule, they were killed by the flames! Prior to the space shuttle accident in 1986, that was the only time Americans lost their lives in the space program.

The first U.S. spacewalk took place in June 1965. As millions of Americans witnessed this event on their televisions, James McDivitt from Jackson piloted the Gemini spacecraft. McDivitt also commanded the Apollo 7 flight. That mission was essentially a five-day test of the equipment which would be used to reach the moon on the Apollo 9 mission in 1969.

James McDivitt (Courtesy NASA)

Al Worden also born in Jackson, commanded the 1971 Apollo 15 flight to the moon. Worden stayed in the spacecraft while two other astronauts explored the surface of the moon in the "moon rover." Since the city of Jackson has a connection with several astronauts, there is a space museum on the campus of Jackson Community College. Called the Michigan Space Center, the museum houses several space capsules and other exhibits about the astronauts and their projects in outer space.

Jack Lousma was another astronaut from Grand Rapids. Lousma spent 60 days aboard the Skylab 2 in 1973. He and the other two crew members performed a long list of experiments while the Skylab orbited the earth.

The latest Michigan astronaut is Brewster Shaw from Cass City in the "thumb" area. Shaw flew in the space shuttle *Columbia* in 1983 and commanded the shuttle *Atlantis* in 1985. He helped with design changes for the space shuttle after the explosion of the *Challenger*.

The McGregor Center on the Wayne State University campus, designed by Minoru Yamasaki. *See story on next page.* (Courtesy Michigan State Archives)

The nuclear reactor at Big Rock Point. The first built in Michigan, it was opened in 1962 and can produce 50,000 kilowatts of electricity. (Courtesy Consumers Power Company)

Beautiful Buildings Designed in Michigan

Besides those exploring outer space, another Michiganian was becoming famous for his work. A young architect named Minoru Yamasaki (min or oo yam ah sock ee) moved to Michigan in 1945. He worked in Detroit and began to design airy, attractive buildings. The public was excited by one of his designs used at Wayne State University in 1958, the McGregor Conference Center. The building became a centerpiece of the campus.

It wasn't long before Yamasaki designed several other interesting buildings in Michigan, including one in Southfield and another in Detroit. As his fame spread, he began to do more work around the world including an airport terminal and government office in Saudi Arabia. But Yamaski's greatest achievement was the design of the World Trade Center in New York City. In 1976 when that building was completed, it was the tallest building in the world! Minoru Yamasaki died in 1986 but he left behind a treasure of creative designs in the buildings he planned.

Electricity from Atoms

While Yamasaki was designing modern buildings, Michigan electric power companies were making plans for a new way to generate electricity. Once the atomic bomb ended World War II, scientists, like Glenn Seaborg from Ishpeming, rushed to find peaceful uses for nuclear energy. In the 1960s, Seaborg became the head of the Atomic Energy Commission. Many thought making electricity would be a good way to use knowledge about the atom. In the beginning there were not too many concerns about the dangers of nuclear power.

The first nuclear power plant in Michigan was built between Charlevoix and Petoskey on the shore of Lake Michigan. It was the Big Rock Point Plant. It opened in 1962 and has operated successfully ever since. Four years later, a second nuclear plant opened along Lake Erie near Monroe, just 30 miles from Detroit. That electric plant was named after the atomic scientist Enrico Fermi.

But the Fermi plant had problems almost from the time it started operation. After running for about three months, it suffered a serious accident. It overheated and some of its radioactive fuel elements melted. Months later, it was discovered a piece of protective metal had come loose in the cooling system and plugged an important pipe. For the first time, Michigan's citizens realized nuclear power brought great risk along with its promise of cheap electricity. In 1970 an attempt was made to restart the Fermi plant but once again it had a serious accident with the cooling system. Without ever getting back into operation, the government closed the plant in 1972.

Questions

1. Why is Rosa Parks known as the "mother of the civil rights movement?"

2. When did Detroit have its most recent major riot? Was the riot strictly between black and white people? List some facts to show how bad the riot was.

3. When was the last time Michigan had a new state constitution? Name one major change made then.

4. Who started the Motown Record Company? Name three musicians who recorded with Motown.

5. How many men and women from Michigan served in the Vietnam War? List one way the Vietnam War affected Michigan.

6. Name the Michigan astronaut who orbited the moon. Which one was at the first U.S. spacewalk? Give the name of the Michigan astronaut who died in a practice launch of the Apollo spacecraft.

7. Where was Michigan's first nuclear power plant built? Was the plant a success?

Chapter 14 Section 3
Part 1

Twists and Turns:
A New Era Is Coming - 1970s & 1980s

Here are the key concepts you will find in this section:

The auto industry has been through many changes in recent years. All of the changes have affected Michigan's industry, its workers, and its future.

In 1979 the Chrysler Company almost went broke. It was saved by a large loan from the federal government and big pay cuts for workers.

In the 1970s and early 1980s several businesses left or shifted operations from Michigan.

Foreign companies have built factories in Michigan. They make cars, car parts and a large number of other products.

In 1980 General Motors created much controversy when it decided to build a new factory in the Poletown section of Detroit.

Much of Michigan's future depends on new high technology businesses.

We Face Many Changes

If there is one word which can be used to describe Michigan in the 1970s and 1980s it is "changes." Michigan's important auto industry faced several problems which changed its structure. Other industries changed as they faced competition from outside the state. Michigan's cities have changed, mostly for the better, as downtown developments have brought new life to old and tired business districts. The population of Michigan changed too. There has been an increase in the numbers of Hispanic people and people from Asian countries. One of the nation's largest concentrations of Arabic people is in the Dearborn area. The environment was changed by the dumping of toxic wastes and the accidental release of chemicals.

Oil Crisis Means Expensive Gas

Very significant changes hit the auto industry in the fall of 1973. The story began with a cutoff of oil to the United States. The Arab oil-producing nations stopped shipments in protest of America's support for Israel. Without Arab oil, the supply of gasoline was reduced. Gas became scarce and expensive. Suddenly everyone wanted to buy small fuel-efficient cars; and Michigan wasn't making those. It took car makers about two years to make changes so they could start producing more small cars.

The oil crisis of the 1970s affected workers who earned their living making cars. (Courtesy Michigan State Archives)

Competition From Imports

Since Michigan's economy was so closely tied with the auto industry, the slowdown in sales had a statewide impact. Roughly 20 percent of the state's workers had auto-related jobs then. American motor vehicle production dropped from about 12.7 million in 1973 to roughly 9 million units in 1975. About one third of those cars and trucks were made in Michigan. There was an explosion in imported car sales. Customers needing small cars quickly switched to Toyotas from Japan and Volkswagens from Germany. Before the oil crisis, the Japanese only sold 180,000 cars a year in the United States. By 1979 the amount was 10 times greater and still growing.

The year 1980 was an important turning point for the auto industry. For the first time in 80 years another country made more cars than the United States.

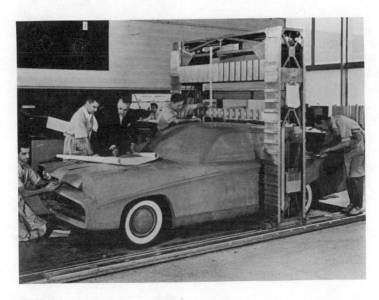

American car companies raced to design smaller models to head off foreign competition. (Courtesy Michigan State Archives)

Japan became the leader. By 1982 about 30 percent of all cars sold in the United States were made by foreign companies. There were many complaints that the Japanese were using unfair trade practices. American companies claimed the Japanese sold their cars for less in the U.S. than in Japan, which is illegal.

Higher Prices Mean Fewer Sales

Meanwhile, Michigan-based car companies worked to bring out new, smaller, and fuel-efficient models. They were "down-sizing" their cars. Cars were made smaller and lighter. By 1985 the largest U.S. car weighed less than the smallest model made in 1975. The government also told car makers they must install devices to reduce exhaust pollution. Such federal requirements were expensive and caused prices to go up. At the same time, inflation increased and everything was more expensive. Car prices went even higher! In one year, between 1980 and 1981, prices for American-made cars increased a whopping 14 percent.

The higher prices again slowed car sales and that had a ripple effect through the economy. The lower demand for tires caused Detroit's Uniroyal plant to close in 1980. Tires had been made in that factory for 74 years. Other Michigan tire companies had to close their plants too. Less steel was used to make smaller cars so additional workers in the Michigan steel industry were out of work. Tourism, another important Michigan business, was affected too. Laid-off workers could not afford to travel.

The Big Three auto makers, General Motors, Ford, and Chrysler, lost $4.6 billion in 1980. That was as much as the entire annual budget for Michigan's state government. The number of cars and trucks actually made in Michigan kept falling. In 1976 the state turned out nearly 4 million vehicles; by 1980, however, it was only 1,981,703— about 50 percent less.

The Chrysler Bailout

The Chrysler company was the smallest of the Big Three, and was in bad shape financially. In 1979 the company announced it would be bankrupt in six weeks and would have to close. Politicians from Michigan were very concerned. As many as 175,000 Michigan workers could be out of work and the jobs of 300,000 more in related industries might be affected too. Men and women from Michigan who were in the United States Senate and Congress rushed to pass a law that had the federal government guarantee a $1.5 billion loan to Chrysler.

Such a loan guarantee, or bailout, was unusual and controversial. There were those who said if the company could not make it on its own, it should go out of business. But help from the federal government saved the company and the jobs. It was also necessary for the workers to accept almost $600 million in pay cuts. Chrysler was, however, back on its feet in record time and in 1983 began to pay back its loans ahead of schedule.

Much of the credit for this recovery

Lee Iacocca. (Courtesy Chrysler Motor Company)

goes to the employees and Lee Iacocca. Iacocca had been the Ford president from 1970-1978 and made his mark there by developing the Ford Mustang. But he was suddenly fired by Henry Ford II. Even though he knew Chrysler had problems, he accepted the top job there in 1979. He became well-known when he made television commercials promoting new Chrysler models. In the process of turning Chrysler around, Iacocca had to make many tough choices, selling off parts of the company to raise money and firing unneeded employees.

The Chrysler company bounced back from the edge of disaster to become a leader in new products. It began making a convertible, something that hadn't been produced for years. It brought out the first mini-van in 1983, which was quite popular. Later, Chrysler even bought the American Motors Company.

Some Businesses Leave Michigan

During the 1970s and early 1980s, Michigan began to lose manufacturing businesses. Many of the companies in Michigan did not want to expand their operations here. Instead, they built new plants in southern states and overseas. That created a crisis and cost Michigan workers their jobs.

Why did the companies leave? There were several reasons. Executives believed wages were too high in Michigan. For example, the 1982 hourly wage for the average Michigan industrial worker was 30 percent higher than similar wages in other states. Michigan car makers were under great pressure to cut their costs. In the mid-1980s experts reported it took U.S. car companies twice as many hours to build a car as it did the Japanese. With fewer working hours involved, each Japanese car cost $1,500 to $2,000 less to make.

Michigan's powerful unions also developed many rules which the car company executives felt made it more difficult to manage the companies. As yet, unions were not so strong in the southern states.

The cost of operating a business was higher in Michigan for other reasons too. The state had some of the highest workmen's compensation and unemployment payment rates in the United States.

Workmen's compensation is a fee charged to employers by the state. It is a form of insurance paid to workers who are injured and cannot work. Unemployment payments are also collected by the state and paid to those who are laid off from their jobs. These programs exist to protect workers, but as long as Michigan had such high rates, companies built their plants somewhere else. It was cheaper to make products in states with lower rates.

In addition, some companies moved to the South because of the increased costs of gas and oil used for heating. Michigan's cold winters made that an important expense.

For various reasons, General Motors decided in 1985 to build its giant Saturn production complex in Tennessee. That loss was a big blow to Michigan. Some jobs related to the project, however, were kept here. The Saturn headquarters office is in Troy and its engineering office is in Madison Heights.

Michigan's car companies developed a trend of buying many parts from factories outside of the state. Building cars with parts not actually made by the auto companies themselves is called "outsourcing." That is to say, buying from an outside source. During the 1970s and 1980s out-sourcing continued to increase. That change in company policy meant more Michigan auto workers lost their jobs.

Union News in the 1970s

Walter Reuther was leader of the United Auto Workers Union for many years. In May 1970 he and his wife died in the tragic crash of a small plane. After Reuther's death, Leonard Woodcock became the president of the UAW. Woodcock served as the leader of the union for seven years. Later, he became the United States ambassador to China.

Walter Reuther had always fought against any involvement by communists or criminals in the UAW. But another Michigan union leader, James Hoffa, tried to get along with gang members although he was strongly anti-communist. Hoffa was the head of the Teamsters Union. Because of the suspicion that gangsters were associated with his union, there were many state and federal investigations of Hoffa during his career with the Teamsters.

In 1975 James Hoffa went to a suburban Detroit restaurant to meet someone. But after his arrival, he mysteriously disappeared. No clues were ever found relating to his disappearance. Police believe he must have been killed. James Hoffa was declared "presumed dead" in 1982.

Michigan and the World

Foreign companies are having an important impact on Michigan and on the state's future. Initially, the national and state governments worried that additional American workers would lose their jobs because of foreign car sales. They put pressure on Toyota, Nissan, Mazda, and other foreign companies to build factories in the United States and make some of their cars here. That program has been successful. In the spring of 1985 Mazda started to build a giant plant at Flat Rock, Michigan. The factory there has jobs for 3,500 workers.

Other foreign companies are building smaller auto-related factories in Michigan too. Ogihara Iron Works has a plant in Howell. Nippondenso is another Japanese plant making automobile air conditioners near Jackson, and a French company is making automotive parts in Port Huron. Those and similar plants may keep auto industry jobs in Michigan, but they won't be controlled by Michigan companies. That could mean workers may be asked to do things differently. Certainly much of the profits made by these companies will leave the state.

There has actually been a boom of foreign companies starting operations in Michigan. They produce a wide variety of products in addition to cars and car parts. Doughnut flour, sugar, musical instruments, and chewing gum are just a few of the items. As of 1987 there were 425 foreign-owned companies in the state. They provide jobs to about 50,000 Michigan workers. Often it cannot be determined just by the company's name that it is foreign-owned. Some are Canadian and British. A few are French, but Japan is the leader with 145 firms.

Trouble in Poletown!

When one of the Big Three auto makers did decide to build a large new plant in Michigan, the project created a great deal of controversy. In 1980 General Motors planned to build a new Cadillac assembly plant. The company selected a location within the city of Detroit known as Poletown. They promised the plant would bring new jobs to the city. Detroit officials were only too happy to see a new factory built in their area. It was the first new auto plant for the city since 1928.

There were problems though. Thousands of homes, plus many churches, stores, and schools in the proud Polish neighborhood stood in the way. All of them would need to be torn down. Naturally, thousands of Poletown residents were very upset. They felt the plant could be built nearby without destroying all their homes.

It turned into a major clash between big government and a big corporation against the ordinary people. The city of Detroit took the drastic step of using its legal power, known as eminent domain, to take control of private property for public use. Normally, cities use such power to buy property needed for new streets and similar public projects. In this case, Detroit paid the owners and then sold the land to General Motors. Lawyers argued it was not a public project and the process was illegal.

After much controversy, the residents of Poletown either left their homes or were evicted by the police. Wrecking balls smashed 1,362 homes, 143 businesses, 16 churches, and 1 hospital. The new Cadillac plant was built where 3,438 people had once lived. Lawsuits and other legal actions were still going on eight years after the plant was started. The city of Detroit may eventually have to pay over $100 million in settlements.

Chrysler also plans to build a new plant in the Detroit area during the early 1990s. Its factory will hire between 2,500 and 3,000 workers.

Robots On the Assembly Line

In the new factories, a change was made in the way cars are assembled. Large numbers of workers were replaced by machines. The car companies installed mechanical robots to do many jobs which had once been done by people. These robots don't look like those from science fiction films. They are just industrial machines with mechanical arms which are designed to do certain jobs in the factory. They are most often used in dangerous or dirty work. Welding and spray painting are two examples. About 30 to 40 percent of Michigan's car painters have been replaced by robots and 15 to 20 percent of the car welders have been replaced too. On some welding lines there is not a single human being to be seen!

Amazing as it may seem, in GM plants the robots know the exact car body on which they are working. Each car body has a circuit chip attached to it. When a body goes into the paint shop, a radio transmitter sends a signal to the chip which sends back a code number. The computer controlling the robot knows what colors the customer ordered for that particular body!

About one third of all the cars and trucks made in the United States come from Michigan. Changes in the auto industry bring major changes for the entire state. The lives of thousands of workers and their families are affected by what happens. The state's businesses have been built around the auto industry for close to 90 years. Over 333,000 Michigan workers still have jobs making cars and trucks for the Big Three companies, but once there were over 500,000.

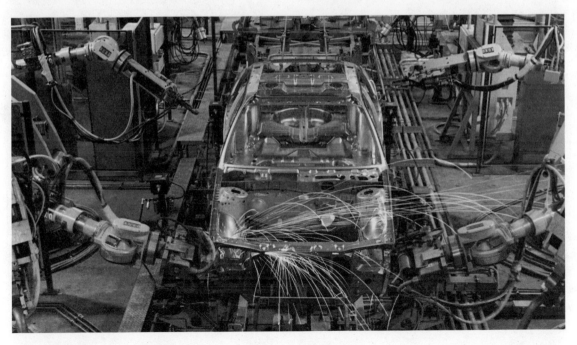

A modern assembly line shows most of the welding work done by robots. (Courtesy Ford Motor Company)

The Assembly Line Today

A. Under-body and other parts are placed on conveyor by workers and robots.

B. Robots weld the under-body together.

C. Robots attach roof, doors, trunk, and hood to frame.

F. Workers install and check wiring and instrument panel.

E. Robots paint body.

D. Workers prime and sand body.

G. Workers install steering wheel and small windows. Robots install large windows and weather striping.

H. Workers install seats, carpeting, dashboard, grill and headlights.

I. Workers and robots assemble and install engine, transmission and wheels.

Art by Theresa Deeter

K. Workers load completed automobiles onto truck for delivery.

J. Computer tests engine and transmission. Workers correct any problems.

Looking Toward the Future

This industry will continue to be an important one for the state no matter what happens over the next 10 to 20 years. But it will not be the same as it was once. It will have more world-wide interaction. American auto companies will have a global focus. They will use more parts made overseas and have partnerships with foreign companies. For example, General Motors is marketing a small car made in Korea. A large number of auto workers will be working for foreign companies right here in Michigan, such as the Mazda plant in Flat Rock. Imported cars will continue to affect Michigan. And there will be more jobs done by robots and automated equipment. Some kinds of jobs will no longer exist for human workers.

When James Blanchard became governor in 1983, he began a strong program to bring more jobs into Michigan. Another goal of his program was to help Michigan industry *diversify. In this case, diversify means to spread out into more than one kind of industry.* Too much of Michigan's business depends on the auto industry. The state opened offices in Japan and Europe to help foreign companies locate here and to find overseas markets for products made in Michigan. State government also helps with loans and money to start new businesses in Michigan.

In 1991 when John Engler became governor, he worked to attract and keep business in Michigan. Some of his main goals were to cut taxes, especially property taxes, and reduce the cost of state government. These plans helped to make Michigan a better place to locate a business; however, the changes and cuts made life more difficult for some people.

In spite of some problems, new industries are developing here. Here are just a few examples. Prab Robots of Kalamazoo makes industrial robots. Stryker Corporation, another Kalamazoo company, makes hip joints and artificial replacement parts for the human body. Ovonic Imaging Systems of Troy produces solar cells; these are devices which change the sun's energy into electricity. Troy's Votrax Incorporated designs machines that understand commands from the human voice. Ann Arbor is the home of many high technology companies and one of these is KMS Industries. At KMS, scientists use powerful lasers to study the possibility of fusion power. To help new

Former Governor James Blanchard (Courtesy Office of the Governor)

industries of tomorrow, the University of Michigan has set up the Industrial Technology Institute, a center to develop thinking robots. The university and its faculty also provide advice to solve industrial problems.

Not every business in Ann Arbor is based on high technology, though. Tom Monaghan built a multimillion dollar headquarters for his Domino's Pizza chain there. Monaghan has included a museum in his headquarters. It displays items he has collected from his favorite architect, Frank Lloyd Wright. Alongside the headquarters is a working farm. Both the headquarters and farm are open to visitors.

376

Michigan also looks toward the future with more minority-owned businesses. For example, a former Tigers pitcher, Henry (Hank) Aguirre (ah gary), is now president of Mexican Industries in Michigan. His company cuts and sews fabric for car interiors. The business began in 1979 with eight workers and now has over 200 employees.

Industry— An Important Part of the State

Michigan's industry is important and significant. Twenty of the nation's 500 largest companies are based in Michigan. The total value of the products produced and services performed places Michigan ninth among all the states. Only eight other states produce more. A worldwide comparison of the value of Michigan's products and services ranks it 25th. That means if Michigan were a separate country instead of a state, only 24 countries produce more.

In the future, even more than in the past, Michigan workers will be affected by events happening far away. Changes in the supply of oil, decisions of foreign companies, and new ideas in technology will be some of the things which control what happens in Michigan.

Hispanic people are an important part of Michigan. Dr. Gumecindo Salas (goo may SIN doe SAH las) served on the State Board of Education for many years.

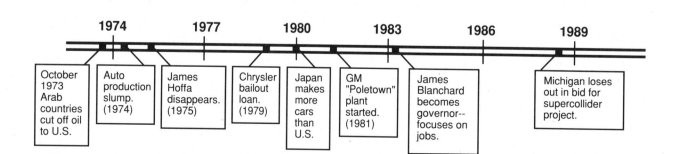

| 1974 | 1977 | 1980 | 1983 | 1986 | 1989 |

October 1973 Arab countries cut off oil to U.S.

Auto production slump. (1974)

James Hoffa disappears. (1975)

Chrysler bailout loan. (1979)

Japan makes more cars than U.S.

GM "Poletown" plant started. (1981)

James Blanchard becomes governor-- focuses on jobs.

Michigan loses out in bid for supercollider project.

Questions

1. Give two examples which show how important the auto industry is to Michigan.

2. What event caused the number of imported cars to increase in this country?

3. Explain what the Chrysler "bailout" was. Do you think this was good for Michigan? Give some specific examples to back up what you say.

4. Who is Lee Iacocca and what did he do in Michigan?

5. What do you think are some good points and some bad points about foreign companies moving to Michigan?

6. What happened in Poletown in 1980? Why were the people in that part of Detroit so upset?

7. How does the value of Michigan's industry and services compare to the value of industry and services from other states and countries?

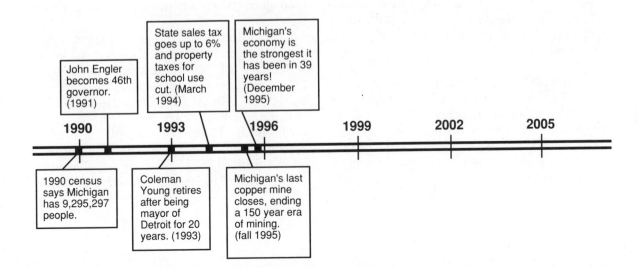

Chapter 14 Section 3
Part 2

Environmental Concerns

Here are the key concepts you will find in this section:

In 1973 a poisonous chemical called PBB was accidentally mixed with animal feed in Michigan. Many people got PBB in their bodies after eating beef or drinking milk from poisoned animals.

Michigan faces the problems of cleaning up toxic wastes and deciding how to dispose of its garbage in the future.

Deciding how electric power is generated will be an important question for the future. Nuclear power can be dangerous, but burning coal in power plants causes air and water pollution.

Acid rain is caused by some Michigan industries and power plants. This rain is carried in the air over Canada, and causes damage to the lakes and forests.

A Tragic Mistake

Several environmental problems face Michigan. One problem developed when a strange chemical accident happened in 1973. That summer a worker at a St. Louis, Michigan, chemical plant was bagging a white powder called Firemaster. It is a toxic chemical used to make material less flammable. Someone picked up some bags for an animal feed supplement and continued to fill those bags with Firemaster, which is also known as PBB. Both chemicals are white powders and the mistake went unnoticed.

The poorly labeled bags were shipped to several Farm Bureau feed mills in Michigan. Once at the feed mills, about 2,000 pounds of the chemical were dumped into machines mixing up a farm animal feed.

A Poison in the Food Chain

Farmers bought the animal feed and gave it to their dairy cows, pigs, and chickens. By fall, many farmers noticed odd things happening to their cattle. Some wouldn't eat; others had calves which were born dead; some lost their hair. Milk production dropped tremendously. No one noticed anything wrong with the milk, however, and most of it was sold. Some of the cattle were butchered and the meat sold too.

Veterinarians could not determine what was wrong with the cattle. Nine months passed before anyone realized what was going on. One farmer had been a chemical engineer. He finally had the animal feed tested and eventually discovered it had been contaminated with PBB, polybrominated biphenol (poly-brom in ate ed- bi fen ol). Further investigation showed the mixing equipment had contaminated all the animal feed going through it, not just the first batch.

Scientists disagreed on what amount of contamination was dangerous. Was there any safe level? How poisonous was PBB? No government agency wanted to be responsible. At first, they did not even issue serious warnings about the problem. By then, many people had PBB inside them because they had consumed contaminated milk, beef, or eggs! When some farmers discovered their herds were contaminated, they shot the cows so the meat would not be sold. Finally the state government tested dairy herds and had all those with PBB killed and buried.

That accident was very expensive to the farmers who lost their herds. It may have an impact on the people of Michigan for a very long time. No one knows what the small amount of PBB in their bodies will do. PBB does not decompose easily and will be around for a long time.

The Disaster in a Nutshell

May 1973— the PBB chemical was mixed with animal feed.

April 1974— A farmer named Rick Halbert spent nearly a year trying to discover why his cows and family were sick. A lab finally finds PBB in the sample he gave it.

May 1974— The Michigan Department of Agriculture begins to quarantine, or cut off sales, from some farms. The number of farms affected is unclear.

March 1976— Farmers go to the state capitol and demand action.

August 1977— A new state law requires cattle and milk be tested for PBB and set lower limits for meat and milk that is sold. The law allows payments for cattle lost due to the poison.

November 1978— Rick and Sandra Halbert write a book about their PBB experiences called *Bitter Harvest.*. Later it became a television movie.

Today— Testing of people continues. The long-term health effects of PBB are unknown.

Nuclear Power— Yes or No?

In the 1980s Michigan faced a controversy that divided its people and may have an important impact on the state in the long run. The controversy was about nuclear power. It was a question of whether a new nuclear power plant should be built in Midland. The Dow Chemical Company and Consumers Power Company planned together to build

The Midland nuclear power plant before the project was scrapped. The project has been changed into a natural gas-fueled power plant which can generate 1,370 megawatts of electricity. This is the first time an American nuclear plant has been changed to use another fuel. (Courtesy Michigan State Archives)

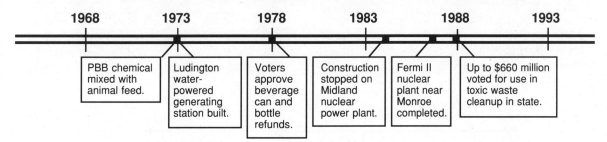

1968	1973	1978	1983	1988	1993
PBB chemical mixed with animal feed.	Ludington water-powered generating station built.	Voters approve beverage can and bottle refunds.	Construction stopped on Midland nuclear power plant.	Fermi II nuclear plant near Monroe completed.	Up to $660 million voted for use in toxic waste cleanup in state.

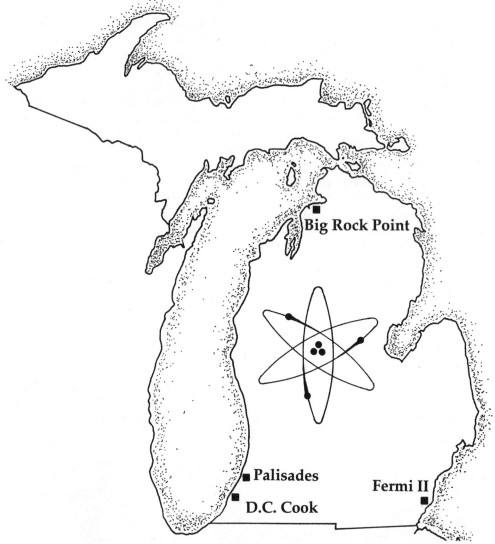

Michigan's Nuclear Power Plants

and use the plant. Consumers Power Company would use the electricity and Dow would get steam from the plant to use in its Midland chemical factories. The plans for the plant were announced in 1967 and much of the construction was finished by 1984.

But even during the time the construction work was going on, many people were demanding the project be stopped. Michigan's attorney general eventually joined their side and the project was stopped after $4 billion dollars had been spent. There was much debate over whether that made sense. On the other hand, many felt the plant would be a potential risk, and they did not want to live near it.

Michigan only has four nuclear plants but they make over 20 percent of the state's electricity and the amount is increasing. The newest plant is Fermi II built by Detroit-Edison near Monroe. That plant also has had many problems but it was ready for operation in 1986. In the past, the federal agency regulating nuclear power plants was upset with some things done at Fermi II.

Meanwhile, Canada has decided to build more nuclear plants of its own. There is a huge new nuclear power complex at Tiverton, Ontario, which is on Lake Huron across from the mouth of Saginaw Bay.

Problems With Other Power Sources

Most of the remainder of the state's electricity is made by power plants burning coal. The air pollution from these plants contributes to acid rain coming from Michigan and falling on Canada. Coal also has small amounts of poisonous and even radioactive materials. When large amounts of coal are burned, the dangerous materials float through the air and settle over the countryside. They can, and do, contaminate lakes and rivers. Fish in several Michigan lakes have unsafe levels of mercury. Most of the

mercury found in fish today probably comes from the burning of coal.

Another debate about electrical power took place in the mid-1980s. In 1973 Consumers Power Company built a water-powered generating station near Ludington. It has a 27 billion gallon reservoir some 350 feet above Lake Michigan. When there is a need for extra power, for instance on hot summer days, water pours out of the reservoir. It flows through six giant turbines generating the needed electricity. At night when the need for power is less, water is pumped back up into the reservoir. This procedure works well and saves about $20 million a year.

Unfortunately, fish are sucked into the pumps along with the water. Some people, including Attorney General Frank Kelley, were very upset by this loss of fish. The power company stated most of the dead fish were alewives and there was no real damage to fish in the lake. The attorney general sued the power company for $147 million. The debate over this pollution-free power supply continues.

The Ludington pumped storage hydroelectric plant. A large man-made lake in the upper right corner supplies the water which flows down through concrete pipes which can be seen just above the highway bridge. This water turns turbines near the lower left which make the electricity. When needed, the process is reversed and water is pumped into the storage lake. (Courtesy Consumers Power Company)

382

It is evident the people of Michigan face several difficult choices about how the state should generate its electrical power. If poor decisions are made, the state might not have enough electricity for everyone who wants it, or when they want it. Nuclear power can be dangerous and produces radioactive waste; on the other hand, burning coal causes air pollution and acid rain.

Chemical Garbage— Toxic Wastes

PBB was an accidental release of a dangerous chemical. But some companies deliberately put toxic chemicals in dumps. Before the 1970s and 1980s, many people did not realize it takes only a small amount of a dangerous chemical to cause health problems. Some of the chemicals in the dumps seeped into the ground and mixed with the water table. From there the chemicals spread into nearby water wells, rivers, and lakes. It took many years for people to realize one of the worst things which can be done with a toxic chemical is to put it in the ground.

At one time the federal Environmental Protection Agency (EPA) announced Michigan had 66 dangerous toxic waste sites which had to be cleaned up. Most experts thought the worst sites were the Hooker Chemical site in Montague

and the Berlin-Ferro site near Swartz Creek. Some of the River Rouge is also badly contaminated by industrial waste. The beautiful areas in the north are not excluded from pollution. Many fish in Houghton County's Torch Lake have cancer and sections of the Menominee River have been contaminated by poisonous metals.

In recent years the state passed new laws against dumping hazardous wastes and toxic chemicals. The Department of Natural Resources (DNR) is in charge of enforcing these tough laws. In the fall of 1988, the people of Michigan voted to borrow up to $660 million to help clean up toxic waste sites in Michigan and for other projects which would protect our environment. It is especially important that the people of Michigan be careful with toxic wastes. Every chemical which gets into a Michigan river or stream will eventually travel into the Great Lakes— the world's largest supply of freshwater!

Running Out of Room— Where Can We Put It?

Not only is it hard to get rid of toxic wastes, but it is also becoming more difficult to find a place for the ordinary things people throw away every day. A large part of garbage does not decompose. The

Groundwater Contamination

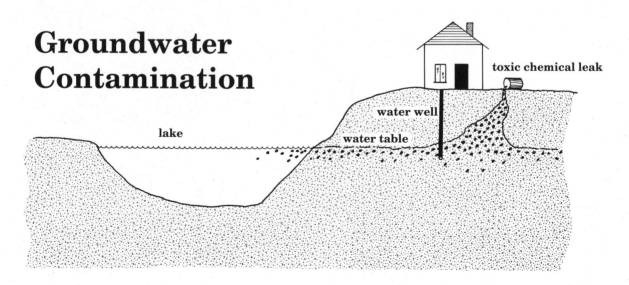

Toxic chemicals which are poured onto the ground can easily travel through the soil and contaminate nearby sources of water. (Art by David McConnell)

plastic bottles, metal cans, and garbage bags just sit in the ground. The DNR estimates that Michigan produces 64 million pounds of solid waste everyday. It all has to go somewhere. In the future we will have to recycle, reuse, and properly burn more of our garbage. More products will need to be wrapped in bio-degradable packaging which can decompose in the ground. In 1978, Michigan government passed a law which put a deposit on many kinds of bottled beverages. In 1986 wine cooler bottles were added to the list. Such laws help reduce the amount of junk people throw out along roads and in parks.

Questions

1. How did people in Michigan get the chemical PBB in their bodies?

2. In the 1980s two new nuclear power plants were started in Michigan. One was stopped before it opened and one has begun to generate power. Give the locations of the two power plants and state which opened and which was closed.

3. What environmental problems are created when coal is used in power plants?

4. Consumers Power Company has a unique way to generate extra power at Ludington. How does this operation work?

5. How do you think Michigan should generate its electric power in the future? What are the good points and bad points of your idea?

6. What laws did Michigan state government pass to help keep junk off roads and highways?

Chapter 14 Section 3
Part 3

Beautiful Places and Interesting People

Here are the key concepts you will find in this section:

Tourism is one of the top businesses in Michigan and millions of people vacation in Michigan each year.

The natural beauty of the state's forests, lakes, rivers, and parks helps attract many visitors every year. People camp, canoe, fish, hike, ski, and snowmobile in Michigan's outdoors.

There are also many interesting historical places that tourists can visit. Mackinac Island, Greenfield Village, and Frankenmuth are just three examples.

Most of Michigan's larger cities have improved their downtown areas with new building projects. Detroit has the Renaissance Center and Grand Rapids has the Amway Grand Hotel.

Michigan has been the home of actors, actresses, sports heroes, and famous writers. These people have made life more interesting for everyone in Michigan and beyond.

Tourists Are Important!

Tourism is considered to be one of the state's top businesses. Millions of people travel and vacation in Michigan each year. They make over 30 million "person trips" here each year. That is, when each trip and each person is counted, the total is over 30 million; of course some people make more than one trip each year. This number also includes trips by Michigan's own people too. Altogether, tourists spend about $7 billion a year. Jobs for over 100,000 of Michigan's work force are in the tourist or travel industries. Within the United States, Michigan ranks eighth as a popular travel and vacation destination.

State government realizes the importance of tourism and works to promote it; in fact, Michigan was one of the first states to do that. It began back in 1910. The Travel Bureau of the Department of Commerce is involved in many promotional activities. They produce Michigan travel posters and print travel booklets. Michigan was the first state to have highway travel information centers, also known as Welcome Centers. There are 13 centers on major highways coming into the state. These centers give away millions of travel pamphlets and other tourist information each year.

Why Do They Visit Michigan?

What attracts millions of people to travel in this state? Many come for the natural beauty they can find here. That is one reason it is so important to protect our environment. When people think about the outdoors and Michigan, the Upper Peninsula is what often comes to mind. Considering that nearly one-third

One of the newer highway welcome centers at New Buffalo just inside the Indiana-Michigan border on I-94. (Courtesy Michigan Department of Transportation)

of the peninsula is recreational area, it is understandable. The Upper Peninsula has 15 state parks, 7 state forests, 3 national forests, and 58 county parks.

But the whole state has natural attractions and outdoor beauty. Michigan has 19 million acres of forest land, 11,000 inland lakes, and 36,000 miles of rivers and streams. Boaters, canoeists, and those interested in fishing love the state's waterways. There are 600,000 boats registered in Michigan, more than in any other state. Michigan also has the most acres of state forests in the United States. The Upper Peninsula has over 100 sparkling waterfalls. The largest is the upper falls on the Tahquamenon River (tah KWAH meh non). It is the second largest waterfall east of the Mississippi River! There are plenty of wild animals

to see; Michigan has one of the largest elk herds east of the Mississippi. A large number of moose can be seen on Isle Royale and in the western Upper Peninsula near Crystal Falls. The Seney National Wildlife Refuge is the largest refuge east of the Mississippi River.

The Value of State Parks

Michigan's 83 state parks and campgrounds are a key part of the tourist business. State parks contain some of the most important attractions. Examples are: Big Spring Kitch-iti-ki-pi—sometimes called the "Boiling Cauldron" (Palms Book State Park), Fayette ghost town (Fayette State Park), Fort Mackinac (Mackinac Island State Park), Fort Michilimackinac (Ft. Michilimackinac State Park), Hartwick Pines

State and National Forest Land in Michigan

(Hartwick Pines State Park see color map-M5), Porcupine Mountains (Porcupine Mountains State Park-M4), and Tahquamenon Falls (Tahquamenon Falls State Park-M5). With a state park system that has so much to offer, it is no wonder there are over 20 million visitors each year. State parks also offer convenient places where tourists can camp. Michigan's state park system has more modern campsites than any other state in the U.S.

Grand Haven State Park, Holland State Park, and Warren Dunes State Park are the ones most frequently used by tourists. They are all located along the southern shore of Lake Michigan. And which state park is the largest? Porcupine Mountains State Park beats out the others with its 58,336 acres.

National Forests, Lakeshores, and Parks

Michigan is also the home of one national park, two national lakeshores, and four national forests. These areas are managed by federal agencies. With 5.5 million acres, the federal system has much more land than the state park system. Isle Royale is the national park. It is an island in Lake Superior about 45 miles from the Keweenaw peninsula. Isle Royale is known for its rugged wilderness and the eerie call of its wolves! The national lakeshores are Pictured Rocks and Sleeping Bear Dunes. (See color map pages M4, M5, and M6.)

The national forests in Michigan are the Hiawatha and Ottawa forests in the Upper Peninsula and the Huron and Manistee forests in the Lower Peninsula.

Most of the land controlled by the federal government in Michigan is in these four national forests.

Besides the state and national parks and forests, the Detroit area has a system of metro parks. A beautiful example is the Kensington Metro Park near Milford. Counting all of the parks plus state and federal land, there are about 7 million acres in Michigan which are open to the public.

Outdoor Recreation

People come to Michigan for the fun of recreation in both summer and winter. White powdery snow brings winter excitement at the state's 45 downhill ski slopes. Only New York and Wisconsin have more slopes. Cross-country skiers have about 1,000 miles of trails they can use. Snowmobile riders can just keep riding and riding on the state's 3,500 miles of snowmobile trails. Another outdoor attraction is the Michigan International Speedway near Brooklyn. MIS is a far cry from the quiet of the downhill ski slopes, but it also attracts large crowds on race days.

With so much water in and around Michigan, fishing is a big drawing card. Sports fishing boomed after the DNR added coho salmon to the Great Lakes in 1966. Since then, there are over five times as many charter fishing boats operating out of Michigan harbors. They number between 900 and 1,000. About 250,000 people charter boats each year to fish in the Great Lakes. That kind of fishing brings a great deal of money into the lakeshore cities and towns. It can cost up to $300 for a day's charter of a boat. That is one reason so many people interested in sports fishing are upset at Indian commercial fishing. There is competition for income between the two groups.

Tourists not interested in fishing can try climbing the Sleeping Bear Dunes. It seems there are miles of sand to cross before reaching the top.

Enjoying fun on the water. (Courtesy Michigan Travel Bureau)

The Pine Mountain ski jump at Iron Mountain. (Courtesy Dickinson County Area Chamber of Commerce)

History is for Tourists too

Tourists also come to learn about Michigan's historic past. Michigan has dozens of interesting places where they can see and hear about history. For example, they can board the huffing and puffing steam train at Crossroads Village near Flint. Once aboard they can smell the coal smoke and feel the sway of the old railroad cars as they travel just as pioneers did over 100 years ago.

Another popular stop is at Dearborn, the location of Greenfield Village and Henry Ford Museum. Going through the gates of the village is just like stepping into a time machine. Visitors hear the clip-clop of horse-drawn carriages as they pass over a covered wooden bridge. The village has many of the actual homes and buildings used by great men and women from America's past.

Mackinac Island is also a favorite place to visit. It is the home of Fort Mackinac and many other historic buildings. Remember, no cars are allowed on the island and people take either a boat or plane to get there.

On the south side of the straits is Fort Michilimackinac at Mackinaw City. The fort has been rebuilt and visitors can see where Alexander Henry trembled in hiding during the Indian massacre those many long years ago. The Mackinac State Historic Parks Commission, which runs the park at the fort and the one on Mackinac island, also has a newer park southeast of the straits. It is Old Mill Creek. Here is a rebuilt sawmill powered by water from a nearby mill pond.

A more modern kind of history can be seen at the aviation history museum on the edge of the Kalamazoo airport. This museum has several WWII fighter planes still in operating condition.

Tens of thousands of visitors go to the Gerald R. Ford Museum in Grand Rapids where they can learn about Gerald Ford's years as president of the United States. A full-sized replica of the President's oval office is included in the museum.

Many more visitors, especially school children, come to the state's capitol building in Lansing. It is a place where

Step back in time 100 years and smell the burning coal and hear the hiss of the steam on the Huckleberry Railroad at Crossroads Village. (Courtesy David B. McConnell)

The Holland Tulip Festival is a major tourist attraction each spring. (Courtesy Michigan Travel Bureau)

they can see history in the making. After seeing the capitol, a perfect ending to the trip is a visit to the state museum, whose new building opened in 1989.

The list of places to see in Michigan goes on and on. One travel expert said he could think of over 100 places just off the top of his head. Besides the locations already mentioned, there are dozens of commercial attractions. The Irish Hills area in the southern part of the state has several commercial operations.

The Most Popular Places

Which places get the prize for the most visitors? Millions stop at some of the most popular tourist attractions in Michigan. The village of Frankenmuth has had three million visitors in one year. Mackinac Island, Greenfield Village and Henry Ford Museum, the Gerald Ford Presidential Museum, Holland at tulip time, Pictured Rocks National Lakeshore, the Soo Locks, and Tahquamenon Falls are among the other top attractions. The tour of the Kellogg's plant in Battle Creek was a top attraction until the tour was discontinued by the company.

Visitors to the Big Cities— Detroit

The money spent by tourists and people going to conventions has been a big help to the downtown areas of several Michigan cities. The downtown areas of the state's large cities hit a low point in the early 1970s. Many buildings were old and little was being done to attract people to visit and shop downtown. Detroit was one of the first cities to begin a major downtown development. It is known as the Renaissance Center. The new project was promoted by Henry Ford II. Before the project began, offices and even churches were thinking about leaving the area. Construction on the Renaissance Center began in 1973 and was completed four years later.

It was built on land where the eastern large wooden stockade of the old fort

Detroit's Renaissance Center and the People Mover. (Courtesy Metropolitan Detroit Convention & Visitors Bureau)

once stood. As the ground was cleared, archaeologists dug into the earth to see what they could find before the new building covered the site. They removed a remarkable collection of broken dishes, old bottles, forks, spoons, bits of clothing, and children's toys— all from long ago. The collection helped historians learn more about what life was like in old Detroit.

The Renaissance Center has five buildings clustered together. There are four 39-story office towers around a gleaming 73-story glass hotel. Twenty thousand people work in the offices, and the hotel has 1,320 rooms.

Detroit already had Cobo Hall. This mammoth convention center can allow about 12,000 people to attend meetings under one roof. In the late 1980s Cobo Hall was nearly doubled in size.

Nearby, Hart Plaza was constructed in honor of former Michigan Senator Philip Hart. Next to the plaza is the Dodge Fountain.

Only a couple of miles from downtown is the 20,000 seat Joe Louis Arena. The arena is home to every kind of activity from rock concerts to tractor pulls to Red Wings hockey games.

Detroit's latest project is the People Mover transportation system. This carries riders in rapid transit cars on an elevated track. The 2.9 mile system curves through the downtown area. It was opened in 1987. Since a subway system does not exist in any of Michigan's cities, this is the only downtown train-like transportation operation. The People Mover stands in contrast to the historic trolleys Detroit began to reuse in the late 1970s. These additions top off the new developments in downtown Detroit.

Lansing

A time machine in Lansing? Well, almost. Visit Lansing and you can step back in time at the Michigan Historical Museum. The museum contains a three-story tall map of the state and ancient Native American artifacts. There is a replica of the first capitol building, and portions of an early Michigan copper mine have been reconstructed. The Library of Michigan and the Archives of Michigan are also in the same building.

The Michigan Library and Historical Center in Lansing. This building houses the State Historical Museum. (Courtesy David McConnell)

Grand Rapids

The Amway Grand Plaza Hotel was built in Grand Rapids. This 680-room hotel combines a new building with an old historic hotel which was decorated and returned to its days of elegance. The city of Grand Rapids rebuilt its convention center, the Grand Center. These two large buildings were finished by 1982. Many other smaller projects started around them. An improved downtown Grand Rapids is alive and busy.

Muskegon

About forty miles northwest of Grand Rapids, Muskegon also improved its downtown area. Sixty-five acres of lakeside factory sites were cleared; grass and trees replaced the ugly brick and concrete buildings. This gave Muskegon's downtown area a beautiful new look.

Pontiac

In the 1970s the city of Pontiac wanted to have a major sports facility in its area. Years of work resulted in the building of the Pontiac Silverdome. Pontiac's residents are proud of the cov-

ered stadium which was finished in 1975. It has one of the largest air supported roofs, measuring a total of ten acres. The building is 770 by 600 feet. Over 80,000 fans can watch a football or soccer match in the Silverdome. The 200- ton dome is held up only with air pressure.

The Silverdome has hosted many events including football's Super Bowl, the Rolling Stones, and Elvis Presley. For a long time the stadium was home for the Detroit Lions and the Pistons. But the Silverdome has had its tough breaks too. The Pistons recently moved out and went to the nearby Palace stadium. One winter, a buildup of ice and snow caused the Silverdome roof to cave in. Now it is back in operation and continues to bring entertainment to thousands.

Traverse City

Traverse City in the northern Lower Peninsula is another area of Michigan which has had tremendous growth and change. It has become a tourist and resort center. A few miles northeast of the city a large golf and recreational hotel complex has been built. It is known as

Michigan's Tourist Attractions

-a selection of many in the state-

Isle Royale

Fort Wilkins

Copper Mines

Quincy Mine Hoist

Porcupine Mountains

Iron Industry Museum

Tahquamenon Falls

Pictured Rocks

Marquette

Soo Locks

S.S. Valley Camp

Sault Ste. Marie

St. Ignace

Mackinac Island

Fort Michilmackinac

Escanaba

Presque Isle lighthouse

Fayette Townsite

Boyne Mountain

Menominee

Alpena

Jesse Besser Museum

Sleeping Bear Dunes

Hartwick Pines

Traverse City

Higgins Lake

Houghton Lake

White Pine Village

Midland

Mt. Pleasant

Fremont

Bay City

Hackley House

Saginaw

Muskegon

Frankenmuth

Crossroads Village

Grand Rapids

Flint

Port Huron

Holland

Gerald Ford Museum

Dossin Great Lakes
Museum

S.S. Keewatin

Lansing

State Capitol

Pontiac

Detroit Zoo

Cranbrook Institute
of Science

Kalamazoo

Battle Creek

Ann Arbor

Detroit

Benton Harbor

Jackson

Renaissance Center

St. Joseph

Fort Wayne

Irish Hills

Henry Ford Museum

Greenfield Village

Kalamazoo Aviation Museum

Boblo Island

Michigan Space Center

© Hillsdale Educational Publishers

the Grand Traverse Resort. This complex and many other new motels house scores of visitors who come to enjoy the scenic beauty of Grand Traverse Bay and the nearby countryside.

About 25 percent of the jobs in the region are tied to tourism. Primarily because of big increases in tourist business, the population of Grand Traverse County jumped 40 percent between 1970 and l980. Not only are Grand Traverse, Kalkaska, and Leelanau counties major growth areas, but almost all sections of the northern Lower Peninsula are growing.

Famous Michiganians!
A President

Two of the best-known Michiganians during the 1970s were Gerald and Betty Ford. Gerald Ford became the 38th President of the United States when he took the oath of office on August 9, 1974.

Grand Traverse Bay at night. (Courtesy Michigan Travel Bureau)

He was the first person to become president without being elected to either the office of vice president or president! That unusual turn of events took place because President Richard Nixon chose Ford to replace Vice President Spiro Agnew. Agnew resigned because of wrongdoing. After the Watergate incident, President Nixon had to resign also, putting Gerald Ford in charge of the United States. President Nixon probably chose Ford to be Vice President because he was well-liked in Congress and had supported Nixon over the years.

Ford won his first elected office when he became the Republican representative of the Fifth Congressional District in Michigan. That district included the Grand Rapids area. He was reelected for 25 years and gained a good reputation in Washington.

President and Mrs. Ford on the back of a campaign train. (Courtesy Ford Library, Ann Arbor)

Gerald Ford grew up in Grand Rapids and attended the University of Michigan and was a star member of their football team. Leaving Michigan, Ford was a coach at Yale and then later attended that same college and received his law degree in 1941, just as World War II began. Rather than be drafted, he joined the navy and served in several actions in the Pacific Ocean.

Just as Gerald Ford was preparing for his first election, he married Elizabeth Bloomer. Betty Ford also grew up in Grand Rapids. She had studied to be a dancer but was working as a buyer for a local department store when she met Ford.

She enthusiastically joined in helping with her husband's political campaigns. Betty Ford is probably best known for her frankness and openness about the problems the family faced. President Ford acknowledged the support his wife had given him when he said at his inauguration, "I am indebted to no man and only to one woman— my dear wife."

Athletes

While Gerald Ford was serving in Washington, D.C., many other Michiganians were making names for themselves. Michigan is a great sports-minded state and always has a long list of top athletes. The four seasons allow Michigan to make the most of nearly every sport. Over the years the state has had some great teams and some great players.

George Gipp was the famous football player from Laurium on the Keweenaw peninsula. The "Gipper's" last season was 1920.

There is a long list of famous Detroit Tigers baseball players going back many years. In 1968 Al Kaline helped win the World Series. Kaline won the American League batting championship when he was only 20 years old. Willie Horton was also on the 1968 World Series team.

Denny McLain won 31 games for the Tigers that year. The Tigers won the Series again in 1984.

"Sparky" Anderson has managed the Tigers for many years. He is known as one of the most successful managers in the Major Leagues. Actually, Anderson has had championship teams in both leagues—the Detroit Tigers in the American League and the Cincinnati Reds in the National League.

The Red Wings hockey team benefitted from Gordie Howe's outstanding ability. Howe, now retired, was considered one of hockey's best players. Howe played hockey for more years than any other player and set many records in the process.

Earvin "Magic" Johnson played basketball during his Lansing high school days. Then he went on to win many games for the Michigan State University Spartans. Johnson continued his career with the Los Angeles Lakers. In a four-year span, Johnson won a high school championship, NCAA championship, and an NBA championship.

Kirk Gibson also played for Michigan State. His game was football. But after college he switched to baseball. Gibson played for the Tigers and later the Los Angeles Dodgers. Then he came back in 1993 to play again for the Detroit Tigers!

The boxing tradition of Joe Louis continued in Michigan with athletes like Thomas Hearns.

Entertainers

When thinking about famous personalities, don't forget many glamorous entertainers started right here in Michigan. Not all movie, television, and music stars come from Hollywood! Michigan has a long list of stars who were born or have lived in the state. The bad thing about being a movie star from Michigan is you usually have to go somewhere else to work.

Some entertainers connected to our state

Tim Allen	Dick Martin
Sonny Bono	Ed McMahon
Alice Cooper	Harry Morgan
Pam Dawber	George Peppard
Aretha Franklin	Gilda Radner
Berry Gordy	Diana Ross
Julie Harris	Tom Selleck
Charleton Heston	Danny Thomas
Arte Johnson	Marlo Thomas
James Earl Jones	Lily Tomlin
Alex Karris	Robert Wagner
Madonna	Stevie Wonder
Lee Majors	

The backgrounds of these entertainers are as varied as their personalities. Pam Dawber went to North Farmington High School and Oakland Community College. She began her career by traveling around the country helping to introduce new car models. Since then she has starred in two television series, "Mork and Mindy" and "My Sister Sam."

Harry Morgan played Sherman Potter, the commanding officer of "M*A*S*H." Morgan was born in Detroit and raised in Muskegon. In an interview he says he still likes to talk about Michigan even though he now lives in Los Angeles, California.

Lily Tomlin was born in Detroit. After going to Wayne State University, Tomlin got her first big break in the "Laugh In" series. More recently she starred in the movie "Nine To Five."

Robert Wagner ("Hart To Hart") and Tom Selleck ("Magnum PI") were born in Detroit too. Danny Thomas was born in the small town of Deerfield. Wyandotte was the first hometown of Lee Majors

Lily Tomlin   Tom Selleck   Pam Dawber

(All photos courtesy Metropolitan Detroit Convention & Visitors Bureau)

("Bionic Man" and "Fall Guy"). George Peppard ("The A Team") went to high school in Dearborn.

What does the voice of Darth Vader, the evil *Star Wars* villain, have to do with Michigan? It was spoken by the actor James Earl Jones who grew up near Manistee! It is interesting to know that stuttering once made Jones so embarrassed that he withdrew into near total silence from the ages of 10 to 14.

Madonna–Louise Veronica Ciccone comes from Bay City. Madonna's mother died when she was only five years old. Her family moved to Rochester. During her days at Adams High School she not only excelled at dance but got mostly A's in her courses. Madonna won a dance scholarship to the University of Michigan. Later, she left the state for the bright lights of New York City and developed an interest in rock 'n roll.

Many Michiganians have gone to Hollywood but in some instances Hollywood has come to Michigan. Eddie Murphy made Detroit's Mumford High School world famous in his movie *Beverly Hills Cop. Somewhere in Time* was filmed on Mackinac Island in 1979. *Anatomy of a Murder* starring James Stewart and Ben Gazzarra was made at the Thunder Bay Inn near Marquette in 1969.

Writers

Not only was the movie *Anatomy of a Murder* made in Michigan, the book was written by John Voelker, a former member of the state supreme court. Voelker wrote his books under the pen name of Robert Traver.

The judge who turned author was only one of several writers from Michigan whose books were made into movies. Judith Guest is the well-known author of *Ordinary People*. Guest was a teacher in Birmingham and Garden City before she became an author. Jim Cash from East Lansing was one of the two screenwriters who wrote *Top Gun*, the movie about jet fighter pilots.

Other recent Michigan authors include Elmore "Dutch" Leonard. Leonard has turned out *Glitz* and other books of crime fiction. Michigan authors write about cars too. Ben Hamper wrote short stories using his pen name "Rivethead" while he worked for General Motors in Flint. Bruce Catton won the Pulitzer Prize for his book about the Civil War entitled *A Stillness At Appomattox.*

Musicians

The Michigan music tradition that started with Motown and the Supremes goes on with Smokey Robinson and other musicians. Today, Bob Seger's beat keeps his fans excited. Seger was originally from Ann Arbor. Other Michigan rock stars also include Alice Cooper and Ted Nugent. Stevie Wonder, the pop-soul singer born in Saginaw, has enjoyed a long career which started with his first recording at the age of 12. Stevie Wonder is interested in more than music. He was one of the leaders behind the hunger relief project for Africa known as "We Are the World."

The long list of famous people from the state is just one more reason to be proud of being a Michiganian. No doubt there are those who will follow in the footsteps of the famous athletes and entertainers from the Great Lakes State.

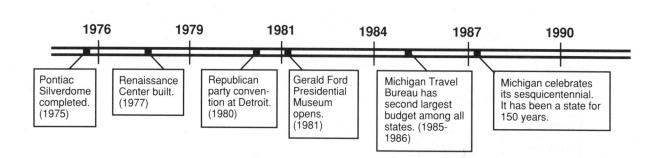

| 1976 | 1979 | 1981 | 1984 | 1987 | 1990 |

Pontiac Silverdome completed. (1975)

Renaissance Center built. (1977)

Republican party convention at Detroit. (1980)

Gerald Ford Presidential Museum opens. (1981)

Michigan Travel Bureau has second largest budget among all states. (1985-1986)

Michigan celebrates its sesquicentennial. It has been a state for 150 years.

Questions

1. List three facts which prove how important the business of tourism is to Michigan.

2. The natural beauty of Michigan's forests, rivers and lakes attracts many tourists to the state. How many acres of forest land does Michigan have? How many inland lakes are there, and how many miles of rivers and streams are in the state?

3. How many state parks does Michigan have? Name six of them and tell where one is located.

4. What fish is responsible for a boom in charter fishing from Michigan's harbors? Was this kind of fish added to the Great Lakes or was it always there?

5. Name four tourist attractions which are historic places in Michigan.

6. State the locations of the following: Renaissance Center, Amway Grand Plaza, Michigan Historical Museum, Silverdome, Joe Louis Arena.

7. Choose the Michigan-related athlete, actor, actress, or writer who interests you the most. Write five interview questions you would like to ask that person. Have at least one question about the time he or she lived in our state.

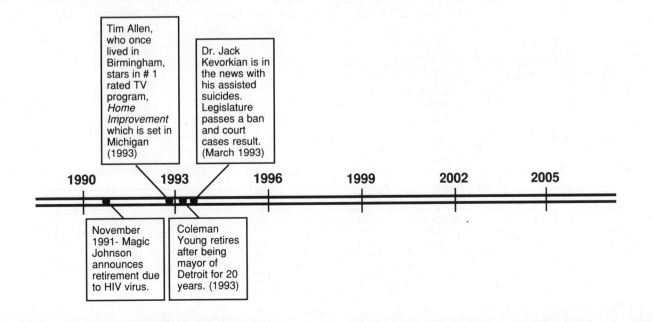

398

page for future additions

Bibliography

If you want to learn more...

How does the author or anyone else learn about Michigan history when it happened so long ago? The answer is by reading! Most libraries are brimming with Michigan materials if you will take time to look for them.

The author consulted the publisher's extensive collection of several hundred books and others from libraries and archives around the state.

This is a list of books and magazine articles you can read to learn more about the subjects in each chapter section. There are also other materials available on most of the subjects, but this list contains many of the best including some old references which are considered classics.

Additional books not listed, but worth reading: *Michillaneous I* and *Michillaneous II* by Gary Barfknecht, and *A Pictorial History of Michigan*, volume I and volume II by George S. May. Also read the *Michigan History* magazine by the Bureau of History in Lansing. Since 1978 each issue includes the history of one of Michigan's counties plus many other fascinating accounts.

Chapter 1 Section 1
Anderson, James M. & Smith, Iva A., ed. *Ethnic Groups in Michigan* (Volume 2—*The Peoples of Michigan* series), Detroit: Ethnos Press, 1983.
Romig, Walter. *Michigan Place Names*. Detroit: Wayne State University Press, 1986.
Santer, Richard A. *Michigan: Heart of the Great Lakes*. Dubuque: Kendall/Hunt Publishing Company, 1977.
Sommers, Lawrence M. *Michigan: A Geography*. Boulder: Westview Press, 1984.

Chapter 1 Section 2
Dorr, John A. & Eschman, Donald F. *Geology of Michigan*. Ann Arbor: University of Michigan Press, 1971.
Heinrich, E. William. *The Mineralogy of Michigan*. Lansing: Department of Natural Resources, Geological Survey Division, 1976.
VanDellen, Kenneth J. "Time on the Rocks." *Michigan Natural Resources Magazine* volume 54 (May-June 1985): pages 52-61.

Chapter 1 Section 3
Fitting, James E. *The Archaeology of Michigan*. Bloomfield Hills: Cranbrook Institute of Science, 1975 (second and revised edition).
Halsey, John. "Miskwabik—Red Metal." *Michigan History* volume 67 (September/October 1983): pages 32-41.
Holman, J. Alan & Gringhuis, Dirk. *Mystery Mammals of the Ice Age*. Hillsdale: Hillsdale Educational Publishers, 1972.
Quimby, George Irving. *Indian Life in the Upper Great Lakes*. Chicago: University of Chicago Press, 1960.

Chapter 2 Section 1
Maxwell, James A., ed. *America's Fascinating Indian Heritage*. Pleasantville: The Reader's Digest Association, 1978, pages 34-41.
McKee, Russell. *Great Lakes Country*. New York: Thomas Y. Crowell Company, 1966, pages 33-41.
Tanner, Helen Hornbeck. *Atlas of Great Lakes Indian History*. Norman: University of Oklahoma Press, 1987.

Chapter 2 Section 2
Clifton, James A., Cornell, George L. & McClurken, James M. *People of the Three Fires*. Grand Rapids: The Grand Rapids Inter-Tribal Council, 1986.
Kinietz, W. Vernon. *The Indians of the Western Great Lakes, 1615-1760*. Ann Arbor: University of Michigan Press, 1972.
Vogel, Virgil J. *Indian Names in Michigan*. Ann Arbor: University of Michigan Press, 1986.

Chapter 2 Section 3
Cleland, Charles E. *A Brief History of Michigan Indians*. Lansing: Michigan History Division, 1975.
Flint Institute of Art. *Art of the Great Lakes Indians*. Flint: Flint Institute of Arts, 1973.
Kubiak, William J. *Great Lakes Indians: A Pictorial Guide*. New York: Bonanza Books, 1970.
Laubin, Reginald and Laubin, Gladys. *American Indian Archery*. Norman: University of Oklahoma Press, 1980.
Rubenstein, Bruce A. "To Destroy a Culture: Indian Education in Michigan, 1855-1900." *Michigan History* volume 60 (Summer 1976): pages 137-166.

Chapter 3 Section 1

Eccles, W.J. *The Canadian Frontier, 1534-1760.* Albuquerque: University of New Mexico Press, 1983, revised edition.

Morison, Samuel Eliot. *Samuel De Champlain, Father of New France.* Boston: Little, Brown and Company, 1972.

Chapter 3 Section 2

Donnelly, Joseph P. *Jacques Marquette, S.J.* Chicago: Loyola University Press, 1968.

Newman, Peter C. "Three Centuries of the Hudson's Bay Company—Canada's Fur-Trading Empire." *National Geographic* volume 172 (August 1987): pages 192-199.

Parkman, Francis. *LaSalle and the Discovery of the Great West.* rev. ed. Boston: Little, Brown and Company, 1942.

Thwaites, Ruben Gold, editor. *The Jesuit Relations, 1610-1791.* 73 volumes. Cleveland: Burrows, 1896-1901.

Chapter 3 Section 3

Bald, F. Clever. *Michigan In Four Centuries.* New York: Harper and Row Publishers, 1961, pages 60-62.

Berg, Harriet Jean. "The Search for Madame Cadillac." *Chronicle* volume 20 (Spring 1984): pages 14-17.

Brown, Henry D., and others. *Cadillac and the Founding of Detroit.* Detroit: Wayne State University Press, 1976.

Havighurst, Walter, ed. *Land of the Long Horizons.* New York: Coward-McCann, 1960.

Chapter 3 Section 4

Gilman, Carolyn. *Where Two Worlds Meet: The Great Lakes Fur Trade.* St. Paul: Minnesota Historical Society, 1982.

Johnson, Ida Amanda. *The Michigan Fur Trade.* Grand Rapids: BlackLetter Press, 1975 reprint.

Stone, Lyle M. *Fort Michilimackinac 1715-1781.* East Lansing: Michigan State University, 1974.

Chapter 4 Section 1

Dunbar, Willis F. and May, George S. *Michigan: A History of the Wolverine State.* Grand Rapids: William B. Eerdmans Publishing Company, 1980, pages 58-71.

Eckert, Allan W. *Wilderness Empire.* Boston: Little, Brown and Company, 1969.

May, George S. and Brink, Herbert J., eds. "Michigan at the end of the French Period." (Contains sections from a report written by the famous French soldier and explorer, Louis Antoine de Bougainville.) *A Michigan Reader: 11,000 B.C. to A.D. 1865.* Grand Rapids: William B. Eerdmans Publishing Company, 1974.

Chapter 4 Section 2

Armour, David A., ed. *Massacre at Mackinac-1763.* Mackinac Island: Mackinac Island State Park Commission, 1966.

Keller, Allan. "Pontiac's Conspiracy." *American History Illustrated* volume 12 (May 1977): page 4.

Peckham, Howard H. *Pontiac and the Indian Uprisings.* New York: Russell and Russell, 1970 reprint.

Chapter 4 Section 3

Armour, David A. and Widder, Keith R. *At the Crossroads - Michilimackinac During the American Revolution.* Mackinac Island: Mackinac Island State Park Commission, 1978.

Havighurst, Walter. *Three Flags at the Straits: The Forts of Mackinac.* Englewood Cliffs, NJ: Prentice-Hall, 1966

O'Neil, Paul. *The Frontiersmen.* Alexandria: Time-Life Books, 1977, pages 121-140.

Chapter 5 Section 1

Farrell, David. "Settlement Along the Detroit Frontier, 1760-1796. *Michigan History* volume 52 (Summer 1968): pages 89-107.

Quaife, Milo M. and Glazer, Sidney. *Michigan: From Primitive Wilderness to Industrial Commonwealth.* Englewood Cliffs, NJ: Prentice-Hall, 1948, pages 103-108.

Chapter 5 Section 2

Commager, Henry Steele, ed. *Documents of American History.* New York: Appleton-Century-Crofts, 1949, pages 131-132.

Gilpin, Alec R. *The Territory of Michigan (1805-1837).* East Lansing: Michigan State University Press, 1970.

Horsman, Reginald. *Matthew Elliott, British Indian Agent.* Detroit: Wayne State University Press, 1964, pages 106-110.

Woodford, Frank B. and Woodford, Arthur M. *All Our Yesterdays*. Detroit: Wayne State University Press, 1969.

Chapter 5 Section 3 Part 1
Edmunds, R. David. *The Shawnee Prophet*. Lincoln: University of Nebraska Press, 1983.
Nelson, Larry L. *Men of Patriotism, Courage, and Enterprise! Fort Meigs in the War of 1812*. Canton: Daring Books, 1985.
Scott, Leonard H. "The Surrender of Detroit." *American History Illustrated* volume 12 (June 1977): pages 28-36.
Sugden, John. *Tecumseh's Last Stand*. Norman: University of Oklahoma Press, 1985.

Chapter 5 Section 3 Part 2
Barry, James P. "The Battle of Lake Erie." *American History Illustrated* volume 11 (July 1967): page 4.
Wood, Eleazar D., Lieutenant Colonel. *Journal of the Northwestern Campaign of 1812-1813*. Defiance: Defiance College Press, 1975.

Chapter 6 Section 1
Dunbar, Willis F. *Lewis Cass*. Grand Rapids: William B. Eerdmans Publishing Company, 1970.
Edmunds, R. David. *The Potawatomis: Keepers of the Fire*. Norman: University of Oklahoma Press, 1978, pages 220-221.
May, George S. and Brinks, Herbert J., eds. "A Fortnight in the Wilderness" by Alexis De Tocqueville. *A Michigan Reader: 11,000 B.C. to A.D. 1865*. Grand Rapids: William B. Eerdmans Publishing Company, 1974.
Nowlin, William. *The Bark Covered House or Back in the Woods Again*. Detroit: Herald Printing House, 1876.
Troester, Rosalie Riegle, ed. *Historic Women of Michigan*. Lansing: Michigan Women's Studies Association, 1987.
Woodford, Frank B. *Lewis Cass, the Last Jeffersonian*. New Brunswick: Rutgers University Press, 1950.

Chapter 6 Section 2
"Farming in Michigan." (Special Issue) *Michigan History* volume 68 (March-April 1984).
Fuller, George N., ed. *Historic Michigan*. volume 1, National Historical Association, 1924, pages 292-314.
Lewis, Ferris E. *Michigan Yesterday and Today*. Hillsdale: Hillsdale Educational Publishers, 1980, pages 151-178.

Chapter 6 Section 3
Brown, Alan S. "The Northwest Ordinance and Michigan's Quest for Excellence in Education." *Michigan History* volume 71 (November-December 1987): pages 24-31.
McClary, Andrew. "Don't Go to Michigan, That Land of Ills." *Michigan History* volume 67 (January-February 1983): pages 46-48.
Schultz, Gerard. *The New History of Michigan's Thumb*. Elkton: Gerard Schultz, 1969, pages 29-37.
Widder, Keith R. *Dr. William Beaumont, the Mackinac Years*. Mackinac Island: Mackinac Island State Park Commission, 1975.

Chapter 7 Section 1
George, Emily, R.S.M. *William Woodbridge: Michigan's Connecticut Yankee*. Lansing: Michigan History Division, 1979.
George, Sister Mary Karl. *The Rise and Fall of Toledo, Michigan...The Toledo War!* Lansing: Michigan Historical Commission, 1971.
Hagman, Harland L. *Bright Michigan Morning: The Years of Governor Tom Mason*. Brighton, MI: Green Oak Press, 1981.
Sagendorph, Kent. *Stevens T. Mason, Misunderstood Patriot*. New York: E.P. Dutton, 1947.

Chapter 7 Section 2
Anderson, James M. and Smith, Iva A., editors. *Ethnic Groups in Michigan Volume 2*. Detroit: Ethnos Press, 1983.
Dodge, Roy L. *Michigan Ghost Towns Volume 1*. Troy: Glendon Publishing, 1970.
Fitzpatrick, Doyle C. *The King Strang Story*. Lansing: National Heritage, 1970.
Fuller, George N. *Economic and Social Beginnings of Michigan: A Study of the Territorial Period, 1805-1837*. Lansing: State of Michigan, 1916.
Lane, Kit. *Singapore, the Buried City*. Saugatuck: The Commercial Record, 1975.

402

Chapter 7 Section 3
Burt, John S. *They Left Their Mark*. Rancho Cordova, CA: Landmark Enterprises, 1985.
Dickinson, John N. *To Build a Canal: Sault Ste. Marie 1853 and After*. Columbus: Miami University, 1981.
Dunbar, Willis F. *All Aboard! A History of Railroads in Michigan*. Grand Rapids: William B. Eerdmans Publishing Company, 1969.
Elliott, Frank N. *When Railroad was King*. Lansing: Michigan Historical Commission, 1966.
Hatcher, Harlan. *A Century of Iron and Men*. New York: Bobbs-Merrill Company, 1950.
Maltby, Lawrence J. "The Quest for Michigan's Ontonagon Boulder." *Chronicle* volume 18 (Fall 1982): pages 5-9.
Murdoch, Angus. *Boom Copper: Story of the First U.S. Mining Boom*. Reprint. Calumet: Drier and Koepel, 1964.
Lankton, Larry D. and Hyde, Charles K. *Old Reliable: An Illustrated History of the Quincy Mining Company*. Hancock: Quincy Mine Hoist Association, 1982.

Chapter 8 Section 1
Ducey, Jean. *Out of this Nettle*. Grand Rapids: Baker Book House, 1983.
Harris, Fran. *Focus: Michigan Women 1701-1977*. Lansing: Michigan Coordination Committee on the Observance of Women's Year, 1977.
McRae, Norman. "Crossing the Detroit River to Find Freedom." *Michigan History* volume 67 (March-April 1983): pages 35-39.
Woodford, Frank B. *Father Abraham's Children*. Detroit: Wayne State University Press, 1961.
Yates, Dorothy L. "Michigan's Female Abolitionist." *Chronicle* volume 17 (Fall 1981): pages 28-31.

Chapter 8 Section 2
George, Sister Mary Karl. *Zachariah Chandler*. East Lansing: Michigan State University Press, 1969.
Oates, Stephen B. "God's Angry Man." *American History Illustrated* volume 20 (January 1986): pages 10-21.
Seavoy, Ronald E. "Borrowed Laws to Speed Development: Michigan, 1835-1863." *Michigan History* volume 59 (Spring-Summer 1975): pages 39-68.

Chapter 8 Section 3
Frost, Lawrence A. *The Custer Album: A Pictorial Biography of General George A Custer*. Seattle: Superior Publishing Company, 1964.
McKee, Russell. *Great Lakes Country*. New York: Thomas Y. Crowell Company, 1966, pages 198-202.
Rosentreter, Roger L. "We Are Coming Father Ab'ram." *Michigan History* volume 67 (May-June 1983): pages 34-42.
Williams, Frederick D. *Michigan Soldiers in the Civil War*. Lansing: Michigan Historical Commission, 1960.

Chapter 9 Section 1
Anderson, David D., ed. "They Knew Paul Bunyan" *Michigan: A State Anthology*. Detroit: Gale Research Company, 1983, pages 125-138.
Chrysler, Don. *The Story of the Grand River*. Grand Rapids: Grace Publications, 1975.
Lewis, Ferris E. *Our Own State Michigan*. Hillsdale: Hillsdale Educational Publishers, 1987, pages 79-91.
Maybee, Rolland H. *Michigan's White Pine Era*. Lansing: Bureau of History, Michigan Department of State, 2nd edition, 1988.
Wells, Robert W. *Daylight in the Swamp!* Garden City: Doubleday, 1978.

Chapter 9 Section 2
Beck, William. "Law and Order During the 1913 Copper Strike." *Michigan History* volume 54 (Winter 1977): pages 16-20.
Boyum, Burton H. *The Saga of Iron Mining in Michigan's Upper Peninsula*. Marquette: Marquette County Historical Society, 1977.
Dersch, Virginia Jonas. "Copper Mining in Northern Michigan: A Social History." *Michigan History* volume 61 (Winter 1977): 291-321.
Lankton, Larry D. "Died in the Mines." *Michigan History* volume 67 (November-December 1983): pages 33-41.
Pyle, Susan Newhof, ed. *A Most Superior Land: Life in the Upper Peninsula of Michigan*. Lansing: Two Peninsula Press, 1987, page 41.

Chapter 9 Section 3
Barnett, LeRoy. "Mint in Michigan." *Michigan History* volume 68 (March-April 1984): pages 16-20.

Fuller, George Newman. *Michigan, A Centennial History of the State and Its People.* volume 1. Chicago: The Lewis Publishing Company, 1939.

Lewis, Ferris E. *Michigan Yesterday and Today.* Hillsdale: Hillsdale Educational Publishers, 1980, pages 114-141.

Massie, Larry B. "Celebrated Celery City Quacks." *Michigan History* volume 66 (September-October 1982): pages 16-23.

Meek, Forest. *Michigan's Heartland 1900-1918.* Clare, MI: Edgewood Press, 1979, pages 1-31.

Michigan Department of Agriculture. *Michigan Food and Fiber Facts-1984.* Lansing: State of Michigan, 1984.

Chapter 9 Section 4

Bogue, Margaret Beattie and Palmer, Virginia A. *Around the Shores of Lake Superior: A Guide to Historic Sites.* Madison: University of Wisconsin Sea Grant College Program, 1979.

Cobb, Charles E., Jr. "The Great Lakes' Troubled Waters." *National Geographic* volume 172 (July 1987): pages 2-31.

Sommers, Lawrence M., et al. *Fish in Lake Michigan.* Washington, DC: National Oceanic and Atmospheric Administration and Sea Grant Program, 1981.

Van Oosten, J. "Michigan's Commercial Fisheries of the Great Lakes." *Michigan History* volume 22 (1935): pages 107-143.

Chapter 10 Section 1

Armstrong, James W. "Dr. Upjohn's Company." *Michigan History* volume 70 (May-June 1980): pages 33-39.

Campbell, Murray and Hatton, Harrison. *Herbert H. Dow: Pioneer in Creative Chemistry.* New York: Appleton-Century-Crofts, 1951.

Holli, Melvin G. "Before the Car." *Michigan History* volume 64 (March-April 1980): pages 33-39.

May, George S. *Michigan: An Illustrated History of the Great Lakes.* North Ridge, CA: Windsor Publications, 1987.

Powell, Horace B. *The Original Has This Signature—W.K. Kellogg.* Englewood Cliffs, NJ: Prentice-Hall, 1956.

Schwarz, Richard W. *John Harvey Kellogg, M.D.* Berrien Springs: Andrews University Press, 2nd printing, 1981.

Chapter 10 Section 2

Babson, Steve. *Working Detroit.* New York: Adama Books, 1984.

Gross, Stuart D. *Saginaw, A History of the Land and the City.* Woodland Hills, CA: Windsor Publications, 1980, pages 34-36.

Havira, Barbara Speas. "A Treasure and a Challenge—Michigan Bureau of Labor Reports." *Michigan History* volume 72 (September-October 1988): pages 36-43.

Lydens, Z.Z., ed. *The Story of Grand Rapids.* Grand Rapids: Kregel Publications, 1967, pages 350-365.

Starring, Charles R. and Knauss, James O. *The Michigan Search for Educational Standards.* Lansing: Michigan Historical Commission, 1969, pages 43-44.

Chapter 10 Section 3

Cleland, Charles E. *A Brief History of Michigan Indians.* Lansing: Michigan History Division, 1975.

Weeks, George. *Stewards of the State: The Governors of Michigan.* Edited by Robert D. Kirk. Ann Arbor: Historical Society of Michigan, 1987, pages 66-71.

Ziewacz, Lawrence E. "The Eighty-first Ballot: The Senatorial Struggle of 1883." *Michigan History* volume 56 (Fall 1972): pages 216-232.

Chapter 10 Section 4

Barry, James P. *Ships of the Great Lakes.* Berkeley: Howell-North Books, 1973.

Boelio, Bob, ed. "Maritime Museums." *Chronicle* volume 18 (1982): pages 24-28.

Clary, James. *Ladies of the Lakes.* Lansing: Michigan Department of Natural Resources, 1981.

Lesstrang, Jacques. *Lake Carriers.* Seattle: Superior Publishing Company, 1977.

Lesstrang, Jacques. *The Great Lakes St. Lawrence System.* Maple City, MI: Harbor House Publishers, 1984.

Peters, Scott M. "The Gales of November 1913." *Michigan History* volume 64 (November-December 1980): pages 11-16.

Pott, Kenneth Roger. "Investigating a Lake Michigan Shipwreck." *Michigan History* volume 69 (July-August 1985): pages 36-42.

Ratigan, William. *Great Lakes Shipwrecks and Survivals.* Grand Rapids: William B. Eerdmans Publishing Company, 3rd edition, 1980.

404

Chapter 11 Section 1
Baker, Jim. *Get Out and Get Under*. Marlton, NJ: Periods and Commas, 1974.
Brough, James. *The Ford Dynasty: An American Story*. Garden City, NY: Doubleday and Company, 1977.
Conot, Robert. *American Odyssey*. New York: William Morrow and Company, 1974, pages 82-84, 120-155.
Editors of Automobile Quarterly Magazine. *General Motors, the First 75 Years*. New York: Crown Publishers, 1983.
May, George S. *A Most Unique Machine*. Grand Rapids: William B. Eerdmans Publishing Company, 1975.
Motor Vehicle Manufacturers Association of the United States. *Automobiles of America*. Detroit: Wayne State University Press, 1961.
Olson, Sidney. *Young Henry Ford*. Detroit: Wayne State University Press, 1963.

Chapter 11 Section 2
Edmunds, Henry E. *Henry Ford—A Personal History*. Dearborn: Edison Institute, 1953.
Lacey, Robert. *Ford, the Men and the Machine*. Boston: Little, Brown and Company, 1986.
Nevins, Allan and Hill, Frank Ernest. *Ford: Expansion and Challenge 1915-1933*. New York: Charles Scribner's Sons, 1957.

Chapter 11 Section 3
Boelio, Bob. "Automotive Landmarks." *Chronicle* volume 16 (Fall 1980): pages 19-21.
Boucher, Ed. "Of Tags and Plates and Licenses." *Michigan History* volume 69 (November-December 1985): page 52.
Hyde, Charles K. *Detroit: An Industrial Guide*. Detroit: Detroit Historical Society, 1980.

Chapter 12 Section 1
Hartney, Harold E. *Up and At 'Em*. New York: Doubleday, 1971.
South, Amy. "What Camp Custer Brought to Battle Creek." *Chronicle* volume 18 (Winter 1982): pages 28-30.
Works Project Administration in the State of Michigan. *Michigan: A Guide to the Wolverine State*. New York: Oxford University Press, 1941.

Chapter 12 Section 2
Barfknecht, Gary W. *Murder Michigan*. Davison, MI: Friede Publications, 1983.
Grimm, Joe, ed. *Michigan Voices*. Detroit: Detroit Free Press and Wayne State University Press, 1987.
Smallwood, Carol, ed. *Michigan Authors*. 3rd edition. Hillsdale, MI: Hillsdale Educational Publishers and Michigan Association for Media in Education, 1993.

Chapter 12 Section 3
Arrigo, Barbara and Lama, Geri, editors. "Michigan Women: A History of Achievement." *Detroit Free Press* (special supplement). May 21, 1987, pages 12-13.
Magilligan, Donald J., Jr. "Charles Lindbergh's Michigan Connection." *Michigan History* volume 72 (July-August 1988), pages 16-23.
Warner, Robert and Vanderhill, C. Warren. *A Michigan Reader: 1865 to the Present*. Grand Rapids: William B. Eerdmans Publishing Company, 1974, pages 183-195.
Wukovits, John F. "Those Thrilling Days of Yesteryear." *American History Illustrated* volume 23 (October 1988): pages 24-29.

Chapter 13 Section 1
Edmunds, Anthony O. *Joe Louis*. Grand Rapids: William B. Eerdmans Publishing Company, 1973.
Fine, Sidney. *Frank Murphy: the Detroit Years*. Ann Arbor: University of Michigan Press, 1975.
Kestenbaum, Justin L. *Out of the Wilderness*. Woodland Hills, CA: Windsor Publications, 1981.
McGehee, Scott and Watson, Susan, editors. *Blacks in Detroit*. Detroit: Detroit Free Press, 1980. (reprint)
Ruby, Christine Nelson. "Art for the Millions: Government Art During the Depression." *Michigan History* volume 66 (January-February 1982) pages 17-20.
Symon, Charles A. *We Can Do It!-A History of the CCC in Michigan*. Escanaba, MI: Charles A. Symon, 1983.

Chapter 13 Section 2
Babson, Steve. *Working Detroit*. New York: Adama Books, 1984.
Korn, Jerry, ed. *This Fabulous Century 1930-1940: Time-Life Books*, volume 4. New York: Time, Inc., 1969, pages 160-171.
Pflug, Warren W. *The UAW in Pictures*. Detroit: Wayne State University Press, 1971.
Reuther, Victor G. *The Brothers Reuther and the Story of the UAW*. Boston: Houghton Mifflin Company, 1976.

Chapter 13 Section 3

Clive, Alan. *State of War.* Ann Arbor: University of Michigan Press, 1979.

Jensen, Ann. "USS Arizona-The Memories do not Die." *American History Illustrated* volume 23 (December 1988): pages 13-21.

LaRoue, Jim. "A B-24 Liberator Comes Home." *Michigan History* volume 72 (March-April 1988): pages 13-21.

Magnaghi, Russell M. "Ford's Gliders at Iron Mountain." *Chronicle* volume 16 (Fall1980), pages 12-13.

Walker, Thomas C. "Gathering at Mackinac." *Michigan History* volume 72 (September-October 1988): pages 12-19.

Chapter 14 Section 1

Cartwright, Allison S. "Soapy's Michigan Ties." *Michigan History* volume 72 (September-October 1988): pages 44-45.

Ratigan, William. *Highways Over Broad Waters.* Grand Rapids: William B. Eerdmans Publishing Company, 1959.

Rubin, Lawrence A. *Bridging the Straits.* Detroit: Wayne State University Press, 1985.

Chapter 14 Section 2

Alexander, George. *Moonport U.S.A.* 6th ed. Air Force Eastern Test Range Public Relations Association, 1985.

Chrysler, C. Donald and Chaffee, Don L. *On Course to the Stars: The Roger B. Chaffee Story.* Grand Rapids: Kregel Publications, 1968.

Fuller, John G. *We Almost Lost Detroit.* New York: Reader's Digest Press, 1975.

Locke, Hubert G. *The Detroit Riot of 1967.* Detroit: Wayne State University Press, 1969.

Morgan, Hugh. "Martin Luther King, Jr. in Grosse Pointe." *Michigan History* volume 73 (January-February 1989): pages 32-39.

Chapter 14 Section 3 Part 1

Eisenstein, Paul A. "Muscle System: Carmakers Juice up the Lines With V-8's." *Michigan Business* (September 1988): pages 49-50.

Iacocca, Lee and Novak, William. *Iacocca: An Autobiography.* New York: Bantam Books, 1984.

Morrow, Kevin. "Michigan's Top Public Companies." *President's Report—Michigan Business* volume 5 (1989): pages 28-32.

Riegle, Donald. "Working to Save Chrysler." *Special Report to Michigan.* Washington, DC: United States Senate, 1981.

Schwartz, Roberta. "Down on the Farm Domino's Style." *Michigan Living* (September 1988): page 28

Tucker, Jonathan B. "GM: Shifting to Automatic." *High Technology* (May 1985): page 26.

Verway, David I., ed. *Michigan Statistical Abstract* 17th edition. Detroit: Wayne State University Press, 1983.

Chapter 14 Section 3 Part 2

Ciokajlo, Pat. "Hydro power on "mega" scale: but the Fish Kills a Side Effect of Massive Ludington Plant." *Jackson Citizen Patriot,* November 30, 1986.

Egginton, Joyce. *The Poisoning of Michigan.* New York: W.W. Norton, 1980.

Gottlieb, Karen V. "Michigan's Pollution 'Area of Concern'." *Natural Resources Register* volume 6 (August 1986): page 9.

Halbert, Frederic and Halbert, Sandra. *Bitter Harvest.* Grand Rapids: William B. Eerdmans Publishing Company, 1978.

Stanton, Barbara. "Fermi 2." *Detroit Free Press,* July 27, 1986, page B1.

Chapter 14 Section 3 Part 3

Barnes, Leonard R., ed. "Celebrities Talk up Michigan." Special issue. *Michigan Living* volume 71 (April 1989).

Burgoyne, George E., Jr. "Moose" *Michigan Natural Resources* volume 54 (March-April 1985): pages 27-42.

Franklin, Dixie. "Travel and Tourism-From Farm Club to the Major Leagues." *Michigan Business* (March 1988): pages 32-34.

McKee, Russell, ed. *Mackinac, the Gathering Place.* Lansing: State Department of Natural Resources, 1981.

Piljac, Pamela A. and Piljac, Thomas M. *Mackinac Island: Historic Frontier, Vacation Resort, Timeless Wonderland.* Portage, IN: Bryce-Waterton Publications, 1988.

Symon, Charles and Symon, Barbara. *U-P PEOPLE.* Gladstone, MI: RonJon Press, 1987.

page for future additions

Here are definitions of words which relate to Michigan history. Many of these words and terms are *italicized* in the text. Knowing these definitions will help you understand what you are reading.

A.D.-(anno Domini) Means year of our Lord. The time period we are living in now, measured from Christ's birth.

abolitionists-(AB oh LISH un ists) people who wanted to abolish or end slavery.

acre-(Aker) a measure of land. A square about 209 feet on a side.

ague-(AY g'you)a disease caused by parasites in the blood which people got from mosquito bites. A type of malaria.

alewives-a small sardine-like fish.

ammunition-rifle and cannon shells used by the military. Bullets.

Anishinabe-(ah nish in A bey*) an Ojibwa word meaning first man or original man. * There are several ways to say Native American words. Some people drop vowel sounds at the beginning of words. Here the last" a" is said very long. This is our best understanding of the pronunciation from *A Dictionary of the Ojibway Language* by Fredeic Baraga. Baraga spent many years living and working with Native Americans.

anti-slavery-against slavery

archaeologist-(ar key AL uh jist) a scientist who studies about past human life and activities.

architect-(AR kuh techt) a person who designs buildings and homes.

arsenal-(ARS en al) a building for storing weapons and ammunition for the military- army, navy, etc.

assembly line-a system in factories where the work travels on a belt in front of the worker. This cuts down on extra steps in the manufacturing process.

aviation-(ay vee AY shen) the business of building and operating airplanes.

B.C.-before Christ. A measure of years before Christ. Add years B.C. plus the current year to find "years ago."

baggataway-(be gat eh way) a very popular Indian stick ball game. It was a team contest. In a modified form we know the game as lacrosse. Each player had two sticks, measuring between 2 1/2 to 3 feet in length, with one end bent to make a pocket. The ball was animal hair covered with animal skin. The number of players to a side varied. The object was always to hurl the ball between goalposts set up at either end of a field.

bailout-emergency financial assistance provided to save a company or organization.

banking crisis-a time of difficulty which took place because many banks were in bad financial condition.

barn raising-when neighbors got together to help build someone's barn.

base line-a reference line going east and west across the Lower Peninsula used to layout the townships in Michigan.

bay-a large area of water surrounded by land on three sides.

bayonet-(BAY ah net) a sharp knife made to fit on the muzzle (front) end of a musket or rifle.

"bee"-anytime a group got together to accomplish a project which would have been hard for one or two people to do by themselves. Bees were social events too because people could talk to their neighbors while they worked and afterwards.

biased idea-(BYE est) an idea which we have formed without actually studying the facts.

biodegradable packaging-containers and wrapping which decompose over time. Glass is not biodegradable but paper is.

Black Muslims-(MUZ lem) or (MAZ lem) a religious group with political goals developed as an offshoot of the Muslim faith by American blacks.

Black Robes-a nickname the Indians used for the Jesuit priests.

board foot-the standard lumber measurement, one foot long, one foot wide, and one inch thick.

bond-a certificate issued by the government or a company which promises to pay back with interest, money borrowed from the buyer of the certificate.

bootlegger-someone who produced, sold or distributed liquor during prohibition. The term comes from those who hid the liquor in boots when it was being delivered.

brine-water which has a high salt content.

British Northwest Company-a fur trading company once operating in the Michigan region.

bromine- (BRO meen) a volatile, red liquid with a strong chlorine-like odor. It is a very reactive chemical.

bulk cargo-freight or goods which can be poured loose into a ship's hold. Great Lake freighters are specially designed for this kind of freight.

bureau of labor-the government department which kept information about the work force and inspected factories to see if they were safe.

bushel-a dry unit of measure which is about 1.25 cubic feet, or a basket for holding grain or fruit.

Cabinet Counties-the nine counties in Michigan named for members of President Jackson's administration. (see map on page 142)

canals-man-made rivers used for transportation.

cavalry-the part of the army which served on horseback.

census-an official survey of the population of a country, city, or town.

child labor laws-laws which set age limits and standards for the treatment of children in industry or farms.

cholera-(KOL er a) an often fatal disease which caused a loss of body fluids.

cinchona-(sin KONA) a South American tree which provides the antimalarial drug quinine. Some pioneers boiled the bark to make a tea to treat their malaria.

civil rights-the basic rights people have that protect them against discriminatory or unequal action by the government or other individuals.

civilian-a person who is not a member of any of the armed forces—Army, Navy, Air Force, etc.

clan-a group where everyone has a common ancestor.

climate-weather conditions at a place, over a period of years. Shown by winds, rains, etc.

closed shop-where every worker must belong to a union and it usually must be the same union.

colony-a group of people who settle in a new country but remain under the control of their original government.

communist-a person who supports a system requiring all property be owned by the state and shared by all.

conductors-people working on the Underground Railroad who took slaves from one hiding place to another..

Confederate-the name given to the south after those states seceded or left the Union.

conquest-to take over a land or people through war or battle.

conservation-protecting something such as forestland or rare animals from waste or the risk of being used up or destroyed.

constitution-the written set of principles or rules by which the state and national government are run.

constitutional convention-a meeting in which a new constitution is formed.

convoy-a group of ships or vehicles organized into a unit and traveling together.

cooperative-any association for buying and selling which benefits all its members.

coral-the rock-like skeleton of various salt water forms of life which live in colonies.

Cornish Pump-a huge steam-powered pump used to remove water from the Chapin Mine.

Cornish-people from Cornwall who came to work in Michigan's mines.

corps-(KOR) a group of people with special training and who are organized to work together.

Count-a European nobleman whose rank equaled that of an English earl.

county-the largest unit of local government within a state. Counties contain cities, villages, and townships.

coureur de bois-(koo ER deh BWAH) illegal fur trader. It means " woods runner".

court-martial-a military trial of a soldier or officer.

culture-refers to ideas and ways of doing things that a group of people share in common.

democracy-a free form of government run by the people who live under it.

deposit-a large amount of some mineral in rock or in the ground.

depression-severe economic or business slowdown when many people are out of work.

detroit-(in English, DEE troyt; in French day TrWAH) French word meaning "strait", a narrow passageway connecting two large bodies or water.

discrimination-(dis KRIM eh nay shen) showing an unfair difference in treatment of people.

diversity-to spread out into more than one kind of activity or industry.

driver's license-a legal document, usually a card, which allows a person to drive a car.

empire-many lands under the control of one government or king.

environment-generally taken to mean the natural setting around us—the air, water, and land, or more specifically: forests, lakes, ground water, etc.

epidemic-(ep eh DEM ik) rapid spreading of a disease so that many people have it at the same time.

erosion-(ih ROW zhen) the wearing away of soil or rock by wind or water.

ethnic diversity-the variety of customs, ideas, and artistic styles, etc. obtained from several ethnic groups living in the same area.

ethnic groups-those based on race or place of origin. Each group has similar customs and beliefs.

European-a person from one of the countries in Europe (France, England, Germany, etc.)

expedition-a journey made to explore or gather scientific samples.

exports-items made or grown in the United States which are taken to other countries to be sold.

extinct-a breed or group of fish, wildlife or plant, which no longer exists. It has died out.

felt-cloth made of matted fibers. These fibers come from the short hairs close to the skin on the beaver.

file-a hardened steel tool having ridges or teeth on its surface used to cut or shape metal.

flotation-a process using soapy water to separate small particles of iron from powdered rock. The metal powder floated away with the soap bubbles.

forge or **forging**-to form or shape, often out of metal as in a blacksmith's shop.

forge-a place where metal is heated and shaped.

fossil-an impression or trace of an animal or plant which has been preserved in a rock or actually changed into rock itself.

Fugitive Slave Law-(FYOU je tiv) [A fugitive is a person who runs away and hides from the law or a slave master.] A law passed to stop people from helping escaped slaves.

G.I. Bill of Rights-G.I. stands for government issue. A law passed near the end of World War II to help former soldiers and sailors with college expenses, starting businesses and the change to civilian life.

geologist-a scientist who studies rocks and the formation of the earth.

gill net-a net suspended in the water which allows the heads of fish to pass through, but catches them on their gills as they try to escape.

girdle-when farmers cut off a strip of bark around a tree, causing the sap to run out and the tree to die. This was a quick way to let sun light reach crops planted among the trees.

glacier-a very thick ice sheet which slowly covers a wide area of land because more snow falls in the winter than can melt in the summer.

Grange-an association of farmers to further their interests.

griffon-a mythical animal with the body of a lion and wings of an eagle. A carved griffon was placed on the bow of La Salle's ship which was named the *Griffon*.

gristmill-a mill for grinding grain into flour. It was usually powered by water.

harvest-reaping and gathering grain and other food crops.

harvester-a machine to cut and bundle grain.

homestead-public land granted to a settler under certain conditions by the United States government.

horseless carriage-an early name for a car.

ice breaker-a ship which can break up ice and keep lakes and rivers open in the winter.

immigrate-move into a foreign country or region to live there.

imports-products from another country which are shipped to the United States and sold.

internal improvements-any of the projects planned to improve the state and make it more appealing to settlers. Examples are railroads, roads and canals.

inventor-a person who creates new and often practical ideas for products or machines.

Jesuits-(JEZH wits) a highly educated Catholic religious group from Europe.

Ku Klux Klan-an organization against Blacks, Jews, and Catholics who often used unlawful tactics.

lacrosse-(le KROSS) a French name for baggataway. An outdoor game using a ball and long sticks with small nets at the bottom. Each team has a goal net used for scoring.

land speculation-buying or selling land when there is a large risk or without a complete study of the situation.

landlooker-a person hired to find good timber land to log.

latitude-a measurement of the earth going north and south from the equator. The horizontal imaginary lines seen on a map or globe.

lawsuit-a case in a court of law started by one person to claim something from another.

legislative-some activity which relates to the body which makes laws.

lifestyle-the values people have and the way they live, including the kind of homes they have and how they spend their money.

liquor-strong alcoholic beverage.

lock-part of a canal where the water level can be raised or lowered to move a ship from a higher or lower lake or river.

longhouse-a rectangular structure of poles and sheets of bark. Each measured 50 to 150 feet in length, depending on the number of families living inside. The width was from 18 to 25 feet, and roof was arched. There were no windows, but there were smoke holes in the roof. When there was heavy rain or snow, the vents could be closed with sliding panels. Then the longhouse would be filled with eye-stinging smoke. Longhouses were used mostly by the Hurons.

longitude-a measurement of the earth going east and west from a particular city in England. The vertical imaginary lines seen on a map or globe.

Lost Interval-a period of 279 million years for which no fossils or rocks can be found in the Michigan area.

lubricator-a mechanism which oiled moving parts on railroad engines.

lumber barons-those who made fortunes in the lumber business.

mammoth-a large hairy or wooly animal like an elephant with large curving tusks. Mammoths usually lived in grassy areas.

man car-open elevators which raise and lower workers into the deep mines.

martial law-(MAR shul) when basic legal rights have been suspended and the military is given control.

mastodon-an elephant-like animal similar to a mammoth but with tusks which curved only slightly. Probably because mastodons lived in swampy areas, many more of their remains have been found in Michigan.

merchant-someone who has a business selling to the public, usually from a store.

migrate-an entire group of people leave one area and move to another.

militia-(me LISH uh) a group of citizens used as a regular military force only in emergencies.

mineral-a compound which occurs naturally in the ground and usually has an industrial or commercial use.

minimum wage-the minimum amount a worker must be paid as set by state or federal law.

missionary-person who is sent to preach or teach others about a religion.

monopoly-total control of a market.

Morse code-the telegraphic alphabet or code. The alphabet and numbers are represented by dots and dashes (long and short sounds). Messages are sent by audible signals. Named after Samuel B. Morse.

mound-a large rounded earthen burial plot where some early Indians placed their dead.

NAACP-National Association for the Advancement of Colored People. An organization to help Black people have equal rights and equal opportunities.

narrow-gauge-railroad tracks often used in lumbering which were not as wide as conventional tracks.

New England-the English or British colonies in North America.

North America-the land or countries north of, and including, Mexico. (The modern countries of Mexico, United States, and Canada.)

Northwest Territory-land which included Michigan and eventually became the states of Ohio, Indiana, Illinois, Wisconsin, and a small part of Minnesota.

nuclear energy-energy which comes from changes in the nucleus of an atom. Atomic energy.

Ontonagon Boulder-(on ton AH gun) a large piece of almost pure copper which was sacred to the Indians.

open shop-all workers can be given jobs in the factory if they qualify to be hired. They do not have to belong to a union.

open-pit mining-mining minerals in large pits instead of in mines.

ordinance-a law passed by Congress under the Articles of Confederation.

ore-mineral or rock containing enough metal or metals to make mining it profitable.

Orient-the modern countries of China, Japan, India, and the others in that part of the world.

out-sourcing-the process where companies buy parts from other manufacturers.

oxen-full grown cattle which were used to pull loads and do work on early pioneer farms.

pacifist-(PASS ih fist) person who is opposed to war or the use of force.

pageant-(PAJ ent) an elaborate exhibition or ceremony.

Paleo Indians-(PAY lee o) these were the first people who lived in Michigan. "Paleo" means ancient and is a name made up by archaeologists.

panic-a fear spreading through many people. In this case caused by an economic collapse.

parasite-a plant or animal living in, on or with some other organism.

patent-a document which grants a person or company sole rights to make, use or sell an invention.

pelt-the skin and fur from fur-bearing animals.

pemmican-(PEM eh kan) a Native American food—a mixture of venison pounded into a paste with fat and dried berries. Usually used for emergency rations.

peninsula-a portion of land nearly surrounded by water.

Personal Liberty Act-an attempt to extend legal rights to former slaves. It was a counteraction to the Fugitive Slave Law.

pesticides-any substance used to kill insects.

Ph. D.-doctor of Philosophy (philosophy doctor= Ph. D.). The highest degree granted by universities.

pitchfork-a long-handled fork used for lifting hay or straw.

plank roads-roads improved by laying down wooden boards or planks. They were not very satisfactory and soon rotted.

planter-a farm machine which makes a hole, drops a seed in and then covers it.

political party-an organized group of people who support the same ideas.

polybrominated biphenol (PBB)-(poly BROM in ate ed bye FEE nol) also known as Firemaster. A chemical which made materials less likely to catch fire. It is a toxic chemical.

portage-an area along a river where the canoes must be carried because their way is blocked by shallows, rapids, or rocks, etc. Or a short distance of land which has to be crossed between two rivers or lakes.

Postum-(POST um) an 1890s coffee substitute made from sugar and grain which is toasted and caramelized.

priest-a member of the clergy in the Roman Catholic Church.

prime meridian-a reference line running north and south through the Lower Peninsula and Upper Peninsula used to layout the townships in Michigan. In combination with the *base line* it allows for the location of any township and its boundaries.

prisoner of war-person who has been taken captive during war and is held under guard.

Progressive Era-a time when people were concerned about corruption in government and business. They wanted to make the world more responsive to the needs of the people.

prohibition-the period of time when it was prohibited to make or drink alcoholic beverages.

prophet-a person who predicts or foretells the future.

province-an administrative district or division of a country. Canada has 10 provinces which are much like a state in the United States.

quadricycle-(KWAD reh sie kal) the name given to the first cars because they had four bicycle tires.

Quakers-a religious group opposed to slavery

quinine-(KWI nine) medication used to treat malaria.

race riot-when a large number of people become violent and out of control due to hatred of another race.

racism-the assumption that one race is superior or should have special rights compared to another.

radical-a person who favors extreme changes or reforms in government.

radio carbon dating-a test used to determine the age of fossils. It measures the tiny amount of radioactivity left once a living thing has died.

radioactive-something which gives off energy or particles because of nuclear decay. Elements such as radium and uranium are radioactive.

reaper-a machine to cut wheat, oats, or other grain.

recreation-play or amusement. Things done in leisure or done while on vacation, or to relax.

religious freedom-the right to practice the religion of choice without interference from the government or other individuals.

revenge-to hurt someone in retaliation. Return evil for evil.

revolution-the military overthrow of one government so that another may take over.

rigging-ropes or chains that support or raise and lower the masts and sails of a ship.

River Raisin-a river in southeast Michigan.

river drive-floating logs down a river from the forest to the sawmill.

roadside park-a small area by the highway with picnic facilities and rest rooms for travelers to use. The parks spoken of in the book are not like the ones along interstates. If you know where one of these parks is near you, mention it to your class.

robot-a mechanical device that does routine work in response to computer commands given by humans.

rum runners-people who purchased alcohol in Canada and brought it into Detroit.

rush-a gathering of many new people to an area in this case to look for copper.

Rush-Bagot Agreement-an agreement between Great Britain and the United States that no military ships would be used on the Great Lakes.

saint-an honor given by the Catholic Church to a person after death for outstanding dedication and good deeds.

salvation- (SAL vay shen) the saving of a person from the spiritual consequences of sin.

sanitarium-(san eh TAIR ee um) a place for treating people who are sick or recovering from an illness. Diet and exercise are usually emphasized.

Sanitary Commission-an organization which gathered food, blankets, books, and newspapers to be sent to the battlefield during the Civil War.

sault-(SOO) French word meaning rapids in a river.

scalp-the top part of the human head which holds the hair. Indians and Europeans cut or tore scalps from an enemy as a token of victory.

scrip-a replacement for money usually printed by an employer when cash is in short supply.

sea lamprey-an eel-like parasite which feeds off fish by sucking their blood.

secede-(seh SEED) to pull out or withdraw from the United States.

sections-units of land within townships which contain 640 acres.

segregation-the separation of one racial group from others, especially in public places or housing.

self-unloading freighter-a freighter equipped to empty itself of its cargo.

shanty boys-nickname for men who cut down trees. Also lumberjacks or loggers.

siege-(SEEJ) a long battle to gain possession of a fort or town.

sit-down strike-when laborers stop work and refuse to leave the shop or factory as a protest.

skilled workers-those whose work requires considerable training.

slashings-the branches, brush, and limbs left over after logging.

slavery-the practice of owning people who must work without pay.

solar compass-a compass that uses the sun to find direction. It is not affected by the magnetic pull of iron ore.

soul-the spiritual part of the body as opposed to the physical part. Many religions believe that the soul and body are separated at death and that the soul lives forever.

speed up-when bosses at a factory increased the speed of the assembly line, which required workers to do their jobs faster.

squatters-people who did not buy the land where they lived.

statehood-the time when the area became a state.

stereotype-considering everyone in a group to be alike based on actual experience with a few members.

stock market-a place where shares of stock in companies are bought and sold.

stockholder-one who is the holder of stocks in a company. A person who has bought shares of stock which give them part ownership of a company.

strike-when workers stop or refuse to work unless given better pay, shorter hours, or some other demand.

suburbs-smaller towns close to or touching the edge of a large city.

sue-to start a lawsuit against someone; to take someone to court over a problem.

suffrage-(SUF rij) the right to vote.

surveyor-a person who finds boundary lines for maps using special instruments.

tar & feather-to coat someone with hot tar and cover with feathers as a punishment or an insulting act.

tavern-a bar or place where liquor is sold. In early times taverns were key meeting places in many towns and villages.

Teamsters Union-union formed originally by wagon drivers, hence the term teamsters.

telegraph-a device for sending coded messages over wires by using electricity. Until the invention of the telephone it was the most popular way to send messages across the country.

temperance-using little or no alcohol as a beverage.

territory-land under the jurisdiction of a government but not having official representatives.

Thames River-(TIMZ) a river in southern Ontario which empties into Lake St. Clair.

thresher-a farm machine to separate grain from the stalk or stem.

Tin Lizzie-early nickname of Ford's Model T.

Toledo Strip-a wedge of land claimed by both Ohio and Michigan which includes the modern city of Toledo.

Toledo War-the dispute which resulted from each state's claim to the Toledo Strip. It had to be settled before Michigan could become a state.

tourism-business activities connected with people traveling for pleasure.

township-land surveyed so that it is in square blocks, six miles on each side; used for the purpose of land sales or as a government unit.

toxic-poisonous

traction engine-an early steam-powered tractor. It could move under its own power or feed power to other equipment through the use of leather belts.

trader-a person who exchanges one kind of goods for another kind without using money. Fur traders, etc.

trap net-a net which traps fish in a box-like area. This net is less harmful to fish than a gill net because the fish can move about and collect oxygen from the water.

treaty-an agreement between two or more official groups or governments.

tri-county area-tri means three. Wayne, Oakland, and Macomb make up the tri-county area mentioned in the text.

trimotor-(TRY mote er) an airplane which has three engines.

Underground Railroad-a system which was created to help slaves escape from the South. It was not underground and not a railroad. It was called underground because it was secret and a railroad because it was a transportation system.

union-a group of workers who join together to protect and promote their interests and to negotiate as one voice with owners.

Union-the name of the north prior to and during the Civil War. The states that remained united and a part of the United States.

unskilled workers-those who do less complex jobs requiring little training.

veteran-a former or ex-member of the military.

voyageurs-(VOY uh zhahs) Frenchmen hired by the fur companies to transport goods and people by canoe.

wampum belt- a belt made by the Indians. They used tiny tubes which were shaped from shells. The belts were often used in Native American ceremonies to show that sacred pledges were made.

warehouse-a large storehouse for wares or merchandise.

waterwheel-a large wheel turned by the weight of water flowing over it and used to do work. The gristmills used by pioneers were run by waterwheels.

welfare-aid or assistance provided by the government to needy people.

Whig-a political party popular between 1834 and 1854. Its members were often eastern business-men, western farmers, and large southern plantation owners. A key goal of the Whigs was unity of the nation. The party began as a backlash to President Jackson's pro-pioneer policies.

wigwam-dome-shaped framework of poles covered with hides or birchbark used as home by some of the Native Americans.

wildcat bank-when dishonest people decided they could get rich by having a bank office and printing money. These banks usually had no cash to back the money they printed.

windmill-a machine operated by the action of the wind. Windmills are mostly used to pump water.

"wireless"-another name for a radio. Before the radio, most communications came over phone or telegraph wires.

Works Progress Administration-a federal organization which created jobs for the unemployed during the Great Depression.

418

page for future additions

A

Abolitionists, 166
Acid rain, 232, 381
Adrian, 154, 167
Agriculture, development, 214-222, 225; early equipment, 216; fruit, 221; in civil war, 189; pests, 130; pioneer practices, 122-125; top products today, 221; women's role in, 218
Ague (malaria), 128
Aguirre, Hank, 376
Airplanes, B-24, 237; Tri-motor, 307-309; World War I, 293; World War II, 337-338, 341-342
Alewives, 229
Alger, Russell, 183, 187
Algonquian, 26
Allen Park, 349
Allouez, Claude, 46, 48
Alpena, 225, 258, 261
Ambassador Bridge, M7, 313
American Federation of Labor (AFL), 246, 327
American Red Cross, 202
Amherstburg, Ontario, 101, 168
Anderson, "Sparky," 394
Animals, ancient, 14
Anishinabe, 26, 36
Ann Arbor, 151, 166, 168, 237, 375
Anthony, Susan B., 172, 307
Anti-Semitism, 302
Arab oil crisis, 368
Arabic people, 4, 151, 368
Architects, 287, 365-366
Asians, 4, 364
Assembly line, 274, 374
Association of Licensed Automobile Manufacturers (ALAM), 270
Astor, John Jacob, 102, 135
Astronauts, 364-365
Athletes, Michigan related, 394
Austin, Richard, 360
Automobiles, development, 264-268; employment, 285; first in Michigan, 264; import competition, 369; jokes and songs, 267, 282; production, 271, 272, 373; spring-powered, 264
Automobile club, 283-284
Automobile license, 285

B

B-24 bomber, 337-338
Bachman, William, 284
Ballard, Florence, 362
Bank holiday, 316
Baptiste, George de, 174
Baraga, Reverend Frederick, 157
Barclay, Robert, 107
Barnraising, 131
Barry, Thomas, 245
Baseline, 91-92
Bates, Frederick, 95
Battle Creek, 168, 172, 234, 294, 296, 316, 336
Baumfree, Isabella, (*see* Sojourner Truth)
Bay City, 225, 245, 262, 264, 288, 336, 396
Beans, 218, 221
Beaumont, William, 135
Beaver Island, M5, 152
Bedding plants, 221
Beemer, Brace, 311
"Bees," (cooperative projects), 131, 214
Begole, Josiah, 199, 235, 248, 306
Belle Isle, M7, 262, 340

Bennett, Harry, 332, 338
Berkey and Gay Company, 237
Berlin, 294
Berlin-Ferro site, 382
Bias, 22
Big Rapids, 306
Big Rock Point Plant, 366
Big Spring Kitch-iti-ki-pi, 385
Big Three, 370
Big wheels, 198
Bingham, Kinsley, 176-177
Bissell, Melville, and the Bissell Carpet Sweeper Co., 238-239
Black Hawk War, 133
"Black Swamp", 102
Blackburn, Thornton and Rutha, 170
Blacks (Afro-Americans), 286; first in Michigan, 77; in civil war, 185; pre-Civil War, 165-178; right to vote, 175; tension between races, 302, 339, 359
Blair, Austin, 178, 181-182
Blanchard, James, 375
Bliss, Aaron, 199
Bloody Run, Battle of, M7, 74
Blue Jacket, 87
Blue Water Bridge, 313
Boblo Island, 255, 389
Bois Blanc Island, M5
Boom companies, 196
Boone, Daniel, 80, 82
Bootlegging, 298-301
Bottle deposit law, 383
Boundaries, overlapping with Ohio, 140, 144; overlapping with original states, 90-91
Bower, Joseph, 312
Brainard, Elmira, 185
Brine, 197, 241
British Northwest Company, 71
Brock, Isaac, 103
Bronson, 114
Brooklyn, 387
Brown, John, 175
Brucker, Wilbur, 319
Brulé River, 144
Brûlé, Etienne, 42-43
Buckley, Jerry, 301
Buick, David D., 268
Buick Motor Company, 268, 272
Bull Run, Battle of, 182, 186
Bunche, Ralph, 349
Bunyan, Paul, 194
Bureau of Labor, 245
Burt, William, 159

C

Cabinet counties, 142
Cadillac, Antoine de la Mothe, 57
Cadillac, Marie-Therese, 59-61
Cadillac Motor Company, 268, 336
Calumet, 208
Calumet & Hecla Mine, 204, 207
Camp Custer, 294
Campau, Antoine, 147-148
Campbell, Captain Donald, 71
Canada, 85, 110, 166, 170, 193, 231; acid rain, 3, 81; border, 3; bridges, 312; fishing agreement, 226; meaning of name, 39; Patriot War, 144; people moved to, 88; Prohibition, 299; seaway, 259
Canals, 112, 132, 154
Canfield, Captain Agustus, 163
Capitol building, C3, 145
Car ferries, 352

Carleton, Will, 149
Caro, 320
Carp River, 161
Cartier, Jacques, 38
Cash, Jim, 396
Cass City, 365
Cass County, 134, 170
Cass, Lewis, 103, 109, 119, 171, 178; governor of territory, 117; 1820 expedition, 117-118, 155; land sold, 147; secretary of war, 120, 138; speech in Detroit, 184
Cass Technical High School, 308
Cassopolis, 168
Catton, Bruce, 396
Celery, 219
Cement, 258
Cereal, 232-236
Chaffee, Roger, 364
Champion spark plug, 272
Champlain, Samuel de, 40-43
Chandler, Elizabeth, 166
Chandler, Zachariah, 171, 176
Chapin Mine, 209-210
Charlevoix, 225, 366
Cheboygan, 225
Checker Cab Company, 287
Cherries, tart, 221
Chevrolet, Louis, 272
Chicago, 154, 191, 196, 237, 351
Chicago Road, 114, 146
Child labor, 243-244
Chillicothe, 137
Chippewa (*see* Ojibwa)
Cholera, 110, 129, 133
Chrysler Corporation, 336, 370; bailout, 370-371, 373
Chrysler, Walter P., 280
Cigars, manufacture of, 237
Cities, ranked by size, 6
Civil rights, 357, 360
Civil War, 172, 181-190
Civilian Conservation Corps (CCC), 320-322
Clark, George Rogers, 80-83
Clay, Henry, 162, 171, 174
Cliff Mine, 157
Climate, Great Lakes affect on, 1
Closed shop, 326
Coal, 10, 155, 258, 296, 381
Coast Guard, 262, 300
Cobb, Ty, 303
Cobo Hall, M7, 390
Coldwater, 114, 182
Communists, 318
Comstock, Charles C., 237
Comstock, William A., 320
Conservation, 225, 230-231
Constitution, of 1835, 140-141; of 1850, 175; of 1963, 360-361
Consumers Power Company, 380
Cooper, Alice, 396
Cooper, Tom, 269
Copper, 17, 46, 155, 189; "Copper Rush," 157; 1913 strike, 207; (also see mining)
Copper Culture people, 17-18
Copper Harbor, 157
Cork pine, 192
Corn flakes, manufacture of, 235
Cornish, 152, 205
Cornish Pump, 210
Cornwall, 150
Coughlin, Father Charles E., 318, 323
Counties, names, 135; purpose of, 5-7, 150
Coureur de Bois, 64

Court, first in area, 85
Courthouse, 5
Cousin Jacks, (*see* Cornish)
Couzens, James, 268, 291, 318-319
Crapo, Henry, 199
Crary, Isaac, 143
Crossroads Village, 388
Crosswhite, Adam, 170
Crystal Falls, 211, 385
Cuillerier, Angélique, 73
Cumberland Gap, 94
Curwood, James, 303
Custer, Elizabeth, 187-188; George A., 186-188; Tom, 187

D

Dalyell, Captain, 74
Darrow, Clarence, 302
Davis, Jefferson, 133; capture of, 189
Dawber, Pam, 395
Dearborn, M7, 114, 144, 307, 308, 368, 388
Deerfield, 395
Democratic Party, 175
Depression (the 1930s), 310, 315-322
Dequindre, Antoine, 82
Detroit, M7, 88, 155, 168, 296; as capital, 145; aviation, 307; British period, 80; city motto, 95; depression, 317, 319; French period, 58-59, 69; fire, 95; first cars, 264-268; fishing, 223; founding, 58; Fox attack, 59; Freedom March, 358; GM plant, 372; growth of suburbs, 349; highways, 351; industry, 285; Irish population, 151; meaning of name, 55; Prohibition, 298; recording industries, 362; settlers arriving, 146; shipping, 254; siege by Pontiac, 73; urban development, 389; village government, 94; Woodward plan for, 95; World War II, 343; 1773 census, 79; 1880s, 249
Detroit-Edison, 381
Detroit Free Press, 310
Detroit International Bridge Company, 312
Detroit News, 300, 310
Detroit Riot, of 1863, 184-185; of 1943, 340; of 1967, 359-360
Detroit River, 59, 299
Detroit Lions, Red Wings, and Tigers, 322, 375
Detroit-Windsor Tunnel, M7, 313
Devins, "Michigan Bridget," 185
Dewey, Thomas E., 347
Dexter, 168
Dismemberment Bill, 143
Dodge Fountain, 390
Dodge, Horace & John and the Dodge Motor Company, 268, 277
Doe, Mary, 306
Domino's Pizza, 375
Dort, Dallas, 237, 272
Dossin Great Lakes Museum, M7, 262
Douglass, Frederick, 176
Dow, Herbert and the Dow Chemical Company, 241-242, 336
Dowagiac, 240
"Down-sizing," 370
Driver's license, 285
Drummond Island, M5
Duluth, Daniel Greysolon, 60
Durant, William Crapo, 237, 272, 280, 315
Dutch, 4, 37, 41, 151, 220
Dwyer, Jeremiah, 239

E

Eagle Harbor, C6
Eagle River, 152, 158
East Detroit, 349
East Grand Rapids, 349
East Lansing, 349
Eaton Rapids, 251
Edison, Thomas, 178-179, 267, 292
Edmonds, Sara E., 186
Education, college, 218, 346, 375; development, 143; financing, 92; pioneer, 133
"Educational Oak," 143
Edwards, Abraham, 114-115
Edwards, Esther Gordy, 363
Edwardsburg, 114
Eldred, Julius, 156
Elections, 138, 142 ; first American, 94; first in area, 85
Electric power, 217, 379-382
Elevation, of state, M4-M6, 2
Elk, 385
Elliot, Matthew, 97
Empire Mine, 212
Entertainers; Michigan related, 361-362, 394-396
Environmental concerns, 378-383
Erie Canal, 111-113, 116, 124
Erie & Kalamazoo Railroad, 153
Erosion, 200-201
Escanaba, 209, 256
Etherage, Anna, 185
Etherington, Captain, 75-76
Ethnic group chart, 4, (map) 151
Everett, Philo M., 161, 252
Exploration of area, 42-43, 47-50, 52-58
Exports, 261

F

Fairbanks, Erastus, 162
Fallen Timbers, Battle of, 87-88
Farm Bureau (PBB accident), 378
Farming, (*see* agriculture)
Farmington, M7, 395
Fascists, 318
Fayette, 210, 385
Ferber, Edna, 303
Fermi I, 366; Fermi II, 380-381
Ferris, Woodbridge, 208
Ferry, D.M., and Ferry & Company, 235
Finland, 4, 151, 193
Fire, of 1871, 202; of 1881, 202
Fisher Body, 272, 329, 337
Fisher Brothers, 287
Fishing, commercial, 223-231; contamination, 231; quantity, 225; sport, C4, 229-230, 387; tribal rights (*see* Indians)
Fitzgerald, Edmund, 260-261
Five dollar-day, 276
Flat Rock, 288, 372, 375
Flint, 146, 235, 237, 272, 285; in depression, 319; sit-down strike, 323, 328-331
Flu epidemic, 296
Ford, Clara, 293
Ford-Dodge lawsuit, 277
Ford, Edsel, 278, 307
Ford, Gerald and Betty, 393-394
Ford, Gerald R. Museum, C3, 388
Ford, Henry, 265, 267, 288, 291-292, 307
Ford, Henry II, 337-338, 371, 389
Ford Motor Company, 268-270, 275-276, 285, 318, 327, 332, 370
Forests, fires, 201-202; national and state, 386

Forsyth, Fredrick, 264
Fort de Buade, 57
Fort Dearborn, 114
Fort Detroit, 71, 80, 82, 101
Fort Frontenac, 54
Fort Greenville, 87
Fort Mackinac, 82, 101-102, 108, 385
Fort Malden, 102, 107-108
Fort Meigs, 106, 108
Fort Miami, 56
Fort Michilimackinac, C7, 62, 69, 385, 388
Fort Pontchartrain, M7, 71
Fort Sackville (*see* Vincennes)
Fort St. Joseph (Niles), 62; Spanish flag raised, 82
Fort Shelby, 109
Fort Wayne (Detroit), M7, 182
Fort Wayne (Indiana), 87
Fort Wilkins, 157
Fox River, 48
Fox tribe, 59, 133
Frankenmuth, C8, 151, 389
Frankfort, 320
Franklin, Aretha, 362
Fraser, 179
French and Indian War, 66-70
Frenchtown, (*see* Monroe)
Frontenac, Count, 54
"Frost-bitten" Convention, 143
Fruit belt, 221
Fugitive Slave law, 174, 176
Fur trade, 38-40, 62-65; British policy toward Indians, 71-72; monopoly, 40; relative values, 64
Furniture, home, 237; office, 238

G

G I Bill of Rights, 346
Garden City, 349
Gaye, Marvin, 361
General Motors Corporation, 270, 272, 278, 285, 316, 323, 370-372; headquarters, 280; major plants, 288, 372; technical center, 288; Saturn project, 371
Germans, 4, 102, 150
Gerrish, Winfield Scott, 198
Gettysburg, Battle of, 187
Ghost towns, 150, 210
Gibson, Kirk, 394
Gill nets, 225, 231
Giltner, David, 170
Gipp, George, 394
Glaciers, 12
Gladwin, Major Henry, 72
Global community and Michigan, 343
Gogebic Iron Range, 211-212
Gordy, Berry, 361
Government, British, 78-79; French, 39-40, 52-54, 57-58, 66; statehood, 138; territorial, 117-120, 137-145
Governors- state-
(See the following under their own entries: Alger, Russell; Begole, Josiah; Bingham, Kinsley; Blanchard, James; Blair, Austin; Bliss, Aaron; Brucker, Wilbur; Comstock, William; Crapo, Henry; Ferris, Woodbridge; Jerome, David; Mason, Stevens T.; Milliken, William G.; Murphy, Frank; Osborn, Chase S.; Pingree, Hazen S.; Rich, John; Romney, George W.; Williams, G. Mennen,; Wisner, Moses,; Woodbridge, William,)
Grand Blanc, 288, 337
Grand Center, 391

Grand Rapids, 152, 238, 243, 288, 308, 391; auto industry, 285, 391; cavalry unit, 183; depression, 316-317, 319; Dutch in, 152; furniture center, 237; log jam, 195; the 1960s, 364-365; World War II, 334, 336, 343
Grand River, 195
Grand Traverse Resort, 392
Grange, 219
Grant, Ulysses S., 150
Grayling, 192
Great Lakes, affect on weather, 1; coastline, 1; fishing, 223, 225-232; pollution, 231; storms, 260
Great Lakes Maritime Institute, 262
Greeley, Horace, 162
Green Bay, 43, 56
Greenfield Village and Henry Ford Museum, 388
Grenoble, 42
Griffon, 55-57, 253
Gristmill, 125
Griswold, Stanley, 95
Groseilliers, Medard, 52
Grosse Ile, 58
Guest, Edgar, 303
Guest, Judith, 396
Gulf of St. Lawrence, 38, 40-41
Guyard, Marie, 47
Gypsum, 9

H
Hackley, Charles H., 199
Halbert, Rick & Sandra, 379
Hamilton, Henry, 80-82
Hamper, Ben, (Rivethead), 396
Hamtramck, M7, 285
Hamtramck, John Francis, 88
Hancock, 204
Hanks, Porter, 103
Hannah, Perry, 199
Harmar, Josiah, 86, 88
Harper Woods, 349
Harper's Ferry, VA, 177
Harrison, William Henry, 99-100, 105-106
Hart Plaza, 390
Hartwick Pines State Park, 192, 385
Harvey, Charles T., 162-163
Haviland, Laura Smith, 166
Hayden, Tom, 363
Hays, John, (Old Blind Hays), 157
Hearns, Thomas, 394
Hemingway, Ernest, 303
Henry, Alexander, 75
Hiawatha, 134
Highland Park, M7, 285
Highland Park plant, M7, 274
Highway welcome centers, 384
Highways, 312-313, 350-351
Hill, Colonel Bennet, 189
Hillsdale, (map) 169
Hispanics, 376
Hoffa, James R., disappearance, 372
Hitsville USA, 362
Hodunk, 161
Holland (Michigan), C8, 152, 202, 389
Holland (Netherlands), 150
Holly, C8
Homestead act, 214
Hoover, Herbert, 280, 315
Hopewell people, 19
Horses, 122, 217-218

Horton, Willie, 394
Houghton, 152, 204
Houghton, Douglas, 155-156
Howe, Gordie, 394
Howell, 320, 372
Hubbard, Bella, 155
Hudson's Bay Company, 52
Hull, William; Court-martialed, 104; governor, 95-97; surrenders Detroit, 102-103
Huron River, 288
Huron tribe, 25, 27; locations of, 24
Hussey, Erastus, 168, 174

I
Iacocca, Lee, 371
Immigration, 205, 286
Imports, 261,369
Indians, 155-156; (*also see* individual tribes); artwork, 33; attitudes of British toward, 71-77; attitudes of French toward, 40-41, 59-69; clans, 23; crops, 30; diseases, 24; fighting for Europeans, 80; fishing rights treaties, 229-231; fur trapping, (*see* fur trading); government, 32; hunting and fishing, 29-30, 223; in Civil War, 185; Indian names, 35; inventions, 33-34; land treaties, 92; religion, 32; removal of tribes in Michigan, 133-134; reservations, M4-M6, 35-36; sports & games, 33; trails, 34; trapping for food, 29; treaties, 88, 92, 119, 156; tribal names, meanings, 25-26
Industrial Technology Institute, 375
Inflation (1980s), 370
Internal improvements, 132, 214
International Bridge, 313
Ionia, 146
Ireland, 150-151
Irish Hills, 151
Iron, 160-161, 189, 210-212
    (*also see* mining)
Iron Mountain, 209, 211, 288, 320, 336
Iron River, 211
Ironwood, 211
Iroquois tribe, 24, 28, 40
Isabella Indian Reservation, M6, 35
Ishpeming, 366
Isle Royale, 385, 386
Isle Royale National Park, M4, 322
Italian Hall incident, 208
Italians, 286

J
Jackson, 160, 168, 176, 182, 285, 364
Jackson, Andrew, 120, 138, 142
Jackson Mining Company, 161, 252
Japan, 370
Japanese-Americans, Internment of, 336
Jefferson, Thomas, 80, 93, 95
Jeffrey, Mildred, 341
Jerome, David, 199
Jesuit Order (*see* missionaries)
Jesuit Relations, 50
Jogues, Father Isaac, 45
Johnson, Ervin "Magic," 394
Johnson, Lyndon, 359
Johnson, Sir William, at Detroit, 71
Johnston, Jane, 134; John & Susan, 118-119
Jolliet, Louis, 47, 50
Jones, James Earl, 396

Jones, Sara Van Hoosen, 218
Jonesville,133, 287
Joy, Henry, and the Packard Company, 268, 336

K
Kahn, Albert, 287
Kalamazoo Stove Company, 336
Kalamazoo, 296, 316, 336; celery, 219; land office, 146; Lincoln speaks at, 176; manufacturing, 285
Kaline, Al, 394
Kansas-Nebraska Act, 175
Kaskaskia, 80, 82
Kawbawgam, Charlotte, 251
Kedzie, Dr., 218
Kelley, Frank, 381
Kellogg, John Harvey and the Kellogg Company, 233, 336
Kellogg, Will Keith, 234
Kelsey-Hayes Wheel Company, 328
Kensington Metro Park, 387
Kentucky, 109
Kettering, Charles F., 279
Keweenaw Peninsula, M4, 156, 204, 209
Kickapoo tribe, 25
King, Charles, 264, 266-267
King, Martin Luther, Jr., 357-358
Kingsford, 288
Knight, Francis, 324
Knights of Labor, 244-246
Knox, Frank, 335
Knudsen, William S., 335
Korean War, 353
Ku Klux Klan (KKK), 302

L
L'Anse, 46
Labadie, Charles Joseph Antoine, 245
Labor unions, 244, 326-332; American Federation of Labor, 246, 326; Knights of Labor, 244-246; United Auto Workers, 326, 331; Western Federation of Miners, 207
Lacrosse *or* baggataway, 75
La Framboise, Magdelaine, 117
Lake Champlain, 41
Lake Erie, 113, 139, 188, 254, 366
Lake Erie, Battle of, 106-108
Lake Huron, 225, 254, 351, 381
Lake Michigan, 225, 254, 351
Lake Michigan Maritime Museum, 262
Lake Ontario, 45
Lake Orion, 288
Lake Superior, 46, 161, 228, 254
Lambert, William, 174
Lamprey, 227-229
Landlooker, 199
Land Ordinance of 1785, 91
Land sales, 115, 146, 150
Land speculation, 147-149
Langlade, Charles, 67-68, 76
Lansing, C3, 145, 390; auto industry, 287, 336; depression, 317; the 1960s, 358, 360, 363, 390
Lapeer, 185
Lardner, Ring, 303
LaSalle, Robert Cavelier de, 53-57; march across lower peninsula, 56
Latitude and Longitude, lines crossing Michigan, M4-M6, 3
Laughing Whitefish (*see* Charlotte Kawbawgam)

Laurium, 394
League of Women Voters, 307
Lee, Robert E., 177; surveyor, 141
Leland, 225
Leland, Henry, 268, 298
Lend-Lease Act, 335
Leonard, Elmore, 396
Les Cheneaux Islands, 225
Limestone, 9, 258
Lincoln, Abraham, 172, 176, 178, 181-182, 190
Lindbergh, Charles, 308, 334
Liquor, in fur trade, 57, 64; prohibition, 298-301, 306
Little Turtle, 86-87
Livonia, M7, 6, 349
Log cabin, description of, 123
Log jam, 195
Log marks, 199
Lone Ranger, 311
Longfellow, Henry W., 134
Longhouse, 31
Lost Interval, 10
Lost Peninsula, 144
Louis XIV, 54
Louis, Joe, 322-323; Arena, 390
Lousma, Jack, 365
Lower Peninsula (general), 2-6, M6, M8, 10-13
Ludington, 256, 381
Lumber barons, 199-201
Lumber camps, 193
Lumbering, 191-203; rivers, 192; river drive, 194; terms, 202; thieves, 195

M
Mackinac Bridge, C7, 351-355
Mackinac Island Conference, 343
Mackinac Island, 85, 117, 135, 349, 388
Mackinaw City, 215, 261-262, 352, 388
Macomb County, 338-339
Macomb, William, 88
Madison Heights, 371
Madison, James, 104
Madonna, (Louise Veronica Ciccone), 396
Malaria, (see Ague)
Malcolm X, 358
Malcolmson, Alexander Y., 268
Mammoths, 14
Manchester, 182
Manistee, 200
Manistee River, 199
Manitou Island, M5
Manufacturing, (see automobiles, cereal, furniture, selected cities, and companies) foreign owned plants, 372; high tech companies, 375; railroad cars, 239; stoves, 239
Marji-Gesick, 161, 252
Marne, (MI), 294
Marquette, 161, 209, 212, 254, 256, 320, 396
Marquette, Father Jacques (Pere), 46-48; accompanies Jolliet in discovery of Mississippi River, 48; death, 50; founds missions at Sault Ste. Marie and St. Ignace, 47
Marquette Iron Range, 212
Marshall, (MI), 143, 170
Marx, Oscar B., 319
Mascouton tribe, 25
Mason, Emily, 185
Mason, John T., 138
Mason, Stevens T., 138-145, 155

Massachusetts, 91
Mastodons, 14
Maumee River, 81, 87, 139
Mazda, 372, 375
McCoy, Elijah, M7, 180
McDivitt, James A., 364-365
McGee, Jim, 200
McGregor Conference Center, 365
McLain, Denny, 394
Meigs, Return Jonathan, 102
Menard, Father Rene, 46
Menominee, 225, 262
Menominee Iron Range, 209, 212
Menominee River, 202
Menominee tribe, 25, 27, 48
Mexican Industries, 376
Miami tribe, 25, 27
Mice, 130
Michigan, economic output ranked, 376; meaning of name, 1; land area, 2
Michigan Agricultural College (see Michigan State University)
Michigan Anti-Slavery Society, 166
Michigan ax, 198
Michigan Central Railroad, 154, 180
Michigan Historical Museum, 390-391
Michigan International Speedway, 387
Michigan Relief Association, 185
Michigan Space Center, 364
Michigan State Prison, 364
Michigan State University, 218, 347, 363
Michigan Stove Company, 239
Michigan Territory, 95-98
Michilimackinac, 57, 62, 64, 75
Midland, 241, 336, 379
Migration, settlers, 112; tribal, 23-24, 28
Milford, 288, 387
Milliken, William G., 348, 364
Minavavana, Chief, 75
Mining, accidents, 206; ancient, 17; copper, 17, 153-160, 204-209; gold, 212; iron, 160-161, 210-212; silver, 11, 159
Mint, 220
Missionaries, 44-50
Mississippi River, 48-49, 54
Model A, 278
Model T, C2, 270-271, 274, 284
Monaghan, Tom, 375
Monroe, 146, 186-188, 366, 381; battle and massacre, 105
Montague, 382
Montcalm, General, 69
Moose, 385
Mormons, 152
Mosquitoes, 128-129, 157
Motown Industries, 361
Mott, Charles Stewart, 279
Mott, Lucretia, 172
Mound-builders (see Hopewell)
Mountains, ancient, 8; current, M4, 2, 386
Mt. Arvon, 2, M4
Mt. Clemens, 179, 295
Mt. Curwood, 2, M4
Mt. Pleasant, 35
Mumford High School, 396
Murphy, Frank, 302, 323-324, 331, 335-336
Muskegon, 319, 351, 391

N
NATO, 344
Nankin Mills, 288
National Association for the Advancement of Colored People (NAACP), 302

National Guard, 208, 323, 330-331, 359
Native Americans, (see Indians and individual tribes)
Naylor, Isaac, 100
Neguanee, 161
Netherlands, (see Dutch/Holland)
Neutral tribe, 25
New England, 112
New France (also Canada), 40, 66
Niagara Falls, 55, 258
Nicolet, Jean, 43
Niles, 82, 168
Northland shopping mall, 349
Northville, 288
Northwest Ordinance of 1787, 137, 140, 165, 170
Northwest Territory, 83, 91, 93-94
Norway, 4, 151, 193
Norway, (MI), 211
Nowlin, William, 113-114
Nuclear power, 366, 379-382
Nugent, Ted, 396

O
Oats, 218
O'Cavanaugh, Father Bernard, 151
Ohio, 94, 116, 139-142
Ojibwa tribe, 24-26, 134
Old Mill Creek Park, 388
Oldfield, Barney, 269
Olds, Ransom E., and the Oldsmobile Co., 266-268, 270, 280
Ontario, 3, 168
Ontonagon Boulder, 155-157
Open shop, 326
Osborn, Chase S., 306
Ottawa River, 42, 47
Ottawa tribe, 25-27
"Out-sourcing," 267
Overpack, Silas, 198
Overpass, Battle of the, 332
Owosso, 303, 347
Oxen, 122, 217

P
PBB (Firemaster), 378-379
Packard Company, 268, 336
Pageant at the Sault, 53
Paleo Indians, 14
Panics; of 1837, 148-150; of 1893, 250
"Paper city," 150
Parks, roadside, 284; state, 385
Parks, Rosa, 357
Parma, 168
Passenger pigeons, 29
Pasty, 205
Patriot War (Canada), 144
Paw Paw, 320
"Payless Payday," 348
Peace Ship (Ford's), 292
Pearl Harbor, 335
Peck, Eli, 257
Pemmican, 30
People Mover, 390
Pere Marquette River, 196
Perrot, Nicolas, 53
Perry, Oliver Hazard, 106-108
Personal Liberty Act, 174
Petoskey, 303
Petoskey stone, 10
Philo Parsons incident, 188
Pictured Rocks National Lakeshore, M4-M5, 386
Pierce, John D., 143

Pingree, Hazen S., 248-251
Pioneer life, diseases, 128-129; food, 131; homes, 123; travel, 112
Plymouth, 288, 320
"Polar Bears," (WW I), 296
Poletown, 372
Polish, 4, 151, 286
Pollution, air, 381; Great Lakes, 231-232; ground water, 382; toxic waste sites, 382
Pontchartrain, Count, 58
Pontiac, Chief, 72-73, 76
Pontiac, (MI), 6, 117, 285, 391
Population, distribution, 4; growth, 119, 139, 144, 146
Porcupine Mountains, C6, 386
Port Huron, 168, 179, 255, 312
Portage Lake, 204
Porter, George, 139
Post, Charles W., 234
Potawatomi tribe, 25-27, 133
Potts, William, 283
Prehistoric animals, 14
Prices, historical, 220, 243
Prime meridian, 92
Prisoner of war camps, (WWII), 342
Proclamation of 1763, 77
Procter, Colonel Henry, 104-106
Progressive movement, 249
Prohibition, 298-301, 306
Property tax, 320
Prophet (*see* Tenskwatawa)
Prophet's Town, 100
Pullman car, 239
Purple Gang, 299

Q

Quadricycle, 265
Quakers, 166-167
Quebec Act, 78-79
Quebec, Battle of, 68
Quebec City, founding, 40
Quincy Mine, C6
Quinine, 129

R

Race car "999", 269
Radio, 307; early stations: WJR, 312; WWJ, 310; WXYZ, 310
Radio-carbon dating, 15
Radisson, Pierre, 52
Railroads, 237, 239; and the grange, 219; first, 153; in farming, 216; in mining, 209-211; narrow gauge, 198
Railroad car manufacturing, 239
Rationing, 338
Raymbault, Father, 45
Religion, Indian, 32; missionary, 44-50
Religious freedom, 66
Renaissance Center, C3, M7, 390
REO Motor Company, 280-281, 287, 336
Republican Party; creation, 175-176
Reuther, Roy, 327; Victor, 327; Walter, 327, 328, 332, 371
Revolutionary War, 78-83
Rich, John, 248
Richard, Father Gabriel, 95, 97
Rickenbacker, Edward, 295
Ripon, (WI), 175
River Raisin (Frenchtown), Battle of, 105
River Rouge plant, 277-278, 288, 294, 316, 332
Rivers (general), M2-M7, 37-42, 47-50, 192, 194, also see names of specific rivers
Roads, maintenance, 214; plank & toll 112;
(toll road picture 154)
Robinson, William "Smokey", Jr., 361
Robotics, 373
Rocks, age of, etc. 10-11
Romney, George W., 359, 363
Roosevelt, Franklin D., 318, 323, 331, 335
Ropes, Julius, 212
Roseville, 349
Ross, Diana, 361
Royal Oak, M7, 318, 363
Ruggles, Charles F., 199
Ruggles, Lt. Daniel, 185
Rum Runners, 299
Running Bulls, Battle of the, 331
Rush-Bagot Agreement, 110

S

Sable, Jean de, 77
Saginaw, 117, 245, 319, 362
Saginaw River Valley, 192, 220
Saginaw Steering Gear, 287, 336
St. Clair River, 3
St. Clair, Arthur, 137
St. Ignace, 55, 62
St. Johns, 220
St. Joseph River, 56
St. Lawrence River, 1, 37
St. Lawrence Seaway, 259
St. Louis, (MI), 378
St. Lusson, 53
St. Martin, Alexis, 135
St. Mary's River, 3, 161
Salas, Gumecindo, 376
Sales tax, 320
Salmon, coho and chinook, 229
Salt, 9, 11, 154-155, 197
"Salties," (oceangoing ships) 259
Sanders, Fred, and the Sanders Candy, 235
Sands, Louis, 199-200
Sandwich, Ontario (*see* Windsor)
Sanitary Commission, 185
Saran Wrap, 241-242
Sassaba, 118
Sauk tribe, 25, 133
Saulteurs, (*see* Ojibwa)
Sault Ste. Marie, 45, 47, 62, 117, 161, 335, 351
Sault Ste. Marie Canal and Locks, (Soo Locks) C5, 162-163, 335
Sawmills, 196-197, 245-246
Scandinavians, 4, 151
Schmid, Reverend Fredrich, 151
Schoolcraft, Henry R., 134-135, 155
Schoolcraft, (MI), 168
Schools, (*see* education)
Schwimmer, Rosika, 292
Scripps, James, 310
Seaborg, Glenn, 366
Seabees, ancient, 8
Sebewaing, 220
Sections, land, 92
Segar, Bob, 396
Segregation, 339
Selden, George, 270
Self-unloading freighters, 258
Selfridge Air Force Base, 295, 342
Selleck, Tom, 395
Seney National Wildlife Refuge, M4, 322, 385
Settlements (early), 47, 53, 57-61, 118-119, 121-135,
Shanty boys, 193
Shaw, Anna Howard, 306
Shaw, Brewster, 365
Shay, Ephraim, 199
Shelley, Rebecca, 291-293
Sheridan, Phillip, 183, 187
Shipping, (Great Lakes), 253-263; bulk cargoes, 256; cost of, 161; types of, 114, 253
Ships, *John B. Aird*, C5; *Roger Blough*, 258; *Chief Wawatam*, 354; *City of Detroit III*, 262; *City of Erie*, 255; *City of Petoskey*, 353; *Alvin Clark*, 262; *Stewart Cort*, 258; *Edmund Fitzgerald*, 260-261; *Greater Buffalo*, 255; *Greater Detroit*, 253; *Griffon*, 55, 56-57, 253; *R. J. Hackett*, 257; *Keewatin*, 262; *Mackinac*, 262; *Madeline*, 262; *Michigan*, the passenger ship, 113; *Michigan*, USS, 188; *Niagara*, 108; *Onoko*, 258; *Philo Parsons*, 188; *Sheadle*, 260; *Tashmoo*, 255; *Vacationland*, 353; *S.S. Valley Camp*, 262; *Vandalia*, 253; *Walk-in-the-Water*, 114, 253; *Welcome*, C5
Shipwrecks, 260-261
Shrine of the Little Flower, 318
Shugart, Zachariah, 168
Sibley, Solomon, 94
Silverdome, 391
Singapore, (MI), 150
Sioux tribe, 25
Sit-down strikes, (*see* strikes)
Skiing, 387
Slavery, 79, 97-98, 132, 165-178
Sleeping Bear Dunes, M5, 386
Sloan, Alfred M., 279
Smith, Harold, 335
Soil types, 13
Sojourner Truth Housing Project, 339
Solar compass, 160
Solid waste (garbage), 383
Soo Locks, C5, 162-163, 335
Southfield, M7, 350
South Haven, 262
Soviet Union, 328
Spanish at Niles, 82
"Speed-up," 328
Squatters, 115, 147
Stanton, Elisabeth Cady, 172
Statehood, steps to, 93, 137-145
Steinman, David, 353
Stereotypes, 23
Stock market crash, 315
Stoneport, 261
Stone, Lucinda Hinsdale, 172, 306
"Stool pigeons," 328
Stout, William B., 307
Stoves, manufacture of, 239-240
Stowe, Harriet Beecher, 172
Straits of Mackinac, 43, 57, 351-354
Strange, James Jesse, 152
Strikes, sawmill, 245-246; sit-down, 323, 328-331
Stuart, J.E.B., 182, 187
Students for a Democratic Society (SDS), 363
Suburbs, 6, 349
Sugar beets, 218, 220
Sunday, Billy, 298
Suomi College, 205
Superconductor supercollider, 375
Superintendent of Public Instruction, 143
Supremes, 361
Surveying land, 91-92, 141, 158-160
Swartz Creek, 382
Sweden, 4, 151, 193, 200

Sweet, Ossian, M7, 302

T

Tahquamenon Falls, C1, M5, 385-386
Teal Lake, 161
Teamsters Union, 371-372
Tecumseh, Chief, 99-101, 106, 108-109
TenEyck Tavern, M7, 114
Tenskwatawa (the Prophet), 99-101
Territorial Road, 146
Thames River, Battle of the, 109
Thomas, Pamela, 168
Thompson, Frank (*see* Edmonds, Sara E.)
Three Fires, 25
Three Rivers, 288
Tiffin, Edward, 116
Tilden Mine, 212
Tippecanoe, Battle of, 100
Tiverton, Ontario, 381
Tobacco, Indian use, 32; products, 237
Tocqueville, Alexis de, 117, 121
Todd, Albert M., 220
Todd, John, 311
Todd, Marion Marsh, 251
Tolan, Eddie, 322
Toledo, (OH), 153
Toledo Strip, 140
Toledo War, 140-141
Tomlin, Lily, 395
Tonty, Alphonse de, 58-59
Tonty, Henri de, 54-56
Torch Lake, 382
Tourists and tourism, 384-397; map, 392; top attractions, 389
Townships, 91-92
Toxic waste, (*see* pollution)
Traction engines, (steam), C2, 217
Tractor, 218, 267, 278
Traffic light, 283
Travel Bureau, 384, 396 (timeline)
Travel Information Center, 384-385
Traverse City, 200, 221, 262, 392
Treaties, (Indian), map 92
Treaty of Greenville, 88
Treaty of Saginaw, 92, 119
Trees, 201; use of bark, 200; clearing of, 121; Christmas, 221; types, 13
Tri-county area, 6
Tri-motor plane, 307-309
Troy, 297, 371, 375
Truman, Harry S., 348
Truth, Sojourner, 171-172
Tulip Festival, 389
Tuskegee Airmen, 342
Tyson, Ty, 310

U

U.S. Steel Corporation, 258
Underground Railroad, 166-169
Unemployment, 316-317
Union City, 161
Unions, (*see* labor unions)
Uniroyal, 370
United Automobile Workers (UAW), 326-332
United Nations, 343-344, 349
University of Michigan, 363, 375
Upper Peninsula (general), 2,
  bridge to- 351-354
  "Copper Culture" people 17-18
  counties in- 5
  ethnic groups- 151-152
  exploration- 42-43, 46-50
  fishing- 225

Upper Peninsula continued ....
  fur trading- 62-65
  Indian tribes- 24-25, 27, treaties- 92, 251-252
  lumbering (general)- 192-203
  maps- M4-M5, 5-6
  mining (map) 212
    copper- 17, 46, 155, 157, 189, 204-209
    iron- 160-161, 210-212
    gold- 212
    silver- 11, 159
  mountains- C6, 2, 8, 386
  settlement (early)- 47, 53, 118-119
  tourist attractions- 386-387, 392 map
  War of 1812- 110

Upjohn, Dr. William and the Upjohn Company, 240, 336
Urban decay, 350
Urban renewal, 389
Urbanization, 304, 339

V

Vandenberg, Sen. Arthur H., attitude toward World War II, 334-335; Mackinac Island Conference, 343; United Nations Conference, 343-344
VanRaalte, Reverend Albertus, 152
Vermont, 116, 162
Vernor, James and Vernor's ginger ale, 235
"Victory Gardens," 336
Vietnam War, 357, 363-364
Vietnamese, 364
Vincennes, 81
Voelker, John (Traver, Robert), 396
Volcanoes, 9
Voyageurs, 63

W

Wabash River, 81
Wages, changes in, 243; five dollar-day, 276; in auto industry, 286, 327-328; in copper mining, 209; one dollar-day, 243
Wakefield, 211
Walker, Captain Jonathan, 170
Walk-in-the-Water, 114, 253
Walloon Lake, 303
Wampum, 72
War of 1812, 102-110
Ward, David, 199
Ward, Eber B., 184
War production, World War I, 293; World War II, 336-338
Warren, 6, 288, 349
Washington, George, 67, 85, 120
Washtenaw County, 338
Wawatam, 75
Wayne County, 4, 6
Wayne, General Anthony, 86-87
Wayne State University, 365
Webb, William, 177
Webster, Daniel, 144
Welfare, 319
Welland Canal, 227, 257
Western Federation of Miners, 207
Westphalia, 151
Whales, fossil remains, 10
Wheat, 124, 189, 218
Wheelock, Julia, 185
Whig Party, 144, 175
Whitefish, 223
White Fish Point, M4
White Pigeon, 146
White Pine Mine, 209

Wigwam, 31
"Wildcat Banks," 148
Williams, Allan, 284
Williams, G. Mennen, 348-349
Willow Run, 337, 342
Wilson, Mary, 361
Wilson, Woodrow, 292
Windmill, 217
Windsor, Ontario, 102, 168, 312
Wisconsin, 144, 47
Wisner, Moses, 186
Wolves, 130
Women, in industry, 237, 244, 293-294; on farms, 294
Women Air Force Service Pilots (WASPS), 341
Women's rights, (*see* women's suffrage and women in industry)
Women's suffrage, 306
Wonder, Stevie, 362, 396
Woodbridge, William, 145
Woodcock, Leonard, 371
Woodward, Augustus B., 95-97
Wool, 189, 218
Worden, Al, 365
Working hours, 243
Workmen's compensation, 371
Works Progress Administration (WPA), 320
World War I, 290-297
World War II, 334-344
Wyandotte, (MI), M7, 395
Wyandotte tribe, (*see* Huron tribe)

Y

Yamasaki, Minoru, 365-366
Yankees, 116
Yost, Fielding, 310
Young, Coleman, 342, 360
Ypsilanti, 114, 154, 168, 180, 182, 288, 337

Z

Zeeland, 152